THE ROOTS OF URBAN RENAISSANCE

The Roots of Urban Renaissance

Gentrification and the Struggle over Harlem

BRIAN D. GOLDSTEIN

HARVARD UNIVERSITY PRESS

Cambridge, Massachusetts & London, England

2017

First printing

 Illustrations in this book were funded in whole or in part
by a grant from the SAH/Mellon Author Awards
of the Society of Architectural Historians.

Library of Congress Cataloging-in-Publication Data
Names: Goldstein, Brian D., 1982– author.
Title: The roots of urban renaissance : gentrification and the struggle over
    Harlem / Brian D. Goldstein.
Description: Cambridge, Massachusetts : Harvard University Press, 2017. |
    Includes bibliographical references and index.
Identifiers: LCCN 2016019286 | ISBN 9780674971509 (hardcover : alk. paper)
Subjects: LCSH: Gentrification—New York (State)—New York. | Community
    development—New York (State)—New York. | Neighborhood leaders—
    New York (State)—New York. | Community organization—New York (State)—
    New York. | African American neighborhoods—New York (State)—
    New York—History. | Harlem (New York, N.Y.)—History.
Classification: LCC HT177.N5 G65 2016 | DDC 307.1/4097471—dc23
    LC record available at https://lccn.loc.gov/2016019286

For Theresa

Contents

THE ROOTS OF URBAN RENAISSANCE

Introduction

ON THE LAST NIGHT OF JUNE 1969, 200 African American demonstrators gathered at the northwest corner of Harlem's Lenox Avenue and 125th Street. The next morning, crews were to begin building a skyscraper to house state offices on this vast, cleared site. Cloaked by darkness, activists cut the construction fence, passed through, and announced the new name they had bestowed on Harlem's central block: Reclamation Site #1. The protesters intended to stop the project but also to claim and control the land as their own. Soon, the site began to reflect the self-determination that its new occupants espoused. Within a few days, they had raised tents and a nationalist red, black, and green flag. Some protesters moved into an old bus that remained on the block. Others built modest wooden shelters. Occupiers were inspired by the ideal of community control that fueled the ongoing Black Power movement, the drive for African American self-determination that emerged from the radical shift of civil rights activism in the late 1960s. They voiced the lofty aspiration that Harlem could be rebuilt by and for its predominantly low-income residents. In staging a cooperative, grassroots redevelopment of these acres, the occupants of Reclamation Site #1 offered a material reality that matched their words.[1]

Forty years later, however, on the site that had symbolized the possibility of community control, loomed Harlem Center, an edifice remarkable for both its immense form and its function. Soaring ten stories above 125th Street and encased in brick, steel, and glass, this was Harlem's newest shopping center, complete with a Marshalls, Staples, and CVS. The development added to the array of national retail chains that were increasingly ubiquitous on

Harlem's main street, vivid symbols for many observers of the neighbor-hood's accelerating gentrification.[2] Yet if the distance between Harlem Center and Reclamation Site #1 seemed vast, the extraordinary fact remained that one of Harlem's largest and best-known community-based organizations, Abyssinian Development Corporation, had built the complex in partnership with a major real estate developer. Harlem Center rose, then, not just as a sign of the increasing ease with which residents could purchase mass-market clothing, cosmetics, and office supplies in the neighborhood. Its construc-tion also pointed to the central role that those very residents had played in the dramatic and widely noted transformation of Harlem in the late twen-tieth century.

The Harlem of the new millennium, marked by increasing privatization, commercial development, and middle-class habitation, did not represent a sudden break from the social movements of the 1960s, I argue in this book, but rather grew from those radical roots. Indeed, profound physical and so-cioeconomic changes on Harlem's blocks were not forced on an unwitting neighborhood by outsiders, but emerged from within Harlem, as the often-unintended outcome of demands for community control. The new kinds of community-based organizations that developed amid 1960s-era radical movements to facilitate broad participation became the vehicles through which activists with a different vision pursued the economic integration and commercial transformation of the neighborhood in succeeding decades. In fact, the very characteristics that initially defined these groups—democratic, experimental, and ambiguous in their means and ends—enabled this evolu-tion. As their history reveals, Harlem's much-remarked-upon gentrification, which came to symbolize the broader transformation of American urban neighborhoods in this era, had origins in some rather unexpected places.

Indeed, American cities underwent a surprising turn of fortunes in these decades. By the 1960s, cities had become for many the very symbols of all that was wrong in America. Urban centers, wracked by crime, joblessness, and poverty, had entered what observers called an "urban crisis." Television screens and newspaper front pages broadcast the decade's turbulent "long hot summers," delivering images that often confirmed the decision many had already made to leave cities behind. Depending on one's perspective, the uprisings that altered the landscapes of Harlem in 1964, Detroit and Newark in 1967, and hundreds of other communities offered distressing evidence that cities were a lost cause, that policies had failed to bring equality to all, or that a bigger upheaval was just around the corner. All agreed that cities were in big trouble. "After our inspections, hearings, and research studies," the National Commission on Urban Problems stated in 1968, "we found conditions much worse, more widespread and more explosive than any of us had thought." In the next decade, as America's biggest city lurched toward bankruptcy, the very possibility that urban centers had tipped past the point of return seemed entirely possible, even probable, at least according to the *New York Daily News*. "Ford to City: Drop Dead," read the paper's famous headline.[3]

Yet by the late 1990s it had become quite clear that American cities had not, in fact, dropped dead. At the end of the twentieth century, many urban centers were, as one national broadcaster explained, "hot again."[4] Reporters followed the stories of families who moved back to city centers to rehabilitate historic buildings, artists who turned overlooked neighborhoods into desirable real estate, and new retail centers that emerged on unexpected streets. Rather than a scapegoat for the country's problems, cities became the very image of cool in the late 1990s and early 2000s. They appeared as the stylish settings of popular TV sitcoms or the unlikely inspiration for new developments that sought to mimic urban lofts and walk-up apartments on the suburban fringe. Observers coined a variety of new terms to describe this turn of events: a "back to the city movement," an "urban renaissance." Their optimism suggested unambiguously that predictions of the city's end had been premature.

Harlem provides a particularly clear lens through which to view this transformation. As the most famous predominantly African American neighborhood in American history—if not the most famous neighborhood in America—and also the most mythologized, Harlem offers a vivid symbol of the many facets of urban change in the latter half of the twentieth century. Encompassing roughly three and a half square miles, Greater Harlem's approximate borders extend north from 96th Street on the east side of Central Park and 110th Street on the west, up to 155th Street, and from the Harlem River at the neighborhood's eastern extent to Morningside Park and the Hudson River at its western edge (see Figure I.1). Harlem's central commercial spine has long been formed by 125th Street, with major secondary streets including 116th, 135th, and 145th Streets, and the neighborhood's north–south

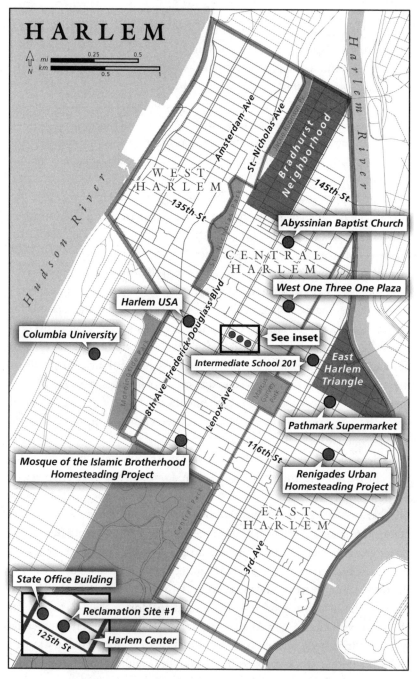

FIGURE I.1. Map of Harlem, New York, showing key sites discussed in book.

boulevards. In between, densely picturesque townhouses, grand apartment buildings, aging tenements, and vast complexes of public housing towers have composed Harlem's variegated residential fabric. Although these blocks had formed the backdrop for many of the most notable people and events in twentieth-century African American history, by midcentury Harlem's streets more typically provided raw material for some of the best-known chronicles of urban crisis. The sociologist and Harlem native Kenneth Clark, for example, used the neighborhood as his laboratory. The title of his 1965 masterwork, *Dark Ghetto,* testified to his bleak findings. So too did the widely seen work of photographer Gordon Parks, whose 1968 *Life* magazine series, "A Harlem Family," chronicled the hunger, poverty, and addiction that haunted his subjects daily.[5]

But Harlem's streets likewise offered a highly visible example of the transformation of so-called inner-city neighborhoods several decades later. Harlem, with refurbished rows of landmark brownstones, new shopping complexes like Harlem Center, and a brightly glowing digital marquee on the Apollo Theater, provided compelling evidence for those who declared the rebound of American cities. Once Manhattan's most infamous enclave, Harlem increasingly appeared as a star in the city's real estate columns. Formerly America's best-known "ghetto," by the end of the century Harlem stood as a symbol that even the most forsaken urban neighborhoods could again become sought-after destinations for a middle-class that had largely deserted them. Harlem's population had approached 600,000 in 1950 before beginning a decades-long descent, bottoming out at 334,000 in 1990. But a marked increase of residents characterized the neighborhood thereafter, reaching nearly 380,000 in 2010. More remarkably, rising wealth spoke to Harlem's new status, with median household income in Central Harlem growing by over 250 percent between 1950 and 2010, from $13,765 to more than $35,335, adjusted for inflation. Indeed, this physical and demographic transformation even earned its own moniker, hearkening back to the era that put African American Harlem on the map. This was, commentators explained, the neighborhood's "Second Renaissance."[6]

Observers often remarked on this apparent revival with surprise, but the story had actually been decades in the making. The years between the early 1960s and the early 2000s were marked by profound transformations at the global, national, and local levels. In this era, Harlem became part of a transnational network of capital and ideas that turned places like New York into "global cities." Across America, a variety of factors combined to drive an ascendant middle class "back to the city," including the availability of cheap property, new downtown employment centers, and a cultural vogue that celebrated urban places. In New York City, a new economy that prioritized finance, insurance, real estate, and business services over declining industry brought a recovery from the fiscal crisis of the 1970s, making it once again the country's leading metropolis.[7]

Yet these factors are insufficient on their own to explain the physical, social, and economic transformation of communities like Harlem. Individuals who developed a new preference for urban living and abstract forces such as globalization both contributed to neighborhood change in the late twentieth century, to be sure.[8] But this was never simply a process that happened *to* residents in places like Harlem. A deeper look reveals that Harlemites themselves played a crucial role in creating this seeming renaissance on their streets. Even amid urban crisis, residents remained deeply invested in the persistence of their community. Harlemites inhabited, reimagined, and rebuilt their neighborhood despite federal retrenchment, increasing socioeconomic constraints, and Harlem's diminishing profile in the city. Consequently, they wrought dramatic changes in their community's residential and commercial landscape, including the arrival of more affluent residents and the increasing presence of national retail chains. These hallmarks of economic gentrification and the increasing emphasis on creating "free" markets for private-sector investment grew from Harlem's grass roots. The story of this transformation provides a new perspective on the rise of urban neoliberalism, contextualizing its emergence in the social and political history of the very neighborhoods that felt its effects most acutely.[9]

This era in Harlem's history unfolded in relation to, and often in opposition to, the midcentury development strategy popularly called "urban renewal." As Americans settled back into life after World War II, officials and their private-sector and institutional partners reshaped cities through spatial and policy tools emblematic of the conjoined projects of modernism and liberalism. In an effort to keep cities viable in an era of rapid suburbanization, the federal government subsidized the large-scale reconstruction of urban centers to build housing, commercial enclaves, expanded universities, and new cultural centers. Such projects relied on stock modernist forms—tower block housing, austere marble pavilions, and prismatic glass skyscrapers. Though urban renewal involved complex techniques and diverse outcomes that scholars have increasingly uncovered, the age of large-scale redevelopment nonetheless proved remarkably consistent in its means and ends: projects typically cleared vast urban acreage, displaced thousands of residents, and constructed monumental structures in their stead.[10]

While urban renewal sought to sustain cities in an era when their foundations were increasingly crumbling, the policy often proved quite counterproductive. Renewal ruptured communities with deep social ties as they fell to the force of the bulldozer. In turn, the public housing towers that held displaced residents often became vast centers of concentrated poverty. In effect, if not intent, redevelopment disproportionately harmed low-income, minority populations. For both uprooted residents and outside observers, the failures of urban renewal came to symbolize the failures of the New Deal welfare state. Indeed, many pointed to it as a crucial factor in precipitating America's urban crisis.[11]

By the mid-1960s, urban renewal had received widespread condemnation from all corners, including libertarian opponents of government intervention, liberals who objected to its social costs, and radicals who included a denunciation of this large-scale, generally top-down strategy in the larger demand for self-determination emanating from the New Left. In Harlem and many other American neighborhoods, this radical critique became a central factor in the rise of a more militant approach to gaining civil rights. Civil rights leaders had once looked to redevelopment as a means of achieving the goals of racial liberalism, especially economic and racial desegregation. But a new, younger generation of activists perceived in the failures of urban renewal yet one more symbol of a power structure in which African Americans had little voice in the decisions that most affected them.[12] Instead of seeing their predominantly low-income neighbors as problems to be excised through large-scale clearance, they turned the equation of urban crisis on its head, arguing that the existing community in places like Harlem provided the very basis from which revitalization could occur. Adopting the anticolonial metaphors common in the Black Power movement, Harlem activists explained that the segregated space in which they found themselves could become a source of power, a means to seize control. They expressed an ambitious, communitarian vision of redevelopment by and for the benefit of Harlem's existing population, an ideal intended to both lift the community's residents and demonstrate their self-reliance.

If Black Power inspired an idealistic conception of community control in the built environment, however, the legacy of such radical demands proved quite unexpected. Activists created a dynamic array of new community-based institutions that promised to realize their ideals in physical form, including community design centers, community associations, and community development corporations. Yet these emergent organizations were inchoate, definitionally imprecise, and thus vulnerable to change. Consequently, they depended on financial partnerships with the public sector even as they preached self-determination; remained subject to the whims of strong leaders even as they promised participatory democracy; were influenced by shifting social thought; and were challenged by the simple difficulty of enacting visionary change against powerful countervailing forces. Over time, they came to idealize new objectives: the cultivation of a mixed-income population and integration into an economic "mainstream." In bringing that vision into physical form in the late twentieth century, these organizations demonstrated their attainment of the long-sought power to shape Harlem's built environment. Yet their accomplishments also exemplified the distance they had traveled from the radical ideals that had once motivated their demands at locations like Reclamation Site #1.

The endpoints of this story testify to the complicated nature of city building in the most recent major period in urban history. If urban renewal grew from a foundation of relative intellectual consensus, the consistent monumentality of architectural modernism, and the backing of a largely stable policy apparatus, the period chronicled in this book manifested competing urban visions, an eclectic and often highly pragmatic approach to physical form, and an equally pragmatic approach to the multitude of policies by which residents brought their ideas to life. A social and political history of urban change in this era largely confirms the late twentieth century as an "age of fracture."[13] Activist designers sought new means of democratizing their professions to enable Harlemites to plan their own future. Enterprising residents demonstrated that if the public and private sectors would not rebuild abandoned buildings into much-needed homes, they would do it themselves. Church leaders became developers, while parishioners questioned their motives. Instead of a single, prevailing idea of the future of the city, Harlemites of different stripes offered multiple ideas about what their community should be.

If contention defined the spirit of these decades, however, they share the constant—and crucial—presence of community-based organizations at their center. Through them, residents negotiated fundamental questions that had followed African Americans for nearly a century: about the tensions between self-determination and integration; between the idea that Harlem, with its largely low-income population, already bore the seeds of its revival, and the notion that greater income diversity and entry into a broader economic system were necessary for revitalization.

For the most part, historians have yet to examine the events of these decades in detail, yet doing so offers several major insights. First, analysis of urban development in the late twentieth century demonstrates the fundamental and lasting influence of the upheaval that brought the end of modernist planning in the 1960s. Anger over the human costs of large-scale redevelopment motivated activists, as did frustration over housing discrimination, the slow pace of school integration, and the lack of economic opportunity. By the end of the decade, neighbors and likeminded architects and planners stood together in front of bulldozers, demonstrated at public meetings, and drafted alternate plans, all for the purpose of ending spatial practices that harmed residents in majority-minority neighborhoods. Historians have typically positioned these movements as an endpoint, crediting them with bringing the fall of large-scale urban renewal but leaving their constructive effects unexamined, or argued that hopes for broad transformation faded away in disappointment. Where scholars have considered succeeding decades, they have focused on change within the institutional structures of planning.[14] In examining movements against destructive redevelopment more broadly, however, I argue that their demands both fundamentally shaped the subsequent debates that defined the contemporary city and transformed the practice of urban development in ways that we have yet to fully understand. By positioning radical social movements as the starting point of a new period in urban history, I show their enduring influence over the late twentieth century, as new kinds of community-based organizations became major players in the transformation of American cities.

I thereby reveal the long, complicated, but profound reverberations of the demands for self-determination that arose on a larger terrain in this period. In recent years, historians have taken a closer look at Black Power, examining the radical shift in the civil rights movement as a new phase in the black freedom struggle. Instead of depicting new militancy as the denouement of a larger story of urban decline, historians have uncovered the persistent, often inventive grassroots organizing and activism that suffused Black Power, through which city residents sought to stem urban problems at the community level. In so doing, scholars have revealed the long history of Black Power, demonstrating its deep roots and the diverse forms that it took in the realms of politics, economics, and education. Through examination of black studies programs in major universities and African American electoral politics, scholars have only just begun to bring the history of Black Power forward into succeeding decades, explaining radicalism not as the tragic end of a "heroic period" in the civil rights movement, but as an innovative, often effective shift that brought new forms of participation into American society.[15]

I join this emerging effort through the lens of the built environment. As a sphere that joins politics, society, and culture in a highly tangible form, urban space offers an especially apt terrain for understanding the lasting ramifications of the social movements of the 1960s. By showing the increasing influence of community-based organizations in that context, I uncover a realm in which Black Power profoundly changed—and continues to change— public life in America. Indeed, radical demands for community control helped to establish "community development" as a concept so ubiquitous that many cities now claim a Department of Community Development, not a Department of City Planning. Community developers gained a new role for citizen participation in the construction of the built environment, I argue, extending the gains of the civil rights movement into a crucial and omnipresent realm that encompassed the home, the workplace, and the street.[16]

Yet by explaining the transformations that occurred under the umbrella of community development in the decades that followed the 1960s, I also demonstrate the unstable and often ironic afterlife of such radical social movements, as Black Power's means and ends proved mutable and multifaceted over time. Indeed, Harlem's history reveals the shifting bodies that donned the cloak of "community development," whether through formal efforts like community development corporations or informal struggles to rebuild the city through the collective labor of urban residents. Black Power shaped the vision of cooperation, self-determination, and democratization that made up radical activists' inclusive ideal for Harlem. Over the course of the 1970s and 1980s, that idealistic hope yielded to a pragmatic approach that assembled a patchwork of residents, funding sources, and political allies across the spectrum, and ultimately prioritized the act of building over broad structural transformation. As these goals shifted, many Harlemites feared that they would lose the influence they had gained and, as a result, lose their neighborhood too. But they found instead a third way between their inclusive ideal and its exclusionary antithesis—a gradual diversification of the neighborhood as Harlem-based organizations built new mixed-income housing, supermarkets, and shopping malls that often met long-standing resident needs as well as those of a growing middle-class population.

This story complicates and enriches the accounts and explanations that have thus far stood as the record of the city in the post–urban renewal era. By showing the crucial role that community-based organizations played in building a city that emphasized greater private-sector involvement and economic integration—even gentrification—as normative ideals, I explain that such changes in urban centers did not arise solely through the actions of opportunistic speculators or middle-class outsiders who saw places like Harlem as ripe real estate opportunities. I argue that residents themselves, through the social movements they joined and organizations they shaped, helped to produce the Harlem that we find today. At times the neighborhood that resulted from community-level efforts was an unintended consequence of the alliances that Harlemites accepted to make their ideals a reality. At other times, it was a deliberate result of the changing objectives that they pursued. In demonstrating these diverse outcomes, I explain that the story of community development was not a monolithic tale of pluck, perseverance, and drive toward a single idea of urban revitalization, but one of change, conflict, and, often, contradiction. The city of the early twenty-first century did not emerge fully formed, but was the product of a long history. In Harlem, efforts with radical roots followed a path of transformation that registered in the neighborhood's physical space, from a vision of a low-income utopia to a mixed-income reality, from a goal of wide-ranging structural change to a new pragmatism, and from an ideal of mixed land uses to an approach that prioritized the commercial redevelopment of Harlem's major streets.[17]

Harlem offers a case that is remarkable both for its exceptional history and for the mythology that surrounds it. Always a center of attention, Harlem has served as the ur-type for majority-minority neighborhoods throughout the twentieth century. Harlem's emergence as the heart of New York City's African American population early in the century exemplified the transformative effects of the Great Migration, as white landlords and enterprising African American realtors looked to new arrivals to fill speculative housing built in the late 1800s and early 1900s when mass transit came uptown. These new Harlemites paid dearly to live here, one of the few options they had, but the famed "renaissance" that followed in the 1920s nonetheless suggested the political, social, and cultural flourishing that demographic shifts could bring. Harlem's experience of the Great Depression in the next decade highlighted the disproportionate burden that African Americans bore amid economic collapse, while the neighborhood's streets soon played host to new demands for civil rights as African American veterans returned home from World War II. Harlem political leaders like Adam Clayton Powell Jr. rose to national prominence at midcentury. Here, Malcolm X matured as an intellectual and activist. Harlem also symbolized the deindustrialization, dilapidation, and overcrowding that undermined African American communities in the postwar decades. The neighborhood came to exemplify a period of urban disinvestment and decline.[18]

Despite Harlem's increasing distance from its popular heyday by the early 1960s, and, indeed, despite the neighborhood's diminishing identity as New York City's largest African American community, Harlem retained its role as the symbolic center of black America in the last decades of the twentieth century. The neighborhood's high visibility in many ways proved a self-fulfilling prophecy, the result of Harlem's prominent history and its proximity to the nation's media capital. As a result, things often happened first in Harlem in the years chronicled in this study, and, even when they did not happen first there, often received tremendous attention. The neighborhood became home to the nation's first community design center, for example, an effort by activist architects and planners to empower residents with the tools to plan their community. Likewise, Harlemites founded one of the nation's first community development corporations in the late 1960s, an entity that aspired to own and shape Harlem's land. When a new generation of community development corporations emerged in the 1980s, Harlem's garnered extensive press coverage and soon became exemplars at the national level. Harlem served as a site for innovative social movements, a destination for prominent national and international officials, and a favored target of public investment throughout this period. Unsurprisingly, then, when middle-class residents began to move back to Harlem at an increasing rate and national retailers like the Disney Store and Starbucks looked to make the neighborhood home, social scientists and journalists took notice. Harlem became a national symbol of inner-city reinvestment and gentrification.[19]

Harlem's history in the last four decades of the twentieth century was undeniably unique as a result of the signal importance of its setting, its cast of notable characters, and the early onset of its physical and social transformation. Yet Harlem offers a telling case through which to understand development in the aftermath of urban renewal precisely because it often served as the leader in techniques and practices that would likewise transform, and that continue to transform, majority-minority neighborhoods elsewhere in the United States. If Harlem provided particularly visible examples of grassroots social movements, community-based organizations, and demographic shifts, those phenomena proved noteworthy not because they were exceptional, but because they soon came to characterize similar communities in other major cities, including the U Street Corridor in Washington, DC, Bronzeville in Chicago, Over-the-Rhine in Cincinnati, and West Oakland. This history of Harlem not only illuminates the mechanics of change in one important place, but also reveals the social and political forces, conflicting ideals, and transformational events that help to explain the dynamics in parallel neighborhoods across the United States. If these places lack the attention that Harlem has long attracted, they share socioeconomic commonalities, a cyclical history of disinvestment and reinvestment, and a tradition of community-level activism. Understanding Harlem helps to explain the complex stories unfolding throughout American inner cities.

Though Harlem's grassroots activists often fixed on the built environment as a site and a stake for their demands, their role as spatial thinkers has not received the historical attention it deserves. Harlemites, including those with and without formal training in architecture and urban planning, did much more than take oppositional stances in their activism. Over the course of these forty years, radical design professionals, charismatic community leaders, and interested residents often expressed their highest ideals about equality and democracy, their "freedom dreams," in the words of historian Robin D. G. Kelley, in the language and material of the built environment.[20] These ambitious, often competing visions of the future city reward detailed analysis. Thus, I combine study of the archival records of community-based organizations and the actors who participated in their activities with close attention to the spaces they produced on paper and in reality. Where the records of architects, planners, activists, and organizations provide a partial history, I have benefited from the intense scrutiny that Harlem received during these decades from both the mainstream and the African American press, and from the memories of the actors in this story.[21]

These sources enable a rich portrait of Harlem's physical spaces during an era in which predominantly low-income, African American neighborhoods, once symbols of decline—if not public pariahs—became symbols of rebirth. Tracing the history of the organizations and individuals who produced this transformation concretizes a process of change that is often described only in amorphous terms, such as "revival," "revitalization," and "renaissance," that fail to capture the social processes, individual decisions, and political dynamics that shaped Harlem at the community level. "Gentrification" itself remains such a term, wielded for diverse ideological purposes, imprecise in its exact meaning, and at risk of obscuring more than it reveals. Yet it remains the predominant word used to describe the demographic and physical changes that swept across neighborhoods like Harlem in these decades and that continue into the present day. Instead of taking one side in ongoing debates over the meaning and implications of gentrification, this book explores and explains its intrinsic complexity and ambiguity. Indeed, examining Harlem from within its boundaries provides an understanding of neighborhood change that goes beyond simplistic frameworks of good and evil, or crude scorecards of winners and losers. As I show here, the gentrification of Harlem was often a two-way street, with chain stores, wealthier residents, and outside money coming into Harlem, and Harlemites themselves creating space for or seeking the growth of those phenomena. Their history demonstrates that one cannot paint neighborhoods with a broad brush and assume that all residents wanted the same thing for their community. Harlemites brought multiple visions and competing aspirations to the project of city building in the late twentieth century. In the process, they debated and reimagined what it meant to construct their ideal city.

CHAPTER 1

Reforming Renewal

IT WAS UNDERSTANDABLE that Gertrude Wilson, a columnist at the *New York Amsterdam News,* looked suspiciously on the October 29, 1964, meeting of the New York Chapter of the American Institute of Architects (AIA). The meeting, on the theme of "Housing Problems in Harlem," took place in the lavish Ponti Auditorium on the eighth floor of what she termed the "plush-lush" Time-Life Building, a midtown skyscraper that marked the extension of Rockefeller Center across Sixth Avenue. Sixty blocks from Harlem, it was far indeed from the neighborhood that participants had gathered to discuss. "The meeting was like a broken record playing all over again—rat-holes, garbage, and yoo-hoo-hoo," Wilson wrote. "I would like to know who is kidding whom and why. It is interesting to see how many white people can attend a nice comfy, cozy meeting in downtown buildings like the Time-Life building to discuss rebuilding Harlem." These architects, Wilson was sure, were after the same prize as the many other professionals who had gazed on Harlem during the past decades. "All the while their collective eye is not on the sparrow, but on the nice lucrative fees to be had in rebuilding such a vast tumble-down area," she wrote.[1]

Indeed, architects and planners had not exactly been good to New York's low-income residents during the postwar period, serving as the shock troops that drafted the plans and designed the buildings that redefined the cityscape in neighborhoods like Harlem. But C. Richard Hatch, the thirty-year-old architect who as a member of the AIA's Housing Committee had organized the October meeting, claimed a different impetus. "It is true that most white architects do not comprehend the problems of the Harlem ghetto," Hatch responded to Wilson. "But that was exactly the rationale for the meeting and for the choice of speakers." The crowd, numbering as many as 400, heard from Harlem tenant activist Jesse Gray; minister Charles Leber, who had led resistance to disruptive urban redevelopment in Chicago; Congress of Racial Equality (CORE) director James Farmer; and architect Albert Mayer, who had assisted residents in East Harlem.[2]

Hatch sought not employment opportunities for his colleagues but the chance to put their skills to the service of Harlem residents. "If [Harlemites] are not to be pawns of the real estate speculators, government bureaucrats, or private institutions seeking cheap land for expansion," Hatch wrote, "they must organize to produce their own urban renewal plans and pressure the city to adopt them." The distance between design expertise and the public had become too vast, leading to plans that followed textbook orthodoxy but did not meet the needs of actual city residents. Hatch acknowledged the faults of his profession, hoping to direct knowledge to new ends. "We in the profession who have followed the pattern of urban renewal (or Negro removal, as it is sometimes called) across the country know what Harlem residents are up against," he said. "We know that technical knowledge equal to or superior to that of the government agencies is necessary to a successful fight. We hope to be able to provide that assistance."[3]

Hatch and the Architects' Renewal Committee in Harlem (ARCH), the organization that he founded and led in the aftermath of the October meeting, tapped into broader currents emerging in Harlem and nationally in the mid-1960s. Residents subject to disruptive redevelopment plans sought the assistance of professionals who could support their activism with design expertise. Likewise, architects and planners like Hatch, who voiced a rejection of the top-down approach of modernist redevelopment from within the profession, sought opportunities to lend their expertise to the communities that renewal reshaped. ARCH joined Harlemites in outlining a new, more humane role for urban renewal. Instead of serving the expansion of institutions and seeking the return of the middle class, its typical objectives, residents called for plans that benefited the existing low-income population of Harlem. They sought to become the beneficiaries of redevelopment, not its victims. In doing so, they turned the assumptions of modernist planning on their head.

Residents reimagined the tenets of midcentury modernism and, consequently, the interrelated project of midcentury liberalism in the mid-1960s.

Yet, paradoxically, their alternative remained within the limits of both. Even as Harlemites offered a dramatic reversal of the typical ends of urban renewal, they remained reliant in two major ways on the traditional means that enabled large-scale redevelopment. First, they called not for an end to publicly funded renewal but for its redirection toward the objectives that they demanded. Second, they continued to rely on the tools of architecture and urban planning and the expertise of the architect and urban planner. These strategies aligned with a broader discourse that emerged in this period, one that sought to expand the range of participants in public life without undermining long-standing liberal institutions. In the realm of governance, this tendency expressed itself in the goals of President Lyndon Johnson's Great Society, which created new avenues for participation without dismantling the state or the role of the experts who maintained it. In the realm of urbanism, this tendency expressed itself in the project of "alternate planning" that Harlem residents pursued, a strategy that fundamentally reinforced the importance of planning and planners even as it sought to make the design disciplines more democratic.

As residents staged a critique of planning orthodoxy, then, they relied on the assistance of experts who could help them translate their ideals into the language of redevelopment. In Harlem, residents turned to ARCH, the first of a new kind of organization that would later come to be known as the "community design center." ARCH's importance lay not only in its location in the iconic community of Harlem but also in its role as a model for dozens of similar storefront efforts in American cities in the mid-1960s and after, which together institutionalized this new function for professional designers.[4] Under Hatch's direction, ARCH partnered with residents in neighborhoods like West Harlem and the East Harlem Triangle. ARCH staked a role for professionals as expert intermediaries. Hatch sought to maintain the designer-client relationship that had long defined the practice of design, but shifted the client role to those whom plans had often harmed. Hatch's organization thus fashioned the strategy of reform that design activism would employ more widely in this era, an approach soon crystallized in the idea of "advocacy planning."[5] Redevelopment, Hatch argued, could work for low-income residents if communities produced their own plans with the help of sympathetic professionals.

If ARCH revealed the fundamental gradualism of efforts toward participatory democracy in the age of Great Society liberalism, however, so too did
it demonstrate the intractable tensions that underlay that project. The right
to shape the built environment represented a civil rights issue equal to the
right to decent education, public accommodations, or employment. Yet the
civil rights movement proved as mutable in this period as planning itself, and
ARCH thus occupied a shifting terrain in Harlem. Outside the windows of
ARCH's Lenox Avenue office, staff saw increasingly radical demands for racial
self-determination by the late 1960s. Though ARCH helped shift the dynamic
of planning from a clearance approach to one that emphasized rehabilitation
and careful redevelopment for the benefit of residents, its persistent reliance
on expert advocates and outside aid increasingly contradicted the demands
that arose with the growth of the Black Power movement. Hatch's attempts
to adapt to such changes within the rubric of gradual reform demonstrated
the dynamism of activist planning in this period. But ARCH's refusal to
fully cede its intermediary role ultimately proved untenable in a neighborhood where the project of participation and the project of radical community control increasingly aligned.

Urban Renewal and the Transformation of Harlem

Though New York's enthusiasm for large-scale urban renewal reshaped
much of the city's landscape in the postwar period, Harlem bore the mark of
redevelopment on an especially vast scale. Here, officials built middle-class
apartments and expansive public housing developments, and expanded the
institutions that ringed the neighborhood. Such projects often claimed be-
neficent ambitions, especially the hope of maintaining New York's prominent
role on national and international stages. Yet they brought disproportionate
harm to and widespread displacement of Harlem's predominantly low-income,
African American residents. Though proponents promised meaningful reforms in the early 1960s in response to criticism of such excesses, Harlemites
found that officials could not resist the bulldozer approach. New plans for
disruptive redevelopment met a mobilized citizenry, however, who expressed
newly strident but also newly constructive opposition in the face of proposals that threatened to reshape their communities. Residents demanded a

voice in the planning processes that transformed Harlem. They called not for urban renewal's end but for its redirection toward new ends, to create a community of decent homes for Harlem's existing population.

In the years preceding these demands, New York City had become the major laboratory for the practice of slum clearance, exceeding all other American cities in both the scale and scope of midcentury urban redevelopment. Two major tools under the Housing Act of 1949 facilitated this reconstruction. The first, the act's Title I, enabled the acquisition and clearance of private land with considerable public subsidy, and its subsequent development by private investors. The second, Title III, provided for the construction of public housing on cleared blocks. New York City pursued both ends enthusiastically under the dominant leadership of Robert Moses, who ensured that New York maintained a steady flow of funding from federal benefactors. By 1960, New York had obtained nearly $66 million in grants under Title I, almost doubling those of the second largest recipient, Chicago.[6] Through Title I, the city supported institutional expansion of its universities, built public facilities like the New York Coliseum and Lincoln Center, and constructed nearly 30,000 housing units for middle-income and affluent New Yorkers. Likewise, officials created 130,000 new public housing units in greater New York between 1945 and 1965 under Title III, rebuilding hundreds of acres in the process.[7]

Such projects disproportionately targeted neighborhoods where low-income New Yorkers of color resided. The law required that cleared sites be predominantly residential, and the subjective nature of "blight," the designation used to justify eminent domain, ensured that officials could mark almost any neighborhood as a slum. Thus, they frequently cleared prime real estate occupied by groups with little political power. Of the sixteen Title I projects built by 1957, seven reshaped largely nonwhite neighborhoods for the benefit of new middle-class residents. Moreover, Moses typically maintained racial and economic segregation in completed projects and gained special exemption from rules requiring oversight of residential relocation. As a result, displaced tenants typically moved to other poor, dilapidated neighborhoods. Residential redevelopment hardened existing racial boundaries, stratified the city's population, and worsened the very conditions that it purported to solve.[8]

Greater Harlem perhaps bore the brunt of such efforts more than any other part of the city. East Harlem, generally the community east of Fifth

Avenue and north of 96th Street, saw New York's largest campaign to construct public housing. Between 1941 and 1965, officials spent over a quarter of a billion dollars there to build projects housing 62,400 residents. They reclaimed massive spaces within the grid. The James Weldon Johnson Houses, opened in 1948, occupied six blocks between Park and Third Avenues, from 112th to 115th Streets. Their scale was grand but not atypical. By the completion of the fifteenth such project, the city had reconstructed 162 acres of East Harlem.[9] Likewise, Central Harlem saw considerable redevelopment, including the Polo Grounds Houses and Colonial Park Houses (now the Ralph Rangel Houses), both large public housing complexes along the Harlem River; and the St. Nicholas Houses, between Seventh and Eighth Avenues and 127th and 131st Streets. Two Title I projects housed middle-income African American tenants—Delano Village, along Lenox Avenue between 139th and 141st Streets, and Lenox Terrace, at Lenox Avenue and 135th Street. Their twenty-four acres had included some of the first speculative townhouses built in Harlem in the late nineteenth century and some of the first homes in Harlem to be sold to African Americans in the early twentieth century.[10] Nearby, in West Harlem, Columbia University and other institutional interests backed the construction of Morningside Gardens, a Title I project that opened in 1957, and two adjoining public housing developments: General Grant Houses, along 125th Street, and Manhattanville Houses, a couple of blocks north.[11]

The intentions behind such projects were never purely negative and their impact on surrounding Harlem was decidedly complex. Redevelopment derived from several motivations: the ambition to restore urban competitiveness in an age of increasing suburbanization, aspirations to stem physical deterioration, and a midcentury faith in the importance of institutions on a national and global stage. For example, Columbia University justified the reconstruction of Morningside Heights by arguing that its continued prominence depended on distance from nearby minority and low-income populations, which leaders perceived as slums. Moreover, proponents sought to temper their actions with steps they viewed as benevolent, including rehabilitation of nearby homes and increased policing.[12] Likewise, the construction of middle-class housing for African Americans in Central Harlem grew from Moses's practice of racial segregation but provided some of the finest housing the neighborhood had yet seen. Lenox Terrace, with its modern towers and elegantly attired doormen, became the go-to address for many prominent Harlemites. Getting to that point was punishing for tenants of the homes that had been located at the site, however, whose neighborhood deteriorated during the five years of delays that preceded construction and, ultimately, their displacement.[13]

Similarly, public housing's legacy is famously mixed: while such housing often became the final destination for those displaced from renewal projects elsewhere in the city, the motivations of backers were initially benign. In the postwar era, officials saw public housing as a valuable tool to replace physically dilapidated buildings with new, affordable apartments, an enactment of the modernist dream of architecture and urbanism as tools of social improvement. Yet the promise behind public housing fractured within only a few years. Tenants found physical problems in the underfunded and undermaintained projects, adjacent neighborhoods faced new social problems, and a pool of low-income New Yorkers either could not qualify for the new housing or spent years on waiting lists.[14]

Regardless of the intentions underlying renewal, then, the fact remained that by the mid-1960s commentators, policy makers, and affected residents largely shared the perception that the means of renewal had brought dramatically negative results.[15] By 1965, social scientist Scott Greer could draw one damning conclusion from his nationwide study of urban renewal: "At a cost of more than three billion dollars the Urban Renewal Agency has succeeded in materially reducing the supply of low-cost housing in American cities."[16] Critics assailed the practice of slum clearance, leveling heavy condemnation from all sides. In her *Death and Life of Great American Cities* of 1961, Jane Jacobs focused on the physical products of renewal. "They seldom aid the city areas around them, as in theory they are supposed to," she wrote. "These amputated areas typically develop galloping gangrene." Sociologist Herbert Gans offered a close study of the Italian Americans in Boston's West End in 1962, revealing a rich social structure in a community that was soon to be cleared for new middle-income housing. In his vividly titled 1964 study, *The Federal Bulldozer*, Martin Anderson, a conservative political scientist, criticized urban renewal's failure to achieve its stated goals of creating decent housing, and condemned the broad government role the program entailed.[17]

Such published works offered the most visible attacks against the predominant city planning practice of the era, but New Yorkers had already begun to push back against modernist redevelopment at the grassroots level. Jacobs herself defended her Greenwich Village neighborhood against street widening plans in 1958. In 1957, she had joined the East Harlem Project, an effort led by social workers Ellen Lurie and Preston Wilcox that attempted to craft a physical alternative to the alienation often associated with immense public housing schemes.[18] In the Lower East Side, too, tenant organizers and residents in the Cooper Square area moved to wrest control of the redevelopment process, forming the Cooper Square Committee in response to a 1959 plan to clear a substantial portion of the neighborhood. They successfully warded off such plans and guided redevelopment of the area over the next several decades.[19]

City officials responded to this rising tide, promising a new approach to the practice of city building. In 1960, Moses resigned his position at the Committee on Slum Clearance, the body most responsible for implementing redevelopment. James Felt, who as chair of the City Planning Commission took over as the top redevelopment official, offered a more nuanced strategy. "The backbone of renewal," Felt said in 1961, "is in conserving and improving our existing structures and relating new development to the character and needs of the community." He promised increased rehabilitation, development on small sites, and selective removal within blocks.[20]

Yet words did not always align with deeds. When Harlem soon found itself the object of renewed attention, proposals frequently relied on the very strategies of large-scale demolition that had come under increasing scrutiny by the late 1950s. In the spring of 1961, the city proposed clearing a neighborhood that would come to be known as the East Harlem Triangle, a predominantly African American community north of 125th Street and east of Park Avenue, which officials called "one of the most blighted and run-down areas in Harlem." In these densely inhabited blocks, the city planned an industrial park including four million square feet of rentable space. Officials called the scheme a "major stimulus to the city's economy," but the massive project also promised the total devastation of the existing community.[21]

Indeed, by the mid-1960s, officials acknowledged a "return to [the] bulldozer," as the *New York Times* described it. William Ballard, chair of the City Planning Commission in early 1964, acknowledged, "We've been trying to do urban renewal without taking down any buildings, moving any people or hurting anybody." But the city emphasized clearance in the projects it was ready to announce. "Now, in a very limited way, we're going again into the areas that have to be bull-dozed." The Morningside General Neighborhood Renewal Plan (GNRP), released in the fall of 1964, described one of those areas. For the ninety-two blocks around Columbia University, the city touted a list of goals, including reducing density and traffic congestion, creating new open space, improving the area's "physical appearance," and enabling the expansion of Columbia and its academic neighbors.[22]

Officials promised a variety of strategies to bring about those ends without severe human costs, but even here, where the city expected to demolish only 17 percent of the project area, or just over thirty-six acres, the city's return to clearance bore profoundly uneven impacts. Then, as now, Morningside Park ran south to north for thirteen blocks, delineating a break in Harlem's landscape marked by dramatic changes in topography, land use, and demographics. Along the park's western flank sat the neighborhood known as Morningside Heights, encompassing Columbia, the Cathedral Church of St. John the Divine, Union Theological Seminary, and the Jewish Theological Seminary, all high up on a bluff looking east over Harlem. Below, West Harlem presented a predominantly residential neighborhood, with dense blocks and commerce along 116th Street and its broad avenues. Almost three-quarters of the residents who lived amid the institutions of Morningside Heights were white. Nearly 99 percent of the residents in the GNRP's designated area of West Harlem were African American and poorer than their counterparts up the hill. Here, officials rendered a bleak diagnosis and, consequently, a harsh cure. In Morningside Heights, they reported, 217 of the 390 surveyed structures had "deficiencies." In West Harlem, however, officials explained that nearly all the housing was unworthy of rehabilitation, especially the many old law tenements—built before 1901 and containing what they deemed insufficient light and "inadequate basic facilities." Planners claimed that 375 of the 393 structures in the West Harlem portion of the plan were unsound. They envisioned clearing 16 of the 50 acres in Morningside Heights, but more than 20 of the 25.7 acres in West Harlem.[23]

The city pledged that the necessary relocation would be a matter of little concern for the residents uprooted by the nearly total demolition of their neighborhood. They noted the hundreds of thousands of housing units that had been completed in the city over the previous decade and projected that hundreds of thousands more could be expected during the ensuing decade. But residents, familiar with the city's heavy-handed approach to redevelopment in Harlem over the past two decades, were deeply suspicious of such pronouncements. In August, just before the Morningside plan's official release, neighborhood leaders including Rev. Eugene Callender, the minister at West Harlem's Church of the Master, and Marie Runyon, a tenant activist in Morningside Heights, circulated a letter asking, "Do you know how the Morningside General Neighborhood Renewal Plan is going to affect you?" Invoking past experience, they noted, "One thing . . . is certain about urban renewal in low income areas: only rarely are the buildings that are torn down replaced by living units that fit the pocket books of those who were living there."[24]

Residents had learned to be disappointed by redevelopment, yet the growing trend of resistance to plans across the city empowered West Harlemites. Indeed, the nature of their early complaints foreshadowed the shape of things to come. Their frustration with the Morningside GNRP was premised on opposition not to redevelopment per se, but specifically to renewal that failed to serve existing residents' needs. In other words, residents did not oppose rebuilding, but rather its use against them. "Urban renewal should improve the life of the community," the neighborhood leaders' letter read, "but it can do this only if its primary allegiance is to the individuals who will be [a]ffected by it. We . . . have not been guaranteed that allegiance, and it is therefore essential that we make sure that the plan benefits us."[25]

Noting that Morningside Heights institutions had helped shape the city's plans, neighborhood leaders demanded a voice in planning decisions too. They hoped to prevent wanton clearance and provide improved, affordable housing for current residents. Runyon's Morningsiders United organized a ten-week seminar led by planner Walter Thabit, who had been instrumental in the effort to transform plans for the redevelopment of Cooper Square. Thabit was to instruct attendees on both the recent history of renewal and his own experience shaping it. These were skills that even a mobilized community could not offer on its own—expertise in the practice of city making, a vocabulary that could match that of officials—but that would prove essential as Harlemites sought to change the nature of urban redevelopment.[26]

Experts as Advocates

It was in this context that Hatch founded ARCH in 1964. Architects and planners conscious of the paradoxes of renewal's liberal aspirations had offered their services to neighborhoods in Harlem and elsewhere on a limited basis since the late 1950s. But ARCH was the first effort to institutionalize this function, creating a new entity, the community design center, and providing a physical space where residents could access professional services otherwise out of reach. Its intentions revealed themselves in the preposition Hatch had chosen to include in the organization's name. The Architects' Renewal Committee was not "of" Harlem—its architects and planners came from throughout the city—but it was "in" Harlem, accessible to residents and at their service. As this suggested, ARCH's staff aspired toward a democratization of redevelopment through reform, not revolution: they maintained both their central role as experts in the process and a faith in renewal itself. But they imagined a dramatically different outcome, arguing for redevelopment that benefited, rather than harmed, existing Harlemites.

Hatch's vision for ARCH had its roots in a range of sources, including ongoing debates about the role of participation in planning and the wider struggle over civil rights for African Americans. Civil rights provided a personal motivation for Hatch, who was white. He had grown up in a conservative Long Island family but maintained Far Left sympathies, representing the American Labor Party in Great Neck and documenting poverty in the town, a campaign published in the *Suffolk County News* in the late 1940s. He studied architecture at Harvard College and the University of Pennsylvania in the 1950s, and in the 1960s became involved with the Student Nonviolent Coordinating Committee (SNCC) and the Mississippi Freedom Democratic Party through his then wife. Hatch watched tides of young people leave to join the civil rights movement in the South, but realized the extent of the problems that persisted in the North. He thus focused his energies on New York, where he was working as an architect. In 1963 and 1964, Hatch became acquainted with Harlem civil rights leaders through Maureen Cusack, who would later become ARCH's first hire and, later still, Hatch's second wife. Through contact with activists Farmer, Gray, Marshall England, and Roy Innis, Hatch began to consider how he might assist Harlemites threatened with disruptive redevelopment.[27]

ARCH aligned with a broader effort to provide new avenues for participation in public life that was gaining momentum at this time. President Johnson had signed the Economic Opportunity Act of 1964 into law in August, launching the Community Action Program and its promise to ensure "the maximum feasible participation of the poor and members of the groups served" in its activities. While it would be several months before the first War on Poverty monies reached Harlem, Hatch, like fellow activists in other American cities, found in Johnson's initiative both a political opening for his civil rights ambitions and new financial support that would help efforts like ARCH get under way. The War on Poverty fueled experiments in participatory democracy and new campaigns for local autonomy by residents of diverse racial and ethnic backgrounds but also by outsiders like Hatch, who sought to organize communities that had suffered without self-determination. Early on, Hatch explained his organization's intention to restore control to Harlem residents. "Ghetto residents must, as a first step toward full participation of our society, be enabled to make the decisions which affect their destinies," he explained. "In our work, they will take the leadership."[28]

Yet in its approach to democratizing planning, ARCH also symbolized the larger paradox that attended such efforts. The drafters of the War on Poverty sought to move beyond the liberalism of the New Deal era, characterized by the sort of federal government–dominated policies that urban renewal exemplified, but President Johnson's Great Society nonetheless remained largely within the parameters of midcentury liberalism. While broadening opportunities for participation, policies continued to maintain the centrality of federal aid and the prominence of professional expertise.[29] Likewise, in pursuing alternatives to clearance-oriented redevelopment, ARCH at once aspired to access a steady stream of public funding and to negotiate a new localism in its use, to bring new participants into the decision-making process and to retain the central role of experts. ARCH's initial board of directors, which included architects Norval White, Mayer, Edward Echeverria, and Edgar Tafel; planner Thabit; and sociologist Gans, exemplified this dependence on highly trained professionals.[30]

Indeed, Hatch sought gradual reform within the traditional architectural relationship of patron and designer, a goal that aligned with the Great Society's ambition to provide citizens with new influence without fundamentally undermining existing institutions. As Hatch explained at the April 1965

Harvard Urban Design Conference, his objective was "to turn the consumers of architectural goods—the poor—into clients, into proper clients." While shifting the patronage role from city officials to residents, designers would retain a primary role as intermediaries in the process, as advocates. "Architects eventually have got to see themselves—I quite strongly feel—as advocates for the poor," Hatch said. "And students coming out of architecture school must be required . . . to go into the neighborhoods of the poor and work with them as lawyers and legal aid societies work with them." ARCH staff members would translate the wishes of their previously disenfranchised clients into the language of architecture and planning.[31]

In describing new modes of engagement within the bounds of the design professions, Hatch's words anticipated those of planner Paul Davidoff's November 1965 article, "Advocacy and Pluralism in Planning." Davidoff's treatise would offer the most famous theoretical backing for the field of activist planning. "The planner should do more than explicate the values underlying his prescriptions for courses of action," Davidoff argued, "he should affirm them; he should be an advocate for what he deems proper." Davidoff envisioned a new role for planners inspired by the adversarial approach of law. Instead of a single "unitary plan," as Davidoff called the traditional medium of planning, he contended that planners should develop multiple plans, each representing the different interests at stake in a given project. These would form the basis for negotiation, with planners serving as advocates for their clients. "Appropriate policy in a democracy is determined through a process of political debate," Davidoff wrote. Though Davidoff's notion of "plural planning" offered a radical departure from the top-down mode of modernist planning, he voiced this solution as a means of strengthening, not undermining, the profession of planning in an era of crisis. "The advocacy of alternative plans by interest groups outside of government would stimulate city planning in a number of ways," Davidoff explained. Advocacy would improve alternatives and increase the quality of work, he argued, and it would force opponents to speak through the tools of planning, not simply vocal opposition.[32]

The paradox intrinsic to ARCH's effort to democratize planning while retaining an intermediary role for professionals suggested itself from day one. ARCH's method required the organization to gain the trust and attention of residents in areas marked for renewal, but staff consisted largely of outsiders to Harlem. "The community will not come to us, we must go to it," Hatch instructed his volunteers. These volunteers formed committees assigned to different Harlem neighborhoods. The committee for the Milbank area, for instance, included young architects and planners, both African American and white; White, ARCH's board president; and Frances Fox Piven, the noted social scientist and poverty scholar. To increase its visibility in Harlem, ARCH had begun to plan federally funded preschools; educational materials, such as a filmstrip on planning; and an exhibition on neighborhood conditions. Its effectiveness depended crucially on finding like-minded local partners and convincing Harlemites that this was a pursuit worth their effort.[33]

Yet with such partnerships commonplace in the political context of the mid-1960s, the perils of this approach remained in the future. In the communities delineated by the Morningside GNRP, ARCH staff found residents who had already begun to organize around the threat of large-scale displacement. Neighborhood leaders, who had sought the assistance of professional experts early on, shared ARCH's approach. In December 1964, Callender formalized opposition with the creation of the Tri-Community Organization, an alliance of tenant activists including representatives from Morningside Heights, West Harlem, and Manhattan Valley, the neighborhood immediately south of West Harlem. With its neighborhoods under threat, Tri-Community asked the newly formed ARCH to analyze the intentions of the Morningside plan.[34]

ARCH's critique of the Morningside GNRP, the organization's first public statement, outlined the approach to redevelopment that would characterize its early work in Harlem. Fundamental to ARCH's denunciation was an extreme distaste for the city's method of urban renewal, but never a rejection of the need for renewal itself. Indeed, ARCH volunteer Ronald Kolbe wrote, their aim was "to improve the plan," to suggest the ways that a wrongheaded strategy could be righted. "The idea that urban renewal is a chance to create a balanced and healthy environment for the present residents is alien to this proposal," Kolbe argued, expressing an ideal for redevelopment even as he criticized the city's neglect of the existing community. The city's plan would harm residents disparately, along class lines. West Harlem would see severe displacement, Kolbe wrote, with more than three-quarters of its tenants uprooted. Even in wealthier Morningside Heights, where fewer homes were to be destroyed, officials intended to displace all tenants of single-room-occupancy (SRO) hotels, typically the poorest and most prob-lem-plagued residents in the city.[35]

Yet ARCH's analysis contended that officials had drawn the boundaries of the redevelopment project too stingily, not too expansively. The plan excluded considerable acreage within its extent, specifically fourteen blocks around Columbia. The exemption of those 17,000 residents from the plan, Kolbe ar-gued, "removes Columbia's actions . . . from public scrutiny, and leaves the interests of the present residents unprotected." Relocation assistance from the city left much to be desired, indeed, but inclusion in the plan would at least provide some aid to the 4,300 households who lived in Columbia-owned property on those blocks, who could otherwise be evicted without any form of compensation. Equally problematic for ARCH activists, the outer boundaries of the plan excluded key areas that could potentially help reduce the burden on displaced residents. In the city's plans for broad clear-ance, a four-block community center, and a widened Eighth Avenue, ARCH saw "a major reduction of residential land" in West Harlem. "The total effect will be to drastically change the character and population of the commu-nity, and to constrict Harlem further as its boundary is pushed eastward from Morningside to Eighth Avenues," Kolbe contended. A larger renewal area would help reduce the scope of these problems by including vacant land on which the city could build new housing for displaced tenants.[36]

Above all, ARCH's critique rested on a fundamentally different concep-tion of redevelopment's beneficiaries from that maintained by officials. The city's strategy grew from an increasingly obsolete approach to urbanism, rooted in the same assumptions that had guided redevelopment in Harlem over two decades—especially a faith in institutions and in the inherent value of the middle class. Returning the middle class to New York City had been Moses's first priority, apparent in the expansion of universities and cultural institutions, and in the dozens of developments intended to provide them with housing.[37] ARCH found the same tendency in the Morningside plan. Staff doubted that the city would house low-income residents in the plan's 4,500 new housing units, noting that officials refused to guarantee affordable rents. Indeed, ARCH forecasted that only a third of displaced tenants would find affordable housing anywhere in the city, let alone in their former neigh-borhood. More distressing still were the dim prospects for SRO tenants.

"Dislocation may be an immediate remedy for Morningside Heights," where institutions hoped to eliminate all SROs, ARCH staff explained, "but it will only force these people into other areas where they will face the same problems and hostilities all over again."[38]

ARCH asked why decent low-income housing couldn't be a solution in itself, even the very objective of redevelopment. "The plan fails to recognize the important need for this type of housing in the city," Kolbe wrote of SROs. Indeed, such housing could be more than a last resort; it could be a means "to restore self-confidence and hope to these people." But, he claimed, the city's priorities revealed a deeper bias. "The plan betrays an almost cynical lack of concern for the deep rooted and serious social problems of the area," Kolbe wrote. His litany captured the full range of issues that ARCH believed were overlooked in the plan: "the housing and social welfare needs of the elderly, unfavorable economic circumstances of many families, the high incidence of drug addiction, and the lack of adequate child care, medical, and educational services." This was a matter of equity. Not only did the Morningside plan reinscribe and worsen existing disparities in uptown's built environment, but the costs were not borne equally. "The plan will offer benefits to certain groups such as the institutions and some middle income families," Kolbe argued, "while others, such as residents of West Harlem, those in rooming houses throughout the area, and the elderly, will suffer an unusually large share of the burdens."[39]

Harlemites echoed Kolbe's criticism, insisting that the city recognize the humanity of existing residents, regardless of their income. Within days of the March 1965 release of ARCH's critique, residents of West Harlem made their way to city hall for a hearing by the Board of Estimate, the body that would vote on the plan. An all-night vigil led by Callender preceded the hearing, where, the *Times* reported, "a parade of the Negro and Puerto Rican poor protested . . . on the ground that it would destroy their homes and simply drive them into other slums." Residents opposed the plan and its backers by pointing to their own value as people. "How much money will you give for a human life?" asked William Stanley, who managed a building in the area and had protested disruptive redevelopment throughout Harlem in the mid-1960s. "These people . . . they know what a rat or a roach infested home is. Bad as it is, they want to keep it." Resident Estelle Edwards wondered whether she and her neighbors were "always going to be a collection of citizens in a minority always categorized by what we haven't got." "We want to be first-class citizens, too," she argued.[40]

But officials reiterated the very approach to redevelopment that activists attacked, demonstrating their fundamental unwillingness to reframe renewal in these new terms. Columbia University officials and their institutional neighbors justified the project with grandiose explanations that had long been central to urban renewal, suggesting that "if the plan did not go forward they would be denied the room for the expansion they desperately needed to serve the city and the nation," the *Times* reported. In response to the pleas of residents, Columbia provost Jacques Barzun voiced concern for the well-being of the university's students. His language angered Harlemites who had publicly objected to the second-class status they repeatedly felt they had been given. As the reporter paraphrased, Barzun argued that his university "had the responsibility of training the leaders that the country would need tomorrow." His actual quote was less delicate, if more revealing. "They must not," Barzun said, "be subjected to an environment that requires the perpetual *qui vive* of a paratrooper in enemy country."[41]

The battle over the future of West Harlem symbolized the broader transformation that redevelopment was undergoing at this time. Urban renewal had long been a paternalistic, top-down policy that viewed a community like this one as a simplified abstraction. ARCH and its partners instead offered an approach that valued the individuals who lived in such places and supported their right to remain. The tension inherent in this shift from an old order to an emergent alternative, and the issues at stake, became vividly apparent when West Harlemites clashed again with Barzun, who personified the standpoint they opposed. Barzun had stereotyped and belittled existing residents with poorly chosen words at an April hearing on the city's proposal. They were "transient, footloose, or unhappily disturbed people," Barzun contended. But the members of the West Harlem Community Organization (WHCO), which these residents founded with the assistance of ARCH, Callender, and Morningsiders United, proved remarkably canny, in fact, staging an uninvited visit to Barzun's office in early May 1965 and notifying a reporter so the encounter would be recorded. "No one, especially an educated man like you, has the right to talk about people the way you did. . . . You insulted me," Stanley opened. "I was not talking about you good people,"

Barzun deflected, "but about addicts and prostitutes." "How do you know what we are?" Stanley asked. "You were talking about a part of our community. About Harlem. About colored people." "We want to help the addicts. They are a part of our community," added Margaret McNeil, a leader of WHCO. "The university, with all its education, should also help the addicts." Barzun objected. "That is a technical problem," he told McNeil. Stanley disagreed vehemently: "No . . . that is a human problem."[42]

Rehabilitating West Harlem

What might a city without displacement look like, one where Stanley's "human problems" were assisted, not excised, through urban renewal? Vocal critique could only go so far, activists learned, spurring modest compromises but not materially lessening the negative impact of the city's plans. Indeed, the Morningside plan made its way through city bureaucracies largely intact in early 1965, with only minor concessions intended to slow displacement and allow the possibility of some relocation housing in the area. Roughly 6,500 people would still be evicted, opponents estimated.[43] Faced with intransigence in response to their pleas, activists increasingly focused on the translation of resistance into physical form through the creation of alternate plans. Alternate planning was premised on the idea that Davidoff would soon voice, that a physical vision could sway opponents in ways that rhetoric could not. Yet as alternate plans for West Harlem took shape, they were remarkable not for any apparent visionary quality but for their resemblance to the existing city. In emphasizing the intrinsic value of West Harlem's residents, ARCH staff likewise emphasized the intrinsic value of its buildings, calling for the wide use of rehabilitation as a means of improving the neighborhood. Stabilizing the existing fabric of the city to decently house low-income residents provided a solution whose very physical continuity revealed its distance from the norm of urban renewal. Despite this departure, however, ARCH's planning strategy reinforced the organization's fundamental gradualism, reemphasizing the centrality of both the state and the professional designer.

Indeed, an increased focus on the physical form of redevelopment bolstered the role of design expertise in ARCH's work. "Our services are free," Hatch wrote to the editor of the *Amsterdam News* in July 1965, announcing

the opening of ARCH's new office at 306 Lenox Avenue, near the major intersection of Lenox Avenue and 125th Street. "We welcome the opportunity to
serve interested neighborhood groups." ARCH added twenty-one additional
architects and planners for the summer, all graduate students supported
through a J. M. Kaplan Fund grant and engaged in research projects focused
on Harlem's physical space. Likewise, ARCH expanded its expertise with
the addition of Jack Bailey, a white architect and Harvard acquaintance of
Hatch, as assistant director. Bailey had previously worked at the Boston Redevelopment Authority, the agency responsible for one of the most prolific
redevelopment programs in the country; had earlier been on staff at the
New York City Planning Commission; and had become disaffected with
urban renewal. Bailey offered a perspective honed on the other side of the
table, an attribute that Hatch recognized would lend ARCH credibility as it
became more involved in the reconstruction of Harlem.[44]

Such changes underscored ARCH's commitment to reforming redevelopment from within the parameters of urban renewal. So too did the very
planning document through which activists drafted their vision for West
Harlem. To lend legitimacy to their project and, indeed, as a clever sleight of
hand, ARCH and WHCO, their community partner, wrote the alternate plan
for what they called the "West Harlem Urban Renewal Area" as a survey and
planning application, the official form required to request federal planning
funds for redevelopment. They submitted their "counter proposal" through
official channels as well, with the help of New York City congressman William Fitts Ryan, who arranged a meeting between ARCH, WHCO, and the
regional director of the Department of Housing and Urban Development
(HUD), the agency that approved urban renewal funding requests.[45]

The application hewed closely to official guidelines, yet emphasized at
every turn a strategy of upsetting the Morningside GNRP's clearance-heavy
approach. Seeking to encompass more West Harlemites in reconstruction,
drafters of the alternate plan outlined an expanded redevelopment area. They
extended the eastern boundary to encompass both sides of Eighth Avenue
and pushed the northern boundary from 119th Street up to 123rd Street. Yet
if these generous boundaries suggested assent to the basic premise of renewal, the alternate plan's physical strategy offered a telling rebuke to the
city's plans. "Rehabilitation" was the architectural watchword of the alternate
plan, an idea that recurred throughout (see Figure 1.1). "The dwindling supply

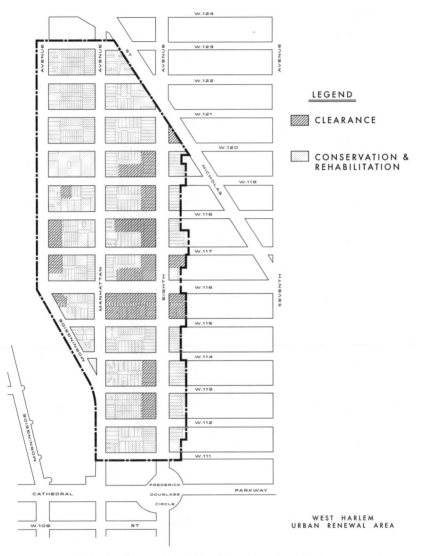

FIGURE 1.1. Plan for the "West Harlem Urban Renewal Area," from the survey and planning application drafted by WHCO and ARCH in January 1966. Their proposal emphasized rehabilitation, a response to and rejection of the city's clearance-heavy approach to West Harlem redevelopment.

of low rent housing in Manhattan . . . and the expanding need for such housing," planners argued, "makes it mandatory that the basic[al]ly sound housing stock of West Harlem be retained through a program of conservation and rehabilitation in varying degrees with spot clearance and redevelopment only where necessary and appropriate." ARCH had conducted its own survey of housing in this area, finding dramatically different results from those described by the city. Against the notion of a neighborhood in dilapidation, planners contended that much of the housing stock was intact. Some building types, such as old law tenements, were not ideal but remained habitable. ARCH staff estimated that more than a third of the neighborhood's buildings required only code enforcement, or basic improvement based on city building codes, and as much as 40 percent could be improved through modest rehabilitation without relocation. ARCH proposed concentrating clearance along Eighth Avenue, the area where staff identified the most dilapidated housing.[46]

Rehabilitation marked a physical response to a practical problem, perhaps the most obvious strategy in a situation where residents were low income and housing was imperfect but salvageable. ARCH did not originate the concept, to be sure. The Housing Act of 1954 had brought rehabilitation under the umbrella of redevelopment, and the city became more open to that approach in the 1960s. HUD had recently embarked on a model rehabilitation project adjacent to West Harlem, on 114th Street between Seventh and Eighth Avenues. The 114th Street effort captivated journalists, who traced the journey of the low-income tenants as they began to move into their new homes in 1965. But the scale of rehabilitation outlined in ARCH's alternate plan for West Harlem, and the exclusive use of this rehabilitated housing for low-income tenants, marked a dramatic departure from precedent. Urban renewal, after all, remained physically deterministic at its core, tying large-scale reconstruction to improved social outcomes. Activists' calls for the retention of obsolete housing types, such as the old law tenement, refuted the idea that the improvement of a neighborhood required starting with an architectural blank slate, just as it rejected the idea that redevelopment required starting with a new population.[47]

Yet even as the alternate plan suggested deep frustration with officials' typical strategy, activists fully exploited the potential resources they could obtain from government at all levels. Just as planners called for urban renewal's reorientation toward new ends, they encouraged the use of public funding for the benefit of existing residents. They would tap every available public resource, ARCH staff explained, to facilitate property acquisition, ease physical improvement, and reduce rent. As ARCH staff wrote in their March 1966 *Government Programs for Community Development,* a guidebook whose very title encapsulated this strategy, "The Federal, State and City governments all offer aids which can enable local organizations, on their own initiative, to make real changes in their neighborhoods." They broadcast the message less subtly in announcing the guide: "This book will help your community organization to get *government money* for neighborhood improvement." They highlighted programs that promised to reduce the cost of housing rehabilitation, subsidize construction labor, or minimize new construction costs, in order to make new housing affordable to low-income tenants.[48] Likewise, the Housing and Urban Development Act of 1965, passed in August, caught ARCH's admiring eye for its focus on rehabilitation and new rent supplements that promised to reduce the costs of private-market affordable housing.[49]

The tenants' rights movement offered an alternative approach to the goal of rehabilitation as a means of ensuring the availability of decent, affordable housing. Tenants' rights battles had a long history in New York, but 1965 and 1966 brought several new tools at the state and local levels that ARCH leaders enthusiastically embraced. The city's Emergency Repair Program, for example, allocated a fund from which officials could draw to make crucial repairs, billing recalcitrant landlords for the costs. Article 7-A of the state's Real Property Actions and Proceedings Law facilitated rent strikes, allowing tenants to gain court protection to put rent money toward building needs, such as heat, water, or electricity, and dangerous structural problems. City Receivership allowed temporary takeover of dilapidated buildings when landlords failed in their responsibilities, again to ensure that essential repairs were made.[50] ARCH's major contribution to such efforts was a comprehensive guidebook, *Tenant Action,* first published in 1965 and distributed widely in Harlem and beyond. The book went into its second printing by March 1966, with 2,500 copies circulated by November. Free publicity in *Times* and *Amsterdam News* articles surely helped. *Tenant Action* "offer[ed] guidelines for minority-group families in dealing with uncooperative landlords—or an uncooperative society," the *Times* wrote.[51] ARCH likewise extended its work beyond guidance to become directly involved in such cases throughout Harlem, even drafting legal claims. Staff testified in court and recruited lawyers and volunteers to target housing violations. By June 1966, staff member Robert Stover, who had prepared *Tenant Action,* had filed fifteen rent strike cases. By the fall, he had assembled ten attorneys and ten architects in a broader effort that encompassed forty actions under Article 7-A and other legislation. Hatch reported that these represented more than half of the cases brought in New York City in 1966.[52]

Such success demonstrated the plausibility of rehabilitating Harlem's housing, an accomplishment that inspired broader ambitions. "We are the *only* housing organization active in this fashion in Central Harlem!" Hatch wrote in late 1966. With more activist legislation on the horizon, Hatch imagined the "potential for substantial city-wide strike action." His dream embodied a prescient vision that would attain ironic reality in the mid-1970s. "The net effect of such a massive, simple, legal rent strike would probably be to drive many marginal slumlords to abandon their buildings—and here we are back at the Neighborhood Housing Corporations which would be created to take over the properties," Hatch said.[53]

Yet as Hatch relayed his hope that the organization's efforts marked only the first step in a sweeping rehabilitation of Harlem, new concerns tempered his enthusiasm. "We feel we need a Negro organizer-housing consultant to oversee this program and seek out clients," Hatch wrote. Indeed, this warning spoke to a broader tension that had begun to surface more frequently. For example, a December 1965 article noted the criticism of one volunteer, an African American architect "in charge of ARCH's activities in the neighborhood where he was reared." In his view, the reporter noted, "too few of the volunteers have or seek direct knowledge of the ghetto community. Too much time is spent on fact-finding reports . . . and too little getting acquainted with community leaders and organizations." One 1965 project, a proposal for a "long range plan" for Harlem, suggested a possible basis for criticism that the organization risked aloofness. "ARCH must begin to think about a long range plan for Harlem as a whole," the proposal began, before outlining a strategy that originated with the trained professionals of ARCH before moving into the Harlem community. "It would . . . be appropriate for a group to start working on total long range ideas of what Harlem could be like and how it might get there," staff wrote, "to stimulate the thinking of local community groups and broaden their concepts of possibilities."[54]

Even as ARCH witnessed these initial stirrings of frustration with its relative gradualism, the support of its first clients endured unabated. West Harlem residents voted on the alternate plan for their neighborhood at its December 1965 unveiling at a "community-wide public hearing," where, in ARCH's words, they "unanimously approved." Yet these changing dynamics would soon confront the organization's predominantly white architects and planners more profoundly. In the following months, Harlem would become the very seat of new demands for racial autonomy and new frustrations with the advocacy model that ARCH, with its emphasis on the intermediary role of professional experts, particularly embodied.[55]

The Emergence of Community Control

The alternate plan for West Harlem and its reception among both federal lawmakers and bureaucrats testified to the gains ARCH had made in reputation and visibility in less than two years. Yet the organization's goal of neighborhood-wide rehabilitation proved unattainable. "A great deal of our energy has gone into this project," Hatch wrote in November 1966, listing the survey and planning application, community meetings, various studies, and the Head Start preschool—perhaps the first in New York City—that ARCH and WHCO organized to provide employment and facilitate community organizing. But momentum had subsided. "The city has all but dropped the project," Hatch observed, an outcome that marked only a partial victory for the activists who had maintained pressure in the hope of improving the neighborhood.[56]

Activist planners still intended to realize their vision of a community reconstructed for low-income Harlemites, however. The East Harlem Triangle, the neighborhood that the city had designated for total clearance in 1961 to make way for an industrial park, offered a new opportunity for ARCH in 1966. Where ARCH had often led the way in West Harlem, as staff helped establish WHCO and then guided the alternate planning process, the East Harlem Triangle had seen an active and tenacious resistance to urban renewal throughout the early 1960s. By the time leaders tapped ARCH's assistance in June 1966, members of the Community Association of the East Harlem Triangle

(CAEHT) already had extensive experience manipulating the urban renewal bureaucracy and grand aspirations for their own alternate plan.[57]

The East Harlem Triangle offered a departure from West Harlem not only because of its long-standing mobilized community, however. Here, ARCH came in direct contact with the leading edge of the transforming civil rights movement. Residents of the East Harlem Triangle sought to balance continued reliance on outside assistance with emerging aspirations toward self-help. Such struggles revealed the larger battle in progress in this era, between enduring gradual approaches to participation and growing demands for radical self-determination. Indeed, as a key site in the emergence of the Black Power movement, with its calls for racial autonomy in education, politics, and the built environment, the Triangle neighborhood became the very crucible in which such demands were forged. The drive for "community control" in Harlem, the rest of New York City, and throughout the United States exposed the intractable dilemma in the work of organizations like ARCH. ARCH's model, premised on the alliance of community members and expert intermediaries, marked the very dynamic that radical activists would come to reject amid widespread calls for unmediated decision making by African American residents.

No figure represented the deep-rooted activist spirit of the East Harlem Triangle as much as Alice Kornegay, whose mischievous greeting at the February 1966 opening of CAEHT's new headquarters encapsulated the modus operandi of the Triangle's driving force. To an audience of social workers, clergy, police, and, especially, government officials, Kornegay exclaimed, "I have to acknowledge that all you city people are here because I'll have to fight y'all later." "Let the city be on notice," she continued. "We intend to press for action on the renewal of our community and along the lines we want, not what they want for us. The time is past where we are willing to let others make our decisions for us." The renovated loft at 130 East 129th Street, until recently another dilapidated building, now housed CAEHT's staff and programs, which included tenant organizing and welfare officer training for residents, a Head Start preschool, and a "planned parenthood center."[58]

Kornegay had loudly demanded equal resources and decent treatment for her neighbors for over a decade. Indeed, she, a resident of the East Harlem Triangle since the 1940s, knew officials well by 1966. Melvin Schoonover, the white minister at nearby Chambers Memorial Baptist Church and Kornegay's eventual collaborator, first learned of her as the central figure in the so-called 130th Street Mafia, a group of residents who served as a de facto social service organization for their neglected block. Kornegay, he was told, was "a real fireball." The *Times* reported that she was feted at the opening of CAEHT's headquarters as their "sparkplug." The metaphor was apt, for her first major public activism involved the dangerous traffic that surrounded the community, which was bounded on one side by busy Harlem River Drive, on the second by Park Avenue, and on the third by 125th Street. The city had constructed a park on the far side of Harlem River Drive in 1953. After several children were injured crossing traffic, Kornegay organized petitions for a stoplight and then a pedestrian bridge, both ignored by officials. In 1957, Kornegay led her neighbors onto Harlem River Drive, where they blocked the major thoroughfare and off-ramps. Kornegay's arrest in the protest's second week sparked a 300-person picket at the local Twenty-Fifth Precinct. Her persistence yielded a meeting with the Manhattan Borough president. "He actually said he didn't know people lived in the Triangle," Kornegay remembered. "He told us, 'Your area has never asked for anything before.' We asked for plenty that day." They gained a temporary footbridge over Harlem River Drive and then "Alice's Bridges," the permanent red steel pedestrian bridges that still connect the neighborhood to the park today.[59]

Conditions in the Triangle were grim, a fact that Kornegay, Schoonover, and officials all agreed on, though they offered contrasting responses. Kornegay's 130th Street Mafia had long challenged ineffective landlords, ousted unresponsive building superintendents, and repaired dilapidated buildings themselves. The city intended to simply bulldoze away the neighborhood's problems, selecting the Triangle as the relocation site for industry displaced by residential redevelopment along the Harlem River, near 107th Street. After the city's announcement of clearance plans in May 1961, Schoonover sought more information about this relatively unknown corner of Harlem. He sent seminarians to survey the neighborhood. "There was no question that the area contained some of the most deplorable housing anywhere in the city," he remembered. "Overcrowding was almost unbelievable, with as many as thirteen people living in two rooms." Surprisingly, Schoonover's assistants also learned that most residents had no idea that a renewal plan was even in the offing.[60]

In many ways, the state of the East Harlem Triangle exemplified the direct and collateral damage inflicted by urban renewal over the previous decade and a half. The very conditions that officials hoped to excise were a consequence of past renewal efforts throughout the city. "People complained of having moved as many as seven times because of 'community improvements,'" Schoonover explained. "One man said that the Triangle was 'endsville' as far as he was concerned—where did the city expect him to go, into the East River?" Faced with the stark reality of a neighborhood full of redevelopment's victims, Kornegay cofounded a Committee for the Preservation of the East Harlem Triangle. Its first effort involved a resident-led study of the neighborhood. With loudspeakers installed on a car, committee members distributed surveys throughout the Triangle. The results confirmed the anecdotal evidence that Schoonover cited. Many neighbors struggled with addiction to drugs and alcohol and many also had criminal records. Sixty percent of children were born out of wedlock, and 70 percent of families were separated without divorce. In the context of urban renewal, these facts meant that few residents could qualify for public housing if they were displaced again. If the Triangle was a "last resort," as the *Times* reported in 1964, then where would residents go to make way for an industrial park?[61]

Anticipating the pleas of West Harlem residents, Kornegay argued that clearance wrought profound harm but was also a missed opportunity. She remembered a mother asking, "Why should I have to move somewhere where people don't understand my kids?" Kornegay insisted that her community should represent "a model for the black poor everywhere." "We must have something we can be proud of and want to preserve," she contended, echoing the name of her committee. At a June 1961 City Planning Commission hearing, residents explained that they did not oppose renewal per se, but rather its use against them. They wanted a plan that would improve the community's housing alongside any industrial development. Later that year, at the Board of Estimate hearing where the city requested approval of the clearance plan, Kornegay's group presented their survey findings and their stance on redevelopment. Seventy residents attended, wearing paper triangles on their collars. "The city has a moral responsibility to . . . help those communities which it arouses to overcome their worst fears," their report stated, "as well as to help them to build a new community that will uplift their lives rather than merely scatter them."[62]

Such calls came as the city showed new willingness to experiment with redevelopment in the aftermath of Moses's departure. But here, as elsewhere in New York City in the early 1960s, officials proved inconsistent in their support for alternate methods. Amid residents' protests, the city seemed to shift away from the clearance approach they had outlined. The Triangle gained the Area Services Program that community leaders had requested to maintain property before redevelopment began, for instance. Yet the city dragged its feet in implementing the effort. Likewise, once the program commenced, Schoonover wrote, "alarm grew that Area Services was really engaged in a program to empty out the neighborhood." Officials moved families out of overcrowded housing, but also often out of the neighborhood entirely. They declined to pressure delinquent landlords and failed to maintain services as basic as garbage pickup. The city moved at a glacial pace in pursuing a study that would serve as the basis for revised renewal plans that met residents' needs. Officials gained federal funding for the study in 1964, but debated details over the next two years with their selected consultant (and ARCH board member), Gans, who eventually withdrew. Adding to residents' frustrations, the neighborhood continued to decay while officials dithered.[63]

Exasperated with the city's inability to follow through on its promises, CAEHT's leaders resolved to produce their own redevelopment plan. In mid-1966, Kornegay and her staff turned to ARCH to outline a vision for their fourteen blocks, an effort they funded with money Schoonover had obtained from an anonymous donor he called Mr. X. June Fields, a new ARCH staff member who had most recently been employed in the city's Department of City Planning, worked with a community planning committee whose participants suggested the diversity of challenges that residents faced. "Several have been residents of the area for more than 20 years," she explained, "four are single individuals; most are from very low-income families; some receive aid to dependent children; one was a high school dropout; four lived in receivership buildings." They met almost daily with ARCH staff throughout the summer and fall, expressing hope that, above all, they could obtain better housing. "They believe . . . that a 'neighborhood' worth preserving exists in the Triangle, but that time is running out," Fields wrote. The committee culled ideas from neighbors and even carried displays to the neighborhood's sidewalks, to gain the perspective of those who did not join the effort voluntarily.[64]

Their alternate plan balanced traditional redevelopment strategies with experimental methods intended to limit disruption and meet resident needs, a hybrid approach evident even in the plan's forms (see Figure 1.2). As in West

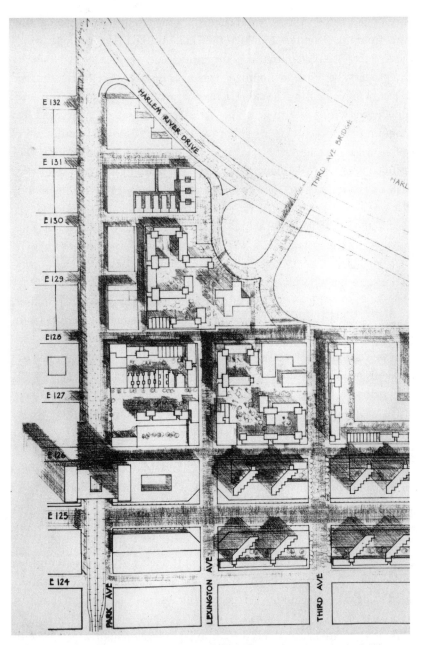

FIGURE 1.2. Preliminary renewal program for the East Harlem Triangle, drafted by
ARCH in collaboration with residents of the neighborhood and completed in October
1966. The plan combined rehabilitation and new construction and incorporated a mixture
of land uses, including residential, commercial, industrial, and public structures.

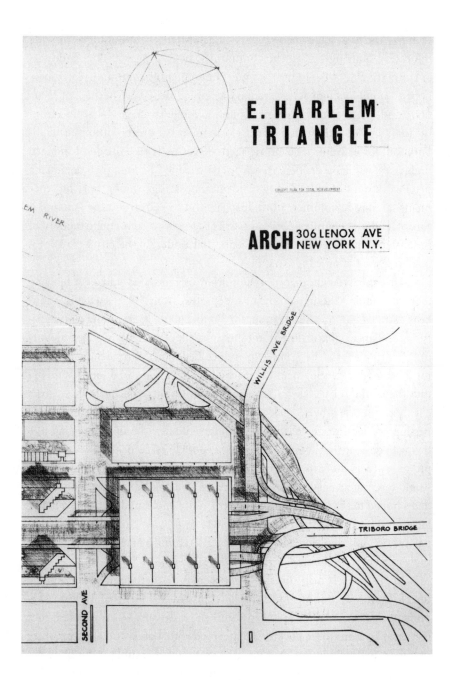

E. HARLEM
TRIANGLE

CONCEPT PLAN FOR TOTAL REDEVELOPMENT

ARCH 306 LENOX AVE
NEW YORK N.Y.

Harlem, the first stage encompassed substantial rehabilitation to provide relocation housing within the community, beginning with five buildings at 130th Street and Lexington Avenue. Subsequently, community members hoped to build a compact elementary school at the center of the neighborhood and a core of new housing around it. Some strategies borrowed from the toolkit of typical urban renewal, closing selected streets within the neighborhood, for example, and lining 125th Street with an enfilade of modern high-rises, while others departed from precedent. The final plan depicted a patchwork quilt of meandering residential buildings among existing tenements, alongside commercial, industrial, and public structures. This mixture of land uses contrasted with the strict segregation common to modernist redevelopment, rejecting the concepts that underlay the city's plan for a neighborhood of only industry.[65]

Just as the Triangle plan's juxtaposition of renovated and new housing marked a subtle—though significant—departure from ARCH's rehabilitation-heavy strategy in West Harlem, so too did this plan's focus on the community's self-reliance signal an important shift from the central role of public support in the earlier effort. The Triangle plan included a mix of residential development, economic development to create jobs, retail, and social services woven into the community's fabric. "The community wants to achieve these goals chiefly through self-help," Fields reported. "It is developing a nonprofit membership corporation to rehabilitate—and eventually to build—housing; it is trying to develop locally-owned businesses both to serve local residents and to produce goods for 'export.'" Committee members envisioned courses that would teach their neighbors how to manage housing as an occupation. Residents hoped to share ownership of a cooperative supermarket, filling a major local need. Community organizations were to provide childcare to working parents, job training, and health services, all to fulfill a mantra that suggested movement beyond intermediaries and external support.[66]

If hopes for self-help foreshadowed demands that would soon emerge forcefully, however, inherent limitations constrained this goal. Indeed, proponents acknowledged, capital to fulfill these dreams was a problem in a corner of Harlem whose poverty likely exceeded that of any other community uptown. "Self-help is not enough," the plan stated frankly. "The financial resources of this area—as of most ghettos—are nonexistent. Considerable help and cooperation from public agencies is needed." While residents hoped self-help would reduce the plan's public costs, they made clear that they still wished for some public housing. Despite the recent disappointments they had experienced at the hands of sluggish bureaucracies, planners explained, they hoped their plan "would go a long way toward persuading the poor everywhere that bureaucracy and administrative regulations are flexible enough to be used to solve critical neighborhood problems." Indeed, even as they dreamed of community-run housing corporations, the committee members sold their plan as a chance to build a model neighborhood for renewal, "a testing ground for the City's intentions in the ghetto."[67]

No aspect of the plan symbolized the tension between dreams of self-determination and continued dependence on outside partners more than the state office building envisioned for 125th Street. In late May 1966, Urban League director Whitney Young had proposed locating the planned World Trade Center in Harlem, an ambition whose hopes echoed those that had long followed urban renewal. "The trickle of antipoverty funds into the ghetto cannot change anything without more visible, tangible signs of willingness to upgrade the ghetto and make it truly a part of the city," Young argued. "What better way than to locate these huge new developments in ghetto areas?" Young, long active in the civil rights movement and an adherent of racial liberalism, imagined that the World Trade Center would blaze a trail for racial integration, employment, and physical rehabilitation. Harlem religious and civic leaders, including Callender, voted unanimously in favor of Young's suggestion.[68] Within days, Wyatt Tee Walker, Governor Nelson Rockefeller's urban adviser, began to encourage a separate state facility for Harlem. After a summer of deliberation and constant pressure from Harlem representatives, Rockefeller announced in September that the state would locate a twenty-three-story office building in Harlem, to be designed by Percy Ifill, a prominent African American architect, Harlem resident, and ARCH board member at this time. The *Times* reported overwhelming support for the building from those on Harlem's streets the day after the announcement. "Maybe it'll make this a better place to live," one shopper suggested.[69]

Moderate leaders publicly backed the skyscraper, but so too did the activists who had most vociferously opposed large-scale urban renewal, a fact that signaled their complex relationship with the public sector in this era. East Harlem Triangle planning committee members endorsed Rockefeller's announcement, as did the members of ARCH, who recognized that the project was not perfect but still saw it as beneficial. "It's a sop to Harlem," Hatch granted, agreeing with borough president Percy Sutton that the project was perhaps a token to the neighborhood. But he nonetheless viewed it as a boon to Harlem's "job base . . . our major problem," believing that it would "help attract good stores, with reasonable prices," as the *Times* paraphrased. Officials were considering several Harlem sites by October, one of them in the Triangle.[70] Residents involved in the planning process hoped that the building might rise in their neighborhood. "The new building would be of great potential benefit to residents, providing jobs and making it possible to support a high quality commercial section," they wrote in their plan, echoing Hatch. "Community members would like to see the building here." But their enthusiasm bore an undercurrent of anxiety, as they insisted that the city ensure that any benefits did not draw wealthier residents who would push the Triangle community elsewhere. The building had to be part of a broader plan, one "that will protect the residents of the Triangle," they explained.[71] The state office building marked a slippery slope. Too much of a good thing, and residents feared they would lose not only affordable housing but also the dream of the ideal community that their plan articulated.

Underlying such hopes and fears were the broader ideological battles sweeping Harlem, between persistent liberal approaches to civil rights, seen in the continued reliance on outside support even in alternate planning schemes, and a growing radical movement centered on the idea of Black Power, evident in rising calls for self-help and self-determination. The East Harlem Triangle found itself at the nexus of this debate at the very moment that community members were completing the plan for their neighborhood. Officials were on the verge of opening Intermediate School 201 (IS 201) in September, at 127th Street between Madison and Park Avenues. They considered the school a "showcase," the *Times* reported, a model for the new fifth-through-eighth-grade city schools that featured curricular innovations, smaller classes, and a "hand-picked staff." Architecturally, too, the school boasted of innovation—its form unabashedly high modernist, a red-brick box elevated on *pilotis* over a vast plaza (see Figure 1.3). Windowless except for occasional brick screens offering views out but not in, the school claimed novel features such as moveable walls and air conditioning. It had already won honors from the New York Chapter of the AIA. But parents in the school

FIGURE 1.3. Intermediate School 201, located on 127th Street between Madison and Park Avenues. Designed by the architecture firm of Curtis and Davis and opened in September 1966, the modernist, windowless school became a catalyst for the demands for community control that emerged in the East Harlem Triangle, in Harlem more broadly, and nationally in this period.

district, most of which encompassed the Triangle community, were less enthusiastic about their new neighbor, promising boycotts before the doors even opened.[72]

Parents who opposed the school were frustrated by the distance between the ideals that officials promised and the reality the project attained. Initially, the city had touted the intermediate schools as models of racial integration, but little in the initial planning of IS 201 in the early 1960s suggested that administrators were pursuing that objective with conviction. Parents and community leaders protested when officials chose the Madison Avenue site, contending that the school's location directly in the middle of an African American and Puerto Rican neighborhood fundamentally undermined aspirations toward integration. Officials denied such charges. In 1965, they blanketed the Northwest Bronx and Queens with 10,000 flyers explaining the school's virtues, an effort intended to attract white students. The *Times* reported that only ten white families expressed interest in the school as a result of the city's campaign, however. *Time* magazine said that none had done so.[73]

Such failures inspired parents and community leaders to seek alternate means to ensure that their children would be best served by a school that, despite promises of innovation, appeared to be more of the same. Indeed, neighborhood debates over IS 201 on the eve of the school's opening charted the ideological transformation under way in the civil rights movement, from the integration model of civil rights liberalism to more radical ideals of racial self-determination. "Either they let us bring white children in to integrate 201 or they let the community run the school," said Helen Testamark, a local parent, in early September. Isaiah Robinson, a leader of the activist Harlem Parents Committee, suggested that segregation might actually be the best choice if it meant that the community could make decisions itself. Soon, integration was no longer a goal sought by picketers. Parents instead demanded veto power over school staff, then dismissal of the school's white principal.[74]

In this way, IS 201 and the adjacent community of the East Harlem Triangle became key sites at which Black Power and its associated ideal of community control burst into the debate over racial justice in America. A September 23, 1966, protest especially symbolized the radical position of autonomy emerging amid increasingly loud conflicts over decision making at the new school. "'Black Power' Moves into Harlem School Battle," the *Amsterdam News* proclaimed across the top of its front page, announcing the arrival to the picket line of Stokely Carmichael, chair of SNCC. Parents had already begun to articulate the meaning of community control in their own terms, but Carmichael, the embodiment of the new militancy that marked civil rights tactics, gave their calls immense weight. "Negroes have a right to run the schools in their areas," Carmichael announced. "White people do. They run the schools in the suburbs where they live and it should be the same in Harlem." The crowd greeted Carmichael enthusiastically. "Freedom, Black Power! We've got to win our fight!" they chanted. Carmichael's arrival marked the culmination of a banner day, which also saw Kornegay arrested from the picket line by eight fifteen that morning. Calls for self-determination had swirled in Harlem for years, but IS 201 marked a critical moment, one that turned philosophical premises into practical strategies.[75]

Education brought community control to Harlem's doorstep, but the debate over IS 201 also crucially played out in architectural terms. Preston Wilcox, a close friend of Kornegay who had worked on the East Harlem Project in the 1950s, declined CAEHT's executive director position, and taught at Columbia University's School of Social Work, became a leading intellectual force behind community control during the IS 201 battle. His belief in his neighbors in the East Harlem Triangle grew out of his larger faith in the abilities of African Americans to run their own institutions. "If one believes that a segregated white school can be a 'good' school," Wilcox explained, "then one must believe that a segregated Negro and Puerto Rican school, like I.S. 201, can be a 'good' school also." Wilcox viewed the heralded architecture of IS 201 as a "palliative for anger," however, a gesture used to distract community members from such aspirations and a means of imposing outside control on the surrounding neighborhood. "I.S. 201 stands as a monument to absentee-decision-making, colonialism, and a personal affront," Wilcox wrote. "It symbolizes the worst in community planning and public education."[76]

Specifically, Wilcox saw the school's aloof form, "loftily perched on stilts," as a symbolic move against local leaders who sought to undermine professional hierarchies—"the professional caste system"—so that residents could shape community decisions themselves. "It epitomizes middle-class paternalism, white control and lower-class compliance and lethargy," Wilcox continued. His critique tied the form of the school to its sociopolitical context: "Passers-by ask the question of I.S. 201 . . . Is it a jail?" Above all, Wilcox condemned the school because its architecture embodied the failure of a liberal approach to community improvement premised on outside approval and the authority of expertise. Wilcox addressed the Board of Education, but his conclusion could encompass the full sweep of outsiders, sympathetic and not, involved in shaping Harlem. "The longing of blacks for positive definitions by the Board has come to an end; blacks are now prepared to exercise and implement their own definitions," Wilcox wrote. "The die has been cast in architectural form. The architecture has soothed the guilt of the Board; it has failed to handle the legitimate anger of the ghetto."[77]

Wilcox's conflation of architectural form and political function at IS 201 undoubtedly grew from his intimate awareness of the failures of this particular project, but likewise suggested more broadly that the means and ends of liberalism, and their formal expression in modernism, could not hold in a new era.[78] Community control rejected the roles of professional intermediaries, however supportive they may have been, since its fundamental principle depended, as Wilcox suggested, on the breakdown of such hierarchies. But many of the gains that activists had made in the built environment up to this point had depended on those intermediaries—on the professional services of ARCH and on the tools and resources of urban renewal. Race added further complications, for community control incontrovertibly relied on the notion of racial self-determination, a hurdle that ARCH's predominately white staff could not clear. Soon after the IS 201 crisis reached its climax, Hatch suggested both his awareness of this limitation and his intention to respect rising demands for autonomy. "Because of our whiteness and our desire to increase the power of indigenous organizations and leadership we have made no attempt to organize in the community," he reported to board members in November 1966. But faced with a rapidly changing context, where did that leave the role of ARCH?[79]

Seeking a Middle Ground

By all appearances, ARCH remained deeply engaged with its partners, even increasingly successful, amid rising demands for Black Power. With an alternate plan in hand, CAEHT gained unexpected support from city officials, who assented to members' proposal to conduct the long-delayed study of the Triangle neighborhood themselves. In June 1967, the city awarded the organization a $164,000 grant for the effort. This was, the *Times* reported, "the first time that the city had retained a community organization to determine how its own neighborhood should be renewed." CAEHT used some of this newfound funding to enlist ARCH to help complete physical planning.[80]

Indeed, despite the emergence of demands for community control, ARCH staff declined to fully cede the role they had evolved in Harlem. Instead, leaders attempted to absorb calls for racial autonomy into their method, seeking a middle ground in a transformation marked by extremes. Hatch sought to diversify the organization's leadership and joined in efforts to introduce new institutional models that would support local movements for self-determination. ARCH's founder and leader found himself in a peculiar position, however. He was both sympathetic to the demands of Black Power and irrefutably the symbol of an organization that sought to expand participation without undermining existing institutions or the role of design expertise. If Hatch recognized the need to evolve from the intermediary position that ARCH maintained, the question remained how much evolution would satisfy emergent radical strands in Harlem.

Consistent with its continued alignment with the broader aspirations of the Great Society, ARCH received its first grant from the federal Office of Economic Opportunity in April 1967. Hatch, however, took this as a chance to bring new racial and ideological diversity to ARCH's leadership. He invited Kenneth Simmons, an African American architect from San Francisco, to join ARCH. Simmons had previously worked in a community action program as part of the War on Poverty and in early 1967 pursued the development of an ARCH-like community design center in San Francisco called Planners and Architects for Neighborhood Regeneration. Simmons hailed from an affluent Oklahoma family—his father, Jake Simmons Jr., had reached unsurpassed heights for an African American oilman—and had attended Harvard College with Hatch. But the arrival of Simmons brought a new perspective to ARCH. In San Francisco he was, as ARCH staff announced, "a CORE militant." He espoused a distinctly nationalist vision, one rooted in the space of the city. "The black people of America—concentrated into communities which are therefore, by definition, black communities—have come to realize that we are *not* part of the mythical homogenous mass," Simmons wrote. "We are a group apart and obviously we are an interest group. We have our survival as a common interest." The solution to the problems that African Americans faced in American cities, he explained, lay in community control of the built environment. "We must . . . control our land; control our geographic community," Simmons argued.[81]

Receptive to the objective that Simmons articulated, and in search of further methods of altering their work to meet emerging ideas, ARCH leaders pursued a second strategy in the spring of 1967, embarking on the foundation of Harlem's first community development corporation (CDC). In Harlem and other predominantly African American communities, residents' lack of control of land often aligned with lack of control of the businesses that occupied that land. Few Harlemites owned either the stores where they shopped or the real property they inhabited. "Why should white people be running all the stores in our community?" Malcolm X had asked in 1964.[82] In 1967, the problem remained equally severe but community control offered a possible way out. Community control's philosophical ideal suggested the need for new institutions that would enable residents to both own their land and determine how that land should be developed. CDCs served as one such model. Though each CDC varied in its specific strategies, such entities typically aspired to build community-owned enterprises that would provide employment and economic resources for community members, thus supporting further development. Amid increasing calls for Black Power, CDCs proliferated in American cities, a movement that ARCH and its community partners joined early on.[83]

CDCs, proponents hoped, would serve the same function for planning and development that locally controlled school boards could serve for education. The Harlem effort involved several components, including skills training and economic research. Its centerpiece was the Harlem Corporation, later called the Harlem Commonwealth Council. The Harlem Corporation, ARCH and its partners explained, was to "[help] Harlem to become increasingly self-sufficient and self-determining through the efforts of its residents." Employing a metaphor common to Black Power and conveying the neighborhood's present lack of economic autonomy, backers hoped "to end Harlem's 'colonial' status and its poverty." The effort brought together major figures in the local Black Power movement, including Wilcox and Robinson, both active in the battle over IS 201, and Innis, who had radicalized CORE, with Stanislaus Wellisz, Roger Alcaly, and Thomas Vietorisz, development economists from Columbia University and the New School. Harlem's residents were disproportionately poor, backers explained, but their density meant that a remarkable amount of potential capital existed in the neighborhood, possibly more than $450 million after taxes. "Properly channeled, this purchasing and investment power could transform the community," they argued.[84]

The proposed tenets of the Harlem Corporation marked a radical departure from prevailing tendencies, a new model that promised a level of self-sufficiency that activists had not seen in either West Harlem or the East Harlem Triangle. Instead of exploiting the federal redevelopment process, proponents hoped to generate their own economic engine for development. They were confident that they could raise an initial $300,000 from within

Harlem in order to procure a federal loan. "To assure that the interests of the poor will be reflected, no more than $200,000 will be raised in large chunks," they wrote. "The final $100,000 will be raised from as broad a group in Harlem as possible in the form of small, perhaps $5, voting shares." Harlemites would each be able to own one share of the corporation, an investment in its success as well as its governance, forming "a mass-based citizen organization with substantial economic power." Their money would go toward "new businesses and industries," intended to provide jobs while expanding the capital from which the corporation could draw. "The Corporation's investment fund will grow steadily, enabling it to move out into new fields including housing, vocational education and health services," backers claimed. Community shareholders offered an intriguing alternative to public aid, suggesting a means to effect self-help over the long term.[85]

Yet despite such lofty long-term aspirations, the paradox remained that in the present the project relied fundamentally on the persistent role of experts like ARCH and academic advisers, and the generosity of the federal government. Though backers hoped to self-finance their effort, they could not resist the pull of readily available funding through the federal War on Poverty. The Office of Economic Opportunity awarded $400,000 to help launch the project. Its enthusiasm for the effort suggested the risks that came with continued reliance on outside support despite calls for self-determination. In agreeing to provide the grant, federal officials considered the Harlem CDC's potential as a model for local elected leaders hoping to stem radical social movements in their cities. "Mayors seeking positive alternatives to turmoil should be able to create a new rapport and working relationship with civil rights groups and militant anti-establishment types," officials suggested. Likewise, while Wilcox, Robinson, and a panel of other local leaders were to "guide the professional research teams," their role remained officially subordinate to the project's academic advisers, who would administer the funding. This arrangement seemed directly contradictory to the goals of autonomy that had motivated the creation of the Harlem Corporation.[86]

With so many potentially competing interests involved, could such efforts provide the community control that Harlemites sought? This stood as the fundamental question that pervaded the model of engagement that ARCH continued to embody. Even as leaders of the organization tried to maneuver around the issues raised by the Black Power movement, they maintained a hold on the very tenets that newly vocal Harlem activists fixed on in their criticism, especially the involvement of outside experts and the persistent, potentially undermining role of outside funding. These principles grew from deep commitments on the part of ARCH's leaders to the project of broadened participation. Likewise, their method of advocacy and reform through official channels marked a clever, often effective strategy of modifying redevelopment without abandoning the resources required for large-scale physical transformation. The vision that ARCH and its community partners voiced, of redevelopment that benefited those most in need, offered a humane alternative to the clearance-oriented methods that had devastated Harlem and predominantly low-income neighborhoods across New York City.

As the goal of community control emerged as a force, then, the differences between Black Power advocates and organizations like ARCH typically concerned means, not ends. If radical activists agreed with figures like Hatch that Harlem could be both a thriving community and one that belonged to its low-income residents, they disagreed about how to get there. Newly empowered African American leaders hoped to radically flatten the process through which decisions in Harlem were made, giving direct control to the neighborhood's residents. Hatch sought a more gradual transformation, supporting increasing degrees of local control in ARCH's work but not quite abandoning the model he had pioneered.

But, as the middle months of 1967 demonstrated, the most radical voices were no longer willing to wait. In June of that year, Hatch appointed Simmons as the codirector of ARCH, a move marking a middle way consistent with the interracial leadership of the Harlem CDC. Hatch and Bailey soon reached out to J. Max Bond Jr., an African American architect and former Harvard classmate, suggesting that he return from Ghana to lead the organization. Hatch believed that the time had come for such change. "A sense of guilt at the disservice which the architectural and planning professions have done to the poor underlie[s] the new profession of advocacy—and it must be sensitive to the need for black leadership," he argued several months later. Indeed, Hatch found "hopeful signs" in "the black ghettos themselves . . . where calls for self-help and self-determination are increasingly heeded by a new breed of black men."[87] Hatch had begun to feel out of place. He increasingly sensed suspicion from community members who had once welcomed ARCH. But while Hatch hoped for a peaceful transition, Simmons had grown impatient with the pace of change. So in late summer, he staged a rowdy demonstration—a "palace coup," Hatch called it—on the steps outside the organization's front door, at 306 Lenox Avenue. Assembling protesters for the spectacle and attracting a crowd, Simmons installed Bond as the first African American director of ARCH. Hatch was out at the organization he had founded.[88]

CHAPTER 2

Black Utopia

BY JUNE 1967, writer and Harlem resident Albert Murray had grown weary of the relentlessly negative depictions of his adopted home. "Mass media images of contemporary Harlem reveal only a part of the actual texture of the lives of the people who inhabit that vast, richly varied, infinitely complex and endlessly fascinating area of uptown Manhattan," Murray wrote. Whether captured through sociological studies or the lens of a camera, such dreary images misrepresented the neighborhood Murray had come to love. "Many photographers seem to use equipment designed especially for assignments in places such as Harlem," he wrote, "especially designed to highlight the bleakness of blackness while obscuring everything else." Along Harlem's boulevards, on its sidewalks, and on the stoops that graced its historic homes, Murray found a community whose members disproved popular stereotypes. "The life-style of Harlem Negroes of all levels already goes with the very best esthetic features not only of Harlem but of New York at large," said Murray. "They do not at all act like the culturally deprived people of the statistical surveys, but like cosmopolites. Many may be indigent but few are ever square." Voicing an appreciation of Harlem taken on its own terms, Murray depicted an idyll in opposition to the dystopia described by many outsiders looking in. "Weather permitting, the sidewalks, the brownstone doorways and steps of most of the streets of Harlem always hum and buzz with people in familiar contact with other people," he remarked. If not perfection, Murray noted, "what Harlemites do with what they have is often marvelous all the same."[1]

Murray's appreciation came from the pen of an observer a generation older than the radicals who had taken over many of Harlem's institutions by late 1967. He was vexed by the separatist perspective of black nationalists.[2] Yet his resistance to the idea of Harlem as a hopeless slum and his faith in the people who populated its streets nonetheless echoed broader currents emerging in the neighborhood in the late 1960s. As organizations like the Architects' Renewal Committee in Harlem (ARCH) shifted from white to African American leadership with the growth of the Black Power movement, they brought not only new demands for community control but also a visionary new conception of the ideal community that Harlem could become. Fundamentally, their dream for Harlem's future rested on the neighborhood's existing residents, those Murray characterized as often "indigent" but rarely "square." Where ARCH had emerged in 1964 as a force advocating the practical goal of preventing the residential displacement of the long-standing, largely low-income residents who made Harlem their home, under African American architect J. Max Bond Jr. the organization advanced a more ambitious vision based on the potential that ARCH and others found in those residents. In the wake of calls for widespread community control, activists shifted their notion of the ideal city from one that simply housed longtime Harlemites into a broader vision of an alternative urban future centered on their daily lives.

This ideal marked continued—and escalating—frustration with two central projects of postwar liberalism: racial integration and urban renewal. Racial segregation had circumscribed the social and geographic parameters of Harlem over the previous half century, but the Black Power movement brought new opposition to the strategy of integration as a means of achieving civil rights. Impatience with its slow pace and the mixed results of its outcomes prompted radical calls to embrace the identity of Harlem as a predominantly African American, low-income space. Adherents to the concept of community control emphasized Harlem's segregated identity as a distinct source of power, even a point of pride. "Integration, as traditionally articulated, would abolish the black community," Stokely Carmichael and Charles V. Hamilton explained in their manifesto, *Black Power*. "The racial and cultural personality of the black community must be preserved."[3]

In that community, activists increasingly found the raw material out of which to build a black utopia as a rebuke to the typical ends of urban renewal.

While activists maintained their reliance on the resources and means of urban renewal—including the tool of the master plan and the financial support of the state—they offered a vision that differed dramatically from the approaches that had generally defined it. Instead of the predominantly commercial, middle-class interests that past plans had emphasized, ARCH and its collaborators sought to accommodate the manifold demands of low-income Harlemites for community-controlled education, affordable housing, social services, and facilities that celebrated African American culture, placing such needs at the center of the community's public life. Their schemes offered human-scale forms unlike the monolithic structures that tended to predominate under urban renewal, mixed the land uses that urban renewal sought to segregate, and emphasized the traditional street grid that defined Harlem. Above all, like artists and writers involved in the contemporaneous search for a "black aesthetic," ARCH staff and their community partners embraced the quotidian vitality of Harlem, celebrating the neighborhood's urban fabric and the vernacular culture they found there. Their vision proposed the radical idea that Harlem's poverty, its literal and figurative isolation from much of New York, served not as a liability but as the means through which Harlemites could achieve empowerment, self-reliance, and self-determination.

To achieve this ideal, the members of ARCH sought radical democratization of the planning process. While activist planners and architects had served as expert intermediaries in the organization's first years, the goal of community control prompted redoubled efforts to bridge the divide between the subjects of planning and the plan itself. Experts like Bond remained at the helm of the organization but pursued less mediated translations of the needs of Harlemites into built form. ARCH came to support a more direct, confrontational style of community engagement and a new focus on minority representation in the design professions. Members idealized widespread participation as a means of ensuring a future for Harlem fashioned collectively by its residents acting on their own behalf. If this goal seemed the most utopian of all those voiced by ARCH, it also appeared entirely within reach in the last months of the decade. In 1969, officials moved to construct the long-planned state office building on 125th Street, intended to be the most consequential redevelopment effort along Harlem's iconic spine and, as Harlem's tallest building, a very literal symbol of the continued power of outside interests in the neighborhood. Activists joined by ARCH vied instead to realize their own idealistic vision at the very center of Harlem, on the block on which the state's building was to rise.

Democratizing Design

When Bond became director of ARCH in the summer of 1967, his arrival marked not only the organization's symbolic transition from white to African American leadership but also a subtle but decisive shift toward more radical strategies in its work on behalf of Harlemites (see Figure 2.1). Though Bond perhaps proclaimed his allegiance to the ideals of racial self-determination less vociferously than did Kenneth Simmons, the ARCH staff member who had led the "coup" that brought Bond's ascension, he nonetheless believed fervently in the power contained in segregated neighborhoods like Harlem. "The ghettos of America reflect the real as opposed to pretended values of that country, and their continued existence gives the lie to all manner of pious statements," Bond wrote in early 1967, while an instructor at the University of Science and Technology in Kumasi, Ghana. "The ghetto, this fact of American town planning (and let no one call it an accident) invariably strikes back at the nation and, as evidenced by the recent upheavals, may yet prove to be its undoing."[4] Bond maintained the goal of turning urban renewal to the advantage of those typically harmed by it and retained the strategies that ARCH had practiced in Harlem's neighborhoods under the banner of "advocacy planning." Yet with Black Power's influence increasing in Harlem, ARCH staff deemphasized their intermediary role and, at the same time, sought to increase minority representation among those who determined urban form. Both approaches indicated a desire to create new routes by which Harlemites could shape their community.

Bond's own biography helps to explain how a member of one of the twentieth century's most distinguished families came to lead the radical architectural vanguard in Harlem in the late 1960s. Born in Louisville, Kentucky, in 1935, Bond moved frequently as his father, J. Max Bond Sr., manned academic posts at Dillard University and Tuskegee Institute, and an American educational post for the U.S. government in Haiti. Bond's father would become president of the University of Liberia, but his achievement was hardly unique in the family. Bond's mother, Ruth Clement Bond, was also an academic, and

FIGURE 2.1. J. Max Bond
Jr. *(left)* with architects
Donald Ryder *(middle)* and
Nathan Smith *(right)*,
circa 1969.

she played an instrumental role in modernizing the art form of the quilt through her work with the Tennessee Valley Authority. Max Sr.'s brother, Horace Mann Bond, held the presidency of Lincoln University in Philadelphia, and his brother-in-law, Rufus Clement, served for two decades as president of Atlanta University. Horace Mann Bond's son, Julian Bond, would become a major civil rights leader and remained close to his first cousin, Max Jr.[5]

Despite his exceptional family, Bond's experience as an undergraduate and architecture graduate student at Harvard in the 1950s was at times difficult due to his status as one of the few African Americans at the university. Other students burned a cross before the dorm where he and eight other African American freshmen lived in 1952, an event that suggested the racial animosity that pervaded the Ivy League. An architecture professor instructed him to choose a different profession—architecture was not for African Americans, he said. Yet Bond also maintained the presidency of the Harvard Society for Minority Rights, the college's NAACP affiliate. After graduation, he moved to France to begin his career in architecture, received a series of interviews at prominent New York firms upon his return, and then received a series of rejections upon showing up for them. Few African Americans had found entry into the design professions, and few firms would make room even for a designer as highly trained as Bond. In 1964, inspired by a liberated Ghana, Bond joined Kwame Nkrumah's government as an architect—a "palace architect," in Bond's words—who designed public buildings and an addition to Nkrumah's estate.[6]

In moving to Ghana, Bond joined a vibrant expatriate community that shaped his worldview. As one of the first African states to escape colonial status, Ghana attracted an international audience from the moment that Nkrumah declared its independence from British rule in 1957. Nkrumah's guests at the ceremonies celebrating Ghana's freedom included Martin Luther King Jr. and Harlem congressman Adam Clayton Powell Jr., for example, as well as Horace Mann Bond, Max Jr.'s uncle. But the Americans who settled there typically skewed toward the more radical end of the political spectrum, compelled to cross the Atlantic by choice or often by necessity. Harlem writer and activist Julian Mayfield and scholar and activist W. E. B. Du Bois moved to Ghana when their search for alternatives to racial liberalism brought increasing state repression. Many others expatriated electively with the same frustrations in mind. When Max Bond Jr. and Jean Carey Bond, his wife, moved to Ghana, they became part of a group of intellectuals and artists—including writer Maya Angelou—pursuing the promise of a newly liberated state run by black leaders.[7]

Ghana offered a symbolic ideal that appealed to increasing nationalism and internationalism among many African Americans in the urban north, who increasingly linked their situation to that of colonized people in African states. "The economic relationship of America's black communities to the larger society also reflects their colonial status," Carmichael and Hamilton wrote. "Historically, colonies have existed for the sole purpose of enriching, in one form or another, the 'colonizer.'" The struggle for decolonization offered the hope and promise that a nation's people could claim the right to self-determination and self-rule. Ghana provided a living example. Within the boundaries of liberated Ghana, expatriates found a state promising collectivism and openness to socialist ideas. Nkrumah described his nation as the center of an international movement toward the liberation of black people, a Pan-African idea that appealed to African Americans frustrated with the slow progress and failed promise of racial integration. If segregation marked the outcome of disadvantage and discrimination, advocates reasoned, so too could it seed a seizure of power akin to that of Ghana. Bond's observation from Ghana that "the ghetto . . . invariably strikes back at the nation" echoed Carmichael and Hamilton's own invocation of "dynamite in the ghettos." Increasingly, it seemed that desegregation offered not a solution to the problems of predominantly African American neighborhoods but a possible threat to the potential for self-determination that radical activists located in the "liberation" of such communities. Before joining ARCH in 1967, for example, Simmons stated, "If, in fact, we are a colony, we must start to think like a colony seeking to throw off the yoke of colonial oppression. . . . We must come to control our own destinies; we must gain our independence."[8]

By the time Bond arrived in Harlem to lead ARCH, then, he had matured as a designer—"As an architect, I sort of grew up in Ghana," he later recalled—but also politically. Under Bond, ARCH immediately changed the nature of its critique, absorbing the language of Black Power into its daily work. Bond launched a new monthly publication, *Harlem News,* which encompassed a broad range of issues related to race—not only urban planning—and espoused a viewpoint focused on community control. Early issues featured articles on the lack of job opportunities for black contractors and continued battles over school decentralization. David Spencer, a leader in the IS 201 protests, wrote, "More and more, we people of Harlem are showing others that we are a let-us-do-it-ourselves community. To be able to do things for oneself, one's family, one's neighbor, one's community is to find and have power. If it be a black community, then it be black power." Under the headline "Black $$$ Power," Roy Innis wrote, "One of the great needs of black people is for control of their own institutions." Invoking the liberatory perspective he had gained in Ghana, Bond criticized the "continued colonialism" he found in policy approaches to Harlem and similar neighborhoods. "It seems to us that the key issue in housing, in the economic development of our communities, in planning our neighborhoods and in educating our children is not simply what decisions are made but who makes them," he wrote.[9]

Bond's quote suggested a position consistent with the community orientation ARCH staff had maintained throughout the organization's first three years, yet significant differences revealed the vast distance that activists had traveled. For Bond's concern was not with outsiders making decisions for the neighborhood of Harlem, but with outsiders making decisions for "our" neighborhood. The possessive pronoun pointed toward a paradigm shift in the perceived role of those who made up ARCH. Though Bond and his staff were not all Harlem natives and claimed expertise that made them unusual among the people they served, they navigated this tension with a new, racialized sensibility. In the charged climate of Black Power, ARCH's staff identified with Harlem not as supportive outsiders but as members of the community. Consequently, they maintained their tactic of advocacy planning, but with new faces in charge. At the same time, ARCH embraced a new commitment to less gradual strategies that staff hoped would expand African American representation among those who reshaped Harlem and allow Harlemites to exert more direct control over their built environment.

In part this shift marked a response to demands emanating from the very residents whom ARCH had assisted. For instance, Ruth Atkins, a member of the Community Association of the East Harlem Triangle (CAEHT), ARCH's longtime partner, called for diminution of expertise in the neighborhood. "Professionals must learn to give the poor the chance to contribute," she argued. "The situation can be compared to a tree growing in a lot. If a building stands next to the tree, it will rob the tree of light and stunt its growth. If that building is moved or torn down, the tree will have a chance to regrow." Equally, ARCH's desire to collapse the distance between the subjects of planning and the plan itself grew from a sometimes anarchistic and always experimental desire emanating from within the design professions. Activist architects and planners, like their colleagues in the New Left as a whole, sought to enable radical forms of participatory democracy. In declaring the necessity to "go beyond representative democracy to participatory democracy," for example, one ARCH supporter, Alan Kravitz, suggested both the urgency to enable broad participation in planning and the paucity of clear answers on how to do so. His "views carry advocacy . . . to the point where planning becomes a matter of total direct citizen participation," a *Christian Science Monitor* reporter explained about Kravitz, a planning professor who defended ARCH at the annual American Society of Planning Officials convention in 1968. "He offered no details on the how and why of such a system," the reporter wrote.[10]

The means to this end were not always clear, but Bond proved willing to experiment with a variety of strategies. The first involved a dramatic change of leadership in ARCH's board of directors, an effort focused on collapsing the distance between the organization and the Harlemites it served. Since at least late 1966, ARCH's board had included architects Norval White, Lowell Brody, and Edward Echeverria; urban planners Paul Davidoff and Walter Thabit; landscape architect Karl Linn; engineer Ewell Finley; and social scientist Frances Fox Piven. All except Finley were white, and all were credentialed "experts" in their respective fields. But new members joined in January 1968, doubling the board's size and not only providing what ARCH claimed was "a strong position within the community but giv[ing] the community a controlling influence on ARCH's policies and programs."[11]

New board members Leo Rolle, Kenneth Marshall, John Killens, John Henrik Clarke, Preston Wilcox, Simmons, Innis, and Isaiah Robinson, all African American, had prominent reputations as Harlem-based activists and long-standing ties to local community organizations. None were professional designers and most had direct involvement with the Black Power movement. Wilcox and Robinson both played central roles in the battle for community control of New York City schools that had begun at Harlem's IS 201, and Wilcox served as one of community control's most active theorists. Rolle led the United Block Association, a technical resource for block associations in Harlem. Marshall helped pioneer early community action programs and served as vice president at sociologist Kenneth Clark's Harlem-based Metropolitan Applied Research Center. Killens was a writer and civil rights activist who cofounded the innovative Harlem Writers Guild. Clarke, also a writer and professor, campaigned for the adoption of black studies curricula. All except Clarke and Killens also served on the board of the Harlem Commonwealth Council (HCC), the community development corporation initially known as the Harlem Corporation, demonstrating both the continued close ties between ARCH and the organization it had helped to form, and the ideology they shared.[12]

Innis's presence on ARCH's board particularly symbolized the increasing prominence of a radical and community-based point of view among the organization's leadership. His rise closely tracked the growth of the Black Power movement both in Harlem and nationally. Floyd McKissick became leader of the Congress of Racial Equality (CORE) in 1966, replacing the moderate James Farmer and marking the emergence of a nationalist orientation in the organization, but Innis had waged the battle of ideas that led to the transition. Innis, whom the *New York Times* described as a "militant black nationalist," rose from director of Harlem CORE to associate national director of CORE in December 1967 to national director in June 1968, touting the same principles of black economic development that underlay HCC. Indeed, Innis served at this time as HCC's founding director, a position through which he managed a major organizational upheaval that reversed the administrative hierarchy of the development project in favor of a structure more conducive to community control. Columbia and New School faculty members had administered the federal grant that initially supported the organization, passing along a small portion of the overall funding to the Harlem activists who developed HCC. But, as officials from the federal Office of Economic Opportunity explained, Innis had "refused to be subordinate to the grantee and . . . proclaimed himself the head of the demonstration grant."[13]

Innis's seizure of control at the helm of HCC mirrored the second strategy by which ARCH sought to facilitate more direct democracy in Harlem planning. Staff members began to adopt decidedly confrontational tactics in opposing unwelcome plans, a decisive turn that often prioritized protest over expertise and broadened participation. "Until Harlem stands together, the City—or some other outside force—will always make the policy decisions," Bond explained. This strategy reflected the fever pitch of the era, in which conflicts over civil rights and the Vietnam War reached greater intensity, sometimes shifting into violence. Activists increasingly expressed their critique of policy along starkly drawn racial lines, emphasizing the broader injustice they sensed in the uneven application of government power. Bond's speech to the Architects and Planners against the War in Viet Nam in May 1968, for example, evinced both the internationalist perspective he had maintained and the vehemence he brought to his task. "The crisis in Viet Nam, the crisis in our cities are really one crisis, the crisis of Black and white," he said. "America is a racist country." War seemed to affect nonwhites most destructively, Bond argued, as did redevelopment. "In our pacification program at home, we do much the same thing. Urban renewal has meant Negro removal, and still does."[14]

Though staff continued to assist with the planning projects in which ARCH had long been involved, they also moved toward a greater engagement with direct action in response to seemingly unjust plans. Active protest itself became a planning strategy, one that found ARCH and residents together at the ramparts. When the city announced plans to build a massive sewage treatment plant on the Hudson River in West Harlem, for example,

ARCH staff supported angry Harlemites in words and actions. Twenty-eight residents testified at an April 4, 1968, Board of Estimate hearing on the $70 million plant. Edward Taylor joined them on behalf of ARCH, alluding to the violence of recent "long hot summers" in Harlem, Newark, and Detroit. "You want a riot this summer, you build the plant!" he proclaimed, a threat that surely took on new urgency as word spread that evening that an assassin had killed Martin Luther King Jr., and civil unrest broke out in American cities. The *Harlem News* offered an editorial whose threat remained veiled but no less potent. "We as black people in Harlem want and will not settle for less than the RIGHT of SELF-DETERMINATION in Harlem," staff wrote. "We have the right as citizens of this community to say what will be and what will NOT be placed in our midst and we will exert this right. Harlem does not want the plant, Harlem does not need the plant, and Harlem will not have the plant." Even as an advocacy-based approach persisted in the day-to-day work of ARCH, these newly confrontational tactics offered a means of achieving community control that was more direct and immediate.[15]

Likewise, ARCH enthusiastically supported the West Harlem community as long-standing tension with Columbia University turned violent in April 1968. Columbia had planned since the early 1960s to build a gymnasium for its own use in Harlem's Morningside Park. ARCH had resisted the project since at least 1966, when staff considered filing suit against it, but Columbia's move toward construction in late 1967 brought the start of more spirited protests.[16] The West Harlem Community Organization (WHCO), ARCH's partner in West Harlem since 1965, burned a Columbia trustee in effigy at the university's front gate in November, setting the tone for resistance that would become increasingly tense into the spring. In February 1968, police arrested twelve residents of West Harlem and nearby neighborhoods as they sat before bulldozers set to clear the site for what ARCH and others termed "Gym Crow." One protester climbed into the maw of a backhoe (see Figure 2.2). ARCH chronicled the subsequent April student and community takeover of Columbia's campus in great detail, dedicating four pages in *Harlem News* to the conflict that would become one of the iconic events of 1968, and in which the planned gymnasium played a central role. "The Battle of Morningside Park," a *Harlem News* article designated it. "Harlem citizens man the supply lines to Hamilton [Hall] and its 120 Black Berets. The sense of tactics, organization, logistics and strategy is superb!" Photos depicted protests on 125th

FIGURE 2.2. A Harlem resident sits in the mouth of a backhoe in February 1968 in an attempt to prevent clearance of the Morningside Park site intended for a Columbia University gymnasium. A figurative and literal symbol of official and institutional neglect of Harlem, residents nicknamed the project "Gym Crow" and launched direct action against it, an effort that ARCH assisted.

Street and police striking students. Most were captured by the lens of Tyrone Georgiou, an ARCH staffer who closely followed events as they unfolded. Linking the gymnasium project to the broader redevelopment plans for West Harlem that ARCH had long opposed, one writer nudged readers to raise their voices too, asking, "Why are you taking all of this lying down?"[17]

Such tactics expanded the range of participants involved in planning the neighborhood, providing direct involvement for Harlemites who feared the consequences of large-scale redevelopment. Roger Starr, executive director of New York's Citizens' Housing and Planning Council, a prominent nonprofit focused on urban policy, and later a housing administrator in New York City, criticized ARCH's role in the protests surrounding the gym. Starr claimed that ARCH had taken a planning issue and made it into a political issue, using the plan as a lever to gain influence for Harlemites. "ARCH . . . interpreted the gym as a symbol of Columbia's indifference to Harlem. ARCH used it not to defeat a bad planning idea," Starr chastised, "but as a means of affecting community organization." But that, of course, was precisely the point, as ARCH shifted from offering planning services to encouraging confrontations intended to empower Harlemites. In direct action, Bond found a strategy that seemed to gain results when measured approaches achieved little. To initially voice its opposition to the sewage plant, for example, ARCH had organized a press conference that few reporters attended. "Max Bond comments that this is just one example of the well-known fact that polite public outcries never seem to do any good," *Progressive Architecture* reported. "Bond feels a physical demonstration of some sort will be necessary before the city and the press will pay any attention to the Harlem citizens' reasoning about the sewage plant, just as there was on the gym."[18]

If ARCH's growing involvement with direct action marked a decided de-emphasis of professional expertise in the organization's work, however, staff likewise pursued a third strategy that stressed the role of trained designers—but with a new focus on increasing minority representation. The two tendencies, seemingly in tension, grew out of the same impulse to diversify the voices involved in the design process. In part, activists tied the disparate burdens of redevelopment to the paucity of minority designers involved in the pro-cess. Bond hoped that greater opportunities for architects and planners of color would generate more enlightened plans. He issued a broad call to mi-nority professionals, for example, touting ARCH's accomplishments in order to compile a list of like-minded designers. "We are trying to make a nation-wide list of every Black (and Puerto Rican, and Mexican American) architect and city planner who would possibly be interested in either working for an organization of this type or starting one in the city in which he resides," Bond said. He acknowledged the inherent difficulty of this task when there were not many minority planners and architects to begin with, but remained hopeful that their involvement could alter the nature of power in the rede-velopment process. "Even if only a few of the architects express interest in the program," Bond wrote, "these few can help to give the minority groups in America who have been trampled on so long, a strong, effective instru-ment with which to control their destiny."[19]

FIGURE 2.3. A student in Architecture in the Neighborhoods, ARCH's design training program, completes an exercise in 1968. The program marked one of the organization's major strategies for increasing racial and ethnic diversity in architecture and planning.

But Bond also looked to address the issue of racial representation at its roots. Education had long been a preoccupation of ARCH, and, indeed, a design-oriented training program for Harlem residents had been discussed as a possible initiative since ARCH's inception, but it was only under Bond that such a program became a reality. Architecture in the Neighborhoods, as ARCH titled the effort that began in the summer of 1968 under the direction of architect Arthur Symes, sought to address "the dearth of Black and Puerto Rican talent in the fields of Architecture and City Planning." ARCH counted "only 14 black architects in the states of New York and New Jersey combined," a sum whose scarcity seemed all the more alarming in the capital city of American architecture. Symes issued calls through churches and schools and posted announcements, seeking applicants eighteen to twenty-five years old, especially those who had not completed high school. Twenty-five students entered an intensive course including design instruction by minority architects and planners, counseling, and remedial education oriented toward GED attainment. Students studied drafting and drawing, learned architectural terminology, and created a range of projects in two and three dimensions focused on planes, texture, and structure (see Figure 2.3). In the fall, staff placed students in full-time jobs that reflected their interests, with leading architecture firms like Skidmore, Owings, and Merrill, and that provided meaningful design work—on drafting tables, not as couriers. Twelve students remained at the conclusion of the first year, a number that satisfied Symes given the program's demands. Graduates were encouraged to attend architecture schools, with scholarship assistance from the program. Eight did so, at universities including Michigan, Kansas, Howard, and City College of New York.[20]

While ARCH's early ideas for a training program had emphasized job skills and advanced education, under Bond and Symes the effort took on a more political dimension, stressing the positive impact that design competency could have in predominantly minority communities. Instructors favored projects that would be relevant to the lives of students. For instance, students initially pursued hypothetical assignments focused on the design of a vacation cottage and the rehabilitation of an urban brownstone. Staff found that the cottage was too foreign to "the students' social and economic backgrounds," however. "A first design problem should be one that is closer to their real experience," staff reported. "For these students a brownstone is such a structure and therefore, a more meaningful experience." ARCH staff apprenticed students in the city's largest commercial firms, but intended that participants would bring their skills back home. "Specific emphasis will be given to developing skills which can be used not only in traditional planning or architecture studios," they reported, "but also by advocacy planning groups (such as ARCH), by community groups, or in the implementation of governmental programs in urban areas." Kenneth Knuckles, a member of the first class of Architecture in the Neighborhoods, had dropped out of high school and worked as a teller at Con Edison before being pointed to the program by a relative. "There's more creativity to this than counting money, that's for sure," he told a reporter. "I have a chance now." Symes emphasized this goal of empowerment through design. "Architecture and planning are just too important to be omitted from the lives of people who happen to be poor," Symes said.[21]

As the first class of Architecture in the Neighborhoods settled into their apprenticeships, ARCH leadership opened a second front in their battle to expand the presence of minority voices among the decision makers who shaped the city. The City Planning Commission, the body responsible for supervising plans, approving all major redevelopment decisions, and funding low-income housing development in New York, had not claimed a single commissioner of color since its founding in the 1930s. Yet the commission held outsize influence over Harlem and other predominantly minority neigh-

borhoods where the city tended to focus its major planning activities. In
ARCH's first public statement decrying the commission's makeup, issued
in late 1968, Bond cited a recent case in which the commission approved
housing subsidies for those Bond characterized as "high income" but not for
"more needy groups." Bond argued, as the *Harlem News* paraphrased, that
"the opportunity to introduce a different point of view must not be lost."[22]

Over the following months, ARCH brought such protests into the open.
Bond and Nathan Smith, who served as assistant director of ARCH, left the
organization at the end of 1968 to found their own, Harlem-based architectural firm. Under Symes, now ARCH's executive director, the organization
encouraged supporters to send telegrams to city officials recommending African American and Puerto Rican candidates for vacant commission slots,
gathered organizations including CORE and HCC to join their campaign, and
met with Mayor John Lindsay's administration officials, including commission chairman Donald Elliott, to plead their case. When Mayor Lindsay appointed white, male commissioners to two open positions in March and
July 1969, ARCH turned to direct action.[23] In August, Symes and fellow activists arrived at city hall to appoint their own city planning commissioners.
Barred from the building's steps, the sixty demonstrators chanted, "Planning
power to the people," as Symes declared, "We've got to have some representation." The assembled group swore in two African Americans and one Puerto
Rican as the people's commissioners: ARCH board member Marshall
England; architect Harry Quintana, director of the Real Great Society/Urban
Planning Studio, an activist planning group in East Harlem and ARCH ally;
and Vernon Ben Robinson, a former leader of CAEHT. The three attended the
open commission meeting a couple of days later, where a member of the audience exposed the all-white commission's lack of representativeness. Speaking
to commissioners in Spanish, he then returned to English, declaring, "You
can't understand me, but he can!" Quintana, the subject of the protester's
praise, addressed the commissioners. "If I catch any of you Commissioners up
in East Harlem, I'll go all the way with you," he declared. "It's a warning and a
threat."[24]

Though the emotional potency of Quintana's words seemed at odds with
the question of who composed an elite city board, they suggested the huge
potential that ARCH recognized in such an appointment. "The Planning
Commission's decisions are vitally important to minority communities," the

Harlem News had explained, describing the commission's influence over public housing, school construction, and the Model Cities program. "Thus it is crucial that the Mayor of this City understand that he can no longer appoint outsiders to positions from which they can determine how black and Puerto Rican people are going to live." Mayor Lindsay finally acceded to protesters' demands a couple of weeks after the city hall demonstration, appointing an African American lawyer and Harlem resident named Ivan Michael to a vacant seat. Michael almost immediately proved the worth of his perspective, expressing opposition to the typical order of urban redevelopment and demanding that plans include the community's voice. "One of the things I am certain that the black and Puerto Rican community does not want," Michael declared, "is more urban renewal."[25]

Michael's concern was with representation, with the resonance between those who made decisions about the shape of New York and those impacted by such decisions. "Black people make up a large part of this city and we shouldn't have to rely upon pressure to have a truly representative body," he said. Intrinsic to his statement, and to the work of ARCH after Bond's arrival, was the idea that a designer's race or ethnicity mattered, that people of color—whether professionals or amateur activists—were particularly attuned to the needs of neighborhoods like Harlem, and that they could thus uniquely plan their future. As Symes explained in the case of Architecture in the Neighborhoods, the goal of diversifying participation in the design process grew from the assumption that doing so would produce a different sort of city. The effort "should be considered a pilot program—the beginning not the end—of a nationwide endeavor to train black and Puerto Rican young people so that they may take the lead in deciding how they and the people in their communities are going to live," Symes wrote in 1969.[26]

Where white architects assisting black Harlemites had inevitably served as intermediaries in a process of translation from concept to form, now ARCH staff—with Black Power principles inflecting every aspect of their work—claimed the possibility of a more direct, even unmediated translation. This project of participatory democracy remained decidedly idealistic, but to proponents like Bond, Symes, and their collaborators, it seemed worth a try. "There is no great danger in seeing whether other ways of determining architecture might work," Bond said. "The people cannot do a worse job than architects have done. How could the people possibly be more parochial and less sensitive to real human needs and concerns?"[27] The question remained what such a city might look like.

The Search for New Forms

In attempting to discern the nature of this future city, ARCH participated in the broader project of defining the cultural implications of Black Power. While artists, poets, writers, and playwrights involved with the contemporaneous Black Arts Movement argued for the existence and necessity of a "black aesthetic," Bond and the members of ARCH extended this discourse into the realm of the built environment. Their pursuit echoed the culminating chapter of Carmichael and Hamilton's *Black Power.* The need for new political, social, and economic institutions necessitated a "search for new forms," they had insisted, a charge that seemed especially apt in the space of the city.[28] Yet the forms that ARCH and its allies pursued did not always prove to be "new." In fact, activists spatialized Black Power in a form whose revolutionary ambitions were sheathed in a familiar skin. Proponents sought to preserve the existing streets, blocks, and building types of Harlem, if not always the buildings themselves. They identified this traditional urban fabric with a vital, collective, and authentic everyday culture that they romanticized. At the same time, they sought to preserve the existing residents of Harlem, in whom Black Power adherents saw value and potential, and build on their basic needs and demands as the foundation for the neighborhood's very renaissance. If this approach seemed modest in its appreciation of existing Harlem and Harlemites, its physical and social tenets remained quite radical. They turned the typical order of urban redevelopment on its head.

Though not the only place where activists sought to determine the spatial implications of community control, Harlem formed a particularly vital realm for such pursuits. This role grew in part from the community's iconic status as the capital of black culture in America, but also from the presence of ARCH, which filtered the broader concerns of Black Power discourse through its specific interest in design and planning, and from Bond, who proved a passionate advocate for the possibility of an alternative urban ideal. Indeed, Bond's articulation of this ideal drew directly from his experience of the uniquely African American space of Harlem. Fundamentally, Bond believed that form—as much as power—could derive from the fact of segregation, and that race mattered tremendously in determining the shape of the city. "The idea of a Black expression in architecture is . . . something that is scoffed at, for which there is little respect," he noted. "This, in the face of the many distinctive contributions that Afro-Americans have made to music, literature and world culture." If critics attributed Gothic form to the culture of its makers or the appearance of Japanese architecture to the nationality of its designers, Bond wondered, why should cities designed by African Americans not also evince fundamental differences? "It seems reasonable . . . to expect that were Black Americans in a position to express their particular condition and values through understanding architects and planners, distinctive buildings and plans would result," he argued.[29]

Bond's claim mirrored broader debates in Harlem at this time, especially among those active within the Black Arts Movement. The Black Arts Movement, described in critic Larry Neal's 1968 manifesto as "the aesthetic and spiritual sister of the Black Power concept," brought the era's nationalist goals into the realm of the written, visual, and performing arts. Its range of protagonists—including Amiri Baraka, Nikki Giovanni, and Ishmael Reed most famously—pursued an array of goals as diverse as their respective media and geographic locales. But a search for a "black aesthetic" marked one common strain in their work. As Neal explained, "A main tenet of Black Power is the necessity for Black people to define the world in their own terms. The Black artist has made the same point in the context of aesthetics." Neal contended that the black and white worlds were intrinsically different, "in fact and in spirit." Frustrated with the prospects for African Americans within what he perceived as an often-contradictory white-dominated world, Neal argued for the necessity of abandoning Western cultural models. "Implicit in this re-evaluation is the need to develop a 'black aesthetic,'" he wrote. As Addison Gayle Jr., another major critical interpreter of the Black Arts Movement, explained, "Unique experiences produce unique cultural artifacts, and . . . art is a product of such cultural experiences."[30]

The possibility of a black aesthetic rested in a fundamental conception of the "community" as the genius loci of creativity. "The Black Arts Movement is radically opposed to any concept of the artist that alienates him from his community," Neal opened his manifesto. His proclamation reflected a tendency ubiquitous throughout the work of the Black Arts Movement—a focus on authenticity that participants discerned in the vernacular culture of economically impoverished African American communities. Proponents of the Black Arts Movement rejected both the idea that the cultural vanguard would be made up of highly trained intellectuals and the expectation that the raw material of cultural production would derive from or lead to "high" forms. Instead, proponents drew their inspiration from popular culture and daily life in communities like Harlem, where a predominantly African American and low-income population defined the neighborhood's identity for both insiders and outsiders. For cultural producers in the age of Black Power, as with those who took Black Power into political realms, the identity of segregated communities like Harlem—with a diminishing middle class but a substantial population of poor residents—served as a source of inspiration, not a weakness.[31]

Similarly, in articulating his spatial vision, Bond pointed to informal urban settlements, whose vernacular culture and seeming self-determination he idealized. Bond romanticized the thriving public realms he identified with such places, describing spaces shaped collectively by "the people," without the mediation of professional experts. "In considering what a 'people-planned' city would be," Bond said, "I think we have to relate to the current fad among architects for studying Greek towns, anything built by the people. In every case we find not only a coherent expression, but one full of individual variety, full of richness, full of life." If ancient civilizations offered one example, however, Bond noted similar qualities in contemporary, often economically impoverished settings. "What we are trying to capture is not Brasilia but that Shantytown next to Brasilia; not Tema (Ghana's new city), but Ashaiman, the shantytown next to it," Bond explained, raising juxtapositions all the more interesting for their comparison of highly planned, modernist new towns with the unplanned settlements on their margins. "They are shantytowns only because they do not have the public services and facilities that Brasilia or Tema have, but they do possess the spirit and life of an urban place that Brasilia and Tema lack. They are in fact the people's creation, full of the vibrancy and color that go with life." Bond condemned Tema for its contrasting emphasis on private ownership and individualism. Why had planners not embraced cooperative housing and the mutual aid and "community pride" he associated with it, Bond wondered, instead of "locking each family in its own little box"?[32]

Though Bond knew Tema well from his time in Ghana, he did not need to look to Africa to find a cooperatively shaped ideal. Indeed, he found similarly idyllic qualities outside ARCH's door, on the streets of Harlem. "Physically, Harlem is terrific," Bond explained. In a description that echoed the portraits painted by both Murray and members of the Black Arts Movement, Bond celebrated Harlem's streets as the stage on which Harlemites protected each other and participated in civic culture. "You can send your children out to play and the neighborhood will take care of them," he said. If Bond's description recalled Jane Jacobs's "ballet of the good city sidewalk," it more suggested the uniquely racialized space in which participants performed, as well as the political potential latent within. "The streets are informal, they're real. They're the place where your friends are, but where the enemy (the police) is too," Bond continued. "Black people enjoy the streets; they like to go for walks. Everyone is at home outdoors." Harlem's streets revealed its contemporary life as well as its radical history, he noted. "Many corners are symbolic places—125th Street and Seventh Avenue where Malcolm X used to speak, Michau[x]'s bookshop used to be—in the struggle for equality, for liberation." Despite Harlem's poverty, Bond argued, its built environment and residents exhibited an everyday, collectivist vitality.[33]

Thus, Bond sought to retain the architectural diversity, mixed land use, and small scale that he celebrated in gazing on Harlem's blocks, a complexity embodied in the neighborhood's traditional urban fabric. This marked a significant turn from the tenets of modernist planning, which had depended on the notion of the tabula rasa, joining the symbolic potential of the clean slate to the physical possibilities of wholesale reconstruction. The modernist city, embodied in the vast projects of urban renewal, prioritized massive, austere forms, the segregation of land uses, and the division of the city into districts. If redevelopment was not wholly antiurban, it nonetheless largely devalued the city as it had grown over time.[34] Bond, on the other hand, celebrated the messiness of urban life, the eclecticism of land use he discovered in Harlem, and the vitality he identified as a consequence of that diversity, qualities he hoped to maintain and reproduce. "I imagine that the Black city would be like a very rich fabric," he explained. "It would not be a fabric with a superimposed pattern but one with multicolor threads running through it. A great mix of housing, social facilities, and working places, rather than a series of distinct zones, each separate, each pure, each Puritanical." Bond positioned this vision against urban renewal's monumentality. "A Lincoln

Center, pompous and dull and completely aloof from the surrounding blocks, simply could not happen in a Black city," he argued. As he later explained in an interview with writer Ishmael Reed, this dichotomy reflected two tendencies, one grounded in popular culture, one in an elite vision that Bond rejected. He referred to the performances of the Miles Davis Quintet in the late 1950s. "Their stuff is so urban it really conveys the sense of the urban environment, and *without the pretense* [emphasis in original]," he said, "and that's the fundamental difference between what the black art forms are doing and the establishment culture—they really deal with what the people are." In drawing an alternative to urban renewal's massive creations, Bond argued for the possibility of a people-centered urbanism.[35]

Despite their disdain for typical redevelopment, however, Bond, ARCH, and their community collaborators did not fully eschew the tool of demolition. In some cases, they argued, physical reconstruction was necessary. But even where they anticipated replacing deteriorated existing buildings, they nonetheless explicitly sought to preserve Harlem's characteristic urban forms and its residents, both of which urban renewal had disregarded. This mentality was evident in the plans that ARCH staff and their community partners completed in 1968 for both West Harlem and the East Harlem Triangle, the two neighborhoods with which the organization had long worked. The plan for the former served as a conceptual vision for the neighborhood in the aftermath of the Columbia gymnasium battle, and that for the latter as an official document submitted in response to the city's contract with CAEHT for a planning study. The West Harlem plan took a dramatically different approach from—even, in a sense, rejecting—ARCH's earlier, rehabilitation-oriented 1966 proposal. "For hundreds of years, Black and poor people in America have settled for secondhand possessions while the more affluent sector had the better things in life," the plan read. "Let us not be fooled by Establishment types who try to cop out on their responsibility by only offering 'rehabilitation' because it is still secondhand housing." It restricted rehab to the neighborhood's most distinctive homes, its brownstones and post-1920s apartment buildings, and called for the wide use of federal subsidies to rebuild West Harlem's blocks (see Figure 2.4). In the East Harlem Triangle, planners imagined the extensive reconstruction of the neighborhood's houses, limiting rehab to only a few small rows. This marked both a practical response

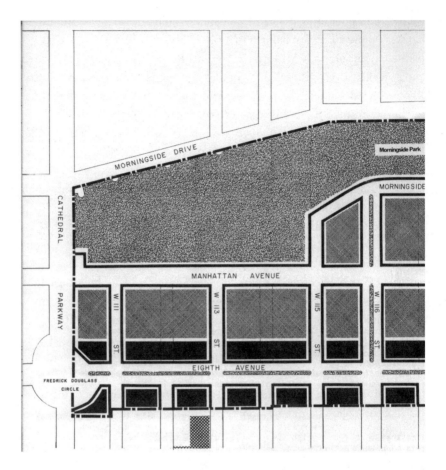

FIGURE 2.4. ARCH and WHCO's 1968 proposal for West Harlem, showing extensive use of new construction *(gray and black)* and limited use of rehabilitation *(light gray)*. Despite its departure from earlier, rehabilitation-oriented plans for the neighborhood, this plan nonetheless emphasized the goal of rebuilding the neighborhood for the benefit of existing, low-income Harlemites.

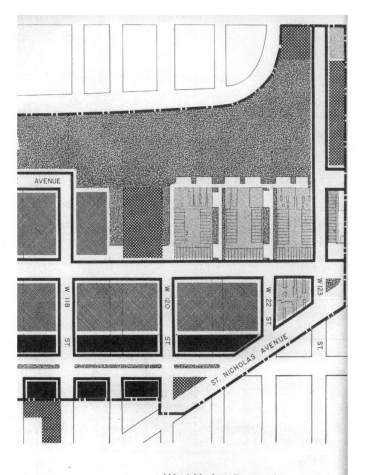

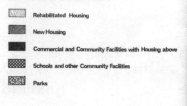

West Harlem Proposal

Rehabilitated Housing

New Housing

Commercial and Community Facilities with Housing above

Schools and other Community Facilities

Parks

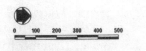

0   100   200   300   400   500

to structures that had physically declined with landlord neglect and a symbolic insistence on housing quality regardless of class, a statement that Harlemites deserved equal treatment no matter their income.[36]

Indeed, both plans redoubled ARCH's focus on the low-income residents of Harlem, emphasizing not just the goal of preventing displacement but also that of rebuilding the neighborhood on a low-income foundation. "With few exceptions, West Harlem must be rebuilt entirely, but this time for the present residents," staff wrote. In the East Harlem Triangle, planners described a population increasingly desperate for improvement. "The people in the Triangle know something is wrong," they wrote. "They simply are not 'bettering themselves.'" Their daily barriers were manifold. "Men and women cannot find decent jobs providing a living wage scale. Children are growing up diseased in mind and body for want of better social services. . . . Housing just can't seem to get built for the poor." But the low-income residents who had opposed the plan to demolish their neighborhood and won the right to reshape it were optimistic about their community's future. "The Triangle Association believes there is a breath of hope remaining; that breath of hope is themselves," the plan explained. "They know they must somehow deliver what all poor people need. Nothing less would suffice." While the plan considered the possibility of eventually attracting middle-income residents to the neighborhood, planners first insisted on the necessity of "a human[e] and decent life style" for *current* residents. Indeed, as members of CAEHT pursued residential construction in the following years, they focused entirely on the development of low-income housing.[37]

It was here that ARCH and its partners diverged most significantly from other contemporary critics of modernist redevelopment. In voicing an ideal of small-scale, diverse urbanism in neighborhoods that had suffered disproportionately from the bulldozer, ARCH shared the architectural paradigm of figures like Jacobs, articulated most famously in her landmark 1961 work, *The Death and Life of Great American Cities*. But these plans differed dramatically in their social conception of this future city. Jacobs's view of ideal urban development in predominantly low-income communities—what she called "slums"—was predicated on economic upscaling or "unslumming," a process of "self-diversification" of the existing residents that she did not detail. ARCH and its collaborators, on the other hand, proposed the radical idea that Harlem did not need class transformation—whether from within

THEORETICAL DESIGN FOR THE PHYSICAL COMMUNITY

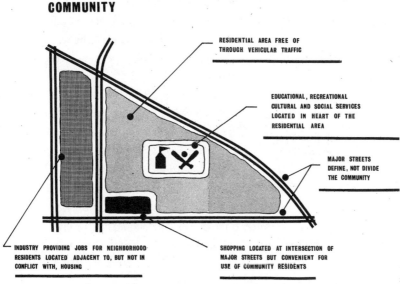

RESIDENTIAL AREA FREE OF
THROUGH VEHICULAR TRAFFIC

EDUCATIONAL, RECREATIONAL
CULTURAL AND SOCIAL SERVICES
LOCATED IN HEART OF THE
RESIDENTIAL AREA

MAJOR STREETS
DEFINE, NOT DIVIDE
THE COMMUNITY

INDUSTRY PROVIDING JOBS FOR NEIGHBORHOOD
RESIDENTS LOCATED ADJACENT TO, BUT NOT IN
CONFLICT WITH, HOUSING

SHOPPING LOCATED AT INTERSECTION OF
MAJOR STREETS BUT CONVENIENT FOR
USE OF COMMUNITY RESIDENTS

FIGURE 2.5. Conceptual plan prepared by ARCH and CAEHT in 1968, showing a mixture of land uses within the East Harlem Triangle neighborhood and needed community and social services at its "heart." Madison Avenue defines the western boundary of this diagram, while 125th Street forms its southern boundary.

or without—to succeed as a community, but could flourish by housing and serving its current inhabitants, however poor they may be. Moreover, while Jacobs's limited discussion of race centered on the objective of desegregation as a prerequisite for "unslumming," ARCH's vision celebrated blackness and the potential activists found in segregated populations like this one.[38]

Quite literally, the needs of these existing Harlemites stood at the center of the reconstructed neighborhoods that ARCH and its community partners envisioned. The plan for the East Harlem Triangle displayed the attributes that Bond had espoused in his description of the "Black city" as "a very rich fabric," especially the varied land uses that had long characterized the small community. Plans maintained a mixture of industry and residences, for example, delineating an industrial area along the Triangle's western flank intended to provide employment for residents near their homes (see Figure 2.5). Instead of hiding residents' unique and often acute social service requirements, the plan's authors located an innovative center called the "Triangle Commons" directly in what they described as the "heart" of the rebuilt neighborhood. This center was to provide a home for the full range of services that residents needed, including welfare and employment assistance, legal services, recreation, addiction treatment, day care, and special education. "An integral part of the whole concept plan is the programming of specific services to meet specific needs of the Triangle community," planners explained.[39]

Likewise, planners sought to retain and reproduce the vernacular character that Bond had so admired on the streets of Harlem. Where structures in ARCH's initial 1966 plan for the East Harlem Triangle had often borrowed the monolithic forms characteristic of urban renewal, the new plan eschewed the "aloof" monumental structures Bond denounced. Buildings took a smaller, variegated form and maintained the neighborhood's existing grid. Pedestrian paths kept the gridiron intact in the few cases of street closings (see Figure 2.6). In new public spaces, planners offered hopeful visions that the civic life of the neighborhood would thrive. One illustration depicted the Triangle Commons as a lively center in the neighborhood, with a modern plaza surrounding a low glass building, children playing, and adults socializing (see Figure 2.7). In Morningside Park, on the already demolished clearing that was to have become the Columbia gymnasium, ARCH and WHCO envisioned a stage set celebrating the cultural and political currents of Black Power (see Figure 2.8). A multiuse amphitheater was to "feature performances by Motown artists, the Negro Ensemble Company, the New Heritage Repertory Theatre, and local musical, singing, and acting groups of all ages," staff wrote. Plans included space to accommodate "avant garde theater," an "African museum," the production and exhibition of "black culture and crafts," and even a "soul food garden," an effort that Harlem residents had begun in the aftermath of the gym battle. The plan's authors imagined a welcoming plaza in which all of Harlem's residents would find space to act out their civic roles—including children, couples, political radicals ("Support Black Panthers," a sign read), and even a neighborhood inebriate (see Figure 2.9).[40]

Above all, idealized visions of Harlem's future preserved the street-side dynamism that Black Power adherents emphasized as the neighborhood's defining feature. ARCH employed a single illustration to depict both 125th Street and Eighth Avenue, a rendering that stood as an ideal type representing aspirations for the neighborhood's famous boulevards (see Figure 2.10). The streetscape's unique qualities revealed themselves immediately. A divided road offered two lanes for buses, taxis, and local traffic. All other vehicles were to be diverted to secondary streets. "Read Muhammad Speaks," the bus urged, touting the official organ of the Nation of Islam. Signifiers of Black Power fashion abounded: passersby raised fists in greeting and wore natural hairstyles. One man sported a dashiki. Yet more evident was the very normalcy of the scene. Though new buildings faced the avenue alongside historic predecessors, they aligned to define an active public realm and an eclectic but unified streetscape. A lush canopy of trees framed the sidewalk, the bearer of the street life celebrated by both Bond and the proponents of the Black Arts Movement, and vividly depicted here.[41]

Planners tied that quotidian activity to the diverse uses that defined Harlem's boulevards. "The strip of residential-commercial uses along Eighth Avenue has a vitality that should be retained in any rebuilding scheme," they argued in the West Harlem plan. They feared the transformation of Harlem's major axes into bland single-use business districts. "All the other crosstown streets are anonymous. What has happened to 8th Street is a good example of what we don't want," Bond said, referring to the community's desires for 125th Street. ARCH's aim, he argued, was to retain the "main street quality" of Harlem's iconic thoroughfare, to prevent the duplication here of what one observer sympathetic to ARCH called "Sixth Avenue stoneland," filled with "maximum-land-utilization office blockbusters." The plan for the East Harlem Triangle abandoned the canyon of identical skyscrapers that the earlier plan had imagined for 125th Street, offering instead a mixture of commercial and residential uses in high-, mid-, and low-rise buildings along the boulevard. The state office building, the skyscraper that planners and residents had once hoped would anchor their transformation of Harlem's major axis, was now nowhere to be seen, as Harlemites instead placed their faith in their own self-reliance. But the state office building was in fact just over the horizon, and workers were soon to begin its construction on 125th Street, at Harlem's center. It proved relatively easy to imagine a portrait of a rebuilt Harlem based on the radical principle that its existing residents and urban forms were the very basis of revitalization. Activists intended to demonstrate that they could also realize Bond's "Black city" in bricks and mortar, even in a community where outsiders still often dominated decision making.[42]

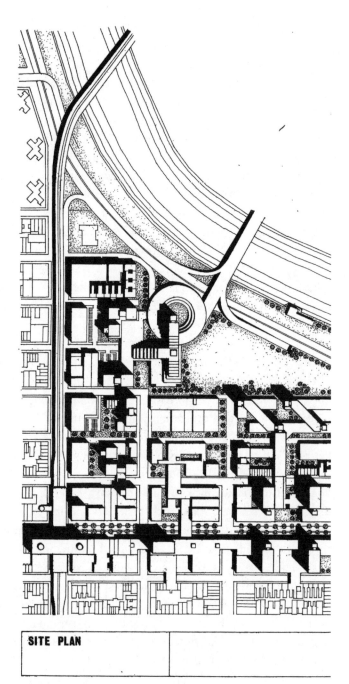

SITE PLAN

FIGURE 2.6. Site plan for the East Harlem Triangle, completed by ARCH in 1968. Despite its wide use of new construction, the plan maintained the neighborhood's traditional street grid, which ARCH and its partners celebrated as one of Harlem's distinctive characteristics.

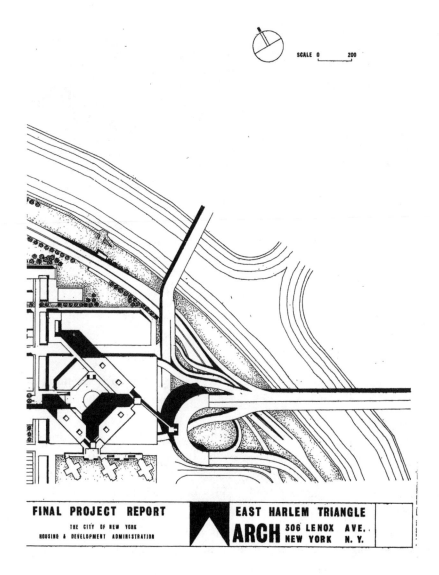

SCALE 0   200

FINAL PROJECT REPORT

THE CITY OF NEW YORK
HOUSING & DEVELOPMENT ADMINISTRATION

EAST HARLEM TRIANGLE

ARCH 306 LENOX AVE.
NEW YORK   N. Y.

Community facilities block from 3rd. Ave.

FIGURE 2.7. ARCH's 1968 rendering showing "Triangle Commons," the community and social service complex to be located at the center of the East Harlem Triangle neighborhood. Planners envisioned its plaza as a vibrant public space that maintained Harlem's civic life.

Reclamation Site #1

In June 1967, the members of ARCH surely watched from their second-floor office as Governor Nelson Rockefeller stood on a platform on the other side of Lenox Avenue to commence the demolition that would clear the block for construction of the state office building. Expressing characteristic assurance, he told a crowd full of dignitaries—including Jackie Robinson, Senators Jacob Javits and Robert F. Kennedy, and civil rights leaders A. Philip Randolph, Whitney Young, and Roy Wilkins—of the lofty goals he held for the skyscraper. "Here will stand the State's 23-story vote of confidence in the future of the community," he announced. "Here will stand a magnet to draw new businesses and new enterprises to this area." This was not to be just any rede-

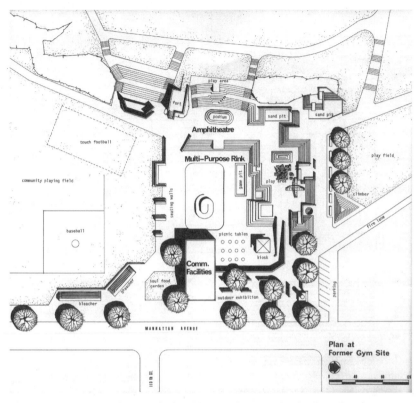

FIGURE 2.8. ARCH and WHCO's plan, completed in 1968, for the cleared site in Morningside Park where Columbia University had planned to build a gymnasium. They envisioned the site as a stage set for the cultural and political currents of Black Power, including an amphitheater, "African museum," avant garde theater space, and "soul food garden" among its uses.

velopment project, he promised, but one as transformative as the midtown commercial campus that bore his family's name, Rockefeller Center. Rockefeller concluded his remarks, took the controls of the demolition crane, launched the wrecking ball, and *hit the wrong building.* The spectators watching from inside the occupied building were shocked, but unharmed. The patrician governor, used to getting his way, struck the right building on the second try. But the wayward wrecking ball was only the first signal to Rockefeller that the previously clear path to redevelopment would be filled with new obstacles amid rising demands for Black Power. During 1968 and 1969, the crucial years in

FIGURE 2.9. Rendering showing residents on the plaza intended for the cleared gymnasium site in Morningside Park. The image, from 1968, suggests ARCH and WHCO's vision of this as an inclusive space welcoming of all Harlemites and supportive of the era's radical politics. Signage includes the advice, "Read Muhammad Speaks" and "Support Black Panthers."

which ARCH underwent its metamorphosis, the site on the north side of 125th Street between Lenox and Seventh Avenues would transform from an inhabited mix of apartments and small businesses into a cleared lot, into the very culmination of the struggle for community control of Harlem. On the neighborhood's central block, where officials intended to build the monumental state office building, radical activists strove instead to bring their vision for Harlem into reality in the last months of the 1960s.[43]

While the walls supporting urban renewal had begun to show substantial cracks well before Bond's tenure at the helm of ARCH, the redevelopment apparatus remained quite powerful in the final years of the decade. When moderate leaders in Harlem gained assurances that the state would build a new office building in the neighborhood in 1966, ARCH had looked on with

FIGURE 2.10. ARCH's rendering of 125th Street, from its *East Harlem Triangle Plan* completed in 1968. ARCH used the same drawing to represent Eighth Avenue in its *West Harlem Morningside* plan of the same year, suggesting this as an ideal type symbolizing the organization's vision for Harlem's major boulevards as active public realms with eclectic but unified streetscapes.

measured approval and the hope that the project would provide needed jobs and improve local retail. But two years later, Rockefeller's bold promises of transformation disturbed many with a different view on Harlem's future. Their objections grew not from lack of faith that the powerful governor's promises would come true, but from confidence and fear that the realization of his vision would undermine their own ideal for both Harlem and its iconic 125th Street. The street marked "Harlem's 'soul center,'" *Progressive Architecture* reported, paraphrasing ARCH, "with a style that belongs distinctly to the people of Harlem." But the state office building plan, which included

FIGURE 2.11. The architectural model of the state office building complex intended for 125th Street, between Lenox and Seventh Avenues, photographed in 1968. The African American–led firm of Ifill, Johnson, and Hanchard designed the skyscraper itself, at left, and architect Philip Johnson designed the adjoining structures. Activists saw the block-filling project as a threat to Harlem's identity and their aspirations for community control.

the modernist skyscraper itself, designed by the African American–led architecture firm Ifill, Johnson, and Hanchard; a state motor vehicle facility; and a vaguely defined cultural building, threatened to change 125th Street fundamentally (see Figure 2.11). "In Harlem, there are many proposals for redevelopment," Bond warned the audience at his May 1968 speech to the Architects and Planners against the War in Viet Nam. "Invariably, these proposals will tend to make 125th Street into a business district which serves the whole of New York and will boost land costs."[44]

Long-term fears about the transformation of 125th Street aligned with immediate realities visible to all who witnessed the clearance of the construction site. As a redevelopment project, the proposal occupied relatively little land, only a single city block in the vast neighborhood. But demolition wiped clean the central space on Harlem's main street and one that had especially defined Harlem's history as a center of racial radicalism. Called both African Square and Harlem Square, the corner of Seventh Avenue and 125th Street had served as one of Harlem's great pulpits, an intersection that offered a soapbox for orators like Malcolm X and Nkrumah, who publicly claimed the civil rights that Harlemites had often lacked. Lewis Michaux's National Memorial African Bookstore, also called the "House of Common Sense and Home of Proper Propaganda," had anchored the corner since the early 1930s, when the ardent Garveyite and political radical began to build the collection that numbered over 100,000 volumes by the time its demolition began. Michaux's bookstore—Harlem's most famous—served as a center of progressive thought in the neighborhood, a space where visitors could buy a book but receive an education for free. "I believe that when the Negro knocks this time and nobody opens the door, he's just going to knock it right in," Michaux told one City College class that stopped by to meet "the Professor" in 1966.[45]

African Square and Michaux's bookstore symbolized the most revolutionary possibilities that Harlemites envisioned for their neighborhood. Their presence marked an intellectual beacon in Harlem. Members of the Black Arts Movement, for example, celebrated the corner as the center of the thought that had inspired their search for alternatives to dominant cultural modes. "The older black nationalists always talked on their ladders across the street in front of the Hotel Theresa," Baraka remembered, describing the hotel on the southwest corner of the intersection. "Larger forums were held in front of Mr. Michaux's bookstore, called, affectionately, the House of Proper Propaganda. Malcolm had spoken in front of the store often and there was a sign in front of the store ringed by Pan-African leaders from everywhere in the black world." Neal melded his memories of the corner with his larger sense of Harlem's celebrated people and places and African American culture at large, rolling together jazz musicians like Duke Ellington and Charlie Parker, Communists like Benjamin Davis, and nationalists like Du Bois. "It was Freedom Square, Garvey Square, Little Africa, Mecca, the University of Timbuctoo, the voice of Nat Turner," Neal wrote. "Du Bois . . . Malcolm X, Mr. Michaux, James Lawson, Richard Wright, Kwame Nkrumah, and Ellison's Ras."[46]

The corner of 125th Street and Seventh Avenue marked the center of the public sphere that Bond, too, had idealized. Its clearance suggested not just inconvenient displacement for the residents and merchants who occupied the block, but a form of cultural violence as well. At the very moment that radical Harlem had seized the mantle of Black Power, the state's promises to bring prosperity through the liberal project of redevelopment threatened to undermine dreams of a neighborhood controlled by African Americans. First the state office building would rise, ARCH and its allies contended, and then the rest of Harlem would slip into the hands of outsiders, typically cast as wealthy whites. "Already demolition is under way for the construction of a state office building on 125th Street," an ARCH brochure warned in the summer of 1968. "The law does not guarantee that Harlem's present residents will live or work in the redeveloped Harlem." The neighborhood's "wide streets" and convenient location were "being eyed by developers who need new building sites for white luxury and middle-income apartments," staff wrote, describing a dystopia directly in opposition to the possibility of a space dedicated to Harlem's low-income residents. The state promised revitalization, one protest flyer read, "but this is not so. Instead, they are physically removing Black people—scattering us, making it impossible for us to effectively vote, making it impossible for the poor to get homes."[47]

Such fears sounded alarmist but were not unfounded. The *New York Amsterdam News* reported a string of projects announced for 125th Street after the start of demolition for the state office building. In August 1968, for example, a white developer proposed to build a thirty-three-story structure containing offices, a hotel, department stores, and a mall on 125th Street at the edge of the East Harlem Triangle, a project that directly contradicted the plan that Triangle residents had developed for their neighborhood. "Again, downtown is trying to dictate to uptown," said Vernon Ben Robinson, executive director of CAEHT (and later nominee as people's planning commissioner). Robinson saw only "colonialists who seek to prostitute our resources, occupy our land and live off nothing but misery." Bond likewise invoked the colonial metaphor in a news conference he held two days later, describing Harlem as a place that outsiders both plundered and used as a dumping ground. "There seems to be a gradual process of nibbling away at the edges of black communities—which are usually very desirable land," Bond said. "Junkyards don't get to choose what they get," he continued, "and that's what's happening here."[48]

Radical Harlemites had their own opinions about what Harlem needed on its central block, but felt entirely excluded from a process that state officials and their partners had dominated from the beginning. As with the plans for

West Harlem and the East Harlem Triangle, activists suggested redevelopment that would meet the immediate needs of current residents, not new middle-class workers that the state hoped to attract. "Why not build something meaningful on the site, something beneficial to the community[?]" asked Symes, ARCH's director by early 1969. Many opponents voiced the goal of a high school on the block. Somewhat remarkably, Central Harlem claimed no general public high school for the 17,000 students that backers estimated lived in the neighborhood. A high school, activists hoped, would not only improve education but also provide an opportunity to realize the community control of schools that radicals had long demanded. Which did residents really want, supporters wondered, "a building that will house the offices of the state of New York, or a community controlled high school that will provide meaningful education for the young people"? The 2,500 jobs that officials promised for the office building would provide only "crumbs" to Harlemites, opponents argued, and the cultural center seemed just another imposition of outside culture at a time when Harlemites increasingly took pride in their own. "How are we to be inspired when they force someone else's culture, someone else's standard of beauty on us[?]" critics asked, echoing the language of those active in the search for a black aesthetic.[49]

Debate over the state office building exposed ideological and generational fissures that often coincided. The politically moderate members of the project's Rockefeller-appointed site selection committee included many of Harlem's leading men and women: for example, the presidents of Carver Savings and Loan and Freedom National Bank, the pastors of major churches, and the publisher of the *Amsterdam News*. State office building protesters made up a much more youthful crowd. The loudest voices opposed to the project belonged to the young residents who had enthusiastically embraced the nationalism coursing through Harlem, and who adopted the militancy and even violence that had increasingly become prevalent as an antiredevelopment technique. A memorial service commemorating the fourth anniversary of the death of Malcolm X in February 1969 marked a fitting inflection point as their opposition increased in intensity. Around 600 students gathered at Cooper Junior High School at 120th Street and Fifth Avenue, the *Times* reported, to watch a film about the assassinated leader, "a skit on the divide-and-conquer tactics ascribed to the power structure," and African dancers. As the program concluded, at least thirty students marched the seven

blocks to the construction site, yelling "State building, no; high school, yes."
The students lingered at the site, continuing their protest, before moving
west to the building where John Silvera and Wyatt Tee Walker, Rockefeller's
aides in Harlem, kept their office. "They smashed and kicked their way
through a locked door," the *Times* explained, before ripping draperies from
windows, overturning a photocopier and desks, and dumping out drawers,
all while continuing to chant their anti–state office building mantra.[50]

The rowdy high school protest set the tone for much of the spring to follow.
Harlem state senator Basil Paterson became a vocal opponent of the project
when the state legislature funded the office building but not the adjacent
cultural center in April 1969. Paterson warned the governor that Harlemites
might justifiably see the stripped-down project as a provocation. But protests
had already escalated regardless of the funding situation. As a projected July
construction date loomed and the site sat empty, the *Times* noted, "the opposition became more intense." Picketers frequented the block and Rockefeller's
staff faced a hostile crowd at a late June meeting, "overwhelming" in its opposition to the impending construction. Then, late on June 30, the night before
construction crews were to at last begin building the skyscraper, 200 African
American demonstrators came down to 125th Street with wire cutters in hand.
Under the cover of darkness, they severed the construction fence that blocked
access to a site that had once served as a center of Harlem's public life. They
moved past the barricade before raising barriers of their own, beginning an
occupation that they intended to halt the state office building project.[51]

These occupants renamed the block "Reclamation Site #1," a moniker that
designated both the fundamental objective of community control that the
seizure signified and the larger project that the occupation was to initiate.
The name, protesters allied as the Community Coalition proclaimed, marked
their "conviction that this is just the first of many such battles." Their objective,
as they stated in their official position statement, was to stop the state office
building at all costs but also to shape the site to their ideal vision of Harlem.
"Under no circumstances will a state office building be allowed to sit on
125th Street in the middle of our community," they proclaimed. As they explained, the building rewarded a few Harlemites "at the expense of the general
welfare of Harlem people." It would bring the transformation of the neighborhood that opponents had long feared, "clear[ing] the present residents
out of the area and into other slums . . . to 'redevelop' Harlem with commercial-

industrial buildings and middle to upper income housing." The state's project undermined long-held planning goals, contradicting both the means by which radical activists insisted that their community take form and the ends that they envisioned as the outcome. The project was "an inappropriate, unwanted and treacherous intrusion on the rights of Harlem residents to plan for redevelopment that will truly suit our needs," the Community Coalition wrote. As with earlier efforts, they emphasized the value of present inhabitants as the foundation for development, not the middle class whom officials and the Harlem establishment sought to attract. "We intend to see to it that the primary concern in all redevelopment designs for Harlem is for the *Human Beings* who live here now," they claimed.[52]

The ensuing weeks saw the site begin to reflect the self-determination that protesters espoused as their ultimate objective. Governor Rockefeller indefinitely postponed the project late on the second day of the occupation, bowing to what he termed "community concern" as well as the city's fear that protests would turn violent if the project continued. The governor promised that the site would become a recreational area for the summer, but occupants objected. They had already "begun clearing the land and planning for its temporary use," they reported. The inhabited site was to display their ideal of radical participatory democracy and its forms that celebrated everyday life. "We intend to demonstrate to many so-called 'community leaders' and the State and City of New York what it means to serve the *basic* needs of Black people," they countered. Within days, the Community Coalition had raised five tents on the site, one as a "field kitchen," and replaced the American flag that flew at the intersection of 125th Street and Seventh Avenue with a nationalist red, black, and green flag, a standard that also flew at multiple places along the site's fence (see Figure 2.12). "Red for the blood we have shed, black for our blackness and green for our land, which we are demanding," an occupant proclaimed to passersby through a loudspeaker. Guards patrolled the outer perimeter of the site.[53]

The block had "been transformed from a brick-strewn lot into a tent and shanty 'liberation' town," a reporter noted, an apt comparison as the site began to resemble the "unplanned" settlements that Bond had romanticized. Reclamation Site #1 became a community without designated architects or planners, one in which all members filled those roles. Several protesters inhabited the hulk of an old bus that had remained on the site. Others added a

FIGURE 2.12. Reclamation Site #1 in the summer of 1969, with its nationalist red, black, and green flag flying in the foreground and a variety of temporary structures, including tents and wooden shelters, that housed residents.

large green-and-white striped tent and simple wooden structures that provided shelter. "The occupiers are digging in," a *New York Post* reporter wrote a month into the occupation. "At the gate of the fenced in area is an information booth with a sign above it requesting food, funds and support. And decorating the 15 foot fence surrounding the site are signs put up by the demonstrators[.] One of them reads: 'What do you want here?'" Site residents planned a health clinic and a day care, inviting community members to see for themselves and take part. "If you come visit us, you will see that our temporary clinic will soon be finished," they said. "If you come to help us, you will see that it will be finished much faster."[54] Their efforts recalled those of civil rights activists in Washington, DC, the previous spring, who settled the National Mall for six weeks as part of Martin Luther King Jr.'s posthumous Poor People's Campaign. Almost 3,000 activists had built and inhabited plywood structures in what they called "Resurrection City." Reclamation Site #1 marked a much smaller effort—media estimated from under fifty up to several hundred people on the site at a time—but nonetheless earned a parallel nickname from one reporter: "Resurrection City, Harlem."[55]

Also like Bond's shantytown ideal, Reclamation Site #1 functioned as a cooperative enterprise. "All work on Reclamation Site #1 is done voluntarily,"

FIGURE 2.13. Exemplifying
the principles of cooperation and collectivism that
residents espoused, occupants
of Reclamation Site #1 cook
and build together in the
summer of 1969.

members of the Community Coalition explained. "We are being fed, clothed,
sheltered, protected, and generally supported by thousands of people in the
community." Coalition members insisted on anonymity and shared responsibilities on site. "It's about working together," they announced. Mealtime
provided a telling example of their collectivism (see Figure 2.13). "The people
occupying the site may be poor, but they're proud," a reporter wrote. "Each
day a hale and hearty meal is cooked over an outdoor, charcoal pit fire. . . . The
meal cost nothing to those who wished to enter and partake." Journalist Charlayne Hunter described a woman in "African-style dress" peeling potatoes
for stew alongside two of the site's security guards, who debated the merits
of removing all of the peel or leaving some on for flavor. "Naw, man, you got
to leave some soul," one guard told the other, a cooking tip that embraced
the language of racial pride that pervaded even the dinner hour. While they
prepared food, others nearby assembled more wooden structures. An African drum circle often played and various events took place for site residents

FIGURE 2.14. A rally at Reclamation Site #1 in the summer of 1969. Other activities
on the site likewise embodied residents' radical politics and their principles of racial
self-determination, including seminars on political topics, an African drum circle, and
performances by artists associated with the Black Arts movement.

and members of the Harlem community, including festivals, Saturday ral-
lies, and informal seminars on political topics (see Figure 2.14). At night, the
occupants of Reclamation Site #1 gathered around bonfires to enjoy read-
ings and performances. Baraka brought his Spirit House Movers to the site
from Newark. Jazz drummer Milford Graves and singer Leon Thomas performed here too, as did Clarence Reed and Jacques Wakefield, both poets
affiliated with the Black Arts Movement.[56]

Politically moderate observers often disparaged the occupiers, suggesting
that they were youth unrepresentative of a Harlem mainstream that supported the state office building. William Hudgins, president of the black-
owned Freedom National Bank, characterized the protesters as a "small
handful of noisy rabble." The *Amsterdam News,* whose publisher backed the
state's project, acknowledged that the occupiers had succeeded in raising the
question whether Harlemites should have been consulted on the plans. But
the paper called Reclamation Site #1 an "eyesore" and cast suspicion on the

occupiers' policy of anonymity, suggesting that the protesters had an ulterior motive other than selflessness. "What have they to hide?" the paper asked. "It gives us pause to wonder."[57]

The occupants of Reclamation Site #1, however, were not alone in their opposition to the project and their support for a community-determined plan. Famed Harlem tenant leader and politician Jesse Gray supported their campaign. Rev. Moran Weston, the influential rector of St. Philip's Church in Harlem, called from the pulpit for the state to sell the land to Harlemites. At the first Afro-American Day parade, held in September, Reclamation Site #1 received a hearty endorsement from the congressional delegation that led the caravan. Harlem representative Powell raised his fist in salute to the occupiers, who offered the same greeting. Representative Shirley Chisholm blew site residents a kiss. A *Manhattan Tribune* reporter found some support for the office building among seven men and women he surveyed. "If it brings jobs and money into the community," one respondent said of the building, "then I'm for it." But others wondered whether such jobs would go to Harlemites, and many focused on the issue of representation. "The government is trying to construct a building in the community without consulting the community or meeting its needs," Edward Brown, a recent college graduate, said. Una Kumani agreed. "The state has a lot of nerve trying to construct an office building on 125th Street without consulting the community," he told the paper.[58]

Where opponents of the state office building disagreed was on the issue of what should go on the site instead. The Community Coalition did not intend their settlement to be permanent, even if they sought to build a subsistent community in the meantime, but purposely left the future contents of Harlem's central block undefined. "It's not up to us to determine what goes on here any more than it is up to Wyatt Walker or any other individual or group," they said, referring to the governor's aide in Harlem. The *Tribune* reporter found that some Harlemites endorsed the high school, while others suggested housing, cultural facilities, industry, or Black-owned businesses. Inverting the top-down approach of the state office building and urban renewal in general, site occupants encouraged Harlem residents to voice this diversity of proposals. "We need you! We need your ideas!" Community Coalition members appealed to their neighbors in July, offering a battery of possibilities. "A health center? Educational center? Low-income housing? A combination of these? What would you like to see on this land?"[59]

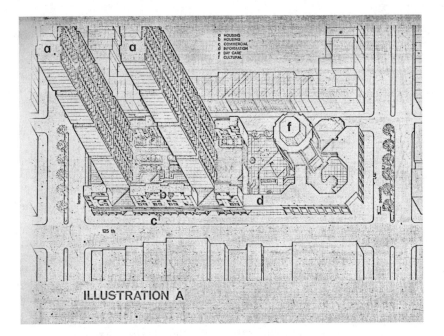

FIGURE 2.15. Three schemes for Reclamation Site #1, prepared by ARCH with assistance from the Real Great Society/Urban Planning Studio, at the request of the site's occupiers. "Illustration A" depicted a proposal emphasizing low-income housing, "Illustration B" centered primarily on a plan for a high school, and "Illustration C" offered a concept focused on commercial uses, yet all three schemes nonetheless embraced a thoroughly mixed-use approach with many different resident-oriented programs accommodated on the site. All likewise adopted a variegated formal strategy that restored Harlem's traditional streetscape. Protesters displayed these illustrations at Reclamation Site #1 throughout August 1969, and asked Harlemites to vote on which ideas reflected their aspirations for Harlem's center.

To answer this question, the residents of Reclamation Site #1 sought a means of decision making different from any that had prevailed before in Harlem, a process that would concretize the notion of participatory democracy that suffused the discourse of the Black Power movement. At the request of occupiers, ARCH presented three conceptual schemes for the site at an open hearing on the block in early August: one emphasizing low-income housing, one focused on education, and a third that combined office space and retail (see Figure 2.15). All departed dramatically from the plan for the state office building in their focus on multiple land uses and on community

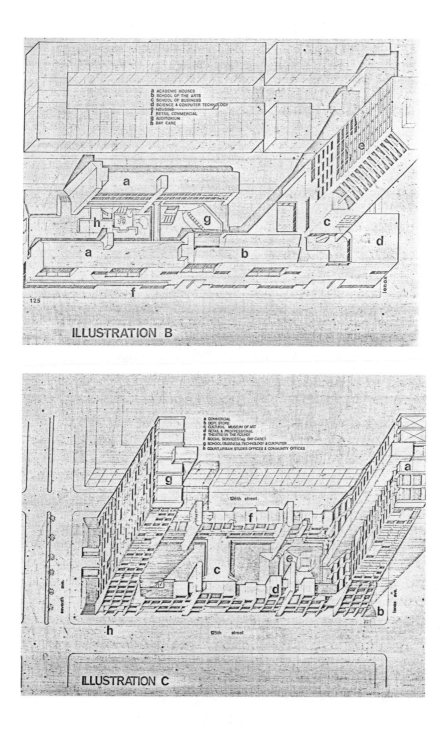

a ACADEMIC HOUSES
b SCHOOL OF THE ARTS
c SCHOOL OF BUSINESS
d SCIENCE & COMPUTER TECHNOLOGY
e HOUSING
f RETAIL COMMERCIAL
g AUDITORIUM
h DAY CARE

125

ILLUSTRATION B

a COMMERCIAL
b DEPT. STORE
c CULTURAL MUSEUM OF ART
d RETAIL & PROFESSIONAL
e THEATRE (IN THE ROUND)
f SOCIAL SERVICES (eg. DAY CARE)
g SCHOOL (BUSINESS, TECHNOLOGY & COMPUTER)
h COURT, URBAN STUDIES OFFICES & COMMUNITY OFFICES

126th street

125th   street

ILLUSTRATION C

needs and desires. The housing scheme, for example, included office space, a "Black cultural center," and an outdoor plaza for festivals alongside almost 1,000 low-income housing units. The high school proposal included an auditorium for public meetings and 200 units of housing. The "office and trade center complex," as ARCH titled the third scheme, added educational facilities, social services, a "gallery for Black arts," and a theater to the most commercial of the concepts.[60]

Each restored the traditional streetscape that demolition had excised, retaining the sidewalk edge that defined 125th Street's public life. ARCH pointed to the retail strip in each plan as an inversion of the high modernism of the state office building. "This feature reinforces pedestrian activity along the street, while large public plazas occupy space away from this prime commercial area," they explained. "In contrast, compare these proposals to the State Office Building proposal where 600 linear feet of prime commercial frontage . . . is wasted on a pretentious lobby and plaza." Even the forms of the three schemes suggested a reversal of the state's plan. Instead of the monolithic slab and wide plaza of the skyscraper, ARCH's plans adopted an eclectic and often experimental approach consistent with Bond's vision of the Black city, including towers alongside low-rise buildings, variegated building forms, and public spaces at different levels. The housing scheme, for example, included townhouses on an elevated deck, each with its own front yard, and floors in the housing towers "left open for play."[61]

Occupiers displayed ARCH's renderings on site, inviting residents to visit and vote for their preference throughout August. They explained the difference between their inclusive ideal and the state's plans in racialized terms. One option reflected the vision of African American residents, they explained, the other the imposition of white outsiders. "If you had a choice of colors, which would you choose?" Their advertisement beckoned Harlemites to participate in the month-long poll (see Figure 2.16). "Well . . . You've got a choice to make NOW! Black or White?" More than 6,000 residents voted, the Community Coalition reported. Their choices largely endorsed the textured, multiuse, and community-oriented ideal that activists had voiced for Harlem. Just over 1,100 participants selected low-income housing as their first choice for the site; equally as many chose an educational facility. Half of the participants envisioned multiple facilities on the block, choosing a diverse array that included education, housing, a medical center, day care, a cultural center, and retail.

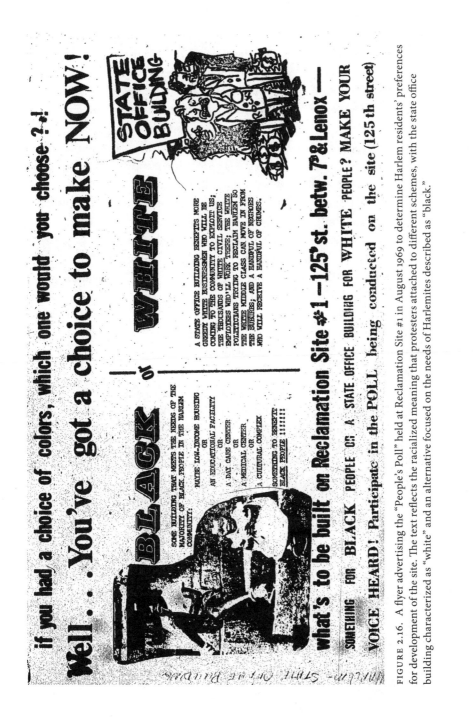

FIGURE 2.16. A flyer advertising the "People's Poll" held at Reclamation Site #1 in August 1969 to determine Harlem residents' preferences for development of the site. The text reflects the racialized meaning that protesters attached to different schemes, with the state office building characterized as "white" and an alternative focused on the needs of Harlemites described as "black."

Just twenty-six voiced their desire for the building that opponents had come to refer to colorfully as the SOB. "The majority of Harlem residents, the poor, the over-worked, the over-looked, do know and understand what they need," a Community Coalition spokesman announced at the conclusion of the poll, "and that need is for housing, an education facility and a day care center."[62]

The fate of this 125th Street block took on epic proportions as the next decade approached. The direction of this site, ARCH insisted, would determine the future of Harlem's main street and, consequently, of the entire community. "Building on this site will establish the tone and policy for development of the whole of 125th St.," staff wrote in August 1969. At stake was the very preservation of Harlem's role as a center of thought and a lively, inclusive public realm. "125th St. has a history as a political arena and an organizing force in the Harlem community. Any new buildings should build on this history." For those with a radical vision for Harlem's future, Reclamation Site #1 marked both a site and a stake in their struggle toward self-determination. The shantytown that activists developed there offered a physical culmination of the flattened, radically democratized process of development that ARCH envisioned in the last years of the 1960s. If imperfect as permanent shelter, the wooden structures and tents that constituted the settlement opened up space to voice alternatives for Harlem's central block. The "People's Poll," as ARCH referred to the on-site referendum, suggested the possibility of bringing planning to its most populist form. Harlem residents elected to fulfill their most acute needs in the very heart of their neighborhood, underscoring their desire that Harlem's spaces and structures reflect its predominantly African American, low-income population. By September 1969, as protesters continued their occupation of the open land that made up Reclamation Site #1, they could claim a vision for Harlem's future, the tools that they hoped would realize it, and physical evidence that their radical ideal could come true. Extending their seeming success from Harlem's central block to reclamation sites throughout the entire neighborhood was their task for the new decade.[63]

CHAPTER 3

Own a Piece of the Block

SEPTEMBER 23, 1969, was an especially long day on the most contested block in Central Harlem. Members of Harlem's Community Coalition and their allies had resisted the construction of the state office building for almost three months, through the simple act of inhabiting the land they renamed Reclamation Site #1. But as summer turned to fall, Governor Nelson Rockefeller sent city police to take back the block. At dawn, a reporter posted at the site's gate notified occupants that authorities would soon appear. A few hours later, police and officials arrived. "Construction work on this location will be starting shortly," a representative of the state Department of General Services called out, "If you leave voluntarily no charges will be placed against you." "We will be free," a squatter responded over a loudspeaker. "Some will die and some others born to carry on the struggle. It will not stop here." Nine refused to move, and police carried them into waiting paddy wagons. Another three dozen crossed the street with black, red, and green flags in hand, watching the last moments of the community they had created at the intersection of Seventh Avenue and 125th Street.[1]

Bulldozers arrived soon, and police thwarted one protester's last effort to stop them with his body (see Figure 3.1). The construction equipment rolled through the most permanent structures squatters had created, the shacks that dotted the site. Then workers cleared protesters' tents, wiping the vast block clean of its provisional homes. A crowd gathered to watch, jeering at police and construction workers for several hours and questioning the motivations of African American officers who were serving the governor's orders. One young protester issued a poignant call that promised the persistence of the

FIGURE 3.1. Police carry John Shabazz, a protester who tried to stop a bulldozer from entering Reclamation Site #1, on September 23, 1969. That morning, on the orders of Governor Nelson Rockefeller, police removed residents from the site and construction crews cleared their tents and the shelters they had constructed.

ideals that had driven the occupation. "This is your land, brothers and sisters," he said. "Freedom is not dead." But many observers were dismayed, as the acreage they had reclaimed transformed so quickly back into a construction site. Crowds gathered throughout the day, watching as parading members of the Community Coalition clashed with police, sparking new arrests. At night, a much larger assembly of several hundred observers saw police subdue rock- and bottle-throwing protesters with nightsticks, sending some to Harlem Hospital. The threat of violence had subsided by midnight, but smaller crowds remained, watching police and watching the site.[2]

The occupation of Reclamation Site #1 marked the apogee of the drive for radical community control over Harlem's built environment, and the plans that activists imagined for that site marked a new confidence in their ability to chart the course of future development. They offered a vision of Harlem built by and for the community's predominantly low-income residents. In this new order, the Architects' Renewal Committee in Harlem (ARCH) and its allies explained, residents would be subject to neither the authoritarian decision making of government officials nor the speculative fervor of private investors who, they feared, would sweep in upon noticing any sign of rebirth on 125th Street. The state's skyscraper would blaze a path for outsiders to take over the neighborhood, opponents argued, rendering meaningless any gains claimed in the campaign for Black Power. "The man wants Harlem for himself since it is one of the most natural Manhattan areas for redevelopment," Omar Ahmed, a site occupier, said. "The state office building was intended as a white outpost at first before the takeover by white power, white strength, and white money." ARCH captured the threat more concisely. "The city and state will make costly expenditures in the name of black people while corporations reap the profits," staff argued, contending that public promises cloaked devious intentions.[3]

Yet the state's rapid eviction of site occupants suggested the difficulties that lay ahead as activists struggled to turn their ideals into reality. Like many aspirations born of the radical movements of the late 1960s, community control captivated adherents but proved quite thorny as believers sought to realize its tenets in physical form. "Let's have the land first and then talk business," ARCH demanded of Reclamation Site #1.[4] But such goals were more easily envisioned than actualized. High hopes sparked the formation of new neighborhood-based organizations in Harlem promising to effect "community development" and identifying self-reliance and self-determination as their ultimate objectives. But in time, such organizations continued to depend fundamentally, and ironically, on the largesse of the public sector at the state and federal levels, across the political spectrum. If these partnerships brought promises that Harlemites would henceforth shape the future of their land, they raised equally serious questions about whether community development would ever achieve the liberated vision to which radical activists had aspired.

Indeed, community development organizations revealed deep contradictions as they took form. These years brought a flood of support for community developers, as remaining liberal political leaders attempted to reform urban renewal without overthrowing it, and ascendant conservative leaders found alignment between demands for local control and their own efforts to devolve urban policy to the local level. Such generous public funding enabled new organizations to become central to the reconstruction of Harlem's built environment. But so too did it consolidate power among a select few moderate community leaders, who took advantage of financial independence from Harlemites, the intransigence of radicals unwilling to compromise their principles, and the intrinsic ambiguity of community control itself to advance a paternalistic approach to the project of community development.[5] Their reliance on the public sector would prove to be something of a devil's bargain, however. Plans—whether bold or prosaic—depended fundamentally on the persistence of such support beyond the 1970s, a condition that became increasingly unlikely amid the political and economic austerity of the next decade.

Struggles to define community development in this era brought a shift at the grassroots level from the communitarian hopes of the 1960s to a greatly tempered, increasingly privatized vision of the future. Without the self-reliance that activists had called for and with moderate leaders dominating decision making, community-based organizations planning development along Harlem's main street turned away from the goals they had once claimed. Instead of the inclusive, cooperative, and mixed-use aspirations of the occupiers of Reclamation Site #1, they advanced an alternate vision that was profit centered, driven by the interests of powerful leaders, and narrowly focused on commercial redevelopment. Their pursuit of this vision in the 1970s would heighten fundamental tensions: between self-reliance and dependence on outside aid, autocracy and participatory democracy, and the individual and the collective. As they reshaped the development landscape in Harlem, new community-based organizations reproduced old inequalities, giving some residents a say without achieving the broad base of support and broad range of benefits to which community control radicals had aspired.

Two organizations, the Harlem Commonwealth Council (HCC) and the Harlem Urban Development Corporation (HUDC), exemplified this transformation most prominently on 125th Street in the 1970s. Both entities followed from the movement for community control that ARCH had helped bring about, but marked the different trajectories available in the aftermath of the occupation of Reclamation Site #1. HUDC, created as a subsidiary of the New York State Urban Development Corporation (UDC), represented the state's attempt to mollify protesters with pledges to redevelop Harlem according to community desires. But HUDC also marked the last best hope of the urban renewal order in Harlem. Promising a foundation that included Harlem's diverse political factions, the organization eventually cast its lot with moderate, middle-class parties who saw HUDC as an opportunity from which they could benefit. HCC, on the other hand, retained many of its original, radical board members but came to align with Richard Nixon's policy agenda, channeling millions of federal dollars into Harlem's real property and remaining industries with the promise that profits would go to Harlem's citizens. While HUDC and HCC initially tracked separate paths, their eventual convergence symbolized the contradictory manner in which the ideal of community development transformed. By the end of the 1970s, HCC held substantial tracts of property throughout Harlem but had failed to pass its equity along to the community at large, and HUDC's promises of community-oriented development adjacent to the state office building remained long unfulfilled. As the 1980s loomed, the highest hopes of community control radicals in Harlem, as in other American urban centers, appeared largely dashed. While they had aspired to find an alternative to both publicly funded urban redevelopment and profit-oriented private development, that possibility had seemingly eluded their grasp. Instead, Harlem's first major community development organizations harnessed fleeting public funds to delineate a largely privatized, elite-dominated future for 125th Street.

Seeking Consensus

The swiftness with which Rockefeller turned Reclamation Site #1 back to rubble indicated the strength that officials maintained at the close of the 1960s. Yet if Rockefeller's crackdown served as a ruthless defense of the urban redevelopment order, in fact leaders understood that their pursuit was taking place in a rapidly changing ideological context. Rockefeller pioneered new innovations in urban renewal even as protests against it grew in strength and number. As he championed the new state office building in 1968, Rockefeller shepherded the legislative passage of UDC. UDC took redevelopment to a new scale, with the ability to build anywhere in the state and supersede the powers of local municipalities. Yet UDC officials also sought a middle ground intended to satisfy both radical critics of urban renewal and moderates who adhered to the view that large-scale public intervention would spur urban revitalization. UDC and its leader, urban redevelopment czar Edward J. Logue, sought to broker calm in Harlem after the occupation of Reclamation Site #1. But their attempts to forge a broad consensus within Harlem's diverse communities ultimately foundered on the same divided ideological terrain that had brought the state office building controversy in the first place. Radicals refused to compromise their demands and thus found themselves increasingly isolated.

UDC marked a watershed in the history of urban redevelopment, an ambitious agency with unprecedented power. Like redevelopment authorities at the municipal level, UDC could take land by eminent domain and build housing, commercial projects, industrial parks, or civic centers. But UDC also boasted unique superpowers, such as the right to build without heeding local land use regulations and even local plans. Moreover, it could issue its own bonds, a fact that enabled the agency to finance its own work and build innovative housing projects throughout the state. Logue, Rockefeller's choice to lead UDC, claimed bona fides that paralleled the agency's position at the vanguard of urban renewal. As the head of redevelopment in New Haven and then Boston, Logue had built his reputation by leading the reconstruction of neighborhoods and downtowns in two of urban renewal's model cities. Logue's presence at the helm of UDC signaled the visibility and prominence of Rockefeller's program, which he expected to set the tone for redevelopment at a never-before-seen scale.[6]

Logue's reputation preceded him. Indeed, ARCH had protested vehemently in 1966 when rumors swirled that Mayor John Lindsay might choose Logue as New York City's new redevelopment executive. "There is some evidence . . . that his coming to New York could mean a return both to the high-handed policies of Robert Moses and to the kind of slum clearance and rehabilitation that spells Negro and Puerto Rican removal," ARCH board member Herbert Gans had warned.[7] But unlike the unyielding Moses, Logue had maintained a flexible approach throughout his career in response to the changing context in which he practiced.[8] UDC's mandate marked the culmination of this adaptability. It set out to reshape New York's cities in a manner that avoided displacement and disparate racial impact: by establishing new towns on open land, building mixed-income tenancy into housing developments, and maintaining racial integration in new suburban housing construction.[9]

Logue's interest in mediating the state office building controversy thus arose out of both his responsibility to Governor Rockefeller and his willingness to adjust to broader social and political transformations that might otherwise derail his redevelopment agenda. Once squatters moved onto the site in the summer of 1969, Logue admitted to Alton Marshall, a Rockefeller aide, that he was "in no sense intimately familiar" with the issue but wanted to help. Responding to protests that in part grew from the state's elimination of any nonoffice land use on the site, Logue offered, "We can put a black-white architectural team to designing a community facility, whether it be a school, a recreational center, or a cultural center." Or, he continued, they could build "housing with built-in community facilities, again with a black-white architectural team." By September, Logue's language began to more explicitly mirror that of site occupants. "The first matter is what is the present desire of the Harlem community with respect to the program for the balance of the site," he told Marshall. "We would of course seek to work out a Harlem community ownership."[10]

Logue's aspirations rested on the fundamental—and still very raw—issue of who exactly constituted Harlem's "community." The state office building had exposed already-existing rifts that often found racial moderates on one side and radical community control advocates on the other. Supporters of the building had coalesced as the Responsible Coalition in Support of the Harlem Civic Center, a group that included members of Harlem's middle-class establishment and religious strongholds. Harlem business leaders, the Negro Labor Council, and the Ministerial Interfaith Association, a group of approximately 150 leaders from many of Harlem's long-standing congregations, made up the core of supporters. Percy Sutton, then the borough president of Manhattan, and Charles Rangel, an upstart on the verge of challenging Adam Clayton Powell Jr.'s congressional seat, sided with supporters as well, while Powell and Harlem political broker Basil Paterson gave clout to those who had seized Reclamation Site #1. Many who continued to oppose the construction of the building made up the radical vanguard in Harlem, claiming roots in the community control movement, and many also maintained direct connections with ARCH. David Spencer, an education activist with a leadership post at IS 201; Eugene Callender, who had worked with ARCH in West Harlem; and ARCH board member Marshall England—as well as ARCH leadership—remained public supporters of the youthful Community Coalition and its allies.[11]

Both sides claimed a mandate in support of their respective positions. Community Coalition leaders maintained that a majority of 6,000 surveyed passersby had supported their stand at Reclamation Site #1, while the

Ministerial Interfaith Association hoped to gather 100,000 petitions to sustain their cause. But Logue remained optimistic that with his broad redevelopment powers he could build a consensus between divided parties.[12] He met personally with project backers including Rangel, L. Joseph Overton of the Negro Labor Council, and James Gunther, leader of the Ministerial Interfaith Association, throughout the fall of 1969, but also with Jesse Gray, the famed Harlem tenant leader and project opponent; Livingston Wingate, an Urban League leader and opposition mainstay; and Callender. Notably, Logue and his staff engaged directly with members of the Community Coalition, ARCH, and Roy Innis, the community control trailblazer who had presided over the transformation of the Congress of Racial Equality (CORE). Logue even sought out the plans ARCH had drafted for Reclamation Site #1, the benchmark of radicals' vision for a new Harlem.[13]

These opposing forces, Logue hoped, would become the representative foundation on which UDC could pursue a much wider role in Harlem. Logue envisioned a Committee of 15 that would help not just plan the redevelopment of the state office building site but also develop a new plan for all of Harlem. He intended to institutionalize the committee's role in a subsidiary corporation, creating a new development entity with semi-independent authority—a decentralized node that retained the unusual powers of its parent body. Logue hoped this group would include the diverse parties he had engaged since September, such as Overton, Gunther, Callender, Wingate, and Rangel, as well as Arthur Symes, ARCH's executive director, and others representing ARCH and the Community Coalition. UDC staff remained realistic about uniting opposed forces but clung to the hope that they could at least garner a critical mass. "You can stress the desire for unanimity on this issue but the realistic prospect is that perhaps it is one of those things that can only go ahead with a majority consensus," one staff member advised Logue. "If this is so, you can indicate a willingness to do business on that basis."[14]

Logue's optimism rested on the belief that reform of the redevelopment process would be sufficient to engage those most frustrated by it. In late 1969, Logue unveiled a series of concessions informed by the meetings he had conducted with Harlem stakeholders. He pledged increased UDC involvement in housing and school construction. He also promised that residents would nominate the members of the committee that was to guide the subsidiary and might even be able to buy shares in the nonprofit corporation. Moreover, the state vowed to yield all land not dedicated to the state office building to the kinds of resident-oriented land uses that radical groups had demanded, including housing and a community center. Logue tapped Bond Ryder Associates, the firm that J. Max Bond Jr. had founded upon leaving ARCH, to plan the site, a move that indicated his willingness to make room for the spatial ambitions of community control adherents.[15]

Likewise, Logue promised a new purpose for the structure that had sparked protests in the first place. The state office building would instead become a state service center, housing functions that served Harlem, such as consumer protection and job recruiting, and providing space to community organizations. Recounting a meeting with Paterson, Logue noted, "His judgment was that the more things that the community wanted incorporated into the building under construction, the more credibility and potential support such a building would have." Yet even as Logue offered to transform the controversial tower to align with radicals' land use demands, and even as he facilitated the involvement of a broader constituency than officials had ever engaged, he refused to abandon the monolithic structure itself. For Logue, the modernist building signified the last vestiges of a redevelopment order that was bending but had not broken.[16]

Community control radicals, on the other hand, opposed Logue's concessions for precisely that reason, as the towering skyscraper's persistence in plans suggested that the struggle for "reclamation" had not yet succeeded. In seeking reform, Logue had overestimated the degree to which opponents were willing to accept compromise. Activists had said as much in their first meetings with Logue and maintained that stance throughout negotiations. The "group indicated that it would not participate in any arrangement with UDC until issue of State Office Building is resolved," Carl McCall, a consultant to UDC and later a state senator, reported of an early November meeting. "Requested Logue to recommend to Governor that construction halt immediately." When they met as the Committee of 15 soon after, opponents listened to Logue's offers but stood their ground. "This was [the] last attempt to meet with a group representing opposite views on this issue," McCall reported.[17]

Community control radicals insisted that only a neighborhood referendum could settle this stalemate, a participatory happening that would truly democratize a process that Logue had largely brokered. Activists vowed to abide by the results of a public vote, but Logue responded cautiously to an invitation that threatened to undermine the structure of governance he maintained. When Wingate announced a community convention for mid-December with the purpose of staging such a referendum, UDC demonstrated its trepidation by sending staff members but not Logue himself. There, ARCH voiced an angry denunciation of UDC's plan. "The change in the name from State Office Building to Harlem Service Center is supposed to be a face-saving device for the community. Who needs it?" They continued, "If we allow the State Office Building to go up, we may as well forget all the rhetoric about community 'participation' in planning and accept the fact that we have been had." Instead, ARCH offered a proposal that would allow community members to replan the *entire* site and stop construction on the state office building immediately. ARCH's position won the day resoundingly, as 55 participants voted for the state's project and 178 against it. Moreover, 167 attendees supported ARCH's plan and only 20 chose UDC's, but the session did little to sway state officials. McCall reported the opposition's success but seemed unconcerned about plans to next stage a Harlem-wide vote. "Construction on the building will probably continue and I do not see any organized effort to prevent that," he told Logue.[18]

McCall's nonchalance suggested the precarious position that community control radicals occupied. While Logue had offered every concession but one, the Community Coalition remained unwilling to concede even that point. Doing so would mean undermining the very principle of self-determination on which the three-month occupation had taken place and abandoning the vision that radicals had crafted. The editors of the *Amsterdam News* appeared perplexed by the Community Coalition's intransigence. "Governor Rockefeller has stated that there is enough flexibility in the project to include all the facilities as recommended at this past weekend's rather raucous convention," they wrote. "To us this should be satisfying to the many adults and young who opposed the building. Or is it that they must have their cake and eat it too?" Indeed, such refusal was bound up in the very tenets of radical community control. "In retrospect we can see that one of the historical problems of black people on American soil is that we have demanded too little too late," ARCH representatives announced at the community convention. "Reclamation Site #1 should belong to the Harlem community and there should be no question about it."[19]

Unwilling to compromise their idealism, however, ARCH and its allies found themselves increasingly isolated from a process that would continue with or without them. Logue had options in the divided community, and while he would go far in adapting the organization he led, he would not preside over the complete upheaval of the top-down method he had pioneered, if not perfected. With hopes for a broad coalition at an impasse, the faction that had always supported the state office building looked to become the community representatives who would negotiate the role of UDC's Harlem subsidiary. "Let me implore you to ignore all pleas for a referendum or other delaying tactics," one member of the Responsible Coalition urged Governor Rockefeller. On the eve of the community convention, Logue met with Gunther's Ministerial Interfaith Association to discuss the purpose of a UDC subsidiary in Harlem, and by March 1970, the Ministerial Interfaith Association—as well as allies including then-assemblyman Rangel and Thomas Sinclair of the Harlem Chamber of Commerce—had begun direct negotiations with UDC. Their interest in fortifying their favored position at least matched their interest in improving Harlem. "State Government should not allow the noisemakers in the community to thwart progress emanating from this agreement in the interest of politics," several members urged. UDC staff advised including less moderate voices, including representatives from ARCH, but leaders tracked toward the middle, drawing from among Harlem officials, ministers, Model Cities committees, and businesses. Consequently, the thirty-one-member negotiating committee formed in May 1970 included Leo Rolle, an ARCH board member selected for his leadership of the United Block Association, and Alice Kornegay, selected for her role in Model Cities, but otherwise consisted of the figures with whom Gunther had worked all along.[20]

By the dawn of the establishment of a new entity promising community development in Harlem, then, Logue had assured the persistence of the state as a major force in the neighborhood. However, he had failed to achieve the diverse coalition he had pursued as an alternative to both the establishment-dominated mode of typical redevelopment and the fully devolved mode that community control radicals had demanded. UDC staff worried about the figures with whom they had cast their lot. "Without Wingate, Callender, Marshall England, Jesse Gray, ARCH, the Community Coalition . . . the group prepared to sign the [Memorandum of Understanding] is not broadly based enough," Dan Miller, a Logue aide, warned.[21]

Those radical figures voiced their agreement, as they watched a process unfold that increasingly excluded them from shaping Harlem's future. England, the president of local community action agency Harlem Youth Opportunities Unlimited–Associated Community Teams (HARYOU-ACT) and an ARCH board member, asked Rockefeller to stop planning for the subsidiary "until a more democratic process is established and more broad-based Harlem representation is reached." Innis disparaged the effort more bluntly. "He said he had heard something about it, but dismissed the 'Pork Chop preachers' as ineffectual," Miller reported.[22] But due in large part to the intransigence of radicals who had refused to cede any ground, the "pork chop preachers" found themselves at the center of the subsidiary that would become HUDC. As it took form over the next year, they consolidated their position. Logue could claim Harlem representation for the new entity but not the collection of diverse viewpoints he had sought. Radicals in the struggle to bring community control into institutional form were left to consider what other means might enable them to gain power over Harlem's land.

"Own a Piece of the Block"

Members of ARCH stood before the community convention in December 1969 to describe their vision for Harlem's main street. "The controlled development of 125th Street could bring benefits to the community. Each project that is developed should be part of a larger process whereby black people generate manpower, information, capital, land and skills which are needed to gain control over their lives," they argued. But if community control stalwarts voiced confidence that redevelopment could help solve the neighborhood's problems of unemployment, housing, and inequality, they pinned such hopes on a dramatic departure from its past methods. *The basic strategy should be ownership of the land and the use of 125th Street as a source of economic development within the community* [emphasis in original]." Activists rejected UDC's offers to facilitate community planning within the rubric of urban renewal, but remained optimistic that they could reshape 125th Street themselves. Self-help offered independence as well as control, and at least the hope that any Harlemite wishing to take part in the neighborhood's reconstruction could do so.[23]

Creating an institutional structure to make such ideas practicable proved complex, but the community development corporation (CDC) offered one possible path. CDCs emerged across American cities in the late 1960s. In Harlem, the members of ARCH, Innis, Preston Wilcox, and other leading lights of the Black Power movement had created one of the first, the Harlem Commonwealth Council (HCC), in 1967. Similar organizations sprouted in places like the Brooklyn neighborhood of Bedford-Stuyvesant, Cleveland, and Philadelphia. As many as seventy-five urban CDCs existed by 1971, and similar corporations came together in many rural areas beset by poverty. Their activities varied dramatically: some invested in local businesses or aided entrepreneurs, while others constructed new housing or provided social services, loans, and technical assistance. CDCs largely aligned, however, in preaching the compelling, if imprecise, notion that, as one observer described, "equality is as much a matter of economic power as it is of political rights," and "that in economics, as in politics, there is strength in numbers."[24]

Indeed, CDCs grew from the hope that cooperation between the predominantly low-income residents of places like Harlem could provide an economic engine for greater self-determination. Communities already bore the resources needed for revitalization, HCC and similar CDCs argued, if only an entity could gather, organize, and direct those resources. Yet despite such dreams of self-reliance, which grew from roots in radical movements for community control, the early history of CDCs revealed a fundamental contradiction in their work: amid continued promises of self-help, these organizations came to depend instead on funds that flowed readily from the federal government in the late 1960s and early 1970s. In the "New Federalism" of the Nixon era, CDCs discovered new opportunity, not new constraints. CDCs calling for local control over development found government officials glad to cede responsibility. Such funding redefined the nature of urban policy, creating a direct path between the federal government and new community-based organizations. This relationship enabled CDCs to become major economic forces in their communities and, soon, dream on a bigger scale. However, this support also ushered in new questions about CDCs' accountability to the residents they promised to serve.

At their beginning, poverty both motivated the formation of organizations like HCC and provided the economic basis for their strategy, which emphasized cooperation and self-help. While individual Harlemites boasted few resources, HCC's founders contended that their combined assets could nonetheless profoundly reshape the neighborhood. Residents' power rested in their role as modest shareholders. Founders estimated that $300,000 would allow HCC to procure an initial loan, one-third of which they intended to raise in tiny denominations, in the form of five-dollar voting shares sold to Harlemites. "The [e]ffect would be the creation of a mass-based citizen organization with substantial economic power," they explained. Profits would return to Harlem, not to the leaders of HCC but into its subsequent ventures. "The Corporation's investment fund will grow steadily," founders promised. As a result, HCC would become largely independent and self-reliant, allowing its activities to expand beyond economic development into housing, education, and social services.[25]

Such an approach struck many residents and observers as novel, but in fact CDCs could claim a deep pedigree in black self-help efforts. Marcus Garvey had founded his Universal Negro Improvement Association in the mid-1910s just ten blocks north of 125th Street. He similarly focused his efforts on business creation throughout Harlem and beyond. Anticipating the very approach that HCC would later promote, he financed his grandest project, the oceangoing Black Star Line—a visionary if ill-fated passenger and cargo line—by offering five-dollar shares to his Harlem neighbors and promising them a portion of profits.[26] Garvey organized within an even wider orbit of self-help, extending back to Booker T. Washington's turn-of-the-century call for black economic self-reliance and encompassing the entire sweep of African American economic pursuits in the early twentieth century, including race-specific businesses focused on personal beauty, news, insurance, and death. Such enterprises, while limited in both scope and scale, offered the promise of a self-sufficient alternate economy that, decades later, organizations like HCC would look to achieve.[27]

Like these predecessors, HCC emerged preaching a gospel combining equal parts market orientation and cooperative mutual aid. At times, HCC leaders espoused undoubtedly capitalist aspirations. "There will be no begging the establishment—the Corporation will compete on the market with its own resources," the founders had vowed. Yet the organization promised to temper the capitalistic pursuit of profits with a communitarian ethos that was to benefit Harlem at large. While economic development remained HCC's primary goal, founders intended that gains would enrich all Harlemites. "The network of businesses that we are building will vastly improve the basic economic structure of our community by creating more financial multipliers, more jobs and better services," leaders argued. Innis, HCC's first director, captured the organization's refusal to chart a dogmatic path. "Blacks must innovate, must create a new ideology," Innis argued. "It may include elements of capitalism, elements of socialism, or elements of neither: that is immaterial. What matters is that it will be created to fit our needs."[28]

The series of small ventures that HCC embarked on in its first years spoke to these coinciding goals. Leaders hoped that through enterprise, the organization could both fill urgent community needs and generate profits to support further efforts. HCC initially operated a small foundry on West 126th Street and a Singer sewing store in the Lenox Terrace housing development, but by the beginning of 1971 had acquired a pharmacy on 125th Street—renamed Commonwealth Pharmacy—launched a travel agency called Commonwealth Tours, and opened a wholesale office furniture store, Commonwealth Office Equipment and Furniture Company. Commonwealth Data Services, incorporated in January 1971, trained keypunch operators and prepared accounting data for computer processing. Other, eventually unrealized plans included a gas station, a record and audio store, and a supermarket. Each business in this seemingly quixotic array served a sector that HCC deemed underserved but crucial. "There is a large institutional market which is not being serviced by existing businesses at present," leaders wrote of the office supply store. Similarly, they justified the pharmacy as the fulfillment of a vital community demand. "For years the Harlem Community has had critical need of a pharmacy that provides twenty-four hour service," they argued.[29]

The name that most of these ventures shared—"commonwealth"— represented more than a connection to the parent Harlem Commonwealth Council. It also signified the idea that success in business would derive from and enrich the entire Harlem community. Leaders frequently reiterated their plan to offer ownership shares to Harlemites, resisting decades of history in which outsiders controlled most of Harlem's economy. "Once we have reversed the ownership trend," explained Donald Simmons, HCC's second director, "we will have the confidence of the Harlem community to continue its growth as a commonwealth." Stock ownership was to provide Harlemites with a stake in HCC's business ventures and control over the organization itself through representation on its board of directors. A foothold in the local economy, Simmons argued, would lead to the widespread influence that residents had lacked. "The economic ownership by the people will serve as the lever to effect changes in Harlem's political and educational institutions," Simmons explained. "Eventually, Harlem's people will be responsible for Harlem's police protection, health services, and education."[30]

Yet despite ambitious promises of self-sufficiency, CDCs like HCC charted a more complicated reality nearly from the moment of their creation. Founders vowed that there would be no "begging the establishment," but in fact the organization launched with support from the federal government. Despite plans to fund its activities through a loan leveraged with the modest donations of community members, for example, HCC's initial seed money came through a 1967 grant from the federal Office of Economic Opportunity (OEO). Simmons, HCC's director by mid-1968, expressed unease with the central role that federal funding had already come to play in the organization's first months. He wished to shed OEO funding within the year, he told a Rockefeller Foundation staff member. "He did not mind receiving Federal assistance but does not want to remain dependent upon Washington," the staffer explained. Yet the organization pursued and received a second OEO grant just a few months later, in early 1969.[31]

Why did HCC so quickly abandon its founding cooperative ethos for a model that depended largely on public-sector support? Two major factors help to explain this transformation. First, the fundamental ideological indistinctness of CDCs—as Innis described, neither capitalist nor socialist—brought a decided flexibility to their work. Despite roots in radical movements for community control, HCC proved more concerned with its intended ends—new business ventures to fuel Harlem's economic prosperity—than with the means of getting there. This expediency grew out of the broader ambiguity of the concept of "black capitalism," a term that contemporary commentators frequently invoked to describe the entrepreneurial outgrowths of the Black Power movement, including CDCs. Innis resisted this label. "In the new focus on economic control, there has been much talk about something called 'black capitalism.' Many of our people have been deluded into endless debates centered around this term," Innis explained.

"There is no such animal." Yet in doing so, he acknowledged the vagueness of an idea that encompassed a wide variety of approaches, from radical demands for reparations to partnerships between multinational companies and African American communities. In a realm of definitional imprecision, in which the very meaning of the CDC remained up for grabs, it proved easy for leaders to shift their approach at will without seeming to abandon the equally ambiguous objective of community control.[32]

Secondly, and relatedly, the ready availability and unconstrained nature of federal funding in this era enabled CDCs to stray from the goal of self-financing. This too arose from the ideological ambiguity inherent in the project of community control. Leaders on the political right and left both saw opportunities in the ascendant mantra of "power to the people." Lyndon Johnson's War on Poverty readily funded community groups in an effort to foster new forms of populist governance. CDCs like HCC, in their eagerness to get off the ground, found such aid difficult to resist. They gladly tapped generous grants in order to avoid the slow, gradual work of gathering resources from low-income residents. Yet if HCC benefited from the last days of the Great Society—its 1969 grant came just a couple of weeks before the inauguration of President Nixon—it found that Nixon's New Federalism hardly staunched the flow of funds. Indeed, CDCs found an eager ally in the new president. As Nixon sought a diminished federal role in urban policy, CDCs offered an appealing outlet with their opposition to the liberal project of urban renewal and their calls for self-help and localism. Through continued support for CDCs, Nixon could appear responsive to African Americans while largely abdicating direct involvement in addressing urban poverty.[33]

CDC proponents viewed the Nixon administration's support for their brand of black capitalism not as a problematic devolution of authority or an attempt at cooptation, but as a policy that coincided with and enabled their demands for self-determination. They were pleased to gain the autonomy implicit in Nixon's effort to chart a path directly from federal coffers to those of incipient organizations. Such seemingly odd bedfellows were common in the complicated political environment of the late 1960s and early 1970s, in which ideals of the libertarian right and radical left often coincided.[34] HCC's first leader, Innis, exemplified this alignment. Innis, who had overseen CORE's shift toward Black Power, found immediate appeal in Nixon's promise to shape a new federal role in cities. Indeed, candidate Nixon had met secretly with Innis in 1968 and supported Innis's attempt to pass the Community Self-Determination Bill through Congress. The bill's proponents hoped to empower and multiply entities like HCC through national financial and administrative support and new powers, including the ability to distribute contracts to other community-based organizations.[35]

Innis's pursuit of such legislation proved unsuccessful, but other mechanisms remained in place to ensure that CDCs like HCC could fuel their activities with generous federal support throughout Nixon's presidency, into Gerald Ford's administration, and under the Democratic administration of Jimmy Carter. Senators Robert F. Kennedy and Jacob Javits had sponsored a 1966 amendment to the Economic Opportunity Act of 1964, Title I-D of which established the Special Impact Program (SIP). Lawmakers created SIP to channel block grants to CDCs in areas with especially high poverty and unemployment, an idea born out of Kennedy's interest in the Bedford-Stuyvesant area of Brooklyn. Kennedy had visited Bedford-Stuyvesant in early 1966 to announce a plan focused on addressing the neighborhood's poverty, and his visit and subsequent sponsorship led to the initiation of the Bedford-Stuyvesant Restoration Corporation, one of the country's first CDCs. SIP funded the corporation and its contemporaries, becoming the major financial support for CDCs once it made its administrative home at OEO in 1969.[36]

HCC's emergence on the national scene, and particularly its elevation through the assistance of SIP, followed closely behind the appointment of the organization's third director, James Dowdy. Dowdy, a Harlem native, had not graduated high school and had no formal training in business. A plumber by trade, he had impressed HCC leaders while working as a contractor for the organization, and soon joined its board of directors as a local business representative. When Simmons departed in early 1970, Dowdy's fellow directors invited him to become HCC's interim leader and, soon, its permanent chief executive officer. Like his predecessors, Dowdy promised that HCC would rebuild Harlem's economy on a foundation of widespread collective ownership. "To achieve this goal we must move in the direction of community control," he explained in early 1971. Yet Dowdy's leadership marked a notable break in HCC's history. His predecessors claimed strong ties to the radical vanguard in Harlem: Innis as a leading Black Power proponent, and Simmons as the brother of Kenneth Simmons, who had led the radicalization of ARCH. But Dowdy, whom leaders tapped specifically because of the fresh perspective he brought to the CDC, claimed no direct ties to either Harlem's radical movements or the cooperative ideals that motivated HCC's foundation. If Simmons expressed reservations about HCC's reliance on federal funding even as he continued to draw from it, Dowdy raised no similar objections. Politically moderate, charismatic, and ambitious, he eagerly pursued partnerships with advocates in Washington.[37]

Indeed, under Dowdy's leadership HCC became one of the country's leading recipients of federal aid through SIP. HCC had financed its early business ventures with SIP grants of $600,000 in 1969 and $800,000 in 1970, both substantial infusions but hardly remarkable compared to the much larger awards given elsewhere. But the organization received $2.3 million in 1971 and $2 million in 1973, both the second-largest grants for their respective years, and $3.5 million in 1974, the largest grant given under SIP that year. By mid-1978, only two CDCs had received more SIP funding than HCC, one a Chicago CDC that edged out their Harlem counterpart by a few hundred thousand dollars, the other the powerhouse Bedford-Stuyvesant Restoration Corporation, which remained the best-funded CDC in the nation long after the death of Robert Kennedy.[38]

HCC received more than 10 percent of the nearly $175 million that SIP had distributed to urban CDCs by the late 1970s, and Dowdy openly acknowledged the fundamental role that federal support played in enabling HCC's work. If Kennedy famously functioned as the patron saint of the Bedford-Stuyvesant Restoration Corporation, Javits in many ways played the same role for HCC. Both New York senators supported HCC's earliest funding requests, but Javits, a liberal Republican and New York's senior senator, became the organization's strongest voice in Washington, ensuring that HCC had ready access to funding throughout the 1970s. Dowdy honored Javits at HCC's first awards dinner in late 1973. "Your presence would mean a lot to me," Dowdy told Javits, whose office complimented HCC's leader. "[Dowdy] is very generous and, I think, sincere in his praise for you and attributes HCC's success largely to your support," a Javits aide wrote the senator. "I think that HCC, even more than Bedford-Stuyvesant Restoration . . . can be considered the showpiece of government-sponsored community development." Javits delivered equally enthusiastic remarks upon receiving HCC's award. "Jim Dowdy has provided exactly the kind of business expertise and quality leadership that was required,"

Javits said. In HCC and Dowdy, Javits found the very embodiment of the urban policy he espoused, which focused on economic enterprise as the means to the broader goal of community development. And in SIP and Javits, Dowdy found the resources to build his organization into the most powerful economic force in Harlem. "I would like to express a personal 'thank you' for all of the good things that have happened to me as a result of your backing," he wrote Javits in 1973. "I hope that in the future I will be able to stand as a testimonial of your efforts in our community."[39]

The flood of federal money that Dowdy accessed enabled HCC to shift its goals to a bigger scale. The December 5, 1970, *Amsterdam News*, headlined "The Story of Two Harlem Buildings," offered material evidence of this decisive transition. The first building mentioned, the infamous state office building, had at last begun to rise after years of tension. The other—similarly modern, just a block away, and also housing government offices (in this case, municipal)—was on the verge of completion. No protesters had attempted to stop what would soon become 125th Street's first new office building in years. "Unlike its sister or brother office building, this City Office Building was not touched by the controversy which befell the state office building," the article pointed out. This was, the author suggested, because of the rumors that had swirled throughout construction stating that HCC would obtain a substantial share of ownership, rumors that would soon prove true.[40]

HCC's move to purchase half, and later all, of the structure that it would rename the Commonwealth Office Building marked a new focus on Harlem's property that would define the organization's work over the next three decades. "This is the first and only piece of real estate owned by the community, and there are going to be many more," Dowdy vowed at the building's inauguration in May 1971. Indeed, a few months later he unveiled a more extensive plan for a "Land Bank Program" dedicated to pouring HCC's resources into Harlem's land. "In most, if not all, of our Special Impact Target Areas lies some of the most valuable real estate in the Nation," he pointed out. But such land was increasingly under siege, Dowdy argued, by redevelopment on one hand and by speculation on the other. CDC-led land banking offered the possibility that residents could control their scarcest resource instead. He proposed putting Harlem's land in public trust and determining its use through a public process. "Whether land is to be devoted to residential, commercial, or industrial uses or is to be left open for park land will be decided by trustees in accord with a general plan, adopted and amended by the community at elections held for that purpose," Dowdy wrote. Redevelopment had spelled the displacement of Harlemites or their exclusion from the profits therein. But land banking, Dowdy argued, would ensure that any development benefited community owners. "The people of the community can, for the first time, gain access to the profits from the physical redevelopment of their community."[41]

Land offered a new frontier for CDCs, but one with both practical and symbolic significance. By the time HCC moved into land banking as its primary activity, its earliest ventures had shown mixed results. Small enterprises demonstrated HCC's aspiration that Harlemites could own more than "race businesses" or the crumbs that white investors left behind, but their monetary and employment benefits remained limited. HCC looked to sell the Commonwealth Pharmacy by the end of 1972; Medicaid reimbursements were slow and expenses too high. Likewise the Sewing Center, affected by Singer's decision not to renew their contract with HCC, soon closed. "The effectiveness of small scale ventures are perhaps more symbolic than real," leaders acknowledged in 1972. But real estate development offered substantial financial benefits, as HCC had already seen in the steady stream of income that city tenants provided through long-term leases in the Commonwealth Office Building. HCC leaders received encouragement, too, from the relative ease with which they moved into larger investments. In mid-1972, they acquired the Shultz Company, a manufacturer of supermarket equipment, employer of one hundred, and one of Harlem's largest remaining industries. Soon, they were proposing to acquire land along Seventh Avenue between 125th and 127th Streets and on 125th Street between Eighth and St. Nicholas Avenues, substantial parcels in Harlem's center.[42]

"Own a Piece of the Block," HCC's newspaper advertisements began to announce in 1972—a promise that the most optimistic hopes of the occupants of Reclamation Site #1 might soon come true. By the time HCC shifted its focus to Harlem's land, it and similar CDCs nationwide had helped to redefine the relationship undergirding development in American cities. Where urban renewal had relied on a network of federal, state, and municipal officials as well as private real estate investors, the funding pipeline that supported HCC ran directly from Washington to the community organization's doorstep. This dependence on outside support even as organizations continued to promise self-reliance did not strike leaders as paradoxical. They maintained their pledge that community members would soon own the corporation themselves, that "this company . . . will be thrown open to Harlem residents," as the *Amsterdam News* put it in 1971. But five years after HCC's launch, as the corporation began to buy up property along 125th Street, this founding principle still remained only a promise.[43]

How Much Power to the People?

Community control activists hoped to fundamentally democratize development in Harlem, but the early history of the neighborhood's community development organizations illustrated the difficulty of such transformation. If the public sector's role in Harlem had changed by the early 1970s, it remained crucially involved in the project of redevelopment. Likewise, as residents soon discovered, if new faces guided emerging organizations, their commitment to the project of participatory democracy proved decidedly uncertain. Dependence on outside aid did not necessarily mean that such groups would stray from goals of empowerment and self-determination, of course, but as the leaders of HUDC and HCC forged close relationships with the state and federal governments, respectively, their work gained increasing distance from founding principles.

Instead of the ideal that radicals had espoused as the basis of community control, a vision of a richly textured neighborhood cooperatively shaped by and for the benefit of its existing residents, HUDC and HCC advanced an alternate vision for Harlem. Their ideal emphasized the commercial development of 125th Street and a paternalistic approach to community control, premised on the assumption that dominant leaders knew best what would benefit their Harlem neighbors. This outcome resulted in part from pressure by outside funders, but more so from the independence that outside funding enabled, leaving leaders of local organizations to chart their own course without reliance on the community members they promised to serve.

Vernon Ben Robinson, who had worked closely with ARCH in the 1960s, summed up the budding doubts of likeminded activists in his critical 1971 study of UDC's work in Harlem. "How Much Power to the People?" he asked.[44] While HCC and HUDC remained separate organizations with separate agendas—HUDC still guided by the Ministerial Interfaith Association, HCC still claiming a board including many community control proponents—

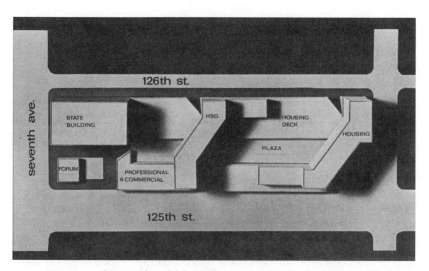

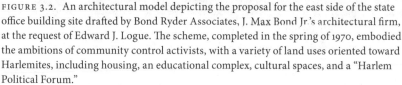

FIGURE 3.2. An architectural model depicting the proposal for the east side of the state office building site drafted by Bond Ryder Associates, J. Max Bond Jr.'s architectural firm, at the request of Edward J. Logue. The scheme, completed in the spring of 1970, embodied the ambitions of community control activists, with a variety of land uses oriented toward Harlemites, including housing, an educational complex, cultural spaces, and a "Harlem Political Forum."

Robinson's question increasingly pertained to the work of both. As HCC turned millions of dollars into real property and HUDC got down to the task of planning 125th Street's center, serious questions surfaced about whether, in fact, most Harlemites would ever own a piece of the block.

For HUDC, finally launched in mid-1971, this dilemma played out most visibly on the site adjacent to the rising state office building. Bond's firm, Bond Ryder Associates, had completed their plan for the half block surrounding the state's building in the spring of 1970 at the request of Logue (see Figure 3.2). Bond described his complex program as the "Harlem Town Centre," a "'central place' in Harlem reflecting the needs, interests, and talents of the local population." In this small portion of vast Harlem, architects found room for up to 500 units of housing; the central piece of a neighborhood-wide educational complex; theaters, studios, galleries, rehearsal space, meeting rooms, a library, and a restaurant constituting a cultural center; commercial space including a communications center; small businesses; a medical center; a gymnasium and swimming pool; and even a "Harlem Political

Forum" that reflected the historical role this block had played as a site of debate and discourse. The plan left loose ends and offered provisional ideas. It was meant "as a step towards the development of a program to be done in conjunction with a group representative of Harlem," the designers wrote. But at the same time, Bond emphasized that his plan did not take an ideological middle road. "We are not offering a rigid proposal, nor is it our intention to suggest a political compromise," he argued.[45]

Indeed, Bond's plan suggested the possibility of realizing community control's spatial vision at the center of 125th Street. Its diverse array of land uses echoed the schemes radical squatters had unveiled at Reclamation Site #1, as well as the more recent public pronouncements that ARCH had voiced in calling for a community of many functions, built by and for its low-income residents. Mixed use reflected the spirit of community control, especially the notion that Harlem's main street belonged to all of its citizens, not only those with the most resources. ARCH and its allies reserved special condemnation for the possibility that 125th Street would be dominated by commercial development. "Black commercial interests would have to be balanced against the other needs of the community," ARCH leaders had declared in 1969, "and large scale developments would include residential as well as educational and cultural components." They reiterated this point in 1971. "The strategic location of 125th Street makes it vulnerable to pressure for commercial development," staff wrote. "However, like 14th Street, 86th Street, and others, its use cannot and should not be entirely commercial."[46]

Early debates within HUDC indicated support for the principle of community-oriented development that occupiers had called for and that Logue had backed. When the state commissioner of general services suggested in December 1971 that his department, responsible for constructing the state office building, was growing less committed to the idea of a state service center with dedicated space for community groups, HUDC's newly appointed president, Jack Wood, responded angrily. "A decision now to revise understandings reached with the community . . . could, in my judgment, trigger a reaction so violently in opposition as to seriously destroy the good faith and commitment of the Governor's administration," he wrote.[47]

The politically moderate board members at the center of HUDC, however, who viewed themselves as the true representatives of Harlem's interests, proved unconcerned with maintaining Logue's earlier attempts to bridge the community's ideological divide. Just a couple of weeks after his stand on behalf of the state service center, Wood reported to UDC leaders that the HUDC board did not share his view. "The Directors made it clear that they were not in favor of using the State Office Building for anything but public agencies," a UDC staffer explained. Their reasons were both imprecise and tentative. "If they did they would then be in the position of having to explain to the many who did not get space why a few were given preferential treatment," he said. Wood increasingly retreated in the course of discussions with HUDC's board, resorting to justifications that further revealed the board's focus on expedience, not principle. Activists' demands for control of the site had reduced the overall square footage of the project, he explained, which reduced the income it could generate. Community offices in the building would only diminish rent further, a concern that seemingly moved the HUDC board more than the issues of equity that had motivated the crisis.[48]

On the land east of the state office building a similar story unfolded, as officials initially backed a plan consistent with Bond's vision and then retreated amid HUDC board deliberations. "The project can combine housing and commercial space with a broad range of Community facilities," the working Memorandum of Understanding between UDC and the negotiating committee stated in April 1971.[49] "We are afforded a one-time opportunity to develop certain much-needed facilities," Wood told HUDC's board early the next year, describing a flexible proposal that he called "a Harlem Center for Culture and Commerce." He felt that Bond's plan physically included too much, but emphasized "making certain that we will end up with a combination which provides the maximum possible social and economic benefit to Harlem." As such, his vision combined housing, a hotel, an auditorium, convention space, "cultural facilities and exhibit space, restaurants, shops, boutiques, small businesses, offices," and parking on the nearly three-acre site. Yet only weeks later, HUDC board members reoriented the wide-ranging mix of uses that Wood had outlined, vastly simplifying the plan and prioritizing commercial functions over the diverse program that Bond and his allies espoused. By the time Logue announced the HUDC board's progress to Governor Rockefeller in February 1972, the project had narrowed to a hotel and convention center. "Other civic, cultural, and residential facilities" had been demoted to secondary importance, "space permitting."[50]

Board members dramatically altered the direction of plans for Harlem's center, but so too did Logue press his own shifting agenda on HUDC's staff. While he had initially promoted development that met the competing demands of Harlem's diverse political communities, Logue's commitment diminished as he grew impatient with a slowly unfolding process. Consistent with his reputation as a redevelopment dynamo, Logue became most concerned with making sure something would be built on the site during Rockefeller's tenure, no matter its symbolism. As the acres to the east of the state office building lay fallow over several years, Logue grew frustrated with Wood's attempts to balance the board's interests and those of Harlem's radicals.

The cultural center intended for the site became the crucible in which this debate played out. Wood understood that it served more than a programmatic role. "Harlem in general would be likely to take a dim view of the eastern portion [of] development if cultural facilities were excluded," Wood argued. "There simply will have to be something in this complex that the people in the community can relate to as non-business, non-commercial." The cultural center connected the project back to Harlem's history as a cultural capital but also to the neighborhood's more recent cultural awakening, a movement in which many state office building opponents had played a major role. Wood realized the symbolism associated with such a center by progressive voices like W. Joseph Black, a Harlem architect with ties to ARCH. "The ravages of urban decay and slum clearance by the wrecker's ball, the social upheavals and economic plights that contributed to environmental ruin . . . in addition to the lack of funding from both public and private sources to support cultural endeavors, all account for the near death of cultural life in Harlem," Black wrote, linking the neighborhood's cultural decline with urban renewal, among other factors. But movements for community control had reversed the trend. "The revival of cultural life came with the determination of the community to control its own destiny," he argued.[51] Redevelopment projects like this one provided a vital opportunity to support outgrowths like the Black Arts Movement, ensuring that the site took more than the commercial cast it increasingly displayed. The cultural center, Bond argued, would "give vital expression to the heritage and continuing life style of the Black people—an institution which will take its cues from the Black community and, at the same time, give to all who come within its sphere of influence."[52]

Logue's concern with implementation, however, demonstrated a drawback of HUDC's dependent position. Because the state would ultimately pay for development, the parent organization retained the final word over its subsidiary. While Logue had earlier supported Bond's site concept, he grew irritated as deliberations produced no physical results. After Logue met with HUDC staff in May 1972, participants agreed the conclave had been a "disaster." Logue put his muscle behind the elements he felt would be most expedient. "Logue is very interested in putting up the hotel, the office space, and the convention hall but wants to dismiss the cultural center as not feasible because he feels it would not pay for itself," a staff member wrote. "A heated discussion ensued about our responsibility to the community to at least investigate the possibility of a cultural center." But Logue's word left staff scrambling for funding through political connections, foundations, or private donors. While the idea of a cultural center would recur periodically over the next several years, Logue's ultimate refusal to provide aid ensured its absence as a viable component in any subsequent plans.[53]

Logue's authority caused HUDC's board to bristle, raising demands that they should be independent from their state benefactor. "Directors argued that the time had come to change what presently exists and go forward with a plan which would enable HUDC to operate on its own," their secretary recorded in September 1972. "It was generally felt that the Board as it now stands is a rubber stamp with no real power." But board members seemed to miss the irony of their demand for self-determination, for such protests mirrored precisely those of the radicals they had rejected in offering their alliance to Logue. Upon formation of the subsidiary, Penn Kimball, a staffer at UDC, had raised alarms about how the organization would be perceived. "To knowledgeable outsiders it is likely to seem to be an Old Guard–Old Politics arrangement," he wrote. "The dominance of the self-appointed Harlem-UDC Negotiating Committee is all too transparent." Indeed, to a great extent the increasingly commercial nature of plans for Harlem's central block resulted not only from outside pressure but also from the outsized influence of one viewpoint within the leadership of HUDC. Though board members complained that they lacked autonomy from their parent organization, their vision for the site largely validated Kimball's concerns about democratic representation. Few, if any, of the moderate voices that dominated HUDC's boardroom would speak up for the communitarian ideals that radicals had advanced.[54]

The figures who controlled HUDC's board pushed a narrower vision for the state office building site because they stood to gain from a profit-oriented approach to the development of 125th Street. As plans unfolded, the behavior of board members raised persistent, sometimes comically absurd red flags suggesting this underlying motivation. In May 1973, for example, HUDC's board received its first proposals for development adjacent to the state office building, unanimously selecting one submitted by Center City Communications, an entity that included Sutton, McCall, and Clarence Jones, the publisher of the *Amsterdam News*. By June, however, as additional proposals came in, board members wished to reconsider. After much debate between a flustered Wood and directors, the board resolved to reopen the process. Jeff Greenup, counsel to the board, raised a question: "Would it be a conflict of interest for members of the Board to be participants in proposals submitted for consideration?"[55]

Greenup foreshadowed what would become an increasingly bizarre situation, one that raised serious questions about whose interests HUDC's leaders were really serving. The proposal that had caused directors to reverse their earlier unanimous decision came from a group that included George Miller, an assemblyman and HUDC board member; Greenup, HUDC's counsel; his brother, Henry Greenup; and Arnold Johnson, a board member and chairman of the very committee charged with reviewing proposals.[56] Wood, who often found himself at the mercy of his capricious board but here reached a new level of frustration, appealed to Logue for assistance. He had been shocked by the request to reopen consideration and further shocked that the board's debate had focused on whether Johnson should continue to sit as chair of the review committee, not the much more obvious question of whether board members should personally profit from HUDC's activities. "People should not be faulted for wanting to do business with HUDC," he told Logue, "they simply must be told that that preference forecloses their eligibility to sit as a member of the board." But discussion at the next board meeting instead centered on parsing UDC's conflict-of-interest policy, a debate to which Jeff Greenup audaciously contributed a written opinion as counsel, contending that "there is nothing in our By-Laws or in fact in the New York State Urban Development Act that prevents Directors from participating as long as their interest is openly declared." Directors aimed their irritation not at Greenup but at Wood, who had forwarded Logue's request that Greenup resign as counsel. While Greenup agreed to withdraw from the development team, directors continued to insist that they should be able to financially participate in HUDC's projects. Kornegay viewed the recommended dismissal of Greenup as a symptom of UDC's power over HUDC, not of HUDC's increasingly apparent self-interest. "UDC had no right to dictate to Harlem," the minutes recorded.[57]

Wood questioned whether HUDC could ever fulfill its mission as long as it defined community development as commercial development that enriched the organization's leaders. "HUDC, in my judgment, can never hope to be effective in Harlem if it carries the image of a corporation which allows its Directors to actively and publicly participate in and benefit from the business of the Corporation," he told Logue.[58] Such motivation appeared to be pervasive in the organization, however, even as its directors promised to serve Harlem's wider interests as HUDC's official community representatives. Even Gunther, who had helped to found HUDC and remained a key member of its board, sought the organization's aid for an effort that claimed high aspirations—"Our group is attempting to foster the revitalization of Harlem," he wrote to Wood—but also served Gunther's own interests. Gunther proposed a 40,000-square-foot retail and office development as well as new churches on land that his Transfiguration Lutheran Church owned on the block immediately east of the state office building block. Two other HUDC directors, Nathaniel Gibbon of the United Mutual Life Insurance Company and Richard Greene of the Carver Federal Savings and Loan, co-signed the request, which read as if it were written by perfect strangers to HUDC. "Our coalition of civic and business organizations in the Harlem community is very interested in the fact that the Harlem Urban Development Corporation is investigating the development opportunities in our community," they wrote, using the third person to refer to the organization in which they served. "We ask that HUDC assist us in the most generous manner possible," they concluded. Wood declined to provide such aid, but his exasperation surely mounted.[59]

Though HCC's leaders demonstrated less brazen self-interest in their evolving approach to community development, they too raised parallel questions about representation and accountability as their investment program increased in scale and ambition. The organization's shift toward land banking had marked something of a leap of faith, but in the mid-1970s HCC took major steps toward achieving its goal of extensive property ownership on and near Harlem's main street. By the fall of 1973, HCC had obtained a parcel that leaders had eyed on Seventh Avenue between 126th and 127th Streets as well as two additional properties along 125th Street, between Seventh and Eighth Avenues and adjacent to the Apollo Theater. The following year, the organization acquired the Braddock Hotel, adjoining the parcels they already owned on 125th Street, and a substantial portion of the land between 125th Street, Eighth Avenue, and St. Nicholas Avenue. The organization owned more than half of that block, which staff called "the prime blockfront on 125th Street," and planned to purchase additional parcels to ensure nearly complete control of its extent.[60]

With its entrance into Harlem's real estate market, HCC's attention shifted from Harlem's small businesses to the development of its land. While Dowdy had initially explained land banking as a cooperatively determined community trust, however, the organization's expansion into real estate instead brought increasing reliance on its own leadership and on a growing partnership with HUDC. In 1972, HUDC had solicited HCC's involvement in the development of the state office building site and in an effort to prepare a comprehensive redevelopment plan for 125th Street. Subsequent efforts to draft a development agenda for 125th Street joined what Dowdy described as "the respective interests" of HCC, HUDC, the Uptown Office of City Planning, and the New York City Economic Development Administration.[61]

HCC came to profess a vision for 125th Street that echoed that of its counterpart. Like HUDC, HCC emphasized the commercial redevelopment of Harlem's prime land. The CDC's major project by mid-decade encompassed the 125th Street block between Eighth and St. Nicholas Avenues, where leaders anticipated a large, 70,000-square-foot development with retail, commercial space, parking, and a market for relocated street vendors. This effort formed only a small portion of the much broader commercial transformation that HCC imagined. The organization projected that it would help plan and develop an additional 300,000 square feet of office space in Harlem by the late 1970s. "The 125th Street Corridor is the best location for a major retail and commercial concentration," Dowdy wrote.[62]

The organization's business investments, too, shifted toward HCC's increasing commercial real estate development activities, creating a structure whereby all of its ventures intertwined. In 1973, HCC purchased a fifty-year-old construction supply business, Ben's Lumber Yard, which occupied property on 124th Street and in the Bronx. Likewise, HCC incorporated a building security and maintenance company as well as a construction company, both intended to assist with future projects. Perhaps the organization's abandonment of the "commonwealth" title of past ventures was merely coincidental, but the names of these new businesses—Telec-Tron Security and Nigel Contracting and Construction—marked a striking departure from the organization's early efforts to emphasize the commonweal.[63]

To a great extent, the increasing prevalence of commercial development as the focus of HCC's activities—and the increasing authority of its leadership—grew directly from the contradictions at the organization's core. In deciding to rely on public funding instead of the pooled resources of local residents, CDCs like HCC severed a fundamental connection tying their interests to those of the constituencies they promised to serve. In an atmosphere of relative freedom enabled by a federal government that took a hands-off approach to urban policy, the proclivities of strong leaders were free to emerge at the helm of their organizations. This was the double-edged sword of policy devolution, which enabled experiments in community development but offered little oversight of the forms they took. In HCC's case, Dowdy embodied the grassroots democracy that CDCs had promised—as he rose from plumber to CEO—but lacked the radical ties of his predecessors. They had linked community control to a communitarian vision of development that first served residents' needs, but Dowdy instead tied community control to a capitalistic vision in which power grew from HCC's successful participation in the activities of the market.

While profits had been an objective of economic-development-oriented CDCs from the start, organizations had maintained a primary focus on the broader impacts of their investments. Thus, HCC had initially chosen to launch business ventures that addressed service or employment deficits in Harlem. But for Dowdy, the pursuit of profits was a self-justifying objective, an end in itself. HCC's obligation, he explained, was to pursue any venture that would yield a lucrative return. "If five years from now it comes out to be paint or tar for roofs," he said, "that is what we will be going after." In the short term, Dowdy found such an opportunity in Harlem's real estate, especially that of 125th Street. "We believe that Harlem is going to be an up and coming community again," he said. "We intend to see to it that this time around . . .

Blacks play a major role in the development of that corridor and get a lion's share of what's developed."[64]

This strategy marked a decidedly paternalistic approach to the project of community development. Organizations that had once espoused ideals of collective ownership and decision making instead came to function much like benevolent private enterprises, with an array of impressive ventures and growing portfolios, but little more than leaders' assurances as a guarantee that benefits would reach all corners of their communities. HCC was hardly alone in this metamorphosis. In the uncharted terrain of black capitalism, many CDCs changed direction at the behest of strong leaders. In Cleveland, for example, the Hough Area Development Corporation similarly transformed with the ascendance of a new director who brought a market orientation to his task. Contemporaneous with HCC, the Cleveland CDC shifted from a socially oriented, communitarian mandate to an approach that emphasized consolidated ownership and the pursuit of lucrative commercial development projects. While such organizations continued to voice an ethos of generosity, the potential pitfalls of this approach were clear. As one observer noted in a study of CDCs, "The reason for the existence of the CDC becomes one of profit rather than one directly beneficial to the target area residents, and the way the CDC operates is much the same as in all other corporations."[65]

Periodic munificent gestures both evinced the concern that leaders continued to maintain for their neighbors and the paternalism that pervaded their work. HCC planned to construct 170 units of senior housing on the property it owned on Seventh Avenue, for example, and purchased the 125th Street YWCA in order to offer its space to community organizations. "Without our acquisition . . . a serious vacuum would have been created since the initial purchasers of the facility were not of the community and had planned to use it for a 'self-serving' purpose," Dowdy wrote.[66] When a fast-approaching deadline threatened state funding for the construction of a new hospital in Harlem in early 1975, HCC provided supporters with the $650,000 needed to take title of the land and secure aid, in exchange for the right to build housing adjacent to the project.[67] But HCC did not maintain a democratic process shaping such decisions, nor did it ever make socially oriented projects a focus of its activities. Indeed, leaders had phased out HCC's Department of Social Services in 1973. "Our primary goal was to do economic development, not so much the social development," Dowdy later explained, suggesting that such work was better left to other organizations that made it their principal task.[68]

An HCC advertisement in the *Amsterdam News* in September 1974 attempted a preemptive response to concerns that the organization's top-down structure would soon evoke, but instead highlighted the disparities that resulted from its approach. "What's the Harlem Commonwealth Council doing for me?" a bold headline read, before a litany of numbers quantifying the organization's achievements. Most evident was the significant scale of HCC's holdings compared to the fairly modest employment it provided in a community of several hundred thousand. HCC held more than $20 million in assets; the organization's real estate holdings alone exceeded $11 million. HCC-owned businesses yielded over $5 million in sales. HCC paid $1.5 million in salaries, provided $260,000 in benefits to its employees, and pumped $140,000 into area minority-owned businesses. Yet its ventures employed a modest 262 people, only 28 of whom maintained management positions. "We're helping you get your share!" the ad promised, but that conclusion was not so clear.[69]

Indeed, HCC both pushed its profit-centered approach to the extreme and demonstrated the risks of this strategy with its 1974 purchase of the New Windward Hotel, a modern, air-conditioned, 145-room, conference-center-equipped accommodation in faraway Saint Thomas, Virgin Islands. Leaders intended the hotel to complement HCC's travel agency, Commonwealth Tours, and capture the dollars of African American tourists. "We believe there is a need for this kind of service, and if the St. Thomas venture is a success, we'll make every effort to duplicate it in other vacation attractions," HCC's vice president said. Leaders acknowledged that the hotel was "a long way from Harlem in terms of distance," but, they maintained, it was "very near in terms of the overall goals of HCC." Such purchases made sense, Dowdy later insisted, whether or not they were within the Harlem community. "We are interested in producing enough profits, so that other organizations will not have to depend solely on the Federal government or anybody else," he said in 1976. "In order to do that we are going to have to start investing our dollars in those things that are going to bring back those profits, and I'm going to tell you, it should not be limited to investments in Harlem, that's another trick bag. . . . I think that as long as the parent corporation has all the profits, all the benefits come back to the people of Harlem, that's all we have to worry about." If Dowdy made such assurances with the New Windward Hotel in mind, however, the argument proved unconvincing. After only a couple of years, HCC was already ridding itself of the distant and unprofitable venture. The domestic economy had worsened, and "the council wants to direct its energy and time to the Harlem community," the *Amsterdam News* paraphrased from an interview with Dowdy.[70]

HCC's long-standing and oft-repeated promises of community ownership were intended to allay concerns that the CDC was putting profits over people. Leaders frequently pledged that when HCC's subsidiary, the Commonwealth Holding Company, became a publicly owned company, Harlemites would gain direct influence over the CDC, elect its board members, and guide its activities. "By September 1971," an HCC ad stated in 1970, "[HCC] plans to sell shares in the holding company to community residents at a maximum of $5.00 per share. . . . Each shareholder will have a voice in controlling the various businesses through the members [of] the Board of Directors." At the unveiling of the Commonwealth Office Building in May 1971, Dowdy took the jubilant occasion as an opportunity to again promise that HCC would soon offer ownership shares. Several years later, a study of the organization reported that "HCC's hope is that divestiture might be initiated during 1974." With such hopes still unfulfilled, HCC's 1975 annual report addressed "Our Potential Stockholders." "The 'Potential Stockholders' of Harlem will soon be invited to participate through the ownership of shares in all of the Council's holdings," wrote Dowdy and Isaiah Robinson, HCC's board chairman, again reiterating the long-delayed but fundamental promise.[71]

But 1975 came and went, and HCC still had not offered shares in the holding company. The reasons given were manifold. HCC leaders genuinely feared that a public offering would lead to takeover by non-Harlem residents, undermining the principle of community ownership. To that end, they investigated a number of possibilities that would both fulfill the promise of shareholding and ensure that they could manage shareholders. Dowdy proposed giving directors first option to buy up to 10 percent of shares. Harlem residents would be able to purchase a majority of 40 percent of the remaining shares, with outsiders allowed to purchase the rest of that allocation. HCC would hold 50 percent of its shares. Leaders also feared the economic recession of the mid-1970s. "We understand that today's climate in the stock market is such that public offerings are generally not recommended and are very likely to fail," Dowdy wrote in 1975.[72]

But leaders also worried that a stock sale would undermine the almost unilateral control they had maintained, and here the danger of HCC's paternalistic approach to community development became clear. Dowdy deserved tremendous credit for the ambitious redirection that he had managed and for HCC's substantial growth in the first years of his tenure. In 1978, the CDC's holding company would make its debut on *Black Enterprise* magazine's list of the top one hundred black-controlled businesses in the United States, at number nineteen. Yet Dowdy also served a practically omnipotent role in HCC, with his fingerprints all over the corporation's decisions. "The present organization is spread very thin. The president . . . is involved in nearly everything," a study noted in 1974. Dowdy agreed. "Working is a part of me. HCC is a part of me. I am HCC. It is not a salary, it is not a 9–5 type of thing," he said in a 1976 interview. "You cannot expect all the employees to be that way, it is me." Opening the company to new investors would introduce new interests to its governance and potentially divergent viewpoints. "If stock were widely held, even the most sound business plan would be subject to the whim of conflicting stockholder factions to the ultimate detriment of the overall program," leaders argued, though such input was precisely the point of community ownership.[73]

Unsurprisingly, then, HCC's reluctance to go public aroused suspicions that its leadership was simply consolidating power and that Dowdy was refusing to share his authority. Though the organization maintained a slate of board members that included many of its radical founders as well as representatives from community organizations, Dowdy's dominant position fit a broader criticism that observers had begun to voice in response to CDCs.[74] "Whereas whites once oppressed the ghetto alone, now the whites have the cooperation of an elite band of black managers and professionals," wrote critic Harry Berndt in considering a group of CDCs including HCC. "These black capitalists aspire to be the new rulers of the ghetto."[75] If this indictment seemed inordinately harsh, even more sympathetic observers criticized HCC's repeated delays. "Continued discussion of the stock sale accompanied by routine deferral of the event could undermine HCC's credibility and interfere with the progress of the sales," wrote Barry Stein, of the Center for Community Economic Development.[76]

Indeed, the banner headline on the front page of the January 29, 1977, *Amsterdam News* confirmed Stein's fears. "Harlem Commonwealth Council Fails to Sell Shares to Residents," the newspaper announced to readers in Harlem and beyond. Reporter Clinton Cox offered a crisp introduction. "Since 1968 Harlem residents have been promised by the Harlem Commonwealth Council that they too 'can own a piece of the block,'" Cox wrote. "But despite HCC's growth from an initial worth of $250,000 to its present worth of over $23-million, the average Harlem resident is no closer to owning stock today than he or she was eight years ago." Cox surveyed the organization's many promises and the acquisitions it had made along the way—the Acme Foundry, Shultz Company, its real estate holdings. He mentioned HCC's plans to develop a commercial center on 125th Street and the soon-to-be-completed purchase of Harlem's largest factory, the Washburn Wire Company. "There would seem to be no insurmountable problems to working out a feasible stock selling plan, just as there seemed to be none in the past." But Barbara Norris, HCC's vice president, offered little hope that such an offering would come soon. "I really don't know when it will happen," she told Cox. The reporter closed with a question that captured years of community expectation and perhaps his own too. "What has held up the sale of stock to community residents since that first promise was made in 1968? And will the average Harlemite ever 'own a piece of the block'?"[77]

Dowdy's rebuttal, in HCC's newsletter, bore his own frustration but also a more troubling undercurrent that evinced the very problem of concentrated power that Cox sought to raise. For while Dowdy expressed the stance HCC had long maintained, that leaders already had residents' best interests in mind, he seemed to take the article very personally too. "One was left to imagine what was really going on," Dowdy claimed. "It was, the article suggested, another Harlem scandal involving the misuse of government money for the enrichment [or] benefit of a select few at the expense of the community." Dowdy staged an angry defense, but curiously focused on claims that Cox had actually never made. "Mr. Cox also alleged that members of the . . . Board of Directors receive big fees for serving on the board. Nothing could be further from the truth," he said. But Cox had never mentioned board members or their compensation. "The Cox story attempted to smear an organization," Dowdy wrote, though Cox had only recorded the promises that HCC itself had made and acknowledged its successes. "It attempted to persuade black people that the 18-member HCC board was crooked and not rep-resentative of the Harlem community," Dowdy argued, but Cox had not mentioned corruption or representativeness at all. The vehemence of Dowdy's anger in the face of measured claims suggested someone who felt threatened. And if that defensiveness was not itself evidence that Dowdy had become more concerned with self-preservation than broad accountability and par-ticipation, the hyperbolic threat with which he closed did suggest as much. "I don't criticize the *Amsterdam News* for holding black organizations to their mandate," he wrote. "But I do criticize them for recklessly endangering the life and work of an organization without the slightest regard for the facts and with no apparent regard for what it would mean to the Harlem commu-nity if the Harlem Commonwealth Council had to close its doors." Ask too many questions, Dowdy seemed to suggest, and HCC would disappear.[78]

Fiscal Crisis

HCC board chairman Isaiah Robinson offered a more measured response to the *Amsterdam News* piece. "How does a corporation, in good faith, offer stock to poor people in a corporation whose every action is subject to the approval of a federal agency with the power to terminate its funding and assume control of all property purchased with federal funds?" Robinson asked.[79] Although Robinson exaggerated the extent of federal oversight, he pointed to a fundamental paradox that community developers faced. Even as the powerful leaders of HCC and HUDC consolidated their hold on their respective organizations, their success depended crucially on continued state and federal support. They thus found themselves in something of a devil's bargain by the mid- to late 1970s. As a result of ample public funding, HCC and HUDC had succeeded in gaining a central role in Harlem's develop-ment. Likewise, they had succeeded in advancing their vision of large-scale, profit-oriented, commercial projects along 125th Street. But because they had not pursued the broad community ownership—both symbolic and financial—that had motivated their foundation, these organizations increasingly found-ered as the new decade approached and government partners withdrew their support.

This was a dilemma that HUDC would face first. Leaders had cast their lot as Logue's reliable allies in forming the subsidiary to the New York State

UDC, but this very interdependence left HUDC vulnerable. UDC's broad powers and borrowing authority met a range of countervailing forces by 1973. Logue's ambition to build low-income housing in Westchester County had raised angry political opposition, pressure that culminated in legislative amendments that curtailed the agency's power to supersede local zoning regulations. At the federal level, the housing moratorium that President Nixon imposed in January 1973 denied UDC a major source of direct subsidy and threatened the tax-exempt status of the bonds that underwrote its work, a characteristic that had formerly made UDC bonds an appealing investment. Governor Rockefeller's resignation to become vice president of the United States further undermined confidence in UDC, the agency that he had created and supported through his extensive familial ties to the banking and real estate sectors. Before Rockefeller even resigned in October 1973, Moody's lowered UDC's bond rating. After the arrival of his successor, banks increasingly refused to underwrite UDC bonds. Greater competition in the bond markets further raised UDC's costs of borrowing, as investors chose more stable options. By the 1974 election, UDC faced mounting debt and fewer options to address it. Upon the inauguration of Governor Hugh Carey in January 1975, with a bond default looming, Logue's position became precarious. Carey installed a Logue opponent as chairman of UDC in early February and the next day requested Logue's resignation. Logue's departure spelled the end of his tenure at the helm of the nation's most powerful redevelopment entity but did not solve the problem of the agency's financial crunch—by the end of the month, UDC would default on debt exceeding $100 million.[80]

UDC's decline and eventual default helped spark the broader fiscal crisis that swept New York City and State in 1974 and 1975, an event that both grew out of and exacerbated the nationwide recession of the period. While the social and economic impacts of the crisis were felt acutely in Harlem, for HUDC the consequences played out most conspicuously on the block containing the state office building. HUDC had requested new proposals for development of the site in early 1974, but the project stalled during UDC's fateful twelve months. By October, Donald Cogsville, HUDC's general manager, realized that New York State would not be a dependable financial partner on the project. Though he asked state officials to donate the land and pay for the cultural center that Logue would again nix, he looked to the federal Economic Development Administration to provide the almost $18 million in grants and loans that construction of a hotel, convention center, and entertainment complex would require. Despite attempts to procure such funding even in the aftermath of Logue's departure, however, the project languished.[81]

HCC's reliance on federal—rather than state—funding left the organization better off, if less certain than it had been in the past. Major bureaucratic changes in the mid-1970s fostered new anxiety among leaders. The Community Services Act of 1974 substantially changed the provisions of the Economic Opportunity Act of 1964, abolishing OEO and creating the Community Services Administration in its stead. HCC leaders were not sure what the dissolution of the agency that had long supported them would mean. "At the end of its current fiscal year, the organization anticipates a difficult round of negotiations with the Community Services Administration," the Ford Foundation wrote of HCC in May 1975. Indeed, the new fiscal year brought bad news, as President Ford vetoed legislation that would have provided the funds HCC depended on for equity investments. Dowdy painted a bleak portrait of the policy landscape at the close of 1975. "1975 . . . gave us a hint as to what is in store for our community if we don't 'get it together,'" he wrote. "From Ford, Rockefeller, and Reagan to Beame, Carey, and a host of Liberal Democrats, one constantly hears the call for the retreat of our government, at all levels, from social activism. There is no greater danger to Harlem and to Black and poor people all over the country."[82]

But against Dowdy's expectations, 1975 proved to be an exception, and with the election of President Carter, a Democrat, HCC continued to be one of the nation's best-funded CDCs in the late 1970s. With federal funding restored, SIP gave HCC the nation's largest grant, $7 million, in 1976, and awarded several million dollars more in 1977, 1978, and 1979. The *New York Times* hailed the organization's purchase of the Washburn Wire Company. The factory, "one of Manhattan's largest industrial employers, was about to go out of business last year," the *Times* wrote. "But the company is alive and well now because it was bought by the Harlem Commonwealth Council."[83] HCC's success sparked bigger dreams, and the 125th Street sites that had supported the visions of HUDC and HCC sprang back to life. The organizations joined together in 1977 and 1978 to propose commercially oriented projects grander than any they had previously envisioned—Harlem's first shopping mall for the land HCC had amassed between Eighth and St. Nicholas Avenues and an international trade center on the site to the immediate east of the state office building. The latter project was to include the hotel and conference center that HUDC had long desired, as well as an office tower dedicated to fostering trade relations between the United States and African and Caribbean nations. Both were to redefine the streetscape of 125th Street, by projecting modern new facades on two of its central blocks.[84]

Yet if these projects marked the optimistic hope that HCC would grow and HUDC would flourish anew in the new decade, they also symbolized the growing prevalence of the very excesses that radical community control activists had sought to escape in the late 1960s. With public-sector funding enabling dominant leaders, organizations founded in the name of broadly democratic community development instead advanced projects that unfolded at the highest levels of power. Far from the input of most Harlem residents, U.S. Representative Rangel stewarded the international trade center through the halls of Washington and into the hands of President Carter. "This is a *priority project for the White House*," Carter's staff wrote, referring to it as "Congressman Rangel's proposed international trade center."[85] The shopping mall, too, depended on the support of political allies in the nation's capital. "It is now up to President Carter—and the Department of Housing and Urban Development—whether the proposed 125th Street Shopping Mall . . . gets the funds to spur its construction," the *Amsterdam News* reported in 1979.[86]

If the manner of decision making and funding for each recalled the top-down, insider-dominated process that underwrote the state office building, only now under the auspices of powerful community-based organizations, even the projects' forms resembled the approach to the city that urban renewal had taken. The international trade center was to be a skyscraper even taller than the adjacent state office building, a monument to commerce and trade without the complex diversity and inclusion that radical activists had envisioned for Reclamation Site #1 (see Figure 3.3). The shopping mall had its own irony. Here, Bond, who had helped to imagine the ideal that inspired Reclamation Site #1, instead designed according to the narrower vision of his clients. Renderings showed an austere modernist structure whose social life existed within its four walls, not on the sidewalks of 125th Street, rejecting the very celebration of traditional street life that Bond had voiced as the leader of ARCH (see Figure 3.4).[87]

But ARCH was not around to criticize such schemes. Bringing the ideals of the 1960s into reality proved difficult for many organizations—this was not a story exclusive to HUDC and HCC. In the case of ARCH, its work took an increasingly professionalized direction in the years after the state office building site occupation. Where leaders had once made dramatic public statements through direct action on 125th Street, in Morningside Park, and at city hall, by 1973 ARCH staff referred to the organization as "a non-profit, community planning and architecture firm" and advertised its activities as "services." At Morningside Park, for instance, ARCH subcontracted with a landscape architecture firm to organize a community planning process and develop a design for the park that activists had once occupied. But ARCH, too, found its options curtailed when OEO stopped funding its work in 1973, and it, too, found itself at the mercy of the dominant leader who had charted its redirection. It is not clear if Leroy McRae, then the executive director of ARCH, fled as the organization ran out of money or fled with its money, but by late 1973, ARCH had stopped paying the landscape architecture subcontractor to whom it owed money; by early 1974, ARCH was writing desperate letters seeking funds; and by late 1974, ARCH found its tax status in doubt and tax bills mounting. The organization, a dependable counterpoint to the top-down redevelopment approach that had returned in the work of HUDC and HCC, soon ceased to exist.[88]

By the late 1970s, CDCs like HCC had been relatively unharmed by the fiscal issues that affected HUDC and ARCH, but that would soon change. Dowdy sent a letter to acquaintances on the eve of the 1980 election that suggested his unease as Carter sought reelection against Ronald Reagan. "I am sure that you appreciate the great importance of the 1980 Presidential election," he began. "The fate of the urban centers in America [is] at stake." Carter had been imperfect, Dowdy acknowledged, but he had supported HCC's work in Harlem. "While Ronald Reagan was praying twice daily for New York to go bankrupt, President Carter made it possible for us to survive," said Dowdy. "We certainly owe him our support." Upon Reagan's election, Dowdy anticipated a rough road ahead. "We at the Harlem Commonwealth Council have begun the process of making contingency plans," he announced in

Powell Boulevard   State Office Building   trade center   parking garage

FIGURE 3.3. View of the 125th Street block between Lenox Avenue and Adam Clayton Powell Jr. Boulevard, showing the state office building *(left)* and the planned international trade center *(right)*, circa 1979. In process and form, the latter project echoed the approach to redevelopment that radicals had opposed, only now under the auspices of powerful community-based organizations.

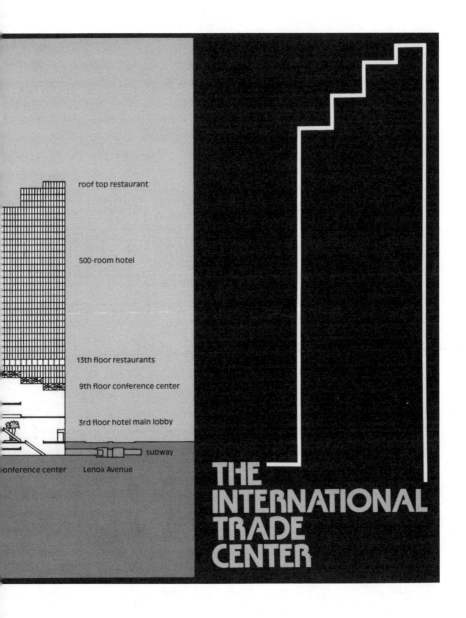

roof top restaurant

500-room hotel

13th floor restaurants

9th floor conference center

3rd floor hotel main lobby

subway

onference center   Lenox Avenue

THE
INTERNATIONAL
TRADE
CENTER

FIGURE 3.4. Exterior and interior renderings of HCC's intended shopping mall for 125th Street, designed by Bond Ryder Associates in the mid-1970s. Bond and his partners devised a structure that met their client's commercially oriented vision for Harlem's main boulevard. Plans for the mall depicted an austere façade, with its social life kept within its walls.

April 1981. Indeed, in September, Reagan eliminated the Community Services Administration, a retrenchment that hit New York City hardest. Before the year was out, the Washburn Wire Factory had shuttered its doors for good, leaving its massive buildings abandoned in East Harlem only five years after HCC had rescued them.[89] The shopping mall and international trade center would remain on drawing boards for the next decade, and Dowdy and Cogsville, the latter of whom had replaced Wood as HUDC's president in 1976, would attract increasing scrutiny of their imperious and autocratic management styles. When Dowdy resigned in 1991, after more than two decades as chief executive, he did so amid a hail of criticism of his personal gain as HCC sank into debt.[90] Reflecting on the 1980s, HCC leaders noted, "The roof caved in!" "We are certain that you are aware of the devastating financial crisis of the past twelve years and the toll suffered by the city government," they told newly elected New York mayor Rudolph Giuliani in 1993. "Well, that devastation had a much more tragic impact in Harlem, and more particularly on HCC where many programs were curtailed, many jobs were lost, as well as some of our prize assets."[91]

The organizations that had set out to realize community control fell far short of the goals that radical activists had voiced in the late 1960s. Perhaps such a fate would have been inevitable in any case, for the distance between ideals and reality was vast, indeed, and the hope that Harlemites could own, manage, and develop their land according to their collective wishes set an especially high bar. But in advancing their own vision for 125th Street, the leaders of HUDC and HCC often reproduced the very phenomena that occupiers of Reclamation Site #1 had rejected: dependence on outside aid, top-down governance, concentrated power, and big, commercial projects as a redevelopment strategy. If such excesses now occurred within a new wave of community-based organizations instead of through the old urban renewal order, that fact offered little consolation to critics.

Radical proponents of community control had envisioned a community-financed, democratic, inclusive ideal as an alternative to both state- and market-driven approaches to development in Harlem. However, by the late 1970s activists' frustrations remained unchanged as new rulers came to dominate the planning of 125th Street. Looking back in the 1990s, Wilcox, the most radical member of HCC's board and long a leading voice in the battle for community control, expressed his disillusionment with the organization he had cofounded. But Wilcox's words could have been referring to any number of community development organizations in Harlem in the 1970s. A "NIGHTMARE . . . has shrouded the original dream," said Wilcox.[92] Harlem residents were left with two empty lots in the center of 125th Street, ambitious—and unfunded—plans for the commercial redevelopment of their main street, and the need to look to other strategies to secure their land.

CHAPTER 4

The Urban Homestead in the Age of Fiscal Crisis

IN "LOVE AND WAR," the August 1973 number of the *Supergirl* comic book, the title heroine finds herself in the middle of a gang war between the Flaming Serpents and the Hustlers. The Flaming Serpents aim to reclaim their turf from the Hustlers, but the Hustlers have gone straight. "I know you once led the greatest street gang of them all," Supergirl tells Rick, leader of the Hustlers. "What 'Once'? I still do!" Rick replies. "Only now—the Hustlers are working for our people—doing good! Instead of wrecking!" Moments later, transformed back into her alter ego Linda Danvers, Supergirl sees the change for herself when Rick takes her to an abandoned tenement with hardhat-wearing gang members repointing brick, patching concrete, and framing new walls. "The city condemned it! We said, 'No—don't knock it down! Let the Hustlers rebuild it,'" Rick tells our heroine. A neighborhood elder stops to kiss Rick on the cheek. "Rick—you are good! You take my boy from the streets and teach him a trade!" "What a change for a street gang," Linda marvels. Yet Supergirl's attempts to broker lasting peace instead spur violent conflict. At the Hustlers' work site, the Flaming Serpents take up sledgehammers, intent on razing the tenement. As the gangs enter into an all-out brawl, Supergirl works quickly to shore up the imperiled building. Turning on the gangs, she wraps the rivals up in the foam insulation that will one day make the building habitable again. Freeing her captives, she demands reconciliation. The leaders agree. Rick offers, "You want to do a little building with us?" Steve, leader of the Flaming Serpents, takes up his challenge. "Okay! We Serpents will show you what building really is!"[1]

If Art Saaf and Vince Colletta's polychrome panels made palpable a tale seemingly too good to be true—full of violence, supernatural strength, and ultimately redemption—the fact remained that far north of the Midtown offices of DC Comics, just such a story was actually unfolding. Without the assistance of Supergirl, the reformed criminals and addicts of the Renigades Youth Gang confronted the impending ruin of their East Harlem neighborhood in 1973. Their homes were falling to pieces, not with the force of the bulldozers that had reshaped the city in the name of urban renewal, but at the hands of the property owners who increasingly left Harlem's buildings behind. "What do you do when your landlord, who has the legal responsibility for maintaining and managing your apartment, has abandoned your building and cannot be located to make repairs? What do you do when the City, which has the moral responsibility to assist tenants when landlords walk out, claims it cannot help??" the Renigades asked. "Do we all surrender our homes and our lives to the advancement of abandonment, the plague of rats, and the final demolition of our community into vacant lifeless parking lots??"[2]

As the tide of abandonment washed over Harlem, the Renigades saw what was quickly becoming a crisis as, instead, an opportunity. "You can own your own home, and finally be rid of the rats, the landlords, the leaks, and the City," they promised. The twenty Puerto Rican members of the Renigades had walked unannounced into the city's Housing and Development Administration only a few months before, convincing officials to sell them one of the many forsaken buildings on their streets. Now that they were busy renovating the six-story tenement at 251 East 119th Street, with the guidance of construction professionals but with their own sweat and labor as equity, they had become early evangelists for a cause that offered hope to low-income residents witnessing the collapse of their neighborhoods.[3]

Housing abandonment shook New York City's neighborhoods in the 1970s. Due to a range of factors, including the city's inability to serve as an effective landlord of the thousands of properties it had obtained, the federal government's diminished role in funding housing development, and the sheer scale of abandonment, thousands of tenants found few places to turn to maintain their still-viable but neglected buildings. But abandonment marked a dream as well as a nightmare. Whether fashioning themselves as "urban homesteaders" or "neighborhood developers," residents throughout Harlem, like the fictional Hustlers and the real Renegades, saw in thousands of abandoned tenements and townhouses a resource that could provide much-needed affordable housing, a chance to learn construction skills that could garner future employment, and a means of achieving the community control that had fueled urban renewal protests but still remained elusive. Though fantastical enough to be a comic book plotline, the promise of self-help spawned the hope that Harlemites could at last claim the collectivist utopia that radical activists had long envisioned.

Self-help emerged from both declining government support and the belief that neighborhood revitalization could better proceed without the intervention of the state, yet activists paradoxically depended on the loans and assistance that government would eventually provide. In crafting an alternative to the private market that had failed Harlem, then, homesteaders shaped a local and national policy infrastructure that supported their demands for improvement through rehabilitation, not replacement, of Harlem's existing urban fabric. Their early successes undermined conventional wisdom about the means of neighborhood revitalization, the meaning of abandonment, and the value of certain building types—the tenement versus the townhouse, for example, or the cooperatively owned multiple-dwelling unit versus the single-family home. Yet if this political and architectural landscape offered a compelling, egalitarian alternative to the much better known middle-class rehabilitation of urban neighborhoods of this era, low-income homesteaders' gains remained circumscribed.[4] Harlem activists and officials agreed about the necessity of reusing still-viable buildings, but ultimately disagreed about who should live in them. The city's decision to begin the sale by lottery of Harlem's most sought-after abandoned homes—its brownstones—in the early 1980s signaled officials' desire to attract the middle class to the neighborhood. In the city's refusal to fully hand over Harlem's stock of abandoned buildings to its enterprising low-income residents, activists saw their opportunity for control slipping away.

I argue, however, that New York's abandonment crisis marked a hinge, not a rupture, in Harlem's history of urban development. In Harlem, as in America, the 1970s was a decade of transition from the radical hopes of the late 1960s. Yet shifts proved more gradual than abrupt in the residential neighborhoods north of Central Park.[5] Two visions of the city collided around the issue of what to do with the thousands of buildings that were rapidly becoming city property. On one side lay the hope that sweat equity and cooperative ownership could provide a path toward abundant affordable housing, the foundation for long-sought neighborhood control of Harlem's built environment. On the other lay the faith that officials placed in the middle-class residents who were returning to New York's neighborhoods. Though observers feared that the sale of city-owned brownstones to outsiders would bring rapid racial and class upheaval in the neighborhood they loved, the reality proved more complicated. Abandonment suggested the possibility of realizing the predominantly African American, largely low-income, and collectively owned community that activists had imagined since the late 1960s, a hope that increasingly dimmed in the 1980s. Yet in its wake followed an outcome that hinted at a third way between that ideal and its exclusionary other—a vision of gradual economic diversification amid increasingly individuated ideals of autonomy.

Crisis and Opportunity

The promise of self-help rested in the hope that the revitalization of New York's hollowing neighborhoods could grow out of their very devastation. Empty homes in communities already suffering from inadequate housing suggested that neither the private nor the public sector was working properly to house New Yorkers. Self-help marked a radical alternative to both, however, an ideal that turned the housing crisis on its head. If people could rehabilitate abandoned homes themselves, advocates reasoned, at once they could fulfill two critical needs: to provide sufficient, decent, and affordable housing, and to equip unemployed workers with useful skills and the job opportunities to use them. Moreover, they could achieve a third, more abstract goal: community control, the hope that low-income Harlemites could themselves determine the shape of their built environment. Abandonment gave rise to new spatial techniques in Harlem as it grew in scale. If the government and landlords would not provide decent housing, perhaps residents could do it themselves.

Abandonment had been a growing problem in New York for years, but it exploded in scale in the 1970s as the city came to be flooded with in rem buildings, or those that became public property due to their owners' non-payment of taxes. Landlords had deserted 7,000 buildings by 1968. Landlord desertion only accelerated in the following decade. Figures were inevitably imprecise as inventory—let alone management—proved a daunting task, but in the 1970s the rate of abandonment reached at least 21,000 units a year and perhaps as many as 40,000 units annually in the first eight years of the decade. By April 1978, the city controlled 8,000 buildings with 90,000 tenants, and estimated that by July 1979 it could be the keeper of 20,000 buildings with 250,000 tenants. In Harlem, the city became the major holder of residential property. Officials estimated that the city owned more than 65 percent of Harlem's property by the early 1980s. Even excepting public housing, the city owned over 35 percent of Harlem's houses and apartment buildings through tax foreclosure—almost 20,000 units.[6]

A perfect storm of local, national, and international events converged to motivate landlords to abandon properties. While postwar suburbanization continued apace, the rapid deindustrialization of this era diminished employment in urban centers. Both drove fundamental demographic shifts throughout American cities. Middle-class residents departed urban homes at an accelerating rate, while the low-income tenants left behind had few employment opportunities and sparse resources with which to pay rent. Some officials blamed New York's rent control laws, claiming they made it more difficult for landlords to maintain profits, and often landlords simply walked away when tenants initiated rent strikes in response to diminished management. Rising maintenance and operations costs also widened the gap between what tenants could afford and what landlords hoped to receive, including skyrocketing fuel prices amid the 1973 world oil crisis. Additionally, many buildings were simply old, with almost two-thirds of New York's housing over fifty years of age by 1978. Buildings deteriorated more quickly as they aged, making residential properties increasingly poor investments. Policy changes only exacerbated these trends. The federal government instituted a housing moratorium in 1973, providing fewer resources to help low-income tenants with rent payment or rehab. And the city changed in rem laws in 1976, taking control of property after one year of unpaid taxes instead of three. It soon found itself inundated with apartments, many of which landlords had "milked" by squeezing out as much rent as possible while neglecting upkeep, before leaving them behind.[7]

Yet as the Renigades themselves had described, a crisis born of the negligence and self-interest of absentee landlords held immense potential for those left behind. "You can rebuild your block, your homes, and your lives," the Renigades promised. Such rhetorically seductive ideals were grounded in efforts emerging across New York City in the 1970s. Though self-help seemed the most obvious response when public support for low-income housing was declining and private landlords proved unwilling to help, the techniques that came to be known as "sweat equity" and "urban homesteading" did not emerge fully formed. Monsignor Robert Fox, a Catholic priest with a position in the New York Archdiocese, offered one precedent. In 1967, he had led East Harlem residents in the restoration of East 102nd and East 103rd Streets after civil disorder damaged those blocks. Their efforts began first with street cleanup and colorful exterior repainting, but soon extended to building projects. Behind the adjoining tenements, tenants installed a swimming pool and built a basketball court, and one basement served as a shared community space for residents. In 1969 and 1970, residents convinced an absentee property owner to sell them three abandoned tenements and began the rehabilitation of one, at 175 East 102nd Street. The city had planned to demolish the apartment building. By the time neighbors acquired it, prospectors had stripped it of its copper pipes and appliances, and broken many of its windows. But in the still-sound structure, residents cleaned out debris and replaced floors, supporting beams, and walls. With funding that Fox arranged through small bank loans and donations, residents purchased and installed a new heating boiler. The city proved less imaginative than the incipient renovators, tying up the project in debates about whether homespun solutions met restrictive building codes. But despite red tape, tenants were able to move into the building in 1973.[8]

A movement of squatters that bloomed across New York City in the spring of 1970 provided even more radical precedents. Squatting was both a pragmatic response to the paradox of abandonment in neighborhoods that lacked decent affordable housing and a political act embodied in the claiming of space. As activists had demonstrated in taking over the site of the state office building in the summer of 1969, control could be gained by simple occupation when other means failed. When squatters began to "liberate" unoccupied homes across New York City, and often on the periphery of Harlem, they quite literally pulled off the tin sheets that covered windows and doors so apartments could return to use. Inside, they found rooms full of dust and debris but frequently in adequate structural condition. Returning such buildings to life addressed both the quotidian and the abstract needs of some of the city's most dispossessed.[9]

Squatters typically occupied buildings that the city and institutions had held vacant for years while awaiting redevelopment projects, and thus constituted a late phase of grassroots opposition to urban renewal. In making such buildings habitable again, squatters offered an alternative development model that depended on neither the public nor the private sector. The first and most prominent squat, in the West Side Urban Renewal Area in April 1970, suggested the upper limits such efforts could reach. A group called Operation Move-In led the occupation of six buildings on the project's Site 30, on Columbus Avenue between 90th and 91st Streets. Site 30 was to be cleared and redeveloped as middle-income housing, part of a larger project that had already contributed to the economic upscaling of the neighborhood. In an effort to resist the displacement of the neighborhood's many poor residents, Operation Move-In introduced 180 low-income, largely Spanish-speaking families to the apartment buildings remaining on the site. "We, the poor community, demand control over our lives," the tenants of Operation Move-In argued. "The home is the first mirror of our lives. We are going to plan an Urban Renewal that will reflect the destiny of our people." By the summer of 1971, squatters had begun to transform the already cleared lots on their block into a park, with gardens, barbecues, and a baseball diamond. Operation Move-In ran a health clinic on a nearby block of Amsterdam Avenue and a housing clinic and day care on Site 30. The Dot Coffee House, constructed and operated by squatters, hosted evening events, fiestas, singing, and dancing. A *New York Post* reporter marveled at the change these blocks represented. "Abandoned buildings usually become havens for addicts and drifters, but the three tenements on Columbus Avenue have given birth to a remarkable community," he wrote. Tenants embraced the self-sufficiency they displayed. "This is the first time we showed the city that poor people can help themselves," one squatter proclaimed. "We might not have diplomas, but we are very skillful people. We became plumbers, plasterers and painters and we've made our own homes here."[10]

Inside their new homes, squatters worked to renovate apartments that had deteriorated through years of disuse. Juanita Kimble's experience typified the process of squatting. Kimble, a single mother of nine, had fallen into a dismal situation when the rent in her Harlem apartment increased beyond her means in early 1970. Since Kimble received public assistance to supplement her income as a nurse's aid, the Department of Social Services moved the ten Kimbles into two rooms in an exorbitantly expensive welfare hotel. Juanita Kimble subsequently quit work to search for an apartment, and her children stopped attending school while they were crowded five to a room in an unfamiliar neighborhood. Friends knew of a Columbia University–owned apartment building at 130 Morningside Drive, however, and its empty units. One apartment had eight rooms and had sat vacant for two years. Columbia had shown no urgency to develop the land, so in May 1970 friends moved the Kimbles into the building. The apartment was big but in poor shape. The floor was piled with old newspapers, dust covered its surfaces, and sinks and even bathroom pipes were missing. Supporters repaired the plumbing and replaced fixtures, while Kimble and her family cleaned and restored the kitchen to working order. Friends lent appliances and fixed broken windows and doors. Classmates of Kimble's children replastered the apartment. Kimble tried to pay rent each month, but Columbia would not accept her money—doing so would have validated her tenancy. But a year later, Kimble and her family nonetheless remained in the apartment. Activists celebrated with a "paint-in," an event intended to both finish uncompleted repairs and rebuke the unwilling landlord. "Roll over Columbia with paint power," an announcement read.[11]

If such efforts achieved a measure of success in returning homes to use, however, their tenants' residence remained nonetheless illegal. Squatters faced constant pressure from the city, which hoped to stem further squatting and reclaim occupied buildings. Officials arrested squatters who attempted to expand Operation Move-In's territory in November 1970 and relocated the Site 30 squatters in 1971, promising that low-income housing would take their place once development commenced (but later recanted that vow). Within two years, the momentum of the squatters' movement cooled. Yet while the community that squatters had constructed disappeared quickly with the advance of bulldozers, they had nonetheless shaped a radical vision of self-help, one promising that vacant buildings could fulfill housing needs, that tenants could become their own redevelopers, and that self-building could provide direct control over the built environment.[12]

Even as squatters' brief momentum dissipated, the practice that would become known as "homesteading" emerged as a legal alternative that embraced the same goals. Homesteading reentered the popular lexicon in the early 1970s, reviving a term with rich romantic associations in American history. The Homestead Act of 1862 had allowed citizens in good standing to claim 160 acres of western land. After settling the land for five years, homesteaders legally obtained title. In time, vast stretches of prairie became settlements, towns, and cities. Settlers gained sustenance from the crops they grew on the acreage and built homes. When homesteading reemerged in the mid-twentieth century, the term indicated a similar use of land, this time in American cities. At least in the popular imagination, the term suggested the promise of unused real property. As residential vacancy proliferated in urban cores, proponents alluded to the western ideal as a strategy encompassing pluck and self-reliance. Cities across the Eastern Seaboard adopted homesteading programs in the early 1970s, with the hope of attracting new residents to neighborhoods with substantial abandonment. Philadelphia adopted the first such policy in mid-1973, offering homes for one dollar to new owners who would renovate them, and Wilmington, Delaware, and Baltimore soon followed.[13]

Such programs favored the middle class by design, intending to bring wealthier residents back into city centers to boost tax revenues and pursue residential rehabilitation. Indeed, as frontier imagery made its way into urban discourse, it overwhelmingly represented the vantage point of the middle class. Brownstone renovators described the neighborhoods they settled as "frontiers" and themselves as "pioneers." As with the settlement of the west, the terms implied a willful elision of the presence of predecessors—Native Americans in the case of the American West or low-income residents in the case of the city—or their conquest. Brownstoners celebrated the economic transformation of neighborhoods they brought about and characterized their poor neighbors, often people of color, as violent undesirables. The reimagination of South Brooklyn, the Upper West Side, and other gentrifying neighborhoods as wild territories necessarily assumed the objectives of displacement and economic upscaling. With settlement, the metaphor implied, the poor people would be gone.[14]

An alternate vision of homesteading emerged in the wreckage of the squatters movement, however, positioning low-income residents as the intrepid pioneers who sought to turn abandoned buildings back into viable homes. Marie Runyon, a squatting supporter and leader in the efforts against Columbia's expansion in Morningside Heights and West Harlem, adopted the romantic allusion early on. When the university commenced demolition of the squatted buildings adjacent to 130 Morningside Avenue in September 1971—with squatters still inside—Runyon's protest invoked America's frontier past. "Defenders of the Pharmacy Site, Morningside Heights' most ancient housing battleground, will take to their rocking chairs . . . to protect the homestead," Runyon announced, like "Americas' homesteaders who guarded their homes with rocking chair and shot gun." In appropriating frontier imagery, low-income self-help advocates reversed the coded language of neighborhood change. Rather than playing the role of savages to be extinguished from the plains of the inner city, existing residents saw abandoned buildings as an opportunity to claim much-needed affordable housing through their own labor.[15]

Harlem formed one important node in this emerging citywide low-income homesteading movement. Groups coalesced rapidly in the early 1970s, representing both the interests of single buildings and the collective interests of like-minded groups. The Renigades were one of many small grassroots organizations to promote self-help rehabilitation. Though a self-described "street gang," its members had turned the group toward neighborhood improvement, with involvement in activities like voter registration and exposure of drug dealers. Indeed, despite claiming criminal records, the Renigades were in many ways typical of homesteaders in general. Homesteaders were mostly young—a majority were under thirty years old—with income below the poverty line. The former squatters of Operation Move-In were among the Renigades' contemporaries. Operation Move-In had taken ownership of an abandoned building just south of Harlem at 948 Columbus Avenue in October 1973, a transaction arranged by sympathetic city employees.[16] In 1974, members of the Mosque of the Islamic Brotherhood began a rehab project in two long-abandoned adjacent Central Harlem tenements, at 55 St. Nicholas Avenue and 132 West 113th Street (see Figure 4.1).[17] The next year, in the spring of 1975, seven low-income Harlem families formed an organization called United Harlem Growth. The families all lived in abandoned housing, public housing, or apartments soon to come out of rent control, and saw in homesteading a chance to own stable, affordable homes. By 1976,

FIGURE 4.1. The abandoned tenements that members of the Mosque of the Islamic Brotherhood rehabilitated as a low-income urban homesteading project, beginning in 1974. The adjacent buildings, located at 55 St. Nicholas Avenue and 132 West 113th Street in Central Harlem, are here seen before construction began.

United Harlem Growth—led by David Robinson, Jackie Robinson's son, and with an expanded membership of fifteen families—had purchased five city-owned abandoned brownstones on 136th Street between Seventh and Eighth Avenues with plans to renovate them into low-income cooperative housing.[18] In a parallel effort, tenants in single buildings across Harlem pursued conversion to cooperative status, to gain control of apartments that negligent landlords had effectively abandoned and to pool rents toward needed repairs.[19]

Organizations with close ties in and near Harlem formed to unite these disparate but likeminded efforts. In 1974, the leaders of the Cathedral Church of St. John the Divine, located just across Morningside Park from Harlem, formed the Urban Homesteading Assistance Board (UHAB), in response to nearby squatters who questioned the church's commitment to its neighbors. The new organization assisted participants in the incipient movement; for instance, UHAB helped the Mosque of the Islamic Brotherhood locate the buildings that members would rehabilitate.[20] Similarly, a collection of community-based organizations came together in 1974 to form the Association of Neighborhood Housing Developers (ANHD), a resource intended to amass collective experience and technical expertise. Members included groups from the Bronx, the Lower East Side, and Brooklyn, as well as West Harlem Group Assistance, UHAB, and the West Harlem Community Organization (WHCO), the long-standing force that had played a central role in opposing disruptive urban renewal.[21]

Such efforts emerged as part of a broader citywide network, whose proponents believed that through their own sweat they could provide decent housing for low-income residents. Philip St. Georges, a homesteading advocate who claimed partial responsibility for inventing the term "sweat equity," became the Zelig of self-help housing, working at times with Msgr. Fox, the city, the Renigades, and UHAB. He explained the potential of abandoned buildings, which for many appeared as only a problem to be excised. "While many abandoned buildings may be structurally sound, and capable of being rehabilitated, they represent an overwhelming public nuisance in the eyes of City policy makers. They are a liability. And increasingly, they are simply demolished," St. Georges wrote in 1973. "However, for many groups of low-income tenants who suddenly see an opportunity to own their own homes, take control over their own lives, and improve the condition of their neighborhood, these vacant and abandoned structures are anything but a liability. They are a true resource. And indeed, they may be the last resource."[22]

Projects that aspired toward St. Georges's ideal were by necessity highly pragmatic affairs. Like squatters, homesteaders who had negotiated the legal acquisition of city-owned buildings were concerned with making them fit for habitation at minimal cost. Expediency and resourcefulness marked such efforts, especially the reuse of structures and materials that could be rejuvenated through minimal transformation (see Figure 4.2). Frequently this meant replacing boilers, repainting, or—in gut-rehabilitation projects—refitting aging buildings as inexpensively as possible. Though sympathetic architects helped prepare the plans needed to obtain permits, homesteaders completed as much construction as was feasible on their own. UHAB encouraged rehabbers to pursue demolition, for instance, by providing guidebooks for this and other construction tasks. UHAB clearly recognized the hazards of such endeavors. "The possible dangers in demolition are almost too numerous to list," one guidebook warned. But nonetheless, structural

1. Fed up with paying rent for a substandard apartment . . . start by calling UHAB for help.

2. The first step is to locate a suitable building for restoration.

3. Then a trip to the Hall of Records to find who owns the building.

4. An estimate is made of the restoration costs.

5. Architectural plans are developed showing the layout of the restored building.

6. An application is made for a rehabilitation loan.

7. Work begins on sweat equity rehabilitation.

8. Project completed: An abandoned tenement has been transformed into homes.

FIGURE 4.2. Instructions for homesteading, published in 1977 by UHAB, one of the major supporting organizations in the sweat equity rehab movement. As these images suggest, homesteading in abandoned buildings required resourcefulness and determination, but could lead to affordable, decent housing.

FIGURE 4.3. A homesteading project under construction at 991 Amsterdam Avenue, just outside Harlem. To save costs, homesteaders performed many tasks themselves, including demolition; reused materials—such as studs—from their buildings; and repurposed fixtures discarded from renovation projects elsewhere.

beam replacement, roof removal, and wall demolition all existed in the realm of the possible for intrepid homesteaders. If dangerous, such work paid well in the currency of sweat equity. UHAB estimated that tenant-led demolition could save $500 of the $800 residents would pay a general contractor for the same labor. Likewise, residents proved clever in procuring building materials. When possible, they reused materials from their own buildings. Studs, for instance, could be cleaned up and employed in reconfigured walls (see Figure 4.3). Others repurposed materials and fixtures from buildings elsewhere in the city. One homesteading group "purchased all necessary tubs, sinks, toilets, louver doors, lighting fixtures, wall-size mirrors, carpets, and furnishings . . . from a contractor remodeling New York's Hotel Croydon," UHAB noted. A homesteader physically unable to participate in the labor-intensive construction instead reconditioned appliances purchased on the cheap as his sweat equity contribution. The unnamed apartment building surely boasted one of the best-appointed interiors in its neighborhood. As UHAB recounted, "Closets were dimensioned and painstakingly built around louvered doors, and bathroom layouts were modified to accommodate the oversized, old-fashioned, but elegant . . . tubs and sinks."[23]

Tenant-laborers were not occupied with the restoration of crown moldings and mantelpieces, yet stabilizing, reconstructing, and reinhabiting an abandoned building nonetheless constituted the most essential form of preservation. In embarking on the rehabilitation of existing buildings with minimal resources, low-income homesteaders formed part of a broader "neighborhood movement" underway in New York and other American cities at this time. While this movement encompassed interests as diverse as those of middle-class brownstoners and low-income tenants, each shared enthusiasm for the promise of self-help as a means of restoring the fabric of their communities. Yet their motivation drew from fundamentally different sources and aspired toward dramatically different ends. Brownstoners celebrated "authenticity," a quality they found in the architectural details of their nineteenth-century homes. They removed finishes and additions that obscured the original appearance of their townhouses, or rebuilt missing decoration. They investigated the histories of their homes and hoped by restoration to grasp a lost past embedded in a building's walls. Low-income homesteaders, on the other hand, feared the loss of affordable housing to abandonment and pursued rehabilitation with the intention of saving a diminishing resource before it was too late. If brownstoners rescued Victorian-era architectural details in order to achieve a nostalgic ideal, low-income homesteaders rescued discarded materials and dilapidated apartment buildings in order to conserve much-needed shelter.[24]

The groups taking on self-help in Harlem voiced hope that renovating a single building might reverberate throughout the entire community. The Renigades stated the case most enthusiastically, promising, "WE CAN REBUILD OUR COMMUNITY OURSELVES!!!!!" By early 1977, the gang had received the certificate of occupancy for the twenty-three-unit cooperative they rehabbed at 251 East 119th Street and, under the more ambitious name of the Renigades Housing Movement, had begun three subsequent projects, at 312 and 316 East 119th Street and 425 East 118th Street. Leaders envisioned their effort extending to the entire block, including "a senior citizens center, several mini parks,

FIGURE 4.4. Members of the Mosque of the Islamic Brotherhood construct their sweat equity rehab project, circa 1975. In addition to fourteen apartments, their effort was to include a day care center, health food store, and new mosque. They intended this to be the beginning of the broader redevelopment of their neighborhood.

vegetable gardens, and renovated brownstones, trees, bushes and flowers on the sidewalks as part of the beautification." The Mosque of the Islamic Brotherhood, too, imagined their initial project to build apartments, a day care center, a health food store, and a mosque expanding into the surrounding blocks of lower Harlem (see Figure 4.4). "These buildings represent the first phase of a redevelopment plan created by the Mosque for this area of Harlem," wrote Imam K. Ahmad Tawfiq, leader of the congregation. "It envisions rehabilitating over 150 units of abandoned housing," more than ten times the impact of the initial fourteen-unit rehabilitation. The families of United Harlem Growth selected their block of 136th Street with the hope that rehabbing five brownstones would start a chain reaction. "It is a neighborhood block, one in which our plans for rehabilitation would have a maximum impact," they wrote.[25]

Such efforts promised the possibility of not only a sheltering roof but also much-needed jobs, both through the individual homesteading effort and the hope that skills learned on-site would transfer to employment in the construction industry. In 1974, with ANHD and two other neighborhood groups, the Renigades proposed a program that combined urban homesteading with job training. In one year, they envisioned, ninety people could learn construction skills while rehabilitating abandoned buildings in East Harlem, the Lower East Side, and Brownsville, Brooklyn. United Harlem Growth, too, envisioned such potential in their homesteading effort. Estimating that half of area residents held job skills that had become obsolete in the deindustrializing economy, they planned for thirty-seven community members to apprentice with construction workers, accountants, and construction managers as they rebuilt the 136th Street brownstones. Though idealistic, homesteading as a route to employment seemed like a genuine possibility. For example, five Renigades worked as paid trainees alongside construction professionals on their rehab effort, while also fulfilling their sweat equity contribution with additional labor outside working hours (see Figure 4.5). Fifteen men learned electrical, plumbing, and construction skills while working on the mosque's homesteading project, through training paid for under the federal Comprehensive Employment and Training Act (CETA).[26]

Anecdotes offered compelling evidence that the seemingly utopian promises of self-help could come true. Carmelo Soria, known as Zorro, had been addicted to heroin for thirteen years when he crossed paths with the Renigades. "He didn't have a job and couldn't get one, didn't go to school, and just hung out," St. Georges recounted. "He had no hope; he had no direction." Zorro frequently passed out on the corner of 119th Street and Second Avenue, where the Renigades rebuilt their tenement. "One day he looked up and saw the Renigades cleaning garbage out of a vacant building which he frequently

FIGURE 4.5. The Renigades of Harlem on their jobsite at 251 East 119th Street, circa 1974. The Renigades, like many low-income homesteaders, saw the rehabilitation of abandoned buildings as a means to learn construction skills and, thus, gain much-needed jobs in addition to housing.

used as a shooting gallery," St. Georges said. Zorro joined the Renigades, learned plumbing, earned an income, and built a home.[27] The historical record does not reveal if St. Georges was embellishing in support of his cause, but redemption narratives recurred frequently in self-help projects. Runyon started the Harlem Restoration Project in 1977 to train the formerly incarcerated to renovate abandoned buildings. Her first effort employed fifty individuals in the rehabilitation of 150 apartments on Seventh Avenue.[28] In East Harlem, Dorothy Stoneman began the Youth Action Program in 1979. Unemployed young people, often high school dropouts, renovated abandoned buildings to provide housing for the homeless while learning construction skills.[29] At least on a small scale, these programs addressed hopes that sweat equity could alleviate pervasive joblessness and housing shortages, while also providing for the less tangible needs of residents who desired influence over the spaces they occupied.

Above all, low-income homesteaders emphasized the objective of control rather than profit in pursuing self-help rehabilitation, an ambition embodied in their focus on the use value of their homes rather than their exchange value. This was especially evident in the near ubiquity of cooperative housing arrangements as a goal, for low-income cooperative housing offered little or no potential for financial benefit but did provide tenants with decision-making authority. Low-income homesteaders pursued what self-building advocate John F. C. Turner at the time called "housing as a verb"—the notion of housing as "process or activity"—instead of "housing as a noun," meaning as a "commodity or product." Housing as a verb, Turner argued, constituted one of the activities that "can act as vehicles for personal fulfillment." As a colleague writing in Turner's classic *Freedom to Build* explained, "Owner-building ... represents participation—the basic human desire to exercise control over the making of one's environment."[30] Turner's theoretical work on the link between self-building and control had real-world impact uptown. He helped organize the efforts that became UHAB, and his student Donald Terner served as the organization's first director. Like his mentor, Terner celebrated the autonomy he discovered in such informal settlements as squatter communities, a quality he contrasted with the lack of control found in the typical landlord-tenant relationship of predominantly minority neighborhoods. "Filling the vacuum created by the absence of public controls is a vital and optimistic sense of direct, independent manipulation of the immediate living environment," Terner wrote of informal settlements.[31] With abandonment creating such an absence of oversight and Harlemites largely left to fend for themselves, homesteading seemed a chance to shape the built environment in previously unattainable ways.

Indeed, self-help enabled an extremely personal engagement with the act of building. Such engagement was evident in the unique opportunity home-steaders had to reflect themselves in the spaces they would occupy. At the Mosque of the Islamic Brotherhood's project, for example, participants incorporated their furniture into the design of apartments, added amenities they desired such as oak flooring and exposed brick, and expressed their cultural and religious identity in the rehabilitated buildings. Intricate tile work decorated several interior spaces in the completed project, and pointed

FIGURE 4.6. Interior details like these, in the Mosque of the Islamic Brotherhood's completed rehab project, suggest the extremely personal engagement that self-help enabled with the act of building, and the role that homesteading played in providing control. Here, pointed arches around apartment doors and tile work in the mosque reflect the cultural and religious identity of occupants.

arches surrounded doors (see Figure 4.6). Such improvements were not merely superficial. Homesteading was difficult work, but residents identified with the process of rehabilitating buildings that were to become their homes. One homesteader recalled the trials of his project as well as the devotion that participants nonetheless maintained. "I remember working in a snowstorm . . . carrying cinder blocks from the street to the cellar, sliding along the sidewalk and down the cellar steps. I remember being upstairs with this little piece of paper, 'How to Change a Beam'—somebody's reading while we have the beam in midair, waiting for instructions," he said. "But I can't remember a time when everybody was down, when everyone thought it was hopeless."[32]

In the modesty of learning a trade and making it physical in the collaborative reconstruction of one's future home, homesteaders expressed feelings of control at the most intimate level. In describing the construction of a window, Charyl Edmonds, the former leader of Operation Move-In and a homesteader at 948 Columbus Avenue, revealed the connection between the building process and her own subjectivity. "You need an upper and lower sash, a pulley and chain, wood for the sides, top, and bottom, a sill, molding behind and in front of the frame," she said. "I measured and sawed and hammered and screwed, and when I was done, I had six windows that actually opened and closed—crookedly, to be sure, but they opened and closed. I felt invincible." Similarly, when St. Georges questioned the Renigades' slow pace, Tom Foskolos, a leader of the rehab effort, retorted, "Don't you understand that we are trying to accomplish something much greater than simply putting a building back together again?" Foskolos explained what he meant while showing the finished building to the *New York Times* in 1975. "It's a dream come true, and it means people in the ghetto can control their own lives, build for the future." Self-help offered the possibility, however idealistic, that Harlemites could gain much-sought-after community control through the collective labor of rehabilitation, the seemingly prosaic but ultimately transformative task of bringing an abandoned building back to life. If the opportunity to reclaim the neighborhood building by building came from desperate circumstances, it remained nonetheless empowering for those who chose to rebuild any way they could manage.[33]

Gains

Self-help marked an attempt to salvage neighborhoods that both the state and the private sector had seemingly forsaken, as well as an opportunistic attempt to create a new mode of development in their absence. Yet grassroots movements to establish self-help housing in abandoned buildings remained fundamentally—and ironically—reliant on the public sector, forging a policy infrastructure that enabled unprecedented growth of their efforts by the late 1970s. While the city supported self-help minimally and largely on an ad hoc basis early in the decade, officials at both the municipal and federal levels came to formalize their assistance as the abandonment problem worsened. With the city grasping to keep up with the management of the thousands of occupied and unoccupied buildings in its possession, the dramatically de-volved solutions under the banner of homesteading appealed to both activists and policy makers. Self-help suggested a radical degree of autonomy, but it was the support of officials that gave proponents hope that their approach could become widespread enough to both counterbalance abandonment and achieve their idealistic vision of abundant affordable housing controlled by Harlemites.

Early homesteaders encountered opposition more often than assistance, as grassroots efforts to stem abandonment ran against a bureaucracy that largely lacked the imagination to support such endeavors. The renovation of 175 East 102nd Street led by Msgr. Fox, for instance, nearly succumbed to a long list of violations, some reasonable but many others constituting little more than red tape. Officials chastised tenants for employing the volunteer services of an architect from Westchester County instead of a licensed New York City architect, and for likewise employing a plumber from New Jersey, not one holding a New York license. Inspectors objected that the wiring of the rehabilitated tenement could not support air-conditioning units, but tenants did not have air conditioners. Tenants sought a modest loan to cover debts they incurred in the course of construction, but their request became delayed as the city cited these violations and sorted out a scandal in the Municipal Loan Program. Yet officials threatened to foreclose on the nearly renovated building because tenants had not paid real estate taxes while waiting for the loan to clear, a threat that puzzled participants who had restored an abandoned building to a habitable state without help from the city.[34]

Support for self-help came from advocates within the bureaucracy, however, whose willingness to experiment with new approaches drew from efforts pioneered by enterprising tenants in declining buildings. Attempts to convert rental buildings into low-income cooperatives in the 1960s interested officials in the John Lindsay administration, who tapped a housing lawyer, Robert Schur, to investigate the viability of such conversions as a strategy for addressing abandonment. Schur's report motivated the city's creation of the Office of Special Improvements (OSI) in the Housing and Development Administration, an office that Schur came to lead in early 1970. OSI supported the creation of low-income cooperatives as well as tenant efforts to refurbish their homes through moderate rehabilitation. Schur provided city loans for such projects, which brought Msgr. Fox to OSI's door. St. Georges became one of Schur's interns in 1972, and while officials tended to point out all that was wrong with Fox's project, St. Georges advocated for the tenants within the Housing and Development Administration. St. Georges, an early evangelist for sweat equity rehab, helped negotiate compromises that the tenants of 175 East 102nd Street could afford to resolve, allowing them to receive their loan and enabling their occupancy in 1973.[35]

St. Georges sought to streamline sweat equity rehabilitation, a cause that the then twenty-one-year-old intern hoped to improve after the experience of Fox and his collaborators. "To a man, the other 'housing professionals' had images of boiler explosions, building collapses, shoddy workmanship, and inept or lazy tenant self-helpers," St. Georges wrote of the officials he encountered in city hall. With Schur's support, he organized a loosely arrayed Sweat Equity Program that helped rehabbers find abandoned buildings, introduced officials into projects early enough to minimize construction violations, and assisted with loans that supported up-front costs and other expenses incurred along the way. St. Georges encouraged the Operation Move-In squatters to become the program's demonstration project. They took official ownership of 948 Columbus Avenue in the fall of 1973, and the Renigades approached St. Georges soon after, seeking to rehabilitate their own tenement. Over the next three years, the city would award loans to eight more projects, constituting thirteen buildings and 151 housing units. Schur similarly cobbled together a bolstered Receivership Program to facilitate tenant management of properties on the verge of landlord abandonment, modifying the program so community organizations could manage and improve such buildings. These initiatives remained highly informal despite their official titles, as Schur and his band of like-minded interns reassembled existing programs in new configurations in order to keep up with emerging grassroots efforts.[36]

Like the window Edmonds constructed at 948 Columbus Avenue, then, supporting policy was characterized by pragmatism and a high degree of improvisation. Sympathetic officials created paths that allowed tenants to assemble a patchwork quilt of measures old and new. As St. Georges noted, homesteaders "'piggyback[ed] every gimmick in the world." A supportive reporter explained the process like so: "Begin with the sale of a building for $1. Add municipal loans at below market interest rates for long terms. Grant full exemption from payment of real estate taxes for eight to ten years. Utilize as much sweat equity as possible. Dovetail these savings with job training and an adequate technical assistance program."[37] Some homesteaders tapped the low-interest financing available through the city's Municipal Loan Program and its successor, the Participation Loan Program. United Harlem Growth borrowed from the federal Section 312 Loan Program, the first sweat equity project to do so. For their second phase of work, the Renigades obtained a mortgage from the city funded by the federal Community Development Block Grant program, initiated in 1974. Many projects paid tenant laborers through the federal CETA. The Mosque of the Islamic Brotherhood and United Harlem Growth partnered to obtain such assistance, which allowed tenants to earn income while they learned construction skills. Private lenders sometimes supplemented public loans. The mosque received small loans from two foundations—Community Funding Inc., funded by Columbia University and Barnard College, and the Consumer-Farmer Foundation, a generous supporter of sweat equity that grew out of a pioneering New York–based milk cooperative. The modest amounts they lent often funded the start-up costs that allowed projects to get underway.[38]

Such creativity proved necessary in an era when the overall level of political and financial support was consistent only in its irregularity. Self-help proponents lost their best ally within government when Mayor Abraham Beame, elected in 1973, fired Schur. But Schur then led the creation of ANHD, and St. Georges joined the efforts that became UHAB.[39] Both organizations pushed the city to affirm its commitment to homesteading even as officials resisted funding new projects. ANHD urged officials to expand programs that supported management by tenants and community organizations to include buildings taken in rem, not only those facing impending abandonment but still under landlord control. As many as a quarter of the buildings on most blocks in Harlem, the South Bronx, and Ocean Hill–Brownsville, Brooklyn, were forsaken, the organization pointed out, and community groups could restore them to a habitable state. In 1975, officials agreed to bring city-owned abandoned buildings under the Community Management Program that Schur had established. This created an income stream for participating community groups, whom the city paid for management and rehab, as well as a new pathway to improved, cooperatively owned, affordable housing. Meanwhile, UHAB lobbied the city to support sweat equity, urging officials to use newly available Community Development Block Grant funds to provide loans for such rehabilitation. Advocates gained that concession early in 1975, and it led to the creation of the Participation Loan Program in 1976. This program, which joined city and private bank funding, provided thirty-year-term, 1 percent interest rate loans that funded construction of the Mosque of the Islamic Brotherhood's project, among others.[40]

In the short term, however, such success proved limited, for the city's severe fiscal crisis, which peaked in the latter half of 1975, ushered in an austerity budget that drastically cut the city's spending—and particularly programs that affected the poor. While ongoing projects continued, diminished generosity undermined efforts to expand the scope of self-help rehabilitation.[41] Advocacy organizations felt such cuts acutely. As Terner assessed UHAB's progress toward its original goal of supporting the homesteading of 200 buildings and 3,000 apartments in its first two years, he reflected on the limitations imposed by reliance on public-sector support. UHAB had made gains—thirty-five buildings with 426 apartments were under way by August 1975—but he lacked confidence that proponents could make up the deficit in the remaining eleven months. "The main obstacle . . . has been our necessity to borrow money from the city," Terner said. "And the city . . . is more a borrower than a lender these days," a *Times* reporter paraphrased. ANHD sounded justifiably gloomy in assessing the period between mid-1975 and the end of 1976. "The city government provided very little in the way of tangible support or encouragement for the preservation of housing or neighborhoods," leaders wrote.[42]

Yet if the fiscal crisis shook homesteaders' confidence in the city as an ally, the federal government proved increasingly responsive in the same period. President Jimmy Carter was drawn to self-help as a revitalization strategy, a result of both the emphasis on neighborhood power at this time and Carter's own interest in voluntarism.[43] Carter's election motivated one city official to tout the Mosque of the Islamic Brotherhood's project as a model that could address nationwide problems. "With the support of a new administration in Washington, every city in America could begin to combat the decline of adequate housing and the staggering increase in urban unemployment," Lucille Rose, commissioner of the Department of Employment, said in November 1976 at a press conference in front of the mosque's buildings. Rose's call went unheeded, but area homesteading advocates did make headway under Carter. UHAB promoted its successes to the federal Department of Housing and Urban Development (HUD), an appeal that garnered a generous, federally funded low-income homesteading demonstration project in

New York beginning in 1977. HUD committed to supply CETA job training funds and federal low-interest Section 312 loans for projects in the Lower East Side, the South Bronx, and Central Harlem, a plan in part based on HUD's experience loaning Section 312 funds to United Harlem Growth. Though Harlem did not remain in the final program, the UHAB-coordinated effort eventually encompassed twelve tenements with over one hundred apartments in New York City, and grew to include Hartford, Cleveland, Chicago, Boston, and Springfield, Massachusetts.[44] Carter famously elevated New York's grassroots revitalization efforts to the national stage with his visit to the South Bronx in October 1977, during which he toured 1186 Washington Avenue, the twenty-eight-unit sweat equity rehabilitation project of the People's Development Corporation. Community organizations gained unprecedented financial support in the wake of Carter's tour.[45]

These gains came as the fiscal crisis ushered in a tidal wave of abandoned buildings. The economic climate of the mid-1970s created greater economic fragility for both tenants and landlords, as low-income residents claimed even fewer assets with which to pay rent, and rising inflation and fuel costs worsened landlords' already tenuous position. Banks, long reluctant to lend in predominantly low-income neighborhoods, became even less reliable as new state laws increased the investment activities in which they could participate. As a result, mortgages in New York City diminished as desirable ventures. The city responded to consequently rising abandonment with passage of a new in rem law in 1976. Local Law 45 allowed the city to foreclose on property for nonpayment of taxes after one year, instead of three. Officials hoped the law would demonstrate to the state and federal governments that the city was addressing its financial woes, arguing that the threat of rapid foreclosure would motivate property owners to pay their taxes and that properties that were nonetheless abandoned would reach the city in a better physical state. But Local Law 45 instead brought a flood of abandoned buildings into the city's possession, as landlords cut their losses and fled. The city owned 8,000 buildings with 90,000 tenants by April 1978. By January 1979, the *Times* estimated, the city had become landlord of 9,500 buildings, more than half partially or fully occupied. City estimates claimed ownership of 11,700 buildings with 166,000 units by April 1979; 4,100 of those properties, with 35,000 units total, were occupied. Harlem's streets held a substantial share of those abandoned, occupied buildings—at least 40 percent by the next year. The onrush of city-owned properties created new difficulties, to be sure. "City-Owned Houses Come Complete with Pandora's Box," Michael Goodwin of the *Times* titled a 1979 article, detailing the city's responsibilities as a landlord: to keep up with heat and repairs in abandoned buildings, to fix the code violations in many of them, and to collect rent from reluctant tenants. The city was not equipped to maintain so many properties.[46]

Yet advocates for the conversion of abandoned buildings into affordable housing saw the in rem flood as a welcome chance to build the inclusive, community-controlled neighborhood they had long envisioned. The Metropolitan Council on Housing, a long-standing New York tenants' rights organization, portrayed the crisis as "an opportunity for tenants to move in the direction of housing for people, not profits—in other words housing in the public domain." Likewise, an array of community groups and advocates came together as the Task Force on City-Owned Property to encourage the newly inaugurated mayor, Edward Koch, to pass city-owned buildings along to self-help organizations. Members included many of the stalwarts of the homesteading movement, including ANHD, UHAB, the Renigades Housing Movement, and WHCO, as well as two Harlem-based politicians, State Senator Carl McCall and Councilman Fred Samuel. The task force cited the portfolio of abandoned buildings as "an opportunity for creative housing and neighborhood development action." Members called for the formation of a "new sector for low income residential management and ownership," with "locally and democratically controlled planning, management and development as its cornerstone." The nonprofits that had shaped grassroots responses to abandonment over the previous decade would back the effort. The programs they had developed, including tenant and community management and homesteading-based rehabilitation, were to function on a newly expanded scale. In conjunction with the expansion of these programs, task force members demanded an end to public property auctions as a means of disposing of city-owned buildings. Such disposal methods, which returned abandoned buildings back to private owners, failed at an alarmingly high rate. One April 1977 study by the city Office of Management and Budget found that a quarter of auctioned buildings never paid taxes, and 94 percent were again in arrears after four years. Rather than making abandoned buildings viable, auctions overwhelmingly kept tenants at the mercy of negligent landlords.[47]

The city took title to the first wave of in rem foreclosures under the new law soon after the task force issued its report, and quickly became, as one reporter claimed, "the world's largest slum landlord." While Koch set out to restore the city's financial footing in his first months in Gracie Mansion, the abandonment problem began to cripple the agency that was responsible for city-owned buildings, the Department of Real Property. In this context, officials were willing to experiment, and they proved receptive to the calls for innovation issued by the neighborhood housing movement. In mid-1978, the city shifted the management of in rem buildings from the Department of Real Property to the newly created Department of Housing Preservation and Development, a move that indicated official endorsement of the view that abandoned buildings represented a housing resource, not a fiscal resource. Under the new agency, the city created the Division of Alternative Management Programs (DAMP), a unit that implemented many of the reforms sought by the Task Force on City-Owned Property. DAMP replicated the patchwork nature of the homesteading movement in general, agglomerating a range of strategies intended to free the city of the buildings it reluctantly owned. DAMP expanded the Community Management Program, introduced a new cooperative ownership program called Tenant Interim Lease, and created programs to allow limited management by the New York City Housing Authority and by private managers. As leader of this new division, officials tapped St. Georges, who returned to the city from UHAB. In November 1978, officials issued the moratorium on property auctions that activists had requested, granting their wish that the city reassess a policy that undermined hopes for a collective housing movement.[48]

These programs expanded beyond the scope of sweat equity but built on its intentions, offering new avenues for low-income tenants to claim control over their homes and, consequently, over Harlem. The enlarged Community Management Program enabled groups like WHCO to take ownership of properties they had managed for the city. In 1980, WHCO purchased four city-owned buildings on 116th Street for $250 each, marking the first such transfer from the city to a community group. Tenants who had assisted WHCO with the buildings' renovation in turn purchased their apartments from the organization, creating four new cooperatives. Tenant Interim Lease quickly became the fastest growing of the DAMP programs, enabling residents to manage their building for at least eleven months while paying rent to the city, after which they had the option to convert to a cooperative at a price of $250 per unit. Tenants responded enthusiastically to the chance to own their homes. Pearl and Ernest Knox, for instance, had lived for decades at 1 West 126th Street, a grand apartment building in the heart of Harlem that had housed Count Basie, Billy Eckstein, and Paul Robeson at times. When the owner abandoned the building, tenants found that the city did not maintain it to their satisfaction. So they pooled rents to pay for repairs themselves, and signed on to Tenant Interim Lease as soon as the program began. "I've seen apartments in all the newer and expensive buildings in Harlem," Pearl Knox told the *Times*, "and those in this building are as beautiful as any I've seen."[49]

By the new decade, then, tenant-led efforts to restore abandoned buildings to affordable housing had achieved a level of institutional support and a scale that far eclipsed the fledgling efforts of the mid-1970s. The dramatic increase of apartments in the city's alternative management programs during this period testified to the gains that proponents had made. The range of those programs demonstrated the innovations that had developed from early sweat equity rehabilitation. According to the Task Force on City-Owned Property, the number of occupied units in alternative management programs rose from 1,611 in July 1978 to 8,060 in July 1979, or 20 percent of the city's occupied in rem inventory. By October 1980, the city claimed, DAMP encompassed 645 buildings with a total of 15,205 units. Twelve thousand of those units were occupied, representing over a third of city-owned occupied apartments. Community groups managed over 3,000 units in the Community Management Program; the Tenant Interim Lease program included 240 buildings and 5,800 housing units across the city. A movement that had begun with the determined efforts of desperate tenants had moved into the political and physical mainstream. Would abandonment enable the radical dream of community control that Harlem activists had long imagined?[50]

Thirteen Brownstones

The city's willingness to bring alternative approaches into its bureaucracy promised unprecedented influence for low-income homesteaders. Yet the momentum of the late 1970s would prove to be less a tipping point than a high-water mark for activists. While Mayor Koch incorporated their strategies as the city became inundated with abandoned buildings, he was reluctant to make such approaches predominant as the city came out of fiscal crisis. The new decade brought conflicts over the future of Harlem, centered on the role of its abandoned buildings. On one side, activists saw city-owned buildings as the path to community control. On the other, officials placed their faith increasingly in middle-class resettlement of the neighborhood's city-owned buildings. As Harlemites and Koch clashed over the fate of the neighborhood, activists feared their opportunity for control was slipping away.

Indeed, officials proved to be fickle allies. While the auction moratorium in late 1978 had raised hopes that the city would cease returning abandoned buildings to private owners, New York retreated relatively quickly to its most controversial disposal strategy. Mayor Koch proposed the revival of auctions in the summer of 1979. Officials understandably wanted to get these thousands of properties off their hands. The city was not prepared to serve as landlord, and management and maintenance were costly. Auctions provided the fastest means to dispose of buildings en masse. Critics from the Task Force on City-Owned Property questioned Koch's motives, however, noting the high risk of subsequent default and what that meant for tenants and the city, which would again find itself landlord of these buildings. "If the City runs its *in rem* buildings at a loss," task force members asked, "why will a profit-making individual be able to pay real estate taxes and make a profit?" Under such pressure, the city altered its auction requirements with the intention of reducing speculation and ensuring more effective management. Reforms required that new owners renovate properties to remove code violations, disclose their history as landlords, and live in or near buildings with four or fewer units for three years after purchase. But auction opponents remained unconvinced, arguing that landlords who had gamed the system before would do so again and that rent hikes permitted under the policy would displace tenants in occupied abandoned buildings.[51]

In questioning the need for disposal back to profit-oriented landlords, advocates pointed to the tremendous success that buildings under DAMP oversight had already achieved. As task force members explained, the city had been initially skeptical of self-help strategies, arguing that "such programs would never contain more than a small percentage of city-owned buildings." But the number of units under DAMP had grown rapidly as the city made bureaucratic space for them, and the remarkable rates of rent payment demonstrated the promise of alternative approaches. More than 90 percent of tenants in the Community Management Program paid their rent, the task force pointed out, and expressed high satisfaction with their community-based landlords. The city itself recognized the sensation it had in DAMP. City-owned buildings had typically yielded rent payment under 30 percent in the past. Yet a remarkable 83.8 percent of tenants under DAMP paid rent during the first year of the program, officials noted, and over 87 percent in fiscal year 1980. Just over 45 percent of tenants in in rem buildings under traditional city management paid their rent in the same year, an increase that officials were glad to note but that paled in comparison to tenants under DAMP.[52]

Task force members called for an expansion of community-based approaches to abandoned housing. Their benefits were manifold, advocates claimed—buildings could function at self-subsisting levels, tenants provided much maintenance and operation themselves, and rents remained affordable. Yet officials proceeded with plans to return properties to the private sector, restarting auctions in May 1980. Early sales avoided Harlem, instead focusing on the outer boroughs. The city hoped to sell around 250 buildings in the first year, largely townhouses in Brooklyn and small buildings in Queens. Koch responded enthusiastically to financial projections for one of the first auctions in June 1980. "Keep it up. We need every million dollars you can find," he told his commissioner of general services. Harlem's reprieve proved only temporary, however. In late 1980, officials shifted their attention uptown, announcing plans to sell thirteen abandoned historic brownstones using a lottery instead of a traditional auction. Most were in the Mount Morris Park Historic District, on West 119th, 120th, and 121st Streets (see Figure 4.7). One brownstone was located on West 139th Street, in Harlem's most famous residential blocks, called Strivers' Row. Two were located farther north, in the Hamilton Heights Historic District.[53]

Despite the success of alternative management strategies, a success that even officials acknowledged, why did Koch nonetheless decide to return Harlem's city-owned homes to the private market? One answer could be found in the headlines that had increasingly appeared in New York papers in the last years of the 1970s. "Middle-Class Blacks Return to Harlem," the *Times* reported in 1976. "People Returning to Harlem," wrote Harlem's own *Amsterdam News* in 1979. That same year, *Daily News* columnist Earl Caldwell

FIGURE 4.7. Abandoned brownstones on West 119th Street, pictured in July 1981. These were among the properties included in the lottery of thirteen abandoned Harlem brownstones that city officials announced in late 1980. The Koch administration saw the lottery as a chance to seed revitalization through middle-class resettlement. Many Harlemites saw it instead as a threat to the promise of community control they found in widespread abandonment.

offered the lively title, "Harlem Is Jumpin' to a New Buy-Buy Blues Beat." "It always was someplace else," Caldwell wrote, chronicling the advance of the middle-class "pioneers." "It was Park Slope and Crown Heights in Brooklyn. It was downtown in SoHo and even in midtown, in the neighborhood that was once Hell's Kitchen." Harlem had remained the exception, but now it was Harlem's turn. The neighborhood claimed streets of beautiful brownstones as ornate as any in New York, many now city property. "Once these were houses that nobody wanted," Caldwell wrote. "They sat empty, windows broken, doors missing and, for the most part, they were shelter only for drug addicts." But increasingly the problem was too much demand, not too little. The city welcomed such interest. As wanting eyes looked to Harlem in the late 1970s, officials realized the assets that had fallen into their hands. For Koch, the appeal was not simply the revenue that sales would bring, though officials did desire such revenue, but also a broader faith in middle-class re-settlement as the key to neighborhood revitalization, a belief that he had maintained from the earliest days of his mayoralty.[54]

Officials recognized the potential threat such a position represented in Harlem, where the community's very identity as a majority African American, largely low-income community had become a source of power. One official with the city's Department of Housing Preservation and Development acknowledged this in noting that Harlem residents maintained "understandable paranoia about losing out." "Harlem is vulnerable to a takeover by whites," he admitted. With high outside demand for Harlem brownstones, the city took the unusual step of negotiating the terms of their disposition with the Harlem establishment—including elected officials and leaders of the Harlem Urban Development Corporation—as early as 1979. The choice of a lottery was intended to address interest in a limited resource while meeting Harlem leaders' concerns that the city was seeding the upheaval of the neighborhood. While a freewheeling, wide-open auction could drive prices as high as bidders would take them, the lottery provided a fixed price between $5,000 and $42,000 for each of the brownstones. Entrants applied to purchase a single building. Moreover, city housing officials agreed to build favoritism into the process based on an applicant's current residence, a concession that implicitly addressed concerns about racial transition. Harlem residents would receive three entries each, while nonresidents would receive only one.[55]

But Harlem's grassroots observers were not convinced that the terms negotiated by city officials and establishment leaders served their best interests.
At issue was not simply the sale of these thirteen homes, a small percentage
in a large neighborhood, but the fear that they were to serve as a gateway to
the sale of everything else the city owned in Harlem. Residents filled planning
board hearings in West and Central Harlem in the spring of 1981, making
for "large and often raucous events" at which opponents voiced concerns
that the lottery marked the first step in the neighborhood's takeover by outsiders. The respective community planning boards sided with resident demands that city-owned properties be sold to tenants through direct sales,
not a lottery. Community Board 10, encompassing Central Harlem, voted
unanimously against the plan.[56] A group of residents opposed to the sale
formed the Anti-lottery Committee of Harlemites in early 1981. Their leader
was Lois Penny, a self-described homesteader and twenty-eight-year-old
activist with a home on West 138th Street. Committee members worried that
if an auction was not immediately on the horizon, it soon would be. "If we
do not voice our opposition, the City will sell over *700* City-Owned brownstones and apartment buildings in our community through this Lottery
process and Auctions," they promised in June. Their warning in July, on the
eve of a crucial city Board of Estimate hearing on whether the plan could
proceed, sounded even more dire. "The first step in the plan is the *lottery*
sale of our brownstones," wrote the Anti-lottery Committee. "The *auction*
sale of our apartment buildings will be next!!!"[57]

Activists worried that the Board of Estimate would seal their fate, but their
fears were largely confirmed even before the meeting began. In an interview
the night before the July 23 hearing, the garrulous Koch explained his distaste for the lottery process and the concessions it reflected. "I've directed the
housing agency henceforth to never have an operation that precludes people
otherwise eligible from coming in and buying property in the City of New
York," he said. Koch, who maintained a career-long aversion to racial quotas,
disliked the racialized nature of the plan. But he especially opposed the idea
that disposal of city-owned property would proceed in a manner that restricted the middle-class settlement he saw as crucial to the city's future.
"They're naturals for buying brownstones," he said approvingly of members
of the middle class, regardless of race. "That's called gentrification."[58]

Koch and Harlem activists represented two different positions on what a neighborhood should be and how it should get there. In articulating his opposition to lotteries, Koch described his beliefs as a product of racial liberalism. "I am an old fashioned liberal," he said. "I still believe that it is in the best interest of the city, state, and country that we follow the principles of integration—meaning every citizen has the right to live in any community provided he or she is able to afford to live there." But in objecting to a strong public-sector role in maintaining Harlem's affordability and racial identity, while upholding the city's right to return property to the private sector to facilitate middle-class settlement, Koch evinced the neoliberal approach that pervaded much of his policy. So too did his premise that access came as a right to those with economic means. Koch's conception of the principle of open housing suggested his deep belief in the ameliorative role of economic upscaling through the free market. "The best thing that could happen to the Harlem community would be the strengthening of its middle class base," he said. In line with this belief, Koch maintained a laissez-faire approach to urban change and its consequences. Economic transition, he explained, was an inevitable occurrence that officials and residents could, and should, do little to stop. "My position is that some middle-class neighborhoods go down economically and some low-income neighborhoods go up and that is the nature of a changing city," Koch told an aide in 1982. Consequent residential displacement, he argued, was just a fact of life.[59]

Opponents of the lottery, on the other hand, maintained the radical view of community control that had shaped perceptions of space in Harlem since the late 1960s. Activists envisioned Harlem's power residing in its predominantly African American and low-income population. Abandonment had at last offered the opportunity for residents to claim the ideal they had long sought, to get out from under exploitive landlords and to own their land. "Blacks now have the opportunity to control a significant portion of Harlem Real Estate now that many whites have abandoned their property," Rev. Calvin O. Butts III of the Abyssinian Baptist Church wrote of the lottery. "These plans are against the notions that persons who now live and do business in Harlem will have a chance to control real estate here." Residents were not simply opposed to wealthier or whiter neighbors, argued Lloyd Williams, chair of Community Board 10. At issue was the prospect that opening up

Harlem's abandoned buildings to any interested outsider would undermine residents' ability to determine the future of their community. "It is our sense that Harlemites should have the major voice in determining that which is best for Harlem," Williams said. "This is a right which other non Black and Hispanic communities simply take for granted." In responding to the lottery, community control stalwart Preston Wilcox put the dilemma in typically more colorful terms: "If this is our community, then we have to find a way to control, upgrade our community. It's like everybody knows that they have to ask permission to go into your refrig unless it has already been established that it's ok for them to do so."[60]

In the collision of these visions, Harlemites feared, they would lose their hold on the neighborhood they had begun to rebuild by transforming aging buildings into affordable, cooperatively owned homes. The lottery threatened to return Harlem to the outsiders who had long controlled its real estate. "When the whites came to Africa, they had the Bible. Now they are coming to Harlem with a new game—A Lottery," Wilcox wrote. "They have not used the lottery to integrate white communities with us. . . . Now they want us to participate in a lottery on our land to insure that we don't keep them out!" Anti-lottery Committee members argued that the three-to-one preference given to residents would not be enough to overcome the flood of entries from outside Harlem and objected to rehabilitation requirements that effectively acted as income limits. City officials recommended a minimum annual salary of $18,000 for lottery entrants due to the costs of rehab and suggested that salaries more than two to two and a half times that would be preferable— far in excess of the average income in the neighborhood.[61]

Lottery opponents argued that Harlemites' persistence amid abandonment deserved the reward of community control they had long demanded. They proposed an alternative to the lottery that, not coincidentally, included many of the key tenets of the self-help movement in an effort to make acquisition and rehab affordable. Property should be sold through direct sales, not lotteries, Anti-lottery Committee members argued, with preference given to community residents. Like properties under DAMP, the purchase price should be a modest $250. Sweat equity should be permitted. Wilcox's advice to his neighbors channeled both immediate concerns about the impending loss of "turf control" and the deeper symbolism underlying the drive to turn abandoned buildings into community assets. "Function collectively/selectively/correctively as *psychological cooperative owners,* and never as *psychological tenants,*" Wilcox urged.[62]

Their pleas gained concessions, but never the stay that lottery opponents had demanded. In the aftermath of the Board of Estimate hearing, in which members passed Koch's lottery plan, the mayor backed down from his provocative statements. He would consider preferential lotteries in the future. But Koch had no intention of heeding the more radical suggestions of activists, and with the lottery in place, opponents were devastated. Caldwell, who just a couple years earlier had written with awe of the sudden speculative interest in Harlem, now worried what the future held. "There are 7,000 other properties, by conservative count, and soon they too are going to be dumped on the market," Caldwell wrote of city-owned property in Harlem. "It has the makings of one of the biggest real estate deals in the history of the city, and it is going down now." Sitting with Noreen Clark Smith, a member of Community Board 10, after the hearing, it seemed the bottom had fallen out. "The real estate developers have it now. . . . They have just delivered Harlem to the real estate interests," she told Caldwell.[63]

Anthony Gliedman, the commissioner of the Department of Housing Preservation and Development, announced more generous lottery terms in October. The city would adjust proportions to ensure that Harlemites had 50 percent of the entries in the final lottery, addressing concerns that outsiders would dominate. Still, as the February 1982 lottery loomed, opponents were sure that the end was near. Entries poured in. The city had distributed 7,500 applications for the now twelve brownstones (the previous owner of one had paid the taxes he owed, unbeknownst to the city), and had already received 3,000 by the end of October. Penny, leader of the Anti-lottery Committee, remained defiant in the months before the lottery. "We're not finished yet. We certainly are not lying down and playing dead," she said. But as 250 spectators watched City College students pick winning entries in an auditorium on their campus in the Harlem neighborhood of Hamilton Heights, and as the crowd cheered Samuel, Harlem's councilman, as he told them he hoped "all the names of winners come from Boards 9 and 10," no opponents were in the room to watch. The hopes that activists had carried for Harlem's many abandoned buildings had faded. The lottery, it seemed, marked a watershed moment in the neighborhood's history and the loss of a dream that radical proponents had maintained for almost twenty years—that Harlem's very poverty and segregation could provide the engine for community control. Abandonment had brought that promise near, but Koch's vision appeared to have won out.[64]

Middle Road

Activists were certain that the brownstone lottery would spell the end of Harlem as they knew it. Yet if activists saw the sale as a rupture in the history of Harlem, in time the lottery, and the city's plans that followed, proved more of a hinge than an upheaval. Debates over the role of city-owned buildings had cast the alternatives in stark terms of good and evil. In the end, however, responses to the abandonment crisis charted a middle road on the way to a more economically complex future for Harlem, an alternative to both the radical community control that activists sought and the total displacement that they feared.

This reality became apparent as soon as the names of the lottery winners emerged from the hopper in the City College auditorium. While activists had doubted that the city's plan would provide a measured outcome, indeed the new owners disproportionately represented Central and West Harlem and their environs. One of the brownstone winners came from Long Island, one from Westchester County, one from Queens, and one from Brooklyn. Three, however, lived in nearby neighborhoods—Manhattan Valley to Harlem's immediate south, Washington Heights to its immediate north, and East Harlem. And five were already Central and West Harlem residents. Blanche Brown lived on Frederick Douglass Boulevard (Eighth Avenue) near the Harlem River. Penny Sherrod also lived on Frederick Douglass Boulevard, just north of Central Park. Alvin and Dawn Martine resided on 147th Street, while Linda Gelpi's home was located just south of City College. Amelia Samuda had lived her entire life in Harlem, most recently in historic buildings on 135th Street that St. Philip's Church had owned since early in Harlem's history as a black metropolis. Eleven of the twelve winners were nonwhite, and if the professions of three new owners were any indication, most were middle-class but decidedly not affluent—one worked as an administrative assistant, another as a systems analyst at New York Blood Center, and a third as an assistant manager at a variety store.[65]

In opposing the lottery, observers had argued that the sale would undermine the control that Harlemites had long sought. Yet for the lucky winners, their good fortune provided a feeling of autonomy much like that self-help advocates had claimed, though one increasingly expressed at the individual level, not as a communal ideal. "It really is a joy to have something of your own. It means you own a piece of the rock," Samuda told a reporter. Priscilla Ashley, who had lived just north of Harlem's unofficial borders, agreed. "I'm floating on air—completely," she said. "It means I'm a homeowner, a property owner. It means that I have tangible assets to give my sons."[66] And though more financially secure than neighbors who had scraped by in order to renovate abandoned buildings, the winners likewise faced a thin line between rehabilitated homes and insolvency. When questions arose about whether state officials would require renovators to carefully restore the dilapidated but historic interiors of their new homes, for instance, many worried that substantial added costs—as much as $30,000—would quickly exceed the limited financing the city provided through low-interest loans and grants. Like low-income homesteaders, lottery winners were focused on creating affordable, habitable spaces, not lush period interiors. "We're not in the business of going in for gold faucets and crystal doorknobs. . . . We're trying to make a decent housing stock, not a luxurious housing stock," said one frustrated city official.[67]

Though the state eventually agreed to relax preservation requirements in order to keep rehab costs down, some lottery winners were ultimately unable to take ownership of the homes they had won, whether for financial or other reasons. Samuda was among the four lottery winners who never moved into their Harlem brownstones, but another Harlem resident obtained ownership of her home instead. Harlemites likewise became owners of two of the three homes never occupied by winners from East Harlem, Long Island, and Brooklyn. By the time occupants signed deeds for eleven of the twelve brownstones in 1984, seven homeowners had moved from elsewhere in Harlem, and two more from neighboring blocks. Only two new homeowners came from elsewhere in the city. After renovation, residents lived in their homes far longer than the three years that the city required as a term of ownership. Nine stayed in their homes beyond 2000. Rather than importing a crop of disruptive outsiders or a group of speculators who sought to cash out after their required residency was up, the brownstone lottery ended up providing dream houses for a group of residents, most of whom had lived in the neighborhood during its most trying years and remained there long after.[68]

The status of techniques pioneered by homesteaders in the mid-1970s similarly suggests the ambiguity of Harlem's fate as the neighborhood began to witness new investment. Officially sanctioned sweat equity programs largely diminished in the early 1980s, limited in scale by many of the same factors that had brought abandonment in the first place. Homesteaders found wild inflation a paralyzing factor as they tried to construct their homes on a shoe-string. In 1980, UHAB estimated that the cost of sweat equity had risen to $22,000 per unit, 50 percent more than just four years earlier. The patchwork nature of funding exacerbated difficulties, as onerous and complex bureaucratic requirements took labor time away from construction. Moreover, the rising fuel costs that challenged landlords likewise affected self-builders. Minimum rents necessary to cover costs in 1980 had doubled from their level in 1973, the year that the idea of self-help housing first caught fire. Public agencies offered loans but few subsidies, meaning that sweat equity increasingly became a pursuit that low-income tenants simply could not afford. "Everything has gone up, and basically our incomes are fixed," rued Luqman Abdush-Shahid of the Mosque of the Islamic Brotherhood. "We find ourselves tightening a belt that has already been squeezed." By early 1980, the Renigades had not paid taxes for months, unable to both keep 251 East 119th Street running and pay the city's bills.[69]

Self-help proponents faced an array of impediments as they brought their work into the new decade. The very institutionalization and public support that had enabled progress through loans and job training diminished the radicalism of a movement that had grown out of the dramatic act of squatting. As neighborhood groups gained more resources in the late 1970s and became larger operations with official mandates, participants took on less political roles. Community groups with management responsibilities functioned essentially as landlords, finding themselves on the wrong side of tenants' ire when things went poorly. In July 1982, for instance, tenants led a rent strike against WHCO in a building the group managed on West 117th Street. The property needed a new boiler and the city would not provide WHCO with the money to replace it, so residents withheld rent for six months. More problematic still, funding diminished substantially upon the inauguration of President Ronald Reagan in 1981. Officials removed restrictions that committed Community Development Block Grant funds to low-income communities, and budget cutting slashed many of the programs that neighborhood developers relied on, including the CETA support that had paid many of the laborers on rehab projects.[70]

Despite strong countercurrents, however, neighborhood developers' efforts were not insignificant, nor in vain. The city retained low-income homesteaders' methods as one minor approach but generally cast their lot with the private real estate market that had long dominated New York City. But DAMP nonetheless persisted into the new decade, and the city continued to boast of gains made under Tenant Interim Lease and the Community Management Program. Buildings under DAMP constituted around a third of occupied city-owned buildings by late 1981. Those numbers remained modest in the face of the still vast inventory that the city owned and the widespread demand for affordable housing, to be sure, but the city continued to sell buildings to low-income tenants at an accelerating pace. Between 1978 and 1982, officials claimed, they sold 112 buildings with a total of 2,800 rehabilitated units to tenants through DAMP. Fifty-seven of those buildings, with almost 1,100 units, were sold in the latter half of 1981. By the fall of 1982, the city had sold nineteen buildings with 426 apartments under Tenant Interim Lease and eleven buildings with 149 apartments under the Community Management Program. Another 569 buildings throughout the city, with 13,600 housing units, remained under DAMP. In Central Harlem, Community Board 10 claimed almost 1,500 units in alternative management programs by August 1982.[71] Though representing a smaller portion of formerly abandoned buildings than activists had hoped for, the inventory nonetheless included enough units to house thousands of families.

For every failure in the movement, a success story suggested the potential that advocates had imagined early on. Residents in low-income cooperatives faced a slew of difficulties, including financial precariousness, a limited scale amid widespread abandonment, and tenant participation that lagged behind expectations. But they expressed overwhelming approval for their living situation. In one 1983 survey, 91 percent of residents preferred their low-income co-op to living in a building owned by a private landlord, and 80 percent considered their buildings successful even if they were fiscally unsound.

FIGURE 4.8. Exterior of the Mosque of the Islamic Brotherhood, after resident-led rehabilitation, circa 1979. Self-help proponents faced a range of obstacles, including institutionalization, diminishing federal support, and inflation, but successes spoke to the promise of low-income homesteading. Members of the mosque gained tenant-controlled, affordable housing, and many subsequently worked in the construction trades or in the businesses they had built on site.

Cooperative members expressed feelings of autonomy and inclusion as a result of their housing and, crucially, a sense of control. David Robinson walked away from United Harlem Growth in the early 1980s, frustrated by the enormity of the task and the lack of assistance he felt the group received on West 136th Street. But on St. Nicholas Avenue, members of the Mosque of the Islamic Brotherhood moved into their new residential and spiritual home in 1979, occupying its fourteen newly refurbished apartments (see Figure 4.8). Though members had incurred a $30,000 cost overrun due to inflation during construction, they were current on their mortgage payments. Most tenants were employed, the director of UHAB reported, many in construction, others in the businesses the mosque had built on-site. Ironically, the city took possession of 251 East 119th Street, the Renigades' tenement, in an in rem tax foreclosure in 1985. But seventeen years later the city sold the building to the

Youth Action Program, one of the many rehab and job training programs that had flourished in the late 1970s in the Renigades' wake and that gained national prominence as the nonprofit YouthBuild USA. UHAB included more than a hundred Harlem buildings in a 1988 list of "self help housing" in Manhattan. The legacy of self-help, whether in successful sweat equity projects such as that of the mosque or in buildings that had passed through DAMP to become low-income cooperatives, provided a core of tenant-controlled, affordable housing in Harlem that persisted long past its origin.[72]

Through debates over the fate of Harlem's abandoned buildings, then, participants foreshadowed a pattern of settlement that would increasingly characterize the community over the next decade. In a period when it seemed that the city's poorest neighborhoods might very well implode, competing visions of Harlem's future had vied to determine the fate of thousands of shells, some occupied, some empty. Enterprising residents had envisioned a widespread movement of the poor that would turn forsaken houses back into homes and bring community control. City leaders had imagined the middle-class resettlement of Harlem, placing their faith in market forces that they could help stimulate. But Harlem took early steps toward a vision that was neither the collectively owned ideal of radical activists nor the private-sector takeover that they feared, but instead a middle path, with new affordable housing footholds alongside increasing homeownership opportunities for those with greater means.

Still, in the years immediately following the 1982 brownstone lottery, many Harlemites remained unsettled as the city continued to return in rem properties to the private market. In 1985, officials proceeded with the large-scale auction of abandoned Harlem brownstones that activists had long dreaded, a 149-property sale that dwarfed the earlier lottery. Residents revived many of the concerns—and techniques—they had pioneered over the previous decade. Officials had agreed to sell 98 of the 149 brownstones to Harlem residents, but critics protested that the auction would nonetheless drive prices beyond what neighborhood winners could afford. Many called for sweat equity as an alternative, demanding direct sales to Harlem residents and tenant labor as an allowable financial contribution. Members of the National Reclamation Project, a Harlem group against the auction, echoed their predecessors in leading poor squatters in the takeover of some of the brownstones. But even such drastic measures were unable to prevent the sale. In his remarks to auction winners in September 1985, Mayor Koch reemphasized his position that New York was an "open city" without restrictions on neighborhood resettlement. Yet at the same time he demonstrated newfound restraint emblematic of the era's emerging moderation, voicing his support for the auction's concession to Harlemites. "The people who stayed," he said, were to be "recognized for their courage." But the people who stayed, even the winners, remained uncertain what lay ahead in their changing neighborhood.[73]

CHAPTER 5

Managing Change

IN 1988, Preston Wilcox began a typically determined and ultimately unsuccessful campaign to gain federal, state, and city historic landmark designation for the full extent of Harlem. "Although Harlem is the best known Black community in the world and is irreversibly tied to the heritage, history and inheritance of African Americans, it seems that the racist practices in America continue to demand that we reassert our relationship with it or that we welcome outsiders into it as though they own it—and not us," Wilcox told Orin Lehman, commissioner of the New York State Office of Parks, Recreation, and Historic Preservation. "'Harlem is our home' is the way in which Harlem is discussed among Harlem-ites," he continued. "It is the attitude that helped to nurture the Harlem Renaissance and is currently unfolding the second one. Only this time we hope to establish in unquestionable terms our claim to Harlem; our contributions consecrated it."[1]

While this crusade marked another stage in a life spent seeking recognition of Harlem's special importance, Wilcox worked against a background in which such concerns had reached a new urgency. Harlem was facing two simultaneous and seemingly contradictory threats by the late 1980s, both of which undermined the hopes that longtime activists held for their neighborhood. On one hand, residents continued to fear that the gradual middle-class resettlement of Harlem would pick up speed, displacing residents and aspirations for community control. On the other, residents continued to suffer amid widespread physical dilapidation and entrenched poverty. Historic landmark designation, Wilcox hoped, would stem both forces by officially sanctioning Harlem's identity as a place apart, a space whose cultural and physical properties merited self-determination. "If respected as being full members of this city and nation, then, our right to define ourselves, name ourselves and govern ourselves will be respected too," Wilcox explained. "Such a designation may serve to increase the possibility that others will come to acknowledge and respect our legitimate claim to speak for, define and govern Harlem."[2]

Wilcox's pursuit marked an especially inspired attempt to stabilize Harlem in a period of deep uncertainty. Harlem's historic credentials were peerless. "I believe that a thematic nomination around the Harlem Renaissance is an important key to recognizing the crucial contribution of Harlem and its residents to the history of this country," Lehman wrote Wilcox, encouraging his dream.[3] But the possibility would remain only on paper. This scale of landmark recognition was unprecedented in its vastness, the effort simply too herculean. Wilcox hoped to truly define Harlem's place as a city within a city, marking a district that included brownstones and tenements alike, but such an outcome was beyond even his determination.

Wilcox's crusade to unify Harlem's hundreds of blocks as a single historic district nevertheless offered a symbolic last gasp of a radical spirit that had its origins in the late 1960s. Twenty years later, he still upheld a sweeping conception of Harlem that provided a dramatic counterpoint to the splintered reality of urbanism by the 1980s.[4] In an era of diminishing public resources, however, Wilcox's long-standing revolutionary fervor seemed increasingly quaint. He reminded his neighbors in 1989 "of our absolute obligation to become our own architects," but the realities of the era demanded different expectations.[5] While Harlemites increasingly evoked their past to promise an impending "Second Renaissance," the scale of their dreams took on a diminished scope and tone in the late 1980s and early 1990s. Hopes for a large-scale transformation of Harlem by its poorest residents had dimmed, as had aspirations that Harlemites could collectively own and develop the land underneath their feet. Instead of seeking the radical ideals of their predecessors, a new wave of community-based organizations emerged in the 1980s bearing the mantle of a new pragmatism.

Indeed, the austerity of this era brought limitations for New York's citizens, but so too did it spawn grassroots efforts that transformed the city's residential blocks. While federal cutbacks in the 1980s undermined the plans of early community development corporations (CDCs) like the Harlem

Commonwealth Council, the same diminishing federal role catalyzed the national emergence of a new wave of church-based CDCs that relied on funding from new sources. The Abyssinian Development Corporation (ADC), affiliated with Harlem's famed Abyssinian Baptist Church, and the Harlem Churches for Community Improvement (HCCI; later called Harlem Congregations for Community Improvement), a coalition of dozens of religious institutions, were the most prominent of such organizations in Harlem and among the most notable nationally. Their efforts epitomized the approach to community development that new CDCs adopted. At a time when Harlemites feared both impending takeover by outsiders and internal deterioration, these CDCs managed the transformation of the neighborhood. In doing so, they evinced a decidedly practical approach to Harlem's redevelopment, whether by rehabilitating the community's existing buildings, tacking a path of political moderation to ensure access to resources, or assembling an array of funding from a combination of public and private sources.

Fundamentally, these organizations followed an ascendant ideal of Harlem as a mixed-income community, a principle with roots in both the new funding landscape in which CDCs worked and a social belief that placed tremendous faith in the ameliorative power of economic integration. While Harlemites warily eyed the forces of gentrification at their door, community organizations themselves argued that more moderate- and middle-income residents could bring Harlem's renaissance. Though their work never neglected the community's most impoverished residents, these CDCs nonetheless constructed apartments and condominiums for economically diverse inhabitants at a newly enlarged scale. Middle-class homeowners acting in the private market played a crucial role in altering Harlem's demographic makeup in the 1980s and 1990s, to be sure. But the work of nonprofit community organizations likewise contributed to the neighborhood's economic transformation to an extent that observers have largely overlooked. Their emphasis on income diversification marked a dramatic departure from the notion that had once been the foundation of community development: that Harlem's very strength lay in its predominantly low-income, majority-minority population. Newly established CDCs produced hundreds of new homes, homes intended for Harlem's low-income residents but also for the economically secure families they hoped to attract to the neighborhood, to whom these organizations tied Harlem's future.

Harlem on the Brink

Understanding the vision that new CDCs pursued in Harlem first requires understanding the paradoxical place in which residents found themselves by the mid-1980s. Harlem teetered on the brink in this decade, confronted by both external and internal threats. As new middle-class residents gradually began to move uptown, longtime Harlemites watched warily, wondering if their blocks were the next to "gentrify." Yet Harlem also persisted as one of New York City's most impoverished communities and one of its most physically deteriorated. The multiple concerns that had stoked fears in the previous decade reached a new intensity in this one. Caught on the knife's edge between potentially dangerous isolationism and the equal threat of unchecked outside speculation, Harlem's lasting institutions, especially its churches, spawned new initiatives to manage the neighborhood's transformation in a time of change.

In this turbulent period, those who chronicled Harlem's changing landscape typically began with a question. The exact nature of the query reflected the particular viewpoint of the observer, but the premise remained consistent: Would Harlem survive the 1980s? In surveying the blocks north of Central Park, for example, Elliott Lee, a journalist with *Black Enterprise*, situated himself amid the community, wondering, "Will We Lose Harlem?" "Unlike any other black community in the world, Harlem exerts a profound influence on how we see ourselves," Lee wrote, linking Harlem's fate with the subjectivity of all African Americans. Peter Bailey, writing in *Ebony*, which largely appealed to a black middle-class audience, similarly framed the issue in terms suggesting the urgency of imminent loss. "Can Harlem Be Saved?" he asked. The necessity of trying to do so seemed self-evident to Bailey, though the answer remained uncertain. "Asking a true Harlemite whether Harlem can be saved is like asking the average Frenchman or Italian whether Paris or Rome can be saved," he offered.[6]

Even *New York* magazine, typically at the forefront of middle-class boosterism in New York's gentrifying neighborhoods, adopted a more reverential tone in the case of Harlem. Its query, "Can Harlem Be Born Again?" suggested the presumption of loss as well as the necessity of revival—resurrection was on the author's mind. Though the magazine's Craig Unger employed the language of real estate investment—Harlem was "underdeveloped," he wrote—

he assessed the costs of neighborhood change with evenhandedness. He offered the case of Wanda Kiely, a lifelong resident of Harlem, a single mother suffering from multiple sclerosis, and a realist who observed new middle-class residents warily. "The yuppies are coming! The yuppies are coming!" she told Unger. "They are not ostentatious. They try to fit in. I don't blame them. I'd like to shop at Zabar's myself." But as Kiely attempted to describe the reality of new neighbors, she grew upset. "Then her voice rises," Unger wrote, quoting Kiely. " 'But I'm shocked. I'm angry. I say, "How dare you. Your kind. You want to live here? How dare you?" ' " As Harlem began to transform economically, residents like Kiely, who had stayed during decades of disinvestment, feared they would be first to lose out. "There have been predictions of a rebirth in Harlem for years, all of them premature," Unger wrote. "If the current ones prove more accurate, just about everyone should be pleased. Everyone, that is, but the likes of Wanda Kiely."[7]

Concerns that had first materialized as the earliest middle-class investors found their way to Harlem in the late 1970s grew as their presence became more evident. If fears about the 1982 brownstone lottery as a tipping point had proven to be largely exaggerated, the reality of creeping gentrification remained nonetheless troubling from the viewpoint of Harlemites like Kiely. Yet accounts of early middle-class homeowners revealed the complicated demographic position most occupied—most were African American, and many were former Harlem residents. Unger described two such cases, a lawyer born in Harlem who had grown up in New Jersey, and a photography technician who had grown up in the neighborhood and recently returned as a homeowner. Many of their new neighbors were also African American, if not originally Harlemites. Craig Polite, a clinical psychologist with a home on West 146th Street, offered a particularly colorful portrait for a *Washington Post* profile of Harlem. As the reporter approached Polite's sixteen-room mansion—purchased for $50,000 in 1979 and still under renovation in 1984—Beethoven blasted from his second-floor windows. Polite's neighbors were busy scraping paint from their mantles too. Four other African American middle-class families had moved to the block, and a white teacher had also taken residence with renovation in mind.[8]

Black middle-class investors provided something of a conundrum for observers of Harlem. Their presence could easily be justified on the basis of race. For example, Charles Rangel, Harlem's longtime congressman, explained that many new residents were simply coming home to Harlem. "There are a lot of people out in the suburbs who are anxious to get back home," he said. Among new African American residents who did not actually claim Harlem as a birthplace, many nonetheless claimed it as a birthright, a symbolic hometown if not a literal one. A couple who purchased a townhouse in 1982 near the City College of New York had long dreamed of being homeowners in what they called the "capital of black America." Polite celebrated the history and heritage of Sugar Hill, the famed Harlem neighborhood he had made his home, and which, as he liked to point out, Duke Ellington also had once inhabited.[9]

But these new residents ultimately evinced much of the same self-interest that motivated many who sought historic homes in impoverished neighborhoods throughout New York, no matter their race. While Polite expressed some regret about the possibility that the renovation of his block would bring residential displacement of poor neighbors, for example, he ultimately dismissed such concerns. "Those people will have to go somewhere else," he explained, naturalizing their predicament. "You'll have nice people go, but that's the way of the world." The couple that bought the townhouse near City College, whose acquisition uprooted its longtime tenants, seemed surprised that these upstairs neighbors were not supportive of their renovation plans. "Our dream house—like much of the rest of our community—seemed far from dreamlike when we took it over. It was then a down-at-the-heels rooming house with eight intransigent tenants, none of whom had a glimmer of an interest in our plans to convert the building into a perfect urban living space," the owners said in 1984. Eviction took five months, during which the couple at least helped their former tenants find housing. Their tale emphasized the hopes such a home held for an ambitious family, but also the pecuniary potential a historic house represented as an asset. "Its market value has soared by 400 percent since we bought it," they explained to *Black Enterprise*.[10]

African Americans made equal claims on Harlem across income levels. Thus, while contemporary accounts suggested the direct costs inherent in gentrification by white or African American homeowners, observers tended to downplay the problem of economic displacement in order to highlight the more volatile, class-spanning issue of racial displacement. The *Baltimore Afro-American*, for instance, offered the alarming headline, "Harlem 'Renaissance' May Push Out Long-Time Black Residents." *Ebony* staged an intense racial drama, with Harlem lying vulnerable to its captors. "The external forces are organized around the menacing and ever-spreading specter of 'gentrification,' the take-over of low-income neighborhoods by middle-class whites returning to the city," the reporter explained. "The basis for this apprehension is the steady northward movement of whites to a position where their next logical move is into Harlem." The "invaders" had been on the march through the Upper West Side, turning its blocks "into havens of quiche-eating, boutique-shopping professionals." Now, Harlem's best assets could bring its own downfall. "Harlem, with its sturdy brownstones, strategic location and ready access to public transportation, sits there, like a black plum, ripe, some outsiders believe, for plucking." "The Yuppies Are Coming," *Ebony* blared in a different headline, "Young, Affluent Whites Are Taking Over Urban Ghettos."[11]

If such observations revealed real fears that Harlem would lose its place as the symbolic heart of black America, they existed in large part only as threats in the mid-1980s, not as present dangers. *New York* poked fun at the media's tendency to exaggerate the degree to which racial change was already underway. "Articles about young white professionals moving into Harlem almost all mention Jeffrey Roualt," the owner of a beautifully restored brownstone near Marcus Garvey Park. "Indeed, since Roualt moved there five years ago, publications all over the world have reported an influx of young white lawyers to Harlem." The roll was indeed long, encompassing papers from New York, Atlanta, Arizona, even England and France. "Yet the only white lawyer ever named is Jeffrey Roualt," the reporter noted.[12]

Roualt was certainly not alone among new white Harlem residents, nor did their relatively minor share of the population mean that further change was not a real possibility. As a study on gentrification prepared for the Harlem Urban Development Corporation (HUDC) in 1982 explained, "It could happen here." For the most part, however, neighborhood change remained most palpable on Harlem's fringes—in the Upper West Side and near Columbia University, and in the northern end of the Upper East Side—or elsewhere in the city, in neighborhoods like SoHo. In Harlem, social scientists found unusual increases in income and rent alongside increased residential sales in only a few areas—south of Marcus Garvey Park, along the western edge of Central Harlem, and in the blocks immediately north of Central Park—and no notable racial change. At mid-decade, gentrification remained a phenomenon that observers could trace in pockets throughout Harlem but one that had not yet dramatically changed its economic and racial composition. Upheaval from outside Harlem's borders remained a real and disruptive prospect that stoked fears in residents' minds, but not a full-fledged reality.[13]

More immediately, Harlem faced severe social, economic, and physical challenges within its borders. Economic upscaling and neighborhood deterioration were not mutually exclusive phenomena; indeed, both could thrive side by side. Abandonment had provided the brownstones that the city distributed by lottery and auction and contributed to the decline in property values that made acquisition possible for middle-class buyers entering Harlem's real estate market.[14] Yet in the mid-1980s, profound population loss created a more pressing dilemma than the possibility of rising property values. In the three community board districts that constituted Harlem, the city estimated a decline of almost a quarter of the area's population between 1970 and 1980, including a loss of a third of the population in Community Board 10, the area that corresponded most closely to Central Harlem. The *New York Times*, employing a more expansive definition of Central Harlem, calculated population loss exceeding 40 percent in the same period.[15] The demographic characteristics within that loss suggested troubling trends as well. Forty-four percent of residents with annual income between $15,000 and $20,000 departed the neighborhood. Almost 6,000 remaining families earned more than $20,000, but more than three times that many households earned less than $5,000 annually at a time when the poverty line for four-person families exceeded $8,000. Harlem was growing substantially poorer.[16]

Meanwhile, the housing abandonment that marked the 1970s continued apace in the new decade. By 1984, the city owned 1,669 buildings in Harlem, more than a thousand of them vacant. Eighteen percent of Harlem's 57,000 housing units were vacant in 1980, one 1986 estimate suggested, and the city had sealed up an additional 20,000 housing units in the first six years of the decade. While Central Harlem contained only 2 percent of New York City's housing stock, it encompassed one-fifth of the city's abandoned residential buildings. In assessing the decline of the African American population in the neighborhood, one reporter matter-of-factly noted the "virtual emptying of wide areas in central Harlem." Historian David Levering Lewis, whose 1981 *When Harlem Was in Vogue* lushly depicted the neighborhood's golden age during the Harlem Renaissance, offered a more poetic, and tragic, depiction of Harlem's present state to *Times* readers. "History reserves a special paradox for great, dead cultures: They survive largely as resonant place names," Lewis began. "That is Harlem's apotheosis now." Harlem had suffered a "slow, sleazy death in the late 1970's," he wrote. Now, in Lewis's eyes, its greatest blocks were falling to pieces. "On once shimmering, ostentatious 'Sugar Hill,' the apartment buildings are fortified or empty, their canopies and doormen long gone, their lobby tapestries stolen and vases smashed." Harlem had suffered no single devastating battle in its streets, but many smaller ones had taken their toll. "Harlem today resembles nothing so much as France after the Great War," Lewis suggested.[17]

If for some the Great War had already shaken Harlem's brick and stone facades, they could never have foretold the tragedies that were still to come. The *New York Amsterdam News* plastered the arrival of one new danger across its front page in February 1986. "Crack, Super Drug Hits New York City Streets," ran the headline, and readers learned that crack, a smokeable, fast-acting, and highly concentrated form of cocaine, had already become ubiquitous among Harlem's dealers and users. Police reported that 90 percent of the cocaine they uncovered in West Harlem came in the form of crack. A few months earlier, Drug Enforcement Administration agents had busted a "crack factory" in Harlem, an operation that produced more than two pounds of crack a day, an amount with a street value of half a million dollars. The mix of abandoned buildings and a burgeoning crack industry produced a dystopian reality when the sun went down. On 140th Street between Adam Clayton Powell Jr. and Frederick Douglass Boulevards, the *Times* reported, "the once-grand brownstones are crumbling backdrops for crack selling. But they are far from vacant. As night draws near, the 'vampires come out,' as one resident puts it. In nearly every doorway, clusters of teen-age lookouts scrutinize customers," the reporter described. "Inside virtually every building on the block are young guards with guns. Their age and their inexperience with the weapons are two reasons for the sharp increase in the shootings and in other violence in those neighborhoods."[18]

Reporters connected the rise of crack to the other epidemic that was sweeping across New York, the acquired immunodeficiency syndrome (AIDS) crisis. Half of New York's AIDS cases were linked to intravenous drug use by 1988, and crack offered a high for those who sought to avoid sharing needles. But plenty of users still passed IV needles filled with heroin in Harlem's abandoned buildings, and sex became a well-known means of procuring crack cocaine. AIDS spread quickly. If the disease had been publicly associated with gay, white men downtown in its first years, by mid-decade experts had begun to realize the speed with which it was moving through Harlem and other predominantly minority neighborhoods. Under a thousand cases had been reported in Harlem by 1986, a number that likely undercounted actual victims. Within five years, health officials guessed, the number of reported cases would approach 5,000. Journalists recognized this emergency but Harlem institutions were slow to respond, whether due to denial, inadequate resources, or overtaxed services. Meanwhile, black men were getting the disease two and a half times more frequently than their white counterparts, and black women were contracting AIDS at a rate twelve and a half times that of white women. AIDS had become the leading killer among African American and Latino men in New York between the ages of twenty-five and forty-four by mid-1988. Twin scourges were ripping through already struggling blocks uptown. As the *Amsterdam News* chillingly titled one report, "Drugs, AIDS Killing Off Harlem Youths." The neighborhood seemed on the verge of implosion.[19]

Only a few landmarks escaped the negative light that Lewis cast on contemporary Harlem. The Apollo Theater, in financial trouble in 1981, still stood on 125th Street. The famed Dunbar Apartments and the townhouses of Strivers' Row remained, once home to many of Harlem's most celebrated residents but now in a diminished state. And Harlem's "venerable old churches" persisted, seemingly innocent of the transformations around them, "present[ing] proud facades to the public and declining attendance to their pastors."[20] Harlem was a city of churches. Literally dozens dotted its blocks, some in converted storefronts, others in neat brick buildings that lined up dutifully with their neighbors, and still others in stone, with strong bell towers anchoring their corner lots.[21] Early in the 1980s, J. Max Bond Jr., by this time a city planning commissioner and chair of Columbia University's architecture department, wondered if Harlem's churches were doing enough to face down the neighborhood's crises. "We have a history of churches, fraternal organizations, and building societies pooling resources, but less and less of that is happening," Bond said. "If we continue to let Harlem fall apart, then it will become a white middle-class community."[22]

But by mid-decade, Harlem's churches could do little to avoid the neighborhood's most vexing problems, for they had a heartbreakingly close vantage point. Preston Washington, the pastor at Memorial Baptist Church on West 115th Street, described the quotidian in a time of high inflation and high unemployment. "Those of us who live and labor in the Harlems, Bedford Stuyvesants and South Bronx's of this Metropolitan area know first hand that hungry bellies and frustrated lives represent the signs and symbols of our times," he wrote in late 1982. Next door to his church, Washington watched the stunning deterioration of the large apartment building at 100 St. Nicholas Avenue. "It was the twilight zone for 100," Washington wrote. "Dope-addicted youth and drug-dispensing adults thrust the building and the neighborhood into chaos. The building itself suffered through all too many winters of despair, leaving busting pipes to flood entire apartments." With no other options, residents had taken to using their kitchen stoves for heat. Likewise, Abyssinian Baptist Church, Harlem's best-known congregation, stood sturdily on West 138th Street between Lenox Avenue and Adam Clayton Powell Jr. Boulevard, just a couple of blocks from troubled 140th Street. But congregants saw the present reality of Harlem every time they left church. "I can look at 138th Street buildings that were completely filled and now have only 40 to 50 percent capacity," Abyssinian's executive minister, Rev. Calvin O. Butts III told a reporter in 1985. Virtually the entire stretch of 138th Street facing the church, the block's north side, was empty, city owned, or both. Six facades hid city-owned vacant buildings, and three more vacant buildings remained in private ownership but behind in tax payments. Only six out of twenty-two lots held any residents at all, and only two of those six buildings remained under private ownership. Seven vacant lots pitted the block, like missing teeth.[23]

In this context, Harlem's churches increased their commitment to redevelopment out of both physical and spiritual necessity. Washington felt hemmed in. The building at 100 St. Nicholas Avenue was an accident away from a conflagration and just on the other side of the west wall of his church. The building on the church's east side, 135 West 115th Street, contained fewer tenants, many long-term residents, but the landlord had left it for dead. Washington feared the physical consequences of letting the apartment buildings rot, but likewise saw them as "the mission field next door," in his words. He sought to gain control of 100 St. Nicholas Avenue, rehabilitate it, and put it under tenant ownership, and to enroll 135 West 115th Street in the Tenant Interim Lease program so tenants could eventually own their units. These strategies were a means of bringing Memorial's ministry into the broader Harlem community.[24] The minister of Abyssinian at this time, Dr. Samuel D. Proctor, likewise worried that the physical deterioration of Harlem threatened the quality of life of Harlem-based congregants, many of whom were elderly. The church thus began to pursue an initial housing venture in the early 1980s, a one-hundred-unit project for these and other senior and disabled tenants. Abyssinian considered sites directly across from the church and nearby, before settling on a city-owned site on 131st Street between Fifth and Lenox Avenues, where the church eventually constructed an apartment building called Abyssinian Towers.[25]

These initial forays into housing development seeded broader efforts to confront Harlem's troubled landscape. Washington had been born in East Harlem, worshipped in a storefront church, and left to attend Williams College before returning to pursue a doctorate in education at Columbia University. He had begun preaching at thirteen, seeking a self-described "practical theology" that he eventually found at Memorial Baptist Church, which he joined as the pastor in 1976. While the church's engagement with its immediate neighbors matched the congregation's moderate size, Washington sought a broader involvement that could stem housing problems on a greater scale. In December 1986, he joined more than fifty other congregations to form HCCI, an ecumenical coalition that encompassed an array of predominantly—but not exclusively—African American church leaders from throughout Harlem, and that Washington led as president. HCCI's first public act involved protests against a bus depot that the Metropolitan Transit Authority planned for West Harlem, a project that Washington decried as a health nuisance and waste of resources. Washington called for the project budget to be redirected instead to new housing construction in the area, a concern that reflected the larger mission of HCCI to address the neighborhood's simultaneous threats. "We . . . are very much concerned about the lack of affordable housing for the people of Harlem," he wrote in a 1987 *Amsterdam News* editorial. "We are also determined to prevent the displacement of the members of our churches through the gentrification of our neighborhood."[26]

Abyssinian likewise expanded its work at Abyssinian Towers into a broader effort that sought to rebuild the surrounding neighborhood. The church had a long and illustrious history as an advocate for social change in Harlem and New York City. Adam Clayton Powell Sr. had moved Abyssinian to Harlem in the 1920s, using his powerful pulpit to advocate for civil rights. His son and successor, Adam Clayton Powell Jr., pursued a more public role as pastor, leader of campaigns against racially discriminatory hiring on 125th Street, and longtime congressman from Harlem's district. Proctor, the church's senior minister since Powell's death in 1972, and Butts, his executive minister, maintained a parallel contrast between gravitas and charisma, poise and bluster. Proctor encouraged congregants to engage with the dilemmas outside the church's doors but skirted politics and confrontational protest. Butts, who took over the pastorate in 1989, sought political involvement and openly challenged Harlem and city leaders.[27]

Abyssinian's work in housing reflected the concern both leaders shared for Harlem's broader community. While their public statements evinced fundamentally different outlooks on engagement, together they encompassed the range of issues confronting Harlem. Proctor saw Abyssinian's task as one of healing wounded souls. "We are going to take some of these homeless young women with children and try to see what love can do for them," he explained. Butts, too, insisted on attention to individuals, not just their homes. "Where is the single mother with two kids going to go? Where is the senior citizen with a modest income going to go?" he asked. But he described the problem in political terms. "Gentrification will destroy a black political base. The poor people who are here deserve to remain." With support from church leadership, volunteers already at work on the senior housing project formalized their housing ministry in 1987, an effort that later became known as the Abyssinian Development Corporation. Karen Phillips, a member of the congregation and landscape architect, served as the de facto leader and became executive director when the organization incorporated in 1989.[28]

While these efforts developed from the experiences of individual congregations reacting to their immediate environments, over time they came to take responsibility for far larger stretches of territory in their respective communities. ADC, for example, defined its range as extending from West 134th Street to West 141st Street and from Lenox Avenue to Edgecombe Avenue. The presence of Abyssinian Towers on 131st Street staked the church's claim on that stretch as well. HCCI, with an array of members across Harlem, claimed responsibility for the Bradhurst area, a Harlem neighborhood north of Abyssinian delineated by 139th Street, 155th Street, Adam Clayton Powell Jr. Boulevard, and Bradhurst and Edgecombe Avenues. Bradhurst encompassed an especially impoverished portion of Harlem. An analysis of the 1990 U.S. Census noted that Bradhurst contained the poorest census tract in the entire city, a five-block area where almost 75 percent of residents lived in poverty and only 33 percent of adults had or were seeking jobs.[29] HCCI joined with established Harlem organizations in late 1988 to propose the redevelopment of the area, an effort that was to include HUDC, the Harlem Business Alliance, and others in an entity called the Consortium for Central Harlem Development (CCHD). Their proposal marked an ambitious, $120 million vision for an area that the city had already designated for a much more modest effort. The ensuing power struggle stretched over the next year, but ultimately CCHD gained the responsibility of overseeing one of New York's largest redevelopment projects during the following decade.[30]

HCCI and ADC represented a new form of CDC in Harlem, the result of a nationwide shift effected in large measure by Reagan-era federal spending cuts. While early CDCs, like the Harlem Commonwealth Council, had grown rapidly in a period when they could count on generous federal support, they suffered profoundly with the elimination of key agencies like the Community Services Administration. Broad cuts undermined the means by which cities typically paid for such necessities as low-income housing construction, job training, and mass transit. The budget of the U.S. Department of Housing and Urban Development, for example, plummeted to $10.2 billion in 1988, less than a third of its 1980 budget, and housing-specific resources declined from almost $27 billion in 1980 to less than $4 billion at the end of Ronald Reagan's second term. Aid to cities in general diminished by 60 percent, with cities over 300,000 in population seeing the federal share of their funding decline from 22 percent in 1980 to 6 percent in 1989.[31]

Without dependable federal support for housing construction, but with an acute need for housing development in many cities, a new wave of CDCs paradoxically emerged in the 1980s. A 1987 estimate suggested that over a thousand new CDCs had formed in the six preceding years. As nonprofits, CDCs provided a bridge between available public funding, now predominantly at the state and local levels, and private sources that increasingly played a role in housing development. With bases in long-standing institutions such as the African American church, such organizations claimed legitimacy as community representatives and maintained a persistent physical presence amid deteriorating blocks. Churches had long played an essential role in development in New York, but such activities proliferated in the years preceding the formation of HCCI and ADC. East Brooklyn Churches, South Bronx Churches, the Association of Brooklyn Clergy for Community Development, the Southeast Queens Clergy for Community Empowerment, and Bronx Shepherds Restoration Corporation, all coalitions of multiple churches, formed by the mid-1980s, and several churches throughout the five boroughs launched individual CDCs akin to Abyssinian's effort. Programs like East Brooklyn Churches' Nehemiah Homes, a homeownership initiative that eventually produced 2,400 row houses, established church-based CDCs as key players in the redevelopment of New York City's neighborhoods.[32]

While HCCI and ADC formed in response to the specific conditions of Harlem, then, they were also part of a much larger movement. Within a few years, each had gained responsibility for the stewardship and development of a broad swath of Harlem. Between them, their domain covered nearly half of Central Harlem north of 125th Street. Both organizations professed a comprehensive strategy. "We're talking about neighborhood revitalization, not simply housing renovation," Washington explained. Abyssinian similarly projected housing development alongside social services, economic development, drug rehabilitation, and care for teenage mothers. While neither CDC focused exclusively on housing development, however, the physical reconstruction of Harlem's residential blocks would mark their most visible impact in a neighborhood undergoing dramatic change. "We're talking about making the area beautiful," Washington said.[33] Their vision for who should fill these homes marked an idealistic dream for Harlem's future, one that differed dramatically from idealistic dreams long past.

The Promise of Economic Integration

In a neighborhood confronted with both internal decline and the threat of external upheaval, CDCs could take any of a number of paths. They could adopt a defensive stance, barring access to Harlem to prevent newcomers from disrupting existing residents. Or they could open the neighborhood's gates wide, hoping that new investors would redevelop Harlem for multiple constituencies. In the late 1980s, however, Harlem's CDCs chose to occupy a middle ground, attempting to manage change in the neighborhood by accommodating both longtime Harlemites and the increasing number of middle-class families knocking on Harlem's door. As Abyssinian explained early on, for example, ADC's goal was "balancing proposed development" while "preserving existing residents."[34] This approach marked a significant departure from the notion that Harlem's revival would grow from its existing, predominantly low-income population, a central idea that had motivated community development advocates in the 1960s and 1970s. The movement to a mixed-income ideal drew especially from developments in the social sciences in this period. With observers increasingly focused on the appearance of an "underclass" in Harlem and other poverty-stricken neighborhoods, community organizations seized on economic integration as a panacea. Rather than viewing the middle class as a looming threat, CDCs placed their faith in income diversification as a means of addressing Harlem's socioeconomic crises.

Mixed-income housing appeared in the plans of Harlem's new CDCs from the outset. In Bradhurst, the city's Department of Housing Preservation and Development proposed 1,200 units of housing in 1988, targeted at residents making no more than $25,000 a year. But CCHD, the coalition that included HCCI, instead envisioned a community with 2,256 newly developed units for residents earning from $11,000 to $35,000 a year. The difference was subtle, but significant. While the city's plan would accommodate incomes exceeding those of many current Bradhurst residents, its vision encompassed a significantly lower income band than did the plan of the ministers and included fewer housing options—the city intended to develop only rental units, while CCHD planned to offer rental housing as well as owner-occupied units. Under the CCHD plan, 834 units were to be reserved for existing residents and 364 units for the homeless. But almost as many were to house families with greater means. Four hundred twelve units were to accommodate moderate-income families in rental or cooperatively owned homes, and 646 units were to be middle-class condominiums. Subsequent plans expanded on this idea, with a mid-1989 proposal encompassing 2,800 units, half as cooperatives and condominiums and half as rentals that would convert to ownership. The ministers intended that Bradhurst would contain decent housing across a range of income levels, but a growing amount for the middle class. Their 1989 scheme projected that the number of residents earning more than

$35,000 would rise by nearly 50 percent, from 8.5 percent to a planned 12.4 percent.[35]

ADC proceeded without a comprehensive plan but nonetheless pursued a vision of economic diversity in neighboring blocks that, like the Bradhurst project, encompassed both existing and new residents. Abyssinian's first projects targeted the neighborhood's most vulnerable inhabitants. Soon after completing plans for senior housing at Abyssinian Towers, the church began renovations nearby to create a twenty-four-unit transitional apartment building for homeless families, called Abyssinian House. The volunteers who would become ADC also planned housing for at-risk young men and for teenage mothers, while beginning to explore options for constructing housing affordable to low- and moderate-income families. And in the late 1980s, the church initiated discussions to build middle-income, owner-occupied housing. This became the church's third development, West One Three One Plaza, begun in 1989 and involving the creation of thirty-four one-, two-, and three-bedroom homes across from Abyssinian Towers. The CDC sought to attract families earning between $(1990)24,000 and $54,000 to the 131st Street block that ADC had begun to reconstruct.[36]

Such plans marked a vision of Harlem's future consistent with HCCI and ADC's goal to "balance" development that seemed inevitable by the late 1980s and turn it to the advantage of existing residents. In assessing Harlem's stock of abandoned buildings, for example, Abyssinian observed that they represented both a potential danger in the hands of speculators and an asset that the CDC could shape. "Many city owned structures in the Harlem community are being made available," leaders wrote. "Institutions in this community like ours need to have mechanisms in place to participate in this and other programs in which developers are being invited into Harlem so that we can guide the redevelopment of this community." Staff overseeing the Bradhurst project echoed ADC's goal of "balancing proposed development" in advocating the use of economically diverse housing as a means of achieving "social and economic balance" in the neighborhood. In describing the mix of homes that would fill Bradhurst's blocks, planners explained their intention to diversify the neighborhood while retaining longtime residents. "The Bradhurst plan involves a variety of conceptual premises that need to be stated," they explained at an early public meeting. "First is the need to develop an income-mixed community without displacing existing tenants."[37]

Income diversification did not originate as a strategy in the late 1980s, to be sure. Indeed, the emergence of economic integration as a planning goal had paralleled racial integration as a means of diversifying socially stratified American neighborhoods. Even later proponents' use of "balance" recalled discussions that had arisen at midcentury, when urban renewal remained ascendant. The "balanced neighborhood" emerged as an alternative to the architectural, economic, and racial homogeneity of large-scale redevelopment, a goal "with many meanings," explained housing expert Elizabeth Wood in 1960, but one that remained constant: "It *always* means mixture or heterogeneity of population . . . [and] also signifies that this heterogeneity is desirable." Heterogeneity offered a counterpoint to racial segregation, a "wrong both practically and morally," and to economic segregation, "equally bad both practically and morally."[38]

Heterogeneity as an end in itself, a concept imbued with intrinsic value, marked a through line in the post–urban renewal period, a vestige of racial liberalism that ran counter to the more radical ideals of the community control movement. The New York State Urban Development Corporation (UDC), for instance, maintained economic integration as a goal in the projects it built throughout the state. UDC's 70 percent moderate- or middle-income, 20 percent low-income, and 10 percent senior citizen balance in part grew from leaders' sense that the failures of public housing arose from its economic segregation. UDC maintained a similar income mix in its highly visible redevelopment of New York City's Roosevelt Island and, in Harlem, at the twin towers that made up the Schomburg Plaza project at Fifth Avenue and 110th Street in the early 1970s. HUDC loosely adopted its parent agency's approach in the projects it sponsored throughout Harlem, which included low-income housing, housing for seniors, single-room-occupancy housing, and, by the mid-1980s, condominium development targeted at middle-income buyers.[39] This trend toward middle-class homeownership in Harlem built on a longer history that dated back as early as the 1910s, when African Americans came to settle Harlem in large numbers and the neighborhood claimed an economically diverse cast that had diminished in recent decades.[40]

The pursuit of such economically diverse housing had roots in both the history of progressive housing policy and the history of Harlem, but it gained new prominence among community developers in the late 1980s with the research of University of Chicago sociologist William Julius Wilson. Wilson's *The Truly Disadvantaged,* published in October 1987, offered a complex analysis of the factors underlying the rise of a so-called underclass in American cities, a group that Wilson characterized as "individuals who lack training and skills and either experience long-term unemployment or are not members of the labor force, individuals who are engaged in street crime and other forms of aberrant behavior, and families that experience long-term spells of poverty and/or welfare dependency." Wilson described the emergence of such a group "outside the mainstream of the American occupational system" as a consequence of broad structural forces in predominantly African American urban neighborhoods.[41] While communities like Harlem had always held a significant portion of residents living in poverty, Wilson contended, the concentration of that population grew substantially in the 1960s due to shifts in the labor market from "goods-producing to service-producing industries," greater wage polarization, and the relocation of jobs out of city centers. Minority urban residents without extensive formal training increasingly found themselves without skills to obtain work in ascendant labor sectors, and available unskilled jobs moved increasingly out of geographic reach.[42]

Alongside rising joblessness, the social composition of majority-minority urban neighborhoods changed as a consequence of African American middle-class migration from the inner city. Wilson ascribed this phenomenon to both increasing movement of African Americans into "mainstream" occupations and the lowering of barriers that had previously limited the housing choice of middle-class African Americans. Such families had provided a "social buffer," Wilson argued, "that could deflect the full impact of the kind of prolonged and increased joblessness that plagued inner-city neighborhoods in the 1970s and early 1980s." This "buffer" included institutions that supported residents in times of high unemployment and "role models" who emphasized the importance of education, employment, and "family stability." Without middle-class residents in neighborhoods like Harlem, Wilson wrote, "a sudden and/or prolonged increase in joblessness . . . creates a ripple effect resulting in an exponential increase in related forms of social dislocation."[43]

Wilson's argument in *The Truly Disadvantaged* hinged on an analysis of the social effects of economic homogeneity in the bounded space of a neighborhood. The "massive joblessness, flagrant and open lawlessness, and low-achieving schools" that Wilson observed in high-poverty environments yielded greater disconnection between residents and those who resided elsewhere. The consequence, he argued, was "social isolation," a term that Wilson offered as an alternative to the controversial notion of a "culture of poverty." Whereas "culture of poverty" assumed destructive characteristics internalized by the urban poor, "social isolation" explained social problems as the outcome of structural forces. Social isolation worsened the problems already present in many inner-city neighborhoods, Wilson argued, such as unemployment, deficient education, low marriage rates, and crime. "Social isolation . . . not only implies that contact between groups of different class and/or racial backgrounds is either lacking or has become increasingly intermittent," Wilson wrote, "but that the nature of this contact enhances the effects of living in a highly concentrated poverty area." As Wilson explained, neighborhoods like Harlem suffered "concentration effects," the negative social outcomes of an increasingly poorer population within a defined space.[44]

Wilson's work quickly reached a high level of visibility, not only in public discourse but also in the kinds of communities he chronicled, including Harlem. The substantial initial impact of *The Truly Disadvantaged* arose in part because its mix of structural and cultural explanations challenged both liberal and conservative orthodoxy—which tended to highlight the effects of racism in the case of the former and behavioral explanations for poverty in the case of the latter. Wilson had already emerged as a prominent public intellectual with his previous book, *The Declining Significance of Race,* published in 1978. He received a MacArthur Foundation Fellowship, a so-called genius grant, in 1987. Unsurprisingly, *The Truly Disadvantaged* garnered a front-page review in the *New York Times Book Review* and an interview in the *Times* in which Wilson articulated many of the book's major arguments. In Harlem, leaders invited Wilson to present his research as the keynote speaker at a major March 1988 conference organized by HUDC, entitled "Building Harlem for Harlem through Unity: A Community-Wide Conference on Development." Background materials distributed to participants highlighted Wilson's work, including his recently published *The Truly Disadvantaged.* Sessions debated Harlem's economic and social dilemmas as well as its future direction. Many of the major figures in Harlem's development during the previous two decades participated, including Wilcox, Alice Kornegay, and James Dowdy. The next generation of community developers attended too. Immediately following Wilson's keynote, Abyssinian's Butts and Washington, of Memorial Baptist Church and HCCI, sat side by side on their own panel, entitled "The Role of Religious Organizations, Businesses, and Political Leaders in the Redevelopment of Harlem."[45]

If Wilson's analysis served as a diagnosis of problems already under way in American cities, for many observers it also became a prescription. This proved true in Harlem as well as in urban policy at large. Wilson's major argument—that joblessness and outward migration of the African American middle class had created unprecedented concentrations of poverty, and that those concentrations in turn worsened the effects of poverty—suggested a logical corollary. If the lack of middle-class residents in neighborhoods like Harlem had worsened those communities' maladies, then the solution to such maladies, many assumed, lay in the pursuit of economic reintegration. While proponents had earlier backed income integration on moral grounds, in this period they increasingly cast it in socially ameliorative, even socially deterministic, terms. Indeed, several of the resolutions that participants adopted at "Building Harlem for Harlem through Unity" involved the neighborhood's housing, and such statements emphasized economic diversification, using Wilsonian language as justification. "The Harlem community is in favor of mixed income housing," one resolution read, "which will impact positively on the schools and education; eliminate isolation of the poor from the job network; and provide formal and informal social controls." A second resolution opposed building housing only for the poor and homeless. "The Harlem community is unalterably opposed to economically segregated housing," it stated. "Sections and neighborhoods relegated to lowest income and homeless individuals reinforce underclass patterns of behavior, deterioration and flight of moderate and middle income individuals."[46]

CDCs looked to mixed-income housing out of a belief that returning middle-class families would provide a foundational base in the community, undoing the "concentration effects" that had arisen as a result of high poverty. ADC's West One Three One Plaza, the first middle-class homeownership project to be built by either HCCI or ADC, especially exemplified this intention (see Figure 5.1). "West One Three One Plaza . . . reinforces our concept of having a mixture of income levels in the housing units we provide," Butts

FIGURE 5.1. West One Three One Plaza, located on West 131st Street and completed in
1993. The first middle-class homeownership project built by ADC, these condominiums
exemplified the ascendant strategy among CDCs, which sought to attract the middle class
back to Harlem out of a belief that a mixed-income population would ameliorate the
social and economic effects of poverty.

explained in 1993. Units were to remain affordable, with subsidies for those who qualified, but backers explicitly sought economically secure, working families. Though four one-bedroom homes were available in the rehabilitated, formerly vacant and city-owned buildings, the majority of units provided more spacious quarters, including thirty larger units with two bedrooms and two duplex units with three bedrooms. Advertising materials promoted Central Harlem's proximity to day care, public and private schools, and buses and subways connecting uptown with downtown and "midtown Manhattan department stores." Amenities attracted buyers who could afford to choose based on comfort and quality, not simply a need for shelter. Units featured "oak-strip flooring," and kitchens boasted oak cabinets and mica counters. Closets were "abundant and spacious," bathrooms "elegant," floor plans "unique," and ceilings "high." The duplexes included fireplace mantles, all homes had intercoms for security, and the buildings contained their own laundry facilities. The units were not opulent or excessive, to be sure, but designed to be equivalent to what a middle-class family might seek elsewhere in the city.[47]

In appealing to such families, ADC seemingly had in mind those who might already be considering a move to Harlem, especially the enterprising African Americans who made up the leading edge of gentrification in the neighborhood. Race remained decidedly—and necessarily—latent as CDCs pursued a mixed-income future for Harlem, but advertising materials subtly targeted the African American middle class, the absence of which Wilson highlighted in his work. Though ads touted units' amenities, Harlem itself remained a prominently advertised feature as developers sought to attract buyers. "Become a Harlem Homeowner!" promotional flyers encouraged, asking buyers to claim their place in the neighborhood. "Take stock in your community" marked an even more personal appeal, drawing on the sentimental associations many middle-class African Americans claimed upon moving to Harlem. Advertisements emphasized the nearby cultural institutions that recorded Harlem's history as an African American community, including the Studio Museum, Apollo Theater, Schomburg Center for Research in Black Culture, and National Black Theater. One advertisement for West One Three One Plaza pictured a smiling young African American couple, professionally dressed and in a domestic environment with pictures hanging on the wall—an image reflecting that of potential residents.[48]

The condominium project signaled the role that CDCs intended new middle-class migrants to play as they attempted to "balance" Harlem's residential landscape. Advertisements appealed to homeowners' independence, promising the ideal of individual control. "Be your own landlord!" they proclaimed, and "Stop Paying Rent!" But CDCs also asked potential residents to share in the collective project of improvement. Ads detailed the buildings' role—and thus, that of the homeowners—in the reconstruction of the surrounding neighborhood. The development was "part of [ADC's] initiative to restore the block," advertisements explained. "Renovation is scheduled for 13 additional buildings on the block." One early homeowner at West One Three One Plaza demonstrated the commitment that ADC hoped residents would make, echoing those who had purchased the twelve brownstones the city lotteried in the early 1980s. "I fell in love with it the moment I saw it," Hope McGarrity said of her new home. "I knew it had to be mine." As McGarrity showed a reporter around, her enthusiasm suggested tremendous pride in the recently refurbished unit. "I like being able to throw back the blinds," McGarrity said. "You should see it when the sunlight comes in in the morning."[49]

Planners remained realistic about the scope of problems Harlemites faced. For example, comprehensive social services formed a central part of the Bradhurst plan, a major goal that proponents prioritized alongside income diversity and homeownership. CCHD emphasized job training, educational programs, day care, and health centers. Plans included a "community service center" that would serve as a hub for programming and service provision. ADC likewise described a "comprehensive approach," including social services for formerly homeless families that moved into its properties.[50]

But alongside such individual-level approaches, proponents placed tremendous hope in the belief that the growing middle-class population in developments like West One Three One Plaza would yield profound socioeconomic benefits. Explanations of the intended structural effects of mixed-income housing directly appropriated Wilson's own language, imagining a future for Harlem with diminished "social dislocation." Many such descriptions involved "stability," portraying Harlem as an architectural frame with deficient supports, a metaphor that suggested Wilson's own argument that those in communities with high concentrations of poverty "seldom have sustained contact with friends or relatives in the more stable areas of the city or in the suburbs." Planners wrote that the goal of Bradhurst redevelopment was to "stabilize the neighborhood by creating an income-mixed community including working class, business and professional people with emphasis on home ownership." Paraphrasing Phillips of ADC, one reporter recorded the hopes contained in West One Three One Plaza: "The goal . . . was to get middle-income house-owners to the area because they would bring a stability that low-income housing could not."[51]

Planners described economically diverse housing as a solution to Harlem's deepest challenges. New "working and middle income households . . . will expedite the stabilization of the area and pull the torn social fabric together," Bradhurst participants explained, conceiving of Harlem as a damaged textile with ruptures that required mending. They noted the "economic isolation that results in poverty and its accompanying social pathologies," invoking the "social isolation" of *The Truly Disadvantaged*. Alluding to Wilson's argument that the loss of the middle class removed crucial role models as a "social buffer," planners explained the introduction of professionals and working people "as a means to foster acceptable social norms by reducing the proliferation of drugs, crime, and related social ills."[52]

ADC later tied Harlem's income diversity to its very possibility of persisting as a community. "A basic conviction guides ADC's Housing Initiative," staff wrote, "for a community to have viability it must have a housing stock that offers opportunities for the participation of diverse groups—low-income, moderate-income, formerly homeless, renters and home owners."[53] Economic integration had emerged as the predominant approach to reconstructing both Harlem's physical and its social environments. This marked a significant refutation of past hopes that Harlem's renaissance would grow from its majority low-income population. Instead, CDCs placed their faith in middle-class resettlement. Rather than pursuing radical transformation, proponents forged a new pragmatism as they brought their vision into physical form.

New Pragmatism Uptown

By the mid-1990s, as the earliest projects of ADC and HCCI took shape, the landscape around Abyssinian Baptist Church and the Bradhurst neighborhood had begun to change, if slowly. Gradually both CDCs built a range of

FIGURE 5.2. By the mid-1990s, ADC and HCCI's efforts had begun to bear fruit, as the completion of their initial projects changed the landscape around Abyssinian Baptist Church and the Bradhurst neighborhood, providing a range of housing options for different incomes. Pictured is Bradhurst Phase I, Site 1B, located at 239–251 West 145th Street and completed in 1993, with apartments for moderate-, low-, and very low-income residents.

housing developments, some targeted at low-income tenants and others at moderate- and middle-income families, some for owners and many for renters. Bradhurst's first phase encompassed 290 units on 145th Street and along Frederick Douglass Boulevard (see Figure 5.2). One hundred fifteen units targeted moderate-income residents, with two-bedroom units for incomes ranging from $(1989)23,000 to $40,500; 112 units were for low-income families, with two-bedroom units targeting those earning $16,380 to $24,300; and 58 units were to house very low-income Harlemites, with two-bedroom units for those earning up to $15,245.[54] HCCI's Rev. Dr. John J. Sass Plaza included 94 rental units, half for the formerly homeless and half for low-income tenants. The 77-unit HCCI Plaza I and 59-unit HCCI Plaza II likewise housed low-income tenants in Bradhurst, while the 281 units of Bradhurst's

Phase II maintained the low- and moderate-income balance of the first phase.[55]

ADC, too, made its mixed-income vision a reality, supporting low-income tenants in its seventy-one-unit Hattie Dodson Houses, in the forty-two-unit George W. Lewis Houses, and in the sixty-six-unit Lilian Upshur Houses, with 30 percent of units reserved for homeless families. In other projects, ADC housed moderate-income residents. For example, the Samuel D. Proctor Apartments, across from the church, included twenty-five affordable rental units for a range of incomes. West One Three One Plaza offered thirty-four units for sale. ADC acted as the marketing partner for twenty-four rehabilitated brownstones on West 126th and West 127th Streets, intended for middle-income owner-occupants. And on Astor Row, the stretch of West 130th Street famed for its unique wooden porches, Abyssinian participated in the rehabilitation of two vacant homes into eight limited-equity cooperatives for low- and moderate-income families.[56] The completion of such projects marked more than a culmination of the work Harlem's church-based CDCs had administered since the mid-1980s. As they rebuilt blocks with economic integration in mind, building by building, the CDCs also made physical an approach to community development overwhelmingly characterized by its economic, political, and architectural pragmatism. The landscape they produced was increasingly fueled by hybridized funding sources that merged the public and the private, marked by an emphasis on political realism over idealism, and characterized by a focus on reusing Harlem's existing buildings.

In reconstructing Harlem's blocks, CDCs responded to the exigencies of housing development in a time of diminished federal aid. Their interest in mixed-income housing coincided with a funding context that increasingly emphasized—and accommodated—such approaches. This was a distinct irony of the decline of the federal role in local housing development. Until the Reagan administration drastically reduced its financial support of American cities, federal programs remained a vital engine for the construction and renovation of low-income housing in New York. By 1980, for example, New Yorkers had built or rehabbed as many as 10,000 low-income units in the city through Section 8, a program enacted under the Housing and Community Development Act of 1974. But Reagan officials eyed changes to the program from their first year in office, eventually replacing its support for construction with a voucher-based approach that subsidized low-income rents in existing buildings and added no new housing stock. This was a major problem for municipal governments that had come to depend on federal aid to provide affordable housing. New York mayor Ed Koch explained the issue in typically blunt terms. "You probably all know that the federal government used to have, and still has the responsibility of providing housing for those who can't afford market rate housing," Koch said in a 1988 speech. "But it has been abandoned by the Reagan administration."[57]

Without the federal government as a major player, but with an acute shortage of affordable housing in New York, city and state officials had little choice but to increase their role in housing provision. For Koch, this provided an opportunity to advance the economic integration he had long favored as his vision of New York City. Koch's Ten Year Housing Plan, announced in 1986, marked the grandest municipal housing program in the United States. He initially promised $4.2 billion for the development of 252,000 affordable units, and expanded support to a staggering $5.1 billion in 1988. Koch's plan in part suggested the evolution of the city's approach to the still-large stock of buildings it reluctantly owned. "The commitment of the Ten Year Plan is that every structurally sound vacant building in the city that we own—that's 5,000 buildings in all—will be rehabilitated and turned into afford-able housing for people making $32,000 a year or less," Koch promised. The plan likewise funded the rehabilitation of city- and privately owned occu-pied apartments and new construction of apartments and owned properties. Many of the latter were intended for middle-income buyers, a demographic that made up a significant portion, though not a majority, of Koch's plan—according to the city, 61 percent of units were to house low-income New Yorkers, 26 percent were to house those of moderate income, and 13 percent were to house middle-income residents.[58]

Economically diverse inhabitants reflected the eclectic participants who helped make the Ten Year Plan a reality. While the city had been near the brink of economic bankruptcy by the mid-1970s, its recovery by the mid-1980s enabled officials to plan boldly from the city's capital budget, a source that the city combined with newly available state funding, including a Low Income Housing Trust Fund initiated by Governor Mario Cuomo and pay-ments gained from the development of Battery Park City. Public funding provided the majority of support behind the plan, but its multitude of programs also depended on a range of private- and nonprofit-sector partners that arrived amid federal austerity.[59]

Entities commonly called "intermediaries" were one such outgrowth of the 1980s that played a central role in the Ten Year Plan. The best-known intermediaries, the Local Initiatives Support Corporation (LISC)—initiated by the Ford Foundation and six corporate partners—and the Enterprise Foundation, begun by developer James Rouse, channeled private funding to local development corporations for the purpose of affordable-housing construction, while also providing technical assistance. Intermediaries convinced insurance companies, banks, and other corporations that low-income housing could be a safe and profitable investment, attracting direct contributions or indirect funding through the federal Low Income Housing Tax Credit, which became available in 1986. The Low Income Housing Tax Credit incentivized private investment in affordable housing, providing a tax credit to corporations that invested in a general fund with close administrative ties to the intermediaries, who in turn lent to neighborhood organizations for housing construction. By 1989, estimated Mitchell Sviridoff, LISC's first president, the organization had garnered 350 corporate investors and more than a hundred million dollars that it invested in 500 projects nationwide.[60]

While such financing supported rental housing, other partners, such as the New York City Housing Partnership, aided the city's efforts to increase homeownership through the Ten Year Plan. Initiated by banker David Rockefeller in 1981 as an outgrowth of the New York City Partnership, a pro-development coalition of business interests, the Housing Partnership backed middle-income housing construction on city-owned land or in city-owned buildings. Major New York banks such as Chase, Chemical, and Citibank provided market-rate loans to such projects, which served the minimum income level that lenders deemed profitable. Though the partnership required a 20 percent public subsidy to receive its assistance, the city eagerly sought such private aid. "The work that organization does in conjunction with [the city] truly illustrates how fruitful a partnership between government and the private sector can be," one city publication read. Housing Partnership developments often followed a suburban model of low-density and low-rise buildings in a dense urban context. In Harlem, however, the Housing Partnership's largest move came at the northwest corner of Central Park, where it helped finance the 599-unit Towers on the Park, a predominantly middle-income project completed in 1988 that involved HUDC and the design hand of Bond, who had been involved with planning for that site since 1970.[61]

The Ten Year Plan's approach to housing—which also included programs targeting private developers and construction firms—expanded the patchwork nature of low-income homesteading to a new scale. In general, pragmatism characterized development in the 1980s, an era demanding innovation in the absence of conventional funding sources. "Explaining the Improbable," one contemporary analyst titled a study of downtown development, writing, "After a long tenure as regulators and donors, cities became dealmakers and co-investors in private development projects."[62] The same flexibility and creativity held true in the realm of affordable housing. City officials packaged intermediary funding with their own low-interest loans to support Ten Year Plan initiatives such as the rehabilitation of vacant buildings into low-income and homeless housing, transferred city-owned buildings to private developers who competed for the right to rehab them, and worked with a range of nonprofit neighborhood organizations, including those in Harlem. A 1989 update on the Ten Year Plan listed fifteen ongoing housing development programs, including initiatives under the Division of Alternative Management Programs. Koch's plan set in motion an effort that brought partners together across the public and private sectors to a new degree.[63]

CDCs like ADC and HCCI thus found themselves facing new limitations as well as new opportunities. In many ways, the very fragmentation of financing in this era enabled the diverse approaches CDCs took. The funding landscape they inhabited shaped their work, but also coincided with their own vision for social amelioration through economic integration. HCCI, for instance, found Koch an initially unwilling ally who needed considerable convincing that CCHD should take on the Bradhurst plan. CCHD only gained that responsibility in the last month of Koch's term. But like Koch, they aspired toward a mixed-income neighborhood makeup, and the policies that Koch launched in part underwrote the projects that they constructed in succeeding years with increased funding assistance from Koch's successor, Mayor David Dinkins. To an even greater extent, ADC—without the state ties that HCCI claimed through its partnership with HUDC—relied on the elements of the Ten Year Plan.[64]

The various programs that CDCs could tap facilitated the economic integration at the heart of their housing ventures. A building for seniors might draw from one source, a building for the homeless from a different program, a low-income housing development from a funding intermediary, and middle-income housing from more direct private sources, providing a collage of both means and outcomes. Funding for buildings in the Bradhurst plan included resources from the Low Income Housing Tax Credit procured through LISC; the Ten Year Plan's Homeless Housing Program; and the New York State Low Income Housing Trust Fund. Near Memorial Baptist Church, HCCI developed low-income housing financed through LISC and senior housing funded through the Section 202 program, one of the few federal resources still available.[65] ADC also leaned on Section 202 and the city's Homeless Housing Program. The Hattie Dodson Houses and Lilian Upshur Houses provided low-income housing financed by LISC and the Enterprise Foundation, in conjunction with the city Department of Housing Preservation and Development. The Ten Year Plan's Special Initiatives Program, which hired private contractors to rehab vacant buildings for a combination of homeless, low-, and moderate-income families, funded ADC's work on 129th and 137th Streets and Fifth Avenue. ADC financed other moderate-income housing through the city's Vacant Buildings Program and with the help of the Enterprise Foundation and the Community Preservation Corporation, another coalition formed by commercial banks. West One Three One Plaza, the middle-income homeownership project on West 131st Street, became possible through the assistance of the New York City Housing Partnership, with further support from the New York State Affordable Housing Corporation and mortgage financing from the Dime Savings Bank.[66]

Instead of a single financing vehicle, ADC and HCCI pragmatically followed any thread that would enable realization of a given project. More often than not, this meant a newly prominent role for the private sector in the work of these community-based organizations. The overall funding that each CDC received through the 1990s suggests the centrality of the public-private hybrid that made their work possible. Each depended on banks and intermediaries for about a third of their support, on corporations and foundations for another 10 percent, and on the local, state, and federal government for the remainder. Their expedient approach to funding housing development emerged in a context in which CDCs had few alternatives to such models, but this strategy had consequences beyond the walls of the buildings they built. The union of public and private support brought new interests to the project of community development and to the work of CDCs.[67]

Indeed, the nature of housing finance at this time shaped the political dimension of CDCs as well. In general, ADC and HCCI took an approach to political action as pragmatic as their approach to funding, and one similarly focused on practical outcomes rather than more abstract ideals such as empowerment or broad structural change. This is not to say that the work of CDCs did not remain progressive in orientation. Besides affordable housing construction—which even with a mixed-income goal remained heavily oriented toward those with low incomes—CDCs remained active in social causes. HCCI, for example, played a major role in bringing serious attention to AIDS in the African American church. The CDC educated member clergy, participated in a yearly Harlem Week of Prayer for the Healing of AIDS, provided housing to people with AIDS through a city program, and organized programming and supportive services for those residents suffering from the disease.[68]

But CDCs evinced a decided professionalization in their work, an orientation in part shaped by the complexity of finance in this era as well as the many parties to whom they answered in developing property. As was the case with the first generation of CDCs, dependence on outside funding influenced internal dynamics and moderated ambitions. Funders looked to local organizations as both partners and brokers who could funnel investment to projects while removing potentially disruptive political barriers. Outside organizations hoping to profit from their involvement in affordable housing finance expected local organizations to smooth the path. The New York City Housing Partnership, for example, in a memo retained by ADC, indicated the essential role that they saw for themselves in Harlem amid federal austerity. "Obviously, the termination of federal housing programs is the single largest factor in the emergence of 'affordable housing' initiatives that depend on private involvement," they explained. "The new funds committed by the City and State . . . cannot begin to provide the dollars necessary to capitalize a volume housing production program serving the current residents of low income areas." But plans for mixed-income development depended on private support that would only come once local partners opened political channels. "Responsible members of the development/finance community often say they are prepared to assume economic risks, but not political ones," the Housing Partnership wrote. "To the extent that Harlem seeks outside investment, local leadership will have to provide support in resolving the political issues (both community politics and government policies) that discourage responsible investment."[69]

If organizations like the Housing Partnership called for such cooperation in part out of their own self-interest, however, CDCs voiced a similarly moderate pragmatism on their own. The HCCI staff's description of the organization's role largely echoed the Housing Partnership's stance. "Harlem leadership often perceives external redevelopment interests as domineering, patronizing, and selfishly motivated," they wrote. "Regardless of one's particular view, the tragic isolation of the Harlem community cannot be overcome while distrust remains the order of the day." HCCI's task, they argued, was to create an alliance that could represent the interests of Harlem neighbors while opening the doors to outside parties. "HCCI apparently has succeeded in creating a coalition of concerned clergy and their congregants who can work constructively with lay groups and politicians to breach the development impasse in the area," staff wrote. Todd Jones, the executive director of HCCI in 1991 and later director of the broader CCHD, struck one foundation representative "as a true politico" who "will probably be quite effective in keeping potential antagonistic forces working cooperatively."[70]

Leaders were political in the sense that they managed their relations with funding partners carefully and staked a middle ground. Their very ideological flexibility, openness to collaboration with all sectors, and professionalized approach defined their politics. Where earlier generations of community development leaders, especially those of the 1960s, had emerged as neighborhood activists who then became prominent at the helm of organizations they founded, by the 1980s CDCs claimed leadership with considerable formal training and close ties to the hybridized public-private landscape they inhabited. While not technocrats, the executives of HCCI and ADC maintained a high level of professional expertise and an emphasis on project execution. HCCI's Jones earned a master's degree in real estate development at the Massachusetts Institute of Technology and previously worked as a private consultant assisting the city with the financing and construction of mixed-income housing. Both Phillips, the chief executive of ADC, and Kevin McGruder, the organization's chief operating officer, had previously worked for LISC, the funding intermediary. Phillips studied at the Harvard University

Graduate School of Design and also had worked at UDC and the Port Authority of New York and New Jersey. She was thus deeply familiar with the city's development scene by the time she joined Abyssinian's community development effort in an official capacity.[71]

CDC leaders praised their funding partners, suggesting an alliance of interests, not a relationship of resentful dependence. In 1996, ADC honored four private and nonprofit collaborators—Bankers Trust, Chase Manhattan Bank, J.P. Morgan, and LISC—at its second annual fund-raising event, for example. "Each of these institutions has been there for ADC since 'day one,'" Phillips wrote. Funders in turn contributed to the professionalization of CDCs, encouraging their organizational sophistication. "The amount of housing development going under the HCCI banner, either as sponsor or developer, is indeed awesome," read a 1993 Ford Foundation assessment. But HCCI needed greater financial rigor, the foundation argued, and more developed bureaucratic infrastructure—the kinds of administrative roles that corporations typically had, but community organizations managed more casually. The Ford Foundation recommended that HCCI hire a chief financial officer, preferably a certified public accountant with an MBA and experience with a Big Six accounting company. They suggested that the CDC hire an executive recruiter and consult with partners like Chemical Bank to vet candidates. They eventually funded the position for HCCI, as part of a larger grant that included money for a fund-raising consultant, a role that Washington had often handled on his own but that the foundation also recommended formalizing.[72]

As affiliates of Harlem-based churches, CDCs largely took their efficacy as community representatives as a given. HCCI "seems to be on the verge of what no other recent organization has been able to do," Washington wrote, "to bring together diverse religious and lay community-based groups within Harlem to create a powerful constituency that insures local residents of a significant role in their neighborhoods." Yet HCCI's board of directors consisted wholly of leaders of member churches until 1993, when it expanded slightly to include a representative from a Harlem social service agency, more women, and greater representation from the Muslim community, including the imam of the Mosque of the Islamic Brotherhood. Similarly, through its first years ADC's eighteen-member board was made up entirely of church congregants selected by Reverend Butts. Boards included stakeholders with deeply held interests in Harlem, to be sure, but remained within the orbit of their sponsoring churches. The persistent questions of representativeness, broad participation, and democratization of expertise that had once motivated community development largely faded in an era when leaders focused on assuring funding for their project-based work.[73]

Indeed, the pragmatic orientation of major CDCs brought a considerably diminished engagement with the sort of radical hopes that had supported neighborhood-based efforts in past decades. ADC's experience with community organizing symbolized the paradox it faced, as more aggressive approaches to improving the lives of nearby tenants ran against the organization's political middle ground. ADC hired a staff member to organize building tenants and block associations in the area around the church in late 1992, for example, but the organizer, Lowell Rodgers, found that ADC's focus on development projects often trumped the interests of tenants within. Initially asked to organize residents of several city-owned buildings, Rodgers learned that his actual task was to assess building condition and tenant "stability . . . so that ADC could determine whether or not these buildings would be worth pursuing for acquisition." Was Rodgers's duty to the tenants in dilapidated buildings or to his employer's development plans? "If tenants in [city-owned] buildings are struggling with repair needs, should the organizer assist the tenants with . . . a rent strike or mediate the tenants' demands with the property manager?" an outside assessment by activist Nellie Hester Bailey asked. "How does the organizer balance the needs of the tenants with the redevelopment goals of ADC?"[74]

ADC's involvement with the Task Force on City-Owned Property, the organization that had led resistance against city auction policies and called for low-income housing in abandoned properties, cast this dilemma in stark relief. ADC formally belonged to the task force but demonstrated considerable ambivalence to its strategy of directly confronting officials. Rodgers pushed to include ADC's name on a flyer for a 1994 housing rally, for instance, but CDC staff refused. "The organizer feels that he was being asked to compromise his political integrity for the sake of political expediency," Bailey noted. Such dilemmas grew out of ADC's relationship with its city funders, whom it did not wish to upset, but also its own political inclination. As CDCs increasingly focused on implementation and professionalization, ambitious political advocacy found less and less room to flourish. The issue over the flyer was more than "poor communication," Bailey wrote, but also marked an "ideological clash." Rodgers sought greater involvement in the expansive project of the task force, which focused on building a broad coalition of tenants in the many remaining city-owned buildings. ADC preferred to skirt such potentially controversial action. "In discussions with Mr. Rodgers he suggested that ADC should assume a stronger advocacy role even taking political positions with respect to tenants' rights," Bailey wrote, summing up the larger dilemma. "On the other hand ADC has presented itself as moderately balancing its role with a low profile political agenda to meet its goals of a redevelopment program that will help to stabilize Harlem." Where activism on behalf of radical political goals and the reconstruction of space had once coincided, community organizations now largely abandoned such idealism in order to smooth execution of their development plans.[75]

This pragmatism could be read in the buildings that CDCs reconstructed as well. In 1988, Ghislaine Hermanuz, a former Architects' Renewal Committee in Harlem staff member, architecture professor at City College of New York, and participant in planning for the Bradhurst area, imagined a visionary transformation of Harlem's landscape that combined rehabilitation of existing buildings and new construction to craft a "new physical order" for the neighborhood. "The dilemma posed by rehabilitation in Harlem is not just the choice between rebuilding a past that was once ruled out as unfit for human needs or replacing it by a brand new housing type," Hermanuz wrote. "More importantly, it implies a choice between reinforcing the expression of class structure in the physical environment, by relegating the poor once again to refurbished tenements, while the new housing is slated for the better-offs, or inventing a new physical order to represent a more equitable distribution of space according to needs rather than ability to consume."[76]

If Hermanuz saw physical reconstruction as a chance to represent the equal value of Harlemites no matter their income, however, CDCs pursued the more workaday task of providing housing as efficiently and practically as possible. CDCs proved egalitarian in the sense that they carried out their mixed-income vision regardless of building type. But with the city both the major state actor in housing production and the major landholder of available property in Harlem, rehabilitation of existing, city-owned buildings ruled the day. Indeed, with only a couple of exceptions, such as ADC's Abyssinian Towers and a portion of HCCI's Sass Plaza, all of the projects constructed by the CDCs in this period focused on the rehabilitation of existing buildings. West One Three One Plaza, for example, involved renovation of four vacant, city-owned old law tenements and two row houses. The eight rehabilitated buildings of ADC's low-income Hattie Dodson Houses also were vacant and city-owned before renovation, as were the three tenements of the Samuel D. Proctor Apartments and the two townhouses on Astor Row. The extensive rehabilitation of Bradhurst Phase I and Phase II likewise involved the substantial reuse of city-owned vacant tenements along Frederick Douglass Boulevard, West 145th Street, and West 150th Street.[77]

Like the low-income homesteaders of the 1970s, then—though without their revolutionary aspirations—CDCs participated in the preservation of Harlem by returning buildings to useful life. Frequently, this role came incidentally. The city made tenements and townhouses available through the Ten Year Plan. CDCs eager to build housing capitalized on these opportunities, making abandoned buildings viable again. At times they embraced this task more explicitly. HCCI, for example, renovated five buildings west of Marcus Garvey Park, two of which were designated historic landmarks. "Though many of HCCI's other projects do not have this designation, HCCI maintains the architectural aesthetic of the buildings in their rehabilitation efforts," staff wrote, explaining that the CDC tried to preserve historic integrity whenever possible. ADC served as the community partner in an effort to rehabilitate the landmark Astor Row, with the cooperation of the nonprofit New York Landmarks Conservancy, the public New York City Landmarks Preservation Commission, and the Vincent Astor Foundation (see Figure 5.3). In addition to the two homes that ADC rehabbed, the project restored the facades and wooden porches that made the block unique not just in Harlem, but in New York City. The Landmarks Conservancy celebrated the attention to historic detail that the townhouse renovation entailed. "The entryways feature Victorian pocket doors, tiled hallways, and balustraded staircases. The parlor floors were transformed into two-bedroom apartments, which boast new wood windows overlooking the front yards, oak floors, and original ceiling moldings and fireplace mantels," they wrote.[78]

Yet with preservation, too, CDCs remained concerned with pragmatism over idealism. Wilcox had imagined landmarking all of Harlem to preserve the power and symbolism he identified with the neighborhood, but ADC expressed a cautious approach to landmark designation, determined to

FIGURE 5.3. Astor Row, the historic block of West 130th Street between Fifth and Lenox Avenues, noted for its wooden porches. In the mid-1990s, ADC participated in the rehabilitation of two vacant homes on Astor Row, creating eight limited-equity cooperatives for low- and moderate-income families.

ensure that development goals would not be constrained by the requirements attached. As city preservation officials focused their attention uptown after years of largely overlooking Harlem, Abyssinian attempted to shape the process to its advantage. The organization commissioned a study, intended to "formulate a strategy for how ADC and generic equivalents elsewhere can guide the landmarks process to minimize negative impact of landmark designation." ADC feared that financing its projects might grow only more difficult with widespread designation. "Landmarks designation and its potential for additional costs and procedures may inadvertently diminish the economic feasibility of important development or community services projects," the report noted. Reverend Butts expressed similar sentiments with regard to the designation of Abyssinian Baptist Church, suggesting not opposition to preservation per se, but insistence that preservation not restrict a living institution, one concerned with fulfilling practical needs.

"[The Landmarks Preservation Commission] needs to recognize that [Abyssinian Baptist Church] has a continuing mission of community and social service," Butts wrote. "The evolving nature of this mission and the fact that this is a 'living, working and breathing' institution which will not remain static over time, should be referenced in the Designation documents." Phillips summarized the organization's position rather succinctly in correspondence with the Landmarks Preservation Commission on the matter. "Community development is preservation," she said.[79]

By the mid-1990s, the particular form of community development that Phillips alluded to had ascended as the dominant mode in Harlem, and, indeed, throughout the work of CDCs nationally. Focused on an ideal of urban neighborhoods as economically integrated spaces, this vision looked forward to a future in which residents of all incomes would fill Harlem's blocks. With the new century fast approaching, proponents explained income diversification as an objective whose necessity was self-evident. "This has to be an economically integrated community," Washington said. Yet community leaders from an earlier generation, who had shaped a different, more radical vision of community development, watched cautiously. Margaret McNeil, longtime director of the West Harlem Community Organization, surveyed Harlem's landscape of residential development. As hopes for Harlem increasingly rested on the presence of the middle class, she wondered, would there still be room for the low-income residents for whom she had long worked? "We're distressed that there isn't a high enough percent of low-income housing for people who were displaced from the neighborhood," McNeil said. "We just can't do enough for those people."[80]

Indeed, in these years a new generation of CDCs succeeded in bringing the physical transformation that their predecessors had failed to accomplish. But their approach to Harlem's reconstruction, if highly effective in providing new and decent housing, narrowed the horizon of possibilities to which community developers aspired. In confronting the vexing social, political, and economic dilemmas of the previous decade, these organizations embraced pragmatism as a strategy of building, a means of getting things done. Instead of seeking ownership models that strove toward the idealistic self-determination and self-reliance that had given rise to community development, they aligned their interests with the private- and public-sector funders that would increasingly fuel their work. Instead of building toward broad structural transformation, CDCs simply built. While Harlem gained revived buildings on some of its most stricken blocks, it lost the sort of ambitious, visionary spatial and social imagination that Wilcox and McNeil had maintained. On the one hand, this was the price of progress: CDCs like ADC and HCCI had the expertise and versatility to navigate an increasingly fractured political and financial landscape and largely succeeded in their goals. On the other hand, their success in building raised its own questions about whether inclusion and autonomy still stood as the central tenets of community development, and what would be the long-term implications of mixed-income housing in a community that felt constantly under threat.

McNeil and Washington offered their divergent perspectives on Harlem's transformation in a 1990 article that posed a different question from that seen in the bleak assessments of the previous decade. Observers had once asked, "Can Harlem Be Saved?" But now they wondered, "Harlem: A New Renaissance?" Despite the points raised by old hands like McNeil, CDC leaders were sure it was on its way. "We can already see more evidence that the next Renaissance of Harlem is even closer," Phillips told attendees of ADC's 1996 Harlem Renaissance Day of Commitment, the organization's annual fund-raiser. Indeed, even amid concerns about the direction of community development, their approach had taken hold. Up in Bradhurst, CCHD completed apartments for moderate-income tenants on Frederick Douglass Boulevard, West 147th Street, and Macombs Place. Meanwhile, ADC only bolstered its commitment to economic integration in Harlem. "Recently, ADC has begun to more aggressively pursue opportunities for developing housing for moderate income residents," staff wrote in 1996. "While there has been a significant commitment by local development corporations to building low-income housing, no such commitment exists to meet the needs of moderate and middle-income residents, who are essential for community stability."[81]

The pragmatic approach that enabled Harlem-based CDCs to expand and redouble their involvement in housing construction would, by the end of the century, likewise enable them to become major players in urban development more broadly. As development moved increasingly toward a hybridized model of collaboration between the public and private sectors, these community-based organizations embraced the view that Harlem's future rested not only on income integration within the neighborhood, but equally on integration into economic markets outside its borders. This vision would underlie their efforts to extend their work from Harlem's residential streets to its main boulevard and symbolic center, 125th Street, through commercial redevelopment.

CHAPTER 6

Making Markets Uptown

IN OCTOBER 1996, the board of the Upper Manhattan Empowerment Zone Development Corporation (UMEZ), the body responsible for administering the majority of a $300 million cache of federal, state, and city funding intended to stimulate private development uptown, announced their first round of funding recommendations. Through grants, loans, and equity investments, UMEZ proposed to spend nearly $13 million to expand a microloan program and establish a credit union in Washington Heights, to assist an after-school program and Latino cultural center in East Harlem, and to support a variety of social service, training, and commercial projects in Central Harlem. To renovate a firehouse into a health center, the board offered nearly $250,000. To fund a study on the feasibility of a community court, they provided $110,000. To assist vendors at the outdoor market on 116th Street, they offered a $300,000 grant. The largest allocation by far, a loan and equity investment of $11.2 million, was to underwrite the construction of Harlem's first shopping mall, called Harlem USA, which developers hoped to build on 125th Street.[1]

Just a few days after their long-awaited announcement, however, UMEZ executives, Harlem congressman Charles Rangel, Mayor Rudolph Giuliani, Governor George Pataki, and even President Bill Clinton received a blistering missive on the letterhead of the Harlem Unity Committee for Social Justice. "The board of the Upper Manhattan Empowerment Zone is removed from the Harlem community," committee members wrote. "This can be seen in its first round of funding projects." Signees included local activists with the Harlem Tenants Council and Harlem Fight Back, a long-standing advocate for minority construction workers. A staff member from the Community Association of the East Harlem Triangle (CAEHT) signed too. Unsurprisingly, Preston Wilcox was also a member of the committee, and the vehemence of the letter's prose suggested that he was very likely its author. Members claimed not just the UMEZ board's detachment from their concerns, but also a purposeful campaign to open Harlem to outsiders. "There is little that represents community economic development and most of the funds are going to outside interests," they wrote. "Restaurants, night clubs, Harlem USA, a grant to the 116th Street Vendors Market are not projects that encourage economic growth but tourism." Committee members saw malevolence at play. "The economic racism of this City is second to none and inviting racist business people and investors from downtown or elsewhere to come into Harlem when they have done nothing in the past to address the exclusion of African people is not only self negating but stupid."[2]

Richard Parsons, the CEO of Time Warner and chairman of UMEZ, offered a brief rebuttal that suggested both his impatience with such complaints and the new era in which Wilcox and his compatriots found themselves. "I would encourage you to ease up on the sixties rhetoric and, instead, share with us any specific proposals you may have for economic development initiatives in Upper Manhattan," he wrote. Deborah Wright, UMEZ's newly appointed president, offered a more thorough response, but the paradox of the commercial development of Harlem's central spine in the late twentieth century was bound up in her very first point. "First, your assertion that the initial round of Empowerment Zone projects are 'outside interests' is just plain wrong," Wright wrote. "All but two projects are organized by local organizations or individuals and all will have significant community participation. For example, Harlem Commonwealth Council, a local non-profit, will not only be Harlem USA's landlord, it will also be a significant equity participant."[3]

In the late 1990s, 125th Street increasingly bore the mark of the national retail chains whose stores were reshaping commercial centers throughout New York City. "Retailers Have Harlem on Their Mind," read the title of one *New York Times* account in 1996. Harlem had long been the province of big, unrealized plans, but now Harlem's grand boulevard was showing new life. "Major retailers woke up to the fact that there was still a lot of pedestrian traffic on the street," the article read. "Consumers, in other words."[4] By the beginning of the next decade, vast construction sites on 125th Street had become big projects—the neighborhood's first supermarket, between Lexington and Third Avenues; Harlem USA, between St. Nicholas and Eighth Avenues; and Harlem Center, a retail and office complex at the corner of Lenox Avenue and 125th Street, on the long vacant—and long contested—lot east of the Harlem state office building. If such projects resembled transformations elsewhere in the city, like that of 42nd Street, and, indeed, throughout American cities, Wright's admonition to Wilcox's group raised a crucial point. The large commercial projects that took shape in Harlem were as much a realization of a specific community development ideal as they were a sign of new global and national economic trends in the late 1990s. Community development organizations stood at the center of such plans.[5]

These projects marked the achievement of the vision that the Harlem Commonwealth Council (HCC), Harlem Urban Development Corporation (HUDC), and other community-based organizations had articulated for 125th Street beginning in the 1970s. In contrast to radicals' ideal of Harlem's central spine as a vibrant corridor serving the housing, cultural, and social service needs of low-income Harlemites, these plans represented a narrower conception of 125th Street as a predominantly commercial district. These schemes had been relegated to drawing boards amid the federal funding cuts of the 1980s. But their realization in the 1990s suggested a dramatic sea change, not just as a result of new funding sources that made large-scale commercial development viable again, but also as a result of demographic and intellectual shifts that created an environment in which supermarkets, malls, and offices could flourish. Commercial development went hand in hand with a vision of Harlem as a mixed-income space. The neighborhood's marked increase in income at this time brought retailers to Harlem's door. At the same time, officials and community developers came to share a new understanding of Harlem as an untapped market, and to see the community's fate tied to their ability to integrate it into a broader economic "mainstream." They agreed that the government's role was to create the conditions for what they perceived as a free market in the neighborhood, a world in which national movie chains, retail stores, and supermarkets could flourish, but small businesses often lost out.[6]

The consequences of such changes were decidedly complex, however, perhaps more so than the Harlem Unity Committee for Social Justice could ever have anticipated in 1996. The reconstruction of Harlem marked the total eclipse of the radical ideal that the Architects' Renewal Committee in Harlem, Wilcox, and others had imagined of a prosperous community built by and for its low-income residents, yet the entrance of Harlem into the American commercial mainstream held divergent meanings. For many Harlemites, middle class and not, the arrival of national retailers, especially a Pathmark supermarket, was a welcome change. They hailed the predictability, access, and value that they associated with such commercial development. Likewise, if Wilcox saw Harlem USA and other big projects as exclusionary, even racist impositions, the centrality of community groups in their development suggested a different conclusion: by the end of the millennium, community-based organizations had achieved the prominence that they had long sought.

No group achieved more prominence than the Abyssinian Development Corporation (ADC), the community development corporation (CDC) that had helped lead the way in crafting a mixed-income vision for Harlem through its pragmatic pursuit of diverse funding sources and its professionalized approach to the project of building. ADC rode its reputation to become a major player in Harlem's redevelopment, but other community organizations did not benefit equally. The late 1990s saw the reconstruction of Harlem in steel, glass, and concrete, but also a shift of power at the community level. If ADC's rise symbolized the ascent of community-based organizations that activists had demanded for forty years, so too did it raise new questions about participation and democracy in the age of promised empowerment.

"Mainstreaming" Harlem: The Mall Comes to 125th Street

UMEZ served as only the most visible symbol of a consensus that formed more broadly around urban development policy in the 1990s. Public officials, private-sector leaders, and community-based organizations came to see neighborhoods like Harlem as potentially valuable markets, as undervalued economic resources that had existed outside the rules of capitalism and suffered for it. Policy in this era, then, was overwhelmingly characterized by a motivation to bring Harlem into the economic "mainstream." While the federal government returned as a player in urban policy, it did so not primarily as a major financial backer but as a resource focused on stimulating private investment in high-poverty neighborhoods. If this notion gained wide support, it was not without its critics. Leaders of UMEZ; federal, state, and city officials; and many community development organizations agreed that making Harlem look more like the rest of New York City through commercial development would revitalize the already changing neighborhood. But Wilcox and others objected that the economic mainstream would leave many Harlemites behind. The central role of Harlem's first CDC in the development of Harlem USA, however—the very organization that Wilcox had cofounded on radical principles in 1967—signaled the dominance at the end of the century of the market approach to Harlem's development.

The federal Empowerment Zone program—which gave rise to UMEZ—grew out of legislation signed in the second year of Clinton's presidency and spoke to a broader tendency that characterized his approach to urban policy. Like his immediate predecessors, Clinton favored strategies based in the private sector, valuing housing vouchers over new low-income housing construction, promoting increased homeownership opportunities, and seeking means to expand private investment in predominantly low-income neighborhoods. Unlike the Ronald Reagan and George H. W. Bush administrations, however, Clinton attempted to reestablish the federal role in urban policy. The Empowerment Zone program, established through the Omnibus Budget Reconciliation Act of 1993, was Clinton's first major gesture toward that end, authorizing over $1 billion in flexible grants and $2.5 billion in tax incentives intended to stimulate development in designated areas. Such resources were made available in six urban and three rural zones. In each, private and nonprofit developers could apply for loans and grants, or benefit by hiring workers from within the area. Employers received a tax credit for 20 percent of the first $15,000 in salary and training expenses paid to each resident. They could likewise claim a larger tax write-off for business-related property than enterprises located outside the zone and gain access to tax-exempt bonds to finance development.[7]

Through such incentives, officials hoped to create a climate attractive to private investors and spur job growth in areas with high unemployment. This policy marked a Clintonian twist on an innovation that had long been on the shelf, one that had transformed from a conservative pet idea to a moderate policy with support from both Left and Right. Originating in Britain

in the late 1970s, the idea of geographically bounded areas with special provisions to attract investment, soon called "Enterprise Zones," had moved
from concept to reality in the early 1980s under Prime Minister Margaret
Thatcher. Urban planner Peter Hall's original formulation had proposed to
radically scale back bureaucracy, immigration controls, and regulatory legislation in neighborhoods of declining growth. As passed in 1981, Britain's
Enterprise Zones offered a narrower prescription of tax amenities and reduced planning controls. The idea immigrated to the United States at the same
time, appearing in unsuccessful bills offered at the state level in Illinois and
at the federal level by Congressmen Jack Kemp, a Republican, and Robert
Garcia, a Democrat. Though Reagan supported the idea—one of the few urban
policies proposed by his administration—a series of bills emphasizing tax
incentives and hiring credits failed throughout the 1980s. Meanwhile, the
vast majority of states passed Enterprise Zone laws in that decade. Kemp's
appointment as the secretary of Housing and Urban Development under
Bush kept wind in the sails of federal Enterprise Zone legislation. Both
houses of Congress approved a bill in 1992, after civil disorder swept Los Angeles in the wake of the Rodney King verdict. President Bush vetoed that
bill, but an incentive-based policy, with the addition of a grant and loan component, finally became law under Clinton. Its major proponent in the House
of Representatives was Harlem congressman Charles Rangel.[8]

With Rangel's involvement at the center of the Empowerment Zone legislation, Harlem's designation in the first round of funding seemed a foregone
conclusion. Indeed, Rangel and David Dinkins, New York's mayor until December 31, 1993, had worked to ensure that Harlem would have a favorable
position against both national competition and any other neighborhoods
that might vie for the city's nomination. Rangel included a "special rule" in
the law that modified stipulations requiring joint state-local government
backing to also allow nominations directly from "an economic development
corporation chartered by the State." In creating the possibility of an end run
around officials, Rangel had HUDC in mind, the entity that had emerged out
of the battle over the state office building in the early 1970s and over which
Rangel exerted control. Mayor Dinkins issued an executive order in his last
days in office, naming HUDC as the leader of the nomination process in
order to guarantee Harlem's priority. Mayor Giuliani pushed for a broader

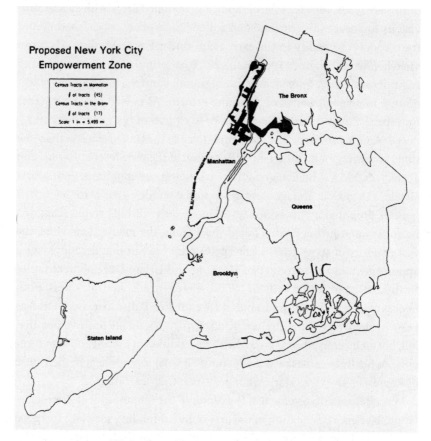

FIGURE 6.1. Proposed boundaries (shown in black) of the New York City Empowerment Zone, from the successful 1994 application for designation submitted by HUDC, the city, and the state. The awarded area included much of Harlem and sections of Washington Heights, together constituting the communities encompassed by UMEZ, as well as portions of the South Bronx.

geographic scope upon his inauguration, resulting in a proposal including sections of Washington Heights—north of Harlem, areas in the South Bronx that encompassed Yankee Stadium, and extensive sections of East and Central Harlem (see Figure 6.1). If Rangel failed to obtain the precise geographic delineation he had in mind, he succeeded in gaining designation for New York's entry, which the Clinton administration selected in late 1994 alongside Atlanta, Baltimore, Chicago, Detroit, and, jointly, Philadelphia and

Camden, New Jersey. Despite the extensive infighting between state, city, and Harlem leaders that preceded the nomination, HUDC's proposal could claim the unique distinction of matching fund commitments from both New York State and New York City. Where the other urban Empowerment Zones drew from a $100 million grant, New York claimed a pot three times as large, with UMEZ responsible for administering over four-fifths of the $300 million total.[9]

For the planners who charted Harlem's role in the Empowerment Zone program, the future direction of development tied directly to the demographic shifts that the neighborhood was experiencing. In part due to the efforts of church-based CDCs, Harlem increasingly claimed economic diversity that it had not seen in decades. "The revitalization of the Harlem community is being led by housing development," staff wrote in a briefing book on the Empowerment Zone nomination presented to U.S. secretary of commerce Ronald Brown. "This activity has provided the opportunity to create a mixed income community with home ownership opportunities." Population had increased only gradually by the 1990 census, HUDC reported, but there were ample signs that Harlem's middle-class constituency had grown in the previous ten years. Thirteen thousand more households earned over $40,000 annually, planners explained, while 34,000 fewer households earned less than $20,000. College graduates in the neighborhood increased by nearly a third, to 62,019, an increase of 15,458 from the 1980 total. HUDC cited decreasing crime statistics too, reporting reduced burglary, robbery, and grand larceny between 1988 and 1991.[10]

With such changes under way, planners argued, Harlem was poised for a boom in commercial development. "Clearly, Harlem has become a place in which to conduct business," HUDC staff explained. "The residential development activities have led to major changes in retail activities and interest of anchor tenants in locating in Harlem." A partnership between government, the community, and the private sector in the form of the Empowerment Zone would "capitalize on this new vision." The widespread vacancy and property abandonment of earlier decades had left its mark on Harlem, the official Empowerment Zone proposal explained. But even such physical vestiges of trying times portended a reversal. More than a million square feet of commercial space sat vacant in the neighborhood, planners wrote, property that awaited new development.[11]

Indeed, proponents argued, Harlem was in a state of commercial immaturity. It was a community, in other words, whose streets were "under-retailed." Between 110th and 153rd Streets, the Empowerment Zone proposal read, "there is approximately $3 billion total personal income and an expenditure potential of $1.1 billion." If Harlem's residents earned less on average than those in other neighborhoods, their collective power on its dense streets added up. But residents were spending that income elsewhere. "Currently, Harlem residents shop in Queens, Westchester County, midtown Manhattan and New Jersey," HUDC explained to Commerce Secretary Brown. "This exodus from the community can only be curtailed by the provision of a variety of community commercial services which will encourage residents to shop in the community." Harlem required "major anchors" on its main streets, planners argued, including Third Avenue, 116th Street, and 125th Street, to attract both Harlem dollars and even more retail. "Biggest assets: 520,000 consumers north of 110 street," UMEZ president Wright told city and state leaders. "Studies at Columbia say we're underretailed by 30%. Pent-up spending power. Retail will be focus." Proponents shared their hopes with the officials who backed the Empowerment Zone, who argued that retail would create an economic engine uptown. "Commercial development is vital to the well being of inner cities," read a summary of the comments Vice President Al Gore and Representative Rangel delivered to Harlem business leaders in March 1995. "With it comes economic stability, jobs and growth."[12]

Empowerment Zone planners hoped that Harlem would join and contribute to what they perceived as the "economic mainstream." They held that Harlem had been isolated from the free market and that the neighborhood's prosperity depended on its return to that market, especially by competing on a larger scale. "With its central location in Manhattan and its superior transportation services," HUDC staff explained, "Harlem has the potential to become a regional shopping center." Harlem's turnaround would measure up to the city's other commercial revivals, contended Wright and Parsons, the UMEZ chairman, even the much vaunted reconstruction of 42nd Street and Times Square. "This is a unique moment of opportunity for Upper Manhattan and hence, the City," Parsons and Wright told Giuliani administration officials in 1997. "We need your personal involvement and that of the Mayor in assisting us to mobilize this City's vast private and public resources

if we are to convert Upper Manhattan's assets into the major economic con-
tributor it is capable of being." Wright's goal, she wrote a year later, was "to
bring our community into America's economic mainstream."[13]

Indeed, in expressing her vision for Harlem, Wright spoke to a larger tendency characteristic of community development at this time. In tying Harlem's fate to its position relative to a broader market, Wright, HUDC, and
their allies both anticipated and channeled an idea with growing currency
in the mid-1990s. Increasingly, observers tied the socioeconomic condition
of communities like Harlem to their perceived isolation from the larger
economy. Harvard University professor and economist Michael Porter served
as the major public evangelist of this idea. "The sad reality is that the efforts
of the past few decades to revitalize the inner cities have failed," Porter wrote
in his landmark article, "The Competitive Advantage of the Inner City," in
1995. Policy makers had typically offered remedies targeted at the social service needs of residents in high-poverty neighborhoods, Porter argued, or
focused on "piecemeal approaches" through subsidies or large public expenditures intended "to stimulate economic activity in tangential fields such as
housing, real estate, and neighborhood development." Such approaches
failed, Porter claimed, because they misunderstood the nature of economic
competitiveness. "Lacking an overall strategy, such programs have treated
the inner city as an island isolated from the surrounding economy and subject to its own unique laws of competition," Porter wrote. "They have encouraged and supported small, subscale businesses designed to serve the
local community but ill equipped to attract the community's own spending
power, much less *export* outside it."[14]

Economic revival demanded "a radically different approach," Porter contended, that depended fundamentally and primarily on the private sector,
and that relied on the rules that proponents associated with the free market. "A
sustainable economic base *can* be created in the inner city," he wrote, "but
only as it has been created elsewhere: through private, for-profit initiatives
and investment based on economic self-interest and genuine competitive
advantage—not through artificial inducements, charity, or government
mandates." Instead of starting with subsidies and hoping economic success
would follow, Porter claimed, policy makers should follow the principles that
governed business development elsewhere. "An economic model must begin
with the premise that inner city businesses should be profitable on a regional,

national, and even international scale," he wrote, echoing those who had called for Harlem to compete on a vaster terrain. Economic development in high-poverty neighborhoods should be guided by the same factors that motivated profit-making businesses in any other geographic context, Porter argued—that is, by the specific locational features that gave such businesses a competitive advantage. Despite its reputation, Porter explained, the inner city had fundamental competitive advantages: a central location, proximity to distinctive regional business clusters, an underemployed labor pool, and an underserved market. This last attribute, the feature that Harlem leaders had pushed forcefully in making a case for the Empowerment Zone, "represent[ed] the most immediate opportunity for inner-city-based entrepreneurs and businesses," Porter wrote. "At a time when most other markets are saturated, inner city markets remain poorly served."[15]

In the pursuit of competitive advantage, Porter called for new private- and public-sector roles. The private sector, he explained, should not approach development in neighborhoods like Harlem with the intention of charity or with the goal of tapping "preference programs." "The private sector will be most effective if it focuses on what it does best," Porter wrote, "creating and supporting economically viable businesses built on true competitive advantage." Such enterprises could take any form that capitalized on those advantages, Porter argued, but he highlighted several that he deemed especially apt. "In particular, retailers, franchisers, and financial services companies have immediate opportunities," he wrote. Large chain retailers were "an especially attractive model for inner city entrepreneurship because they provide not only a business concept but also training and support," he explained. The public sector would need to accept a new function, too. Porter, skeptical of any aid that he perceived as counter to the tendencies he identified with the free market, insisted that government would need to take a secondary role. "Government can assume a more effective role by supporting the private sector in new economic initiatives," Porter wrote. "It must shift its focus from direct involvement and intervention to creating a favorable environment for business." The public sector should not withdraw from the field of economic development, he argued, but maintain a policy of noninterference. "Subsidies must be spent in ways that do not distort business incentives, focusing instead on providing the infrastructure to support genuinely profitable businesses," Porter said.[16]

Porter provided an intellectual justification for the growing predominance of the private sector in inner-city revitalization. As was also the case with housing development in this period, those involved with rebuilding 125th Street increasingly approached their work from a mind-set honed in the world of business. Wright followed this approach. A graduate of Radcliffe College, Harvard Law School, and Harvard Business School, Wright had served as the city's commissioner of housing preservation and development before joining UMEZ. Prior to that, she had worked at the New York City Housing Partnership, where she directed marketing for Towers on the Park, the Harlem condominium buildings that the David Rockefeller–backed partnership built with HUDC. After graduating from business school, Wright had joined the investment bank First Boston. As leader of UMEZ, she proudly claimed the influence of her work in finance. "Ms. Wright is not," the *Times* paraphrased, "another traditional social reformer or a politician handing out favors to friends, but a financier who says she holds Harlem to the standards of Wall Street."[17] Similarly, while the UMEZ Board of Directors included affiliates of nonprofit institutions, Harlem residents, and leaders of social service organizations, the appointment of Chairman Parsons—one of the city's most prominent CEOs—tied the organization to the upper echelons of the private sector and spoke to the new prominence of the business world in community development.[18]

If the designation of Empowerment Zones symbolized the national ascent of the market approach to urban development, however, not all Harlemites watched with enthusiasm. Perhaps no exchange symbolized both the wide acceptance of Porter's theorization and the fear it brought forth quite like the 1996 correspondence between Wright and the Harlem Unity Committee for Social Justice, which transpired soon after the initial UMEZ funding announcement. Wright offered a point-by-point refutation of the concerns voiced by Wilcox and his associates, beginning with her observation that community organizations were at the center of the funded projects and ending with a reminder that Harlemites sat on the organization's board. But she closed with a general statement that neatly echoed Porter's arguments. "The very cornerstone of the Empowerment Zone's approach to eradicating poverty is a belief that the private sector must be a prominent partner in this process," she explained. "Countless failed government efforts have shown that sustainability dictates a nod to market forces. As difficult as this transition may be for all of us, the future of Harlem depends on reuniting it with the larger New York City and regional economies. This cannot take place in a climate of close mindedness and parochialism."[19]

Wright, like Porter, saw the free market as a natural force that operated beneficially. She implied that Harlem's failures had emanated from a neglect of the market and, consequently, that a reorientation toward the private sector would bring long-term prosperity. She explained this a year and a half later in response to concerns that large-scale retail would supplant local businesses. "It's scary, frankly, because, as you know, one of the basic tenets of capitalism is that you can't control it. . . . Nor do I think we want to," Wright said. "We want to prepare people to compete in a market-based economy because that is the only thing thus far that has been shown to be sustainable."[20]

Wilcox and Harlem Unity Committee members, however, doubted that market forces functioned naturally, arguing instead that the very unnaturalness of the market bore much of the blame for Harlem's halting progress. "The so called private sector that has excluded Harlem from participating in economic growth and prosperity downtown is racist," they wrote to Wright. "We are not close minded and parochial, but realistic." Fundamentally unequal rules guided development, Unity Committee members contended. They remained deeply suspicious of the nature of the market that Wright hailed, communicating their doubt by holding the terms in question between quotation marks. "What you call a 'nod to market forces' can and probably will be more devastating than ever if we observe what has happened with 'market forces' around the world in so called underdeveloped areas, in Africa, Latin America, the Middle East, Asia, Russia," they wrote. "God save us from 'market forces'!" Wright cited private-sector involvement as the path to "sustainability," but the Unity Committee saw it paving the road to the neighborhood's upheaval. "Thus, we are brought back to our beginning concern," they concluded, "that continued and accelerated gentrification of Harlem through the seeming beneficence of UMEZ, with more power being asserted and carried forward by 'market forces,' where, once again, every one will be empowered but the people."[21]

That Harlem USA would rise as the neighborhood's first large-scale commercial complex, then, and that HCC—of which Wilcox had been a founding member—would play a central role in its development, was deeply ironic.

The project claimed a long history in the work of HCC. The CDC, Harlem's first, had moved increasingly toward profit-oriented, commercial development over the course of the 1970s. The organization first offered plans for a shopping mall with an anchor tenant in 1976, on the land it had amassed on 125th Street between St. Nicholas and Eighth Avenues, a proposal HCC further developed throughout the 1970s with the assistance of HUDC.[22] These plans remained on paper, however, as the federal austerity of the Reagan era removed the economic support on which the leaders of HCC had built their vision. By the early 1990s, Wilcox had grown extremely frustrated with the organization, which had once aspired to facilitate the radical goal of collective ownership of Harlem's land but proved unable to realize even the narrower vision it came to adopt. "I am, frankly, terribly disappointed that HCC never became the economic pump-primer it was intended to become," Wilcox told a reporter in 1991. Wilcox angrily cut ties with the CDC in the mid-1990s.[23]

UMEZ activated dormant plans, however, bringing HCC's commercial vision into physical reality. When the CDC's controversial president, James Dowdy, resigned in 1991, the organization was left with a series of failed enterprises but also a substantial amount of land on 125th Street, just as private developers were beginning to express renewed interest in Harlem. Late that year, two developers jointly proposed a mixed-use commercial project for a 125th Street site in East Harlem that was to become the Pathmark supermarket. The developers, Gotham Organization and Grid Properties, hoped to bring a commercial project to Harlem including a movie theater, retail, a food court, and a supermarket. Though the city declined to choose their proposal for that site, in part because of its speculative nature, the Grid/Gotham joint venture found an interested partner in HCC, which agreed to participate and lease the 125th Street property it had long intended for a shopping center. Sensing the optimism that surrounded Harlem's designation as an Empowerment Zone and the new public support promised for private-sector development, the partners announced their venture in early 1996, a "retail and entertainment complex" called Harlem USA, which the *New York Amsterdam News* touted as "the largest private commercial investment ever made in Central Harlem." Soon after announcing UMEZ's substantial financial commitment to Harlem USA later that year, Wright described her high expectations for the project's impact on 125th Street. "The thing that is going to push this strip over the top has not yet happened. It's going to take something like Harlem USA to take the cover off."[24]

Indeed, Harlem USA's backers espoused the broader celebration of the private sector that increasingly marked development on 125th Street, echoing the view that Harlemites were under-retailed and that the neighborhood thus offered a prime market for investors. "This complex will dramatically increase the availability of retail goods and services to the residents," said Barbara Norris, HCC's president, in announcing the project. "This will be a platform from which retailers and corporations can reach vastly underserved Harlem residents," she explained. "Retailers are realizing they can sell more products if they are located there," said Drew Greenwald, another of the project's developers, "and banks know that there are deposits there and loans to be made." In expressing their vision of commercial development, the project's promoters had in mind the national chain retailers that had already reshaped Midtown Manhattan. "If they can get 42nd Street under way, we can certainly get 125th Street under way," Norris promised, comparing Harlem's main street to Times Square. "Harlem USA will create 700 jobs and bring national retailers to 125th Street," announced Parsons. "Harlem USA is leading a resurgence in commercial and economic development in Upper Manhattan. Its high-profile tenants will increase the area's visibility and enhance business activity in the community."[25]

On the day of Harlem USA's groundbreaking in 1998, a large advertisement in both the *New York Times* and *Wall Street Journal* proclaimed Harlem's arrival into the mainstream that backers touted (see Figure 6.2). "Today, breaking ground for Harlem USA opens the way to a $2.5 billion consumer market in Upper Manhattan," bold text proclaimed. "Yes, Upper Manhattan." The $65 million project would "spearhead a new wave of private investment uptown," the ad promised. "Proof positive that the upside of Manhattan is indeed above 96th street." The image of a still-clean shovel that dominated the page suggested that this was not just an announcement of the start of construction but also an invitation to join the effort. "So whether your business is large or small, we invite you to get in on the ground floor of New York City's next great destination." An inset captured a rendering of the project, all glass and light with stores opening to the street, as spectacular as the luminaries who gathered for the first turning of soil:

Today, breaking ground for Harlem USA opens the way to a $2.5 billion consumer market in Upper Manhattan.

Yes, Upper Manhattan.

One of New York's most anticipated developments, **Harlem USA**, a 275,000 sq. ft. retail and entertainment complex, begins construction today, leading the way to a bright new future for business in Upper Manhattan.

Market-leaders such as The Disney Store, Magic Johnson Theaters, HMV Record Stores, Old Navy, Modells, The Chase Manhattan Bank, New York Sports Club and Jeepers! have signed on. All eager to serve a customer base the size of Seattle.

The $65 million project will create 700 jobs and spearhead a new wave of private investment uptown. Proof positive that the upside of Manhattan is indeed above 96th street.

Other developments are on the way. So whether your business is large or small, we invite you to get in on the ground floor of New York City's next great destination.

To find out more about tax incentives, low-interest financing and available sites, call the Upper Manhattan Empowerment Zone at (212) 410-0030, ext. 240 or visit our web site at www.umez.org. You can also e-mail us at husa@umez.org.

UPPER MANHATTAN
The
Future's
Looking
Up!

This advertisement provided through the courtesy of The Chase Manhattan Bank.

Banking on Upper Manhattan's future are the following partners: Commonwealth Local Development Corp., Grid Properties Inc., Gotham Organization, Inc., The Chase Manhattan Bank and the New York Empowerment Zone Corporation, a federal, state and city partnership.

FIGURE 6.2. A UMEZ advertisement, which appeared in the *New York Times* and the *Wall Street Journal* on the day of Harlem USA's groundbreaking, touted Upper Manhattan as a lucrative market waiting to be tapped by private investment.

Rangel, Governor Pataki, Thomas Labrecque (president of Chase Manhattan Bank, which financed the project), Parsons, Wright, and Norris, and recording artists Dionne Warwick and Mary J. Blige, who paid tribute in song. The advertisement confirmed that proponents' hopes that the center would attract top national retailers had not gone unrequited. "Market-leaders" including Magic Johnson Theaters, HMV Record Stores, Old Navy clothing store, the Disney Store, Chase Manhattan Bank, sporting goods retailer Modell's, and the New York Sports Club had signed on. "All eager to serve a customer base the size of Seattle," the ad read.[26]

The arrival of the Empowerment Zone and the start of construction that would bring Harlem's first shopping mall to life, story by story, marked the broad acceptance in the 1990s of the idea that socioeconomic and physical revitalization required a new openness to the private sector; in other words, that the road to urban transformation was paved with large-scale commerce. If Harlem USA made 125th Street look more like commercial corridors throughout Manhattan, that was precisely the point (see Figure 6.3). While the presence of national retail chains obscured the diverse participants at the heart of such projects, however, the fact remained that community-based organizations, public officials, and private developers together pursued this vision of Harlem with the aim of bringing the neighborhood into a perceived economic "mainstream." As it turned out, the costs and benefits of that strategy were as varied as the polychromatic signs that bedecked Harlem USA's transparent façade.

The Costs and Benefits of Retail Transformation

When Harlem USA first opened its doors in early 2000, the enthusiastic response suggested a community longing for the new shopping options that the complex provided. Despite the frigid February weather on the day of Old Navy's grand opening, residents lined up outside to await entry into the clothing store. Five thousand Harlemites attended the unveiling of the music store HMV a few months later, eager to meet the celebrities who appeared but also to show their approval at the cash registers. The July debut of Harlem's first multiplex cinema, the Magic Johnson Theaters, likewise found patrons excited to view the initial screening, *Shaft*. Harlemites offered generous praise. "It sends a message of upliftedness and a sense of pride and well-being," the

FIGURE 6.3. Harlem USA, the first major shopping mall on 125th Street, located at the intersection with St. Nicholas Avenue. The project opened in 2000 as a symbol of the ascendance of a redevelopment strategy that sought to bring Harlem into a perceived economic "mainstream," as well as a sign of the central role that community-based organizations played in pursuing that strategy.

development director of the Harlem Congregations for Community Improvement said of the movie theater. "I don't think you can encase it in a few words." Others voiced their sentiments in terms more prosaic, but no less approving. An eager Old Navy shopper was "having a ball," she told a *Times* reporter. "It's convenient, so I don't have to go downtown. It's hard to travel with little kids. And I'm within walking distance, so I save money on carfare."[27]

Some, however, watched new development with concern. "We can't compete with an international corporation like HMV," the owner of a decade-old record store explained. "Things are already tight. HMV will be detrimental to my business." One critical commentator likened UMEZ to a Trojan horse. "When all the occupants of the hollow horse finally disembark, Harlem will have much more glitter, but Harlemites will have much less gold," wrote Mamadou Chinyelu, a journalist who saw new commercial development as economic exploitation. "Harlemites, for the most part, failed to ask, Who is going to be empowered by this initiative?" Chinyelu wrote. "Tragically, for those easily seduced by glitter, the question may never come to mind." Likewise, Harlem-based activist Rev. Al Sharpton wondered aloud about the neighborhood's increasing commercial development. "Harlem is on the rise, but who is riding the wave?" he asked. "Are the people of Harlem surfing or being drowned?" The answer proved decidedly ambiguous, dependent in large measure on whom one asked.[28]

Perhaps no project symbolized both the tension and the promise that attended the arrival of large retail in Harlem quite like the Pathmark supermarket that rose on 125th Street between Lexington and Third Avenues. Like Harlem USA, the supermarket had deep roots in the local history of community development. Already in the late 1960s, the leaders behind the effort to gain community control in the East Harlem Triangle had begun to discuss the possibility of attracting modern food shopping. Triangle activists, led by Alice Kornegay, had opposed city plans to demolish their neighborhood—east of Park Avenue and north of 125th Street—for industrial development. Organized as the Community Association of the East Harlem Triangle, they gained official city approval of their own redevelopment plan, which prioritized affordable housing for their predominantly low-income neighborhood. Activists found that above all, Triangle residents hoped for the addition of "a good supermarket." CAEHT identified this as a long-term goal, tied to the completion of new housing in the neighborhood and ideally to be cooperatively owned by residents. By the early 1970s, CAEHT had identified a site for the project and planned to start construction. The project remained at this stage, however, likely due to the 1973 federal housing moratorium that crippled the group's efforts.[29]

Kornegay remained faithful to this early dream over the succeeding decades, though its promise was only hypothetical for much of that time. In the early 1990s, however, the administration of Mayor Dinkins promoted the construction of supermarkets in neighborhoods with limited food retail and extensive housing construction under the city's Ten Year Housing Plan. Both descriptions fit Harlem, which had no large-scale supermarket in its bounds. When the city requested development proposals for a long-vacant parking lot on the south side of 125th Street in 1991, CAEHT submitted a bid in partnership with Pathmark, a supermarket chain that had already launched similar ventures with CDCs in Bedford-Stuyvesant, Brooklyn, and Newark, New Jersey. Their proposal gained the city's approval, especially because of the central role reserved for CAEHT. "The proposal . . . clearly demonstrates that local entities and minority individuals can be involved in the development process not merely as sub-contractors and consultants, but as full equity participants," officials wrote.[30]

Making the Pathmark a reality provided a bridge between the earliest generation of community developers, represented by the scrappy CAEHT, and the most recent generation, represented by the highly professionalized ADC. While CAEHT's plans had gained praise from officials, problems obtaining financing brought the involvement of the Local Initiatives Support Corporation (LISC), the funding intermediary that had helped to bankroll much of the community-developed housing built over the previous decade. LISC had begun to take greater interest in retail development, in part due to the financial difficulties of projects like this one. Through an effort called the Retail Initiative, LISC raised funds from institutional investors, such as large banks and insurance companies, to provide the equity needed to obtain construction loans. LISC, which had worked extensively with ADC and become familiar with the organization's ability to complete projects, requested its addition to the development team "to strengthen [CAEHT's] administrative capacity," city officials explained. While CAEHT maintained many of the traits that characterized community organizations that originated in the 1960s— a charismatic leader, self-reliant nature, and homespun approach—ADC symbolized the sophistication and expertise that marked recent CDCs. The project proceeded as a joint venture of the two organizations, old and new, with a funding structure as complicated as in the housing developments on which ADC built its reputation. The federal government and Pathmark provided grants, the city Economic Development Corporation and private banks gave loans, New York State and LISC provided both grants and loans, and the Retail Initiative supplied the project's equity. Though planning for the supermarket commenced before UMEZ began operations, the effort shared the combination of public- and private-sector funding that was becoming ubiquitous in Harlem development.[31]

Supermarkets may register at the more mundane end of commercial development, but for many Harlemites the Pathmark project marked an extraordinary advance in a neighborhood that was, to put it mildly, poorly served by existing grocery retail. "The Poor Pay More . . . for Less," the city titled its 1991 study of grocery availability in New York's predominantly low-income neighborhoods. In communities like Harlem, officials in the city's Department of Consumer Affairs explained, residents paid an average of almost 9 percent more for groceries than in the city's predominantly middle-class neighborhoods. Grocery stores in underserved areas were smaller, less sanitary, and had less competition for customers, many of whom lacked mobility and thus consumer choice. Smaller stores stocked fewer products and offered fewer services such as automated teller machines, the city wrote. Convenience stores often filled demand but offered a limited selection of fruits, vegetables, and other fresh ingredients. More detailed studies confirmed that Harlemites did, in fact, pay more. The city's Human Resources Administration conducted market basket studies, comparing the largest available stores in Harlem—all served by two wholesalers—with the broader selection of retail available in New York's Lower East Side, including a Pathmark. A September 1994 study found that the lowest-priced sample basket cost over 11 percent more in Harlem and the highest-priced basket over 6 percent more. A November survey found even starker disparities: residents paid over 27 percent more for the lowest-priced market basket in Harlem and almost 17 percent more for the highest-priced basket.[32]

Unsurprisingly, then, Harlemites desired greater retail options in the community. HUDC conducted a survey of Harlem residents as part of the Empowerment Zone planning process. Only 9 percent of respondents evaluated existing stores and supermarkets as "excellent." Forty-four percent considered the availability of stores within walking distance to be "pretty good," and 42 percent rated grocery stores with the same mark. Equally as many residents considered current stores to be "only fair" or "poor," however. Forty-nine percent placed food retail in those bottom-most categories. When staff asked residents which new stores they would like to see, clothing stores and supermarkets proved the leaders, with 22 percent requesting the former and 19 percent selecting the latter. In 1998, Porter's Initiative for a Competitive Inner City, a nonprofit that he had founded to promote his ideas and for which Wright served as an advisory board member, collaborated with the Boston Consulting Group to investigate the potential of retail development in six urban markets, including Harlem. The study emphasized the profitability of such investment. "For growth-oriented retailers seeking revenues and new opportunities in today's global marketplace," it promised, "the inner city is perhaps the last large domestic frontier." Yet even as the authors made a "business case," their analysis nonetheless offered revealing glimpses of the human cost of limited options in Harlem, a market that they estimated did not have retail supply to meet even half of resident demand. One Harlem focus group member suspected that retailers raised prices during the first two weeks of the month, after eligible residents received public assistance checks. "We do not want old, dated, second-rate stores, products, and services," another focus group member said. "Sometimes six or eight of us share a van to New Jersey to go to BJ's [Wholesale Club]," a third explained, suggesting the lengths residents were willing to go to obtain reasonably priced groceries.[33]

If many Harlemites looked on improved food retail with anticipation, however, others feared that a supermarket would expand inequality alongside grocery selection. As he often did, Wilcox staked a position of deep skepticism at the Pathmark's 1997 groundbreaking. "What we have here is a bunch of capitalists coming into our community, but not really showing us how capitalism works," he said. "Harlem is looking more and more like a cash cow, but what needs to be done is for our people to invest in themselves." Wilcox protested the possibility that new development, with private-sector involvement, would bring benefits to outsiders while leaving Harlemites behind. Instead, he highlighted the financial potential of Harlem's poorest residents. "These bankers and what have you should encourage the tenants who reside in some 22 housing projects and possess nearly $3 million to use their money as an investment vehicle," he told a reporter. Similarly, Lloyd Williams, CEO of the Greater Harlem Chamber of Commerce, seemed to overlook the equity role of the community development organizations at the heart of the Pathmark project in advocating for his members. "You have a Pathmark coming here and we need it," he said, "But it's the Pathmarks that are benefiting from the tax credits, employees' benefits and loans that are available, as opposed to the small mom-and-pop stores that really need to benefit from these zones."[34]

Indeed, the small retailers who had sold groceries for years in the absence of a large supermarket, and who now found themselves the subject of criticism, expressed these sentiments most publicly. The Retail Initiative's support for supermarket development brought a hundred East Harlem storeowners to protest at the intermediary's offices in late 1994. The merchants opposed the public and nonprofit support allocated to the Pathmark project and the 50,000-square-foot size of the combination grocery and pharmacy, a feature that they viewed as only bringing a new scale of competition to the neighborhood. "It will make the shopping strip of any commercial area like a ghost town," one proprietor of small food markets explained. "The Pathmark gets everything." A seemingly straightforward protest became complicated very quickly, however. The lobbyist supporting the merchants most vociferously worked for one of the wholesalers that supplied many East Harlem markets, suggesting the multiple interests at play. The issue was also racially charged, as the owners of bodegas and corner stores, mostly Latino, publicly resisted a project whose community backers were largely African American. Council members, who would have to approve the land transfer to enable the project to go forward, consequently sorted along ethnic lines. Meanwhile, Mayor Giuliani, rarely shy in political battles, attempted to dodge this one as support for the project threatened to upset Latino voters he depended on. Protest subsided only after Giuliani publicly stated his approval of the project on two conditions: a loan program for the smaller merchants administered by Chase, a lender to the Pathmark project, and a promised future 49 percent ownership share for a Latino group in the CAEHT/ADC joint venture, which seems never to have materialized.[35]

Though the Pathmark protest rapidly devolved into a battle cast along parochial lines, it nonetheless remained emblematic of a broader frustration among small-business people in Harlem, who felt overlooked amid the increasing focus on large retail projects. The response of record-store owners to Harlem USA expressed such a sentiment, as did the exasperation of those proprietors who felt neglected amid discussion of "empowerment." UMEZ funded a small-business lending program called the Business Resource and Investment Services Center to support equipment purchases, working costs, and modest expansion with loans under $200,000. It likewise supported an effort targeted at area restaurants and funded other modest lending programs.[36] Such aid proved helpful to those who received it, but those who did not saw only official neglect and indifference to their efforts. One Harlemite who opened a small television studio with his own savings applied for a $50,000 loan from UMEZ, but the program denied his application. "To get a loan they said you have to have a three-year track record of being in a business," he told a reporter. "If I'm a new business, how could I have three years of bookkeeping and records?" Dorothy Pitman Hughes, who owned an office supply store on 125th Street, wrote a book about her frustrations with UMEZ, which denied her funding request as well. "We African-American business owners now feel that we have been used," Hughes wrote, "and that our efforts to empower the community may actually have resulted in accomplishing the gentrification of Harlem."[37]

Yet even as such views indicated deeply held anxiety over changes that were readily apparent to any observer on 125th Street, many other Harlemites looked forward to such new development. Pathmark paid a market research firm to conduct a telephone survey of area residents amid the controversy that surrounded the project. The survey, based on 300 random calls, found that 90 percent of respondents agreed that a supermarket was needed, a remarkably high number even for a commissioned study. The involvement of community-based organizations at the center of this and other large retail projects likewise complicated claims that these projects would bring the empowerment of outsiders and the downfall of residents. ADC and CAEHT jointly owned the land on which the supermarket stood. Pathmark paid them rent, funds that the nonprofits used to support subsequent projects in the community.[38]

Indeed, even the basic claim that new, large-scale competition would undermine smaller merchants remained less than certain. A Baruch College study that analyzed the impact of the Lower East Side Pathmark on neighborhood retail in the mid-1980s found that two of seven large food stores in the area closed in the three and a half years after the Pathmark opened, but the sixty-six nearby small specialty stores—which sold food, clothing, and other goods—were unharmed. The city's own study of possible impact in East Harlem, conducted by a planning consultant in 1992 before any controversy had emerged, explained that the area had been underserved for so long that residents could support another 40,000 square feet of food retail and the same amount of pharmacy retail, far in excess of the size of this project. Soon after the Pathmark opened in April 1999, a *Times* reporter found nearby store-owners already improving their product selection, displays, and interior finishes, some with help from the aid program that had grown from their protests.[39]

This new era of commercial development marked the dwindling of the radical ideal of a community cooperatively owned and rebuilt by its

FIGURE 6.4. The Pathmark supermarket that opened at the corner of 125th Street and Lexington Avenue in 1999. Developed by a partnership between ADC and CAEHT, the grocery store raised concerns about the costs to small businesses of increasing chain retail in Harlem. At the same time, many Harlemites, eager to find quality, affordable goods close to home, welcomed its arrival.

low-income residents. But as many Harlemites responded to the arrival of the Pathmark with glee, it became clear that Harlem's community organizations had achieved at least a measure of one of their early goals—that the neighborhood's main street would serve the needs of its residents. If this objective had been attained on the narrower field of consumption rather than as part of an expansive vision of 125th Street as a space of cultural, residential, social, educational, and economic self-determination, the achievement remained consequential. Residents in majority African American neighborhoods had long depended on chain retail for predictable prices and quality goods. As exemplified by the reaction of Harlemites upon first passing through the automated glass doors of the Pathmark, this remained equally true at the close of the century (see Figure 6.4). One visitor admired a head of broccoli, judging its quality worth its price. "We've been waiting a long time for a nice supermarket in Harlem," she said, explaining that she would no longer need her daughter to bring back decent meat from outside Harlem. A mother of two young boys marveled at the simple fact that she could find everything she needed in one place. "I'm just going crazy in here," she told a reporter. "Everything I need in a store is right here."[40]

One longtime Harlemite was not there to enjoy the fruits of her labors, however. Kornegay passed away in May 1996, having lived long enough to see the long-sought supermarket project come together but not to see it built and filled with customers. As one of the figures who had first insisted that residents demand community control over their built environment, her death signaled the closing of a chapter in Harlem's history. Indeed, the transformation of 125th Street in the late 1990s marked not just the arrival of new retail in the neighborhood, but also a changing of the guard among those who steered community development at the close of the century.[41]

Power Lost and Gained at the Corner of 125th and Lenox

The central block of 125th Street, on the north side between Lenox Avenue and Adam Clayton Powell Jr. Boulevard, had witnessed every major phase in the history of Harlem development in the last four decades of the twentieth century. It was here that the state decided to build a skyscraper to house its offices, the last gasp of an urban renewal order that had reshaped the neighborhood in the 1960s. It was here that radical activists constructed a communitarian settlement for three months in the summer of 1969, hoping to stop the state's project. It was also here, in the aftermath of that occupation, that the leaders of HUDC transformed the inclusive, eclectic ideal of activists and the Architects' Renewal Committee in Harlem into a much narrower vision of a commercial future for 125th Street built on a foundation of large projects. This vision had remained on drawing boards over the following two decades.

In the mid-1990s, this site—home by this time to the state office building, a parking garage, and a row of small storefronts—witnessed yet one more transition, from the older generation of moderate liberal leaders represented by HUDC to the younger generation of pragmatic centrists represented by

Rev. Calvin O. Butts III, leader of the Abyssinian Baptist Church. The addition of Abyssinian's CDC to the Pathmark project had suggested the prominence the organization had achieved through its successful housing efforts. "The developer, Abyssinian Baptist Church, is one of the most powerful forces in *black* Harlem," the *New York Daily News* explained. "But it is also one of the most respected institutions in the city, with a proven track record."[42] Abyssinian's involvement in Harlem's commercial transformation would only increase over the last years of the decade, symbolizing the arrival of community-based organizations not merely as participants but as major players in urban development and, consequently, the city and state's political scene.

This story played out at the corner of 125th Street and Lenox Avenue in the form of Harlem Center. When construction began on this office tower and retail complex at the turn of the century, the strands of the forty-year history explored here came together: the long-standing hope that community-based organizations could shape the neighborhood's physical form, the ascendant vision of commercial development in Harlem's core, and the new pragmatism exemplified by the generation of church-based CDCs that emerged in the 1980s. Here, ADC decisively transformed the block that had been the canvas for generations of visions of Harlem's future. Indeed, if the low-slung Pathmark marked the still-growing influence of ADC in the mid-1990s in a correspondingly understated fashion, the commanding bulk of Harlem Center aptly signified the dominant status the organization had achieved by the early 2000s, when the shopping center opened its doors (see Figure 6.5). While ADC's rise—and that of Harlem's newest commercial complex—signaled the central role of community development organizations in shaping the neighborhood by the new millennium, however, so too did it raise new questions about the nature and distribution of power at Harlem's grass roots.

Harlem Center, like the nearby Harlem USA, added national retailers to the neighborhood's major spine, including the clothing stores Marshall's and H&M, a CVS pharmacy, Staples office store, Washington Mutual Bank, and Dunkin Donuts. Officials explained the approximately $80 million project as the latest in the series of large-scale commercial centers that were transforming 125th Street. "Harlem Center is another tremendous project that will create jobs, investment and confidence in one of New York's most storied

FIGURE 6.5. Harlem Center, located at the corner of 125th Street and Lenox Avenue, with the state office building in the background. Completed in 2002 and developed by ADC and Forest City Ratner, the commercial complex demonstrated the influence that some community-based organizations had gained as major players in urban development while raising questions about the nature and distribution of power at Harlem's grass roots.

neighborhoods," announced Governor Pataki in launching the project in 2000. "Harlem Center will continue the economic renewal that this community is experiencing with projects such as 125th Street Pathmark, East River Plaza [a commercial development on the former Washburn Wire site in East Harlem] and Harlem USA." Like its predecessors on Harlem's main street, Harlem Center grew from a partnership between a supportive public-sector partner—in this case, the state of New York; a private-sector developer— here, Forest City Ratner; and a long-standing Harlem community development organization, ADC.[43]

Harlem Center mirrored the collaborative approach and commercial orientation of its new neighbors, but its origin story proved considerably more complicated. Abyssinian's role at the center of the project indicated not simply the organization's emergence as Harlem's go-to CDC, but the broader transformation of the landscape of community development in the last years of the twentieth century. For nearly two decades, the land that became Harlem Center, located to the east of the state office building, had instead fueled dreams of the Harlem International Trade Center, the project that HUDC hoped would instantiate its own vision of large-scale, publicly funded, commercially oriented development as the basis of Harlem's transformation. The Harlem International Trade Center plan marked the eclipse in the 1970s of the eclectic, inclusive vision that radical activists sought for this site. Instead of a community-planned, mixed-use center of culture, housing, education, and commerce, HUDC's moderate board members pushed a hotel, convention center, trade institute, and international bazaar for this land. Backers hoped that the megaproject would both spur development in Harlem and become a trading hub with what proponents described as "Third World" countries abroad.[44]

Yet while the trade center received enthusiastic promotion from Representative Rangel, the steadfast supporter of HUDC who made this his pet project, and gained prominent backers in succeeding years, the development inched along only slowly amid alternating advances and setbacks. Diplomats and world leaders fueled hopes, for example, visiting Harlem to express their interest. Tanzania's president Julius Nyerere, Nigeria's president Shehu Shagari, and Zimbabwe's prime minister Robert Mugabe were among the statesmen who posed for photographs in the late 1970s and early 1980s with architectural models, HUDC's executives, or Rangel. Reagan's election undermined the federal support President Jimmy Carter had offered to the project, but Rangel's own growing influence in Congress and the election of Democrat Mario Cuomo as New York's governor in 1983 buoyed hopes that a skyscraper would nonetheless rise on the fateful 125th Street site. A 1986 request for proposals failed to secure a developer, but by 1988, Rangel had procured a commitment from the federal government to lease one-third of the office space in the structure, and Cuomo dedicated $50 million to the project from the Port Authority of New York and New Jersey. In 1989, the state at last announced the selection of a developer, a public-private collaboration that foreshadowed the later arrangement of Harlem Center, pairing private entities with community partners, including the Harlem Churches for Community Improvement, the CDC that at that time was also actively involved in housing construction. The groundbreaking was finally just over the horizon, backers claimed. "Next year," Rangel promised in late 1990.[45]

But the long-delayed project continued to stand in suspended animation as the new decade began, and soon it outlasted the state officials who provided essential support. Despite visits from twenty different foreign leaders, none had signed on as tenants in the still speculative complex. Meanwhile, the project's private-sector backers took three years to agree on development terms with the state. By late 1993, the site remained untouched and the trade center languished. While backers scrambled to secure assurances from potential lessees, the political winds shifted. Pataki's election as governor in November 1994 came as something of a surprise, ending both Cuomo's three-term rule and the two-decade tenure of the Democratic Party in the governor's office. Pataki, at the time a one-term state senator, benefited from the steadfast support of Senator Alfonse D'Amato, general dissatisfaction with the Clinton administration, and weariness toward Cuomo, who had responded to the ongoing recession with budget cuts and new taxes. Pataki attracted disenchanted suburban and upstate voters with promises of tax cuts and the reinstatement of the death penalty, riding a broader conservative tide that ushered Republicans into office throughout the nation.[46]

Pataki's election owed little to New York City. Mayor Giuliani, though a Republican, had endorsed Cuomo in the gubernatorial race, a wager based on his sense that Cuomo would win and on his bitter, long-standing rivalry with D'Amato. Indeed, Pataki gained from Giuliani's seeming betrayal of his party, painting it as a cynical "deal" that would benefit residents of New York City at the expense of other New Yorkers. Unsurprisingly, then, soon after his January 1995 inauguration, Pataki looked to eliminate state expenditures that especially benefited New York City's residents. His first budget proposed deep cuts to social services, moved funding for urban public transportation to upstate projects, and slashed support for public education and Medicaid.[47]

Likewise, Harlem did not escape the new governor's notice. Pataki promised the end of HUDC, proposing to merge the autonomous but state-funded organization into the state's Urban Development Corporation, soon renamed the Empire State Development Corporation (ESDC). Charles Gargano, Pataki's appointee to lead ESDC, cited HUDC as an inefficiency in the new state development structure and an expenditure—of $3.5 million annually—that the state could not afford. Upon HUDC's closure in August 1995, Gargano chided the "uncontested reign" of the organization, describing what he perceived as its "failure to stimulate economic growth despite an investment of $109 million in state funds over the years." Pataki created a new organization, the Harlem Community Development Corporation, in its stead, an entity that would receive substantially less funding from the state and whose board of directors the governor would largely control. Rangel, who had backed the creation of HUDC from its inception and supported the faction of Harlem leaders who had maintained power over it, recognized the broader transformation that HUDC's termination foreshadowed. "This seems like the end of development in Harlem as we have known it," he told a reporter.[48]

HUDC's termination surely derived from a changing political context in the state. Pataki's rapid move to dismantle the agency despite its relatively modest budget spoke to his interest in undermining an organization that had been a stronghold of Democratic leaders like Rangel. Yet the Pataki administration's criticisms of HUDC as an entity that had dreamed up big projects but built few, and that had often seemed to spend freely in its own self-interest, were apparently not without foundation. The state performed a comprehensive audit of HUDC after shutting it down. As a result of its autonomy from state oversight, the investigation reported, "HUDC spent untold unnecessary amounts of taxpayer funds, failed to properly account for loans and advances to HUDC directors and employees, and pumped millions of dollars into New York's underground economy through 'off-the-books' payments to construction workers, security guards, consultants, and independent contractors." Despite warning signs throughout the organization's twenty-five-year history, these issues persisted, the report claimed.[49]

HUDC's backers brushed off such criticisms as partisan attacks, but the state's findings were consistent with the conflicts of interest and self-interest that had appeared in the organization's operations from its very first years, sometimes even involving the same people. "I have no idea what the findings are based on," Rangel claimed. "You have a bunch of Republicans going through the files of a defunct organization run by Democrats." Yet many of the excesses that the state cited were plainly egregious, if not malicious. HUDC skirted state hiring restrictions by classifying many employees as "consultants," for example, and did not withhold taxes from their salaries. HUDC often paid excessively for services or paid for services not rendered.

The organization paid a computer consultant a six-figure salary to perform what the state categorized as "routine accounting functions," though HUDC had its own accounting staff. It similarly overpaid a consultant to manage the parking garage on the intended Harlem International Trade Center site, yet failed to pay the city the rent it owed for operating the garage. The Temporary Commission of Investigation frequently cited HUDC's failure to maintain standard financial records as an impediment in determining if the agency's expenditures were appropriate.[50]

The case of attorney Jeff Greenup offered one of the most symbolic examples of the endemic conflicts of interest and misspent funds that marked HUDC. Greenup had sat as the general counsel on HUDC's board of directors throughout its history, yet he served at the same time as a paid legal consultant to HUDC's staff, an arrangement that went unquestioned. In HUDC's last three and a half years alone, Greenup billed for more than $600,000, yet his invoices detailed none of the services rendered nor the members of his firm who had worked on assignments. HUDC had been alerted to such discrepancies as early as the 1980s, the state explained, but leaders had never acted to rectify them. The state claimed that Greenup had billed—and received—three times the amount allowed under his contract in 1995 alone. Greenup's implication in the investigation suggested the persistence over decades of the kinds of excesses that had emerged in HUDC from the start. Indeed, it was Greenup himself who, in the early 1970s, had attempted to submit a proposal for the project intended for the corner of 125th Street and Lenox Avenue despite his official involvement with HUDC's board. He had also sought to change HUDC's bylaws to allow board members to profit from the development activities of the purportedly community-oriented organization. Now, Greenup refused to respond to the state's inquiries and provided only cursory documents when officials went through the courts to compel participation. Greenup's case, reported in the *Times* alongside several other provocative anecdotes, undermined HUDC's protests that it had been a necessary agent in Harlem's built environment and detracted from the successes that it had achieved, especially in the realm of housing.[51]

Unsurprisingly, the closing of HUDC reverberated on the block that its supporters had hoped would hold the skyscraper tower of the Harlem International Trade Center. Like federal leaders and those in UMEZ too, Pataki subscribed to the notion that development efforts should arise primarily from the involvement of the private sector. Soon after taking office, Gargano expressed his distaste for big, publicly funded projects, including the trade center. When Gargano instituted a December 1995 deadline on the long-unrealized project, Rangel protested that its backers needed more time. "The Trade Center is the linchpin for economic growth and business development for Harlem and upper Manhattan," he told Pataki. Yet the administration disagreed, favoring the emerging view that Harlem's economic health rested on the use of public funds to attract private investment, with the goal of bringing the neighborhood into a perceived economic mainstream. When the state withdrew its support from the project in late 1995, explaining that "the money can be better spent," Gargano expressed his desire to instead develop the site for retail. The trade center's death spelled the end of the strategy of Harlem development that Rangel had backed, consisting of large projects funded through public support often arranged by the congressman.[52]

If HUDC's end marked a watershed in community development, however, not all Harlemites stood to lose from the increasing focus on making markets uptown. Trade center supporters claimed that the project's termination would hurt Harlem. "This is economic racism," stated Percy Sutton, the chairman of the Harlem International Trade Center Corporation. But the younger generation of community-based organizations, like ADC, which embraced the market-oriented approach to Harlem's redevelopment, gained by HUDC's loss. Political change created an untenable situation for the Democratic-backed old guard of Harlem community developers, but the political free agency that had long marked ADC's approach—emphasizing the task of building over a rigid political dogma—proved remarkably valuable in this new era. While Rangel and others complained about the seemingly political moves that undermined the international trade center, ADC seized the opportunity provided with the election of Pataki.[53]

This sea change, and the consequent prominence accorded ADC, was bound up in the figure of Reverend Butts, the prominent leader of Abyssinian Baptist Church. Butts, who had called from the pulpit for the community engagement that brought the founding of ADC, served as the very symbol of the political pragmatism that suffused its work and the spiritual guidepost of its agenda. Butts had cut an unconventional figure in the usually predictable political landscape of Harlem since his initial ascent as Abyssinian's pastor. Born in 1949, Butts had participated in the civil rights movement while growing up in New York City and taken part in the civil disorder that followed the assassination of Dr. Martin Luther King Jr. Butts continued to associate his work closely with the legacy of leaders like King and Adam Clayton Powell Jr., his predecessor at Abyssinian. Yet Butts eschewed the typical alliances that African American leaders in New York made. In the late 1980s, Butts criticized old-guard Harlem political leaders like Dinkins, who would become New York's first African American mayor, as "overly cautious." In the 1992 presidential election, Butts endorsed third-party candidate Ross Perot, even serving as the cochair of Perot's New York campaign committee. Butts staged bombastic crusades against tobacco and alcohol advertising in Harlem, leading ministers in painting over neighborhood billboards, and against rap music lyrics. In 1993, he supported the mayoral candidacy of Republican Giuliani. The next year, he endorsed Rangel's congressional reelection from the pulpit, citing the Democrat's support for ADC and new prominence on the House Committee on Ways and Means. But he also took the highly unusual step of inviting Pataki, then the Republican gubernatorial candidate, to speak to the members of the church during Sunday services.[54]

The *Times* described "the political dance of Calvin Butts," emphasizing the minister's flexibility and shifting alliances in pursuit of needed resources. Butts sought diverse political partners not out of cynicism, but because he recognized allies in places where many local leaders had not looked. Republicans claimed political power in the mid-1990s that Butts and his organization could benefit from, to be sure. But Butts also saw alignment between the strategy of ADC, which emphasized improvement through building, and leaders like Pataki, who favored opening neighborhoods like Harlem to development. "I think the Republicans are in an excellent position to make the argument and demonstrate that you can do as much through economic development as you can through social welfare programs—in fact more," Butts explained.[55]

At the same time, leaders like Pataki were eager to embrace figures like Butts, who offered a gateway to a community that had rarely formed part of the Republican political coalition. For his invitation to speak at Abyssinian and his refusal to endorse either candidate in the election that Pataki won, the new governor rewarded Butts with a seat on his transition team and, more crucially, membership on the board of ESDC, the reorganized state-wide development entity. Pataki also appointed Butts to the board of the Harlem Community Development Corporation, the successor to HUDC, whose vote determined the fate of the Harlem International Trade Center. Rangel blamed the appointment of Butts for the trade center's demise. One New York paper claimed that Butts had even introduced the resolution to end the project. Regardless of whether that was actually the case, he reportedly voted with the majority, electing termination.[56]

With the official end of the trade center, the Pataki administration wasted no time in pursuing the retail project that Gargano had indicated was destined for the corner of 125th Street and Lenox Avenue. In early 1996, officials requested proposals for the "Harlem Center Mall," a complex that touted the same market-oriented economic logic as the other large-scale commercial projects that would be built on 125th Street during the latter half of the decade. "The absence of major national retailers, as well as the lack of varied mid-priced retailers, causes many of Harlem's residents to make their purchases outside of the area," the request explained. Likewise, the population between ages forty-five and fifty-four, the "peak earning year group" within Harlem, was expected to grow, meaning hundreds of millions of potential spending dollars. "While many retailers have shown an appreciation of Harlem's favorable demographics and a largely untapped market," state officials wrote, "there has not been first class retail space for them to lease." Harlem Center Mall was to provide that retail space. To build it, the state sought development teams with experience on similarly large-scale projects and involvement from Harlem nonprofits or entrepreneurs. ADC, already engaged with commercial development through the Pathmark project, invited a major private developer, Forest City Ratner, to submit a joint bid for the complex.[57]

If the state did not design the project specifically for such a proposal by ADC, the political capital that Butts had built up through his support of Pataki nevertheless continued to pay dividends. In mid-1997, when ESDC selected ADC and Forest City Ratner to develop the project, some eyebrows were raised but few wondered why that outcome had occurred. "The designation is yet another example of the ascension of Rev. Calvin O. Butts 3d . . . under the administration of Gov. George E. Pataki," the *Times* wrote. Rangel explained the selection as an obvious result of Butts's loyalty to the governor. "You support somebody and they in turn support you," he said, "and I think Reverend Butts understands that." Butts, for his part, waved off such insinuations, even if their speakers delivered them without malice. The reverend, eager to ensure that his project was not tainted with the air of impropriety that had stained HUDC's reputation, explained that though he served on the board that made the selection, he did not take part in the decision. "I am first and foremost a clergyperson," he said. "Charles Gargano has been extremely fair. He hasn't doled out any favors I'm aware of." Later, he attempted to distance himself from the success of the church's development corporation, though their fates—and their ascents—were entwined. "I don't think I've been extended any privilege as a member of the ESDC board," he said. "The Abyssinian Development Corporation is a separate corporation with separate boards."[58]

Yet Butts and ADC's growing influence on Harlem development had become undeniable. Butts's close connection to Randy Daniels, the African American senior vice president of ESDC, provided one example. Daniels largely handled the state's affairs in Harlem. He was a longtime Harlemite, a member of Abyssinian Baptist Church, and a friend to Butts. Daniels also administered the Metropolitan Economic Revitalization Fund (MERF), a revolving state loan fund that seeded privately financed development projects. MERF had grown from the ashes of the Harlem International Trade Center. Upon its termination, the state divided up the millions of dollars it had committed to the project, assigning a portion to the Empowerment Zone program and $25 million to MERF, which provided essential funding to ADC and Forest City Ratner's Harlem Center project. Harlem Center did not tap direct grant or loan support from UMEZ—though the state touted the project's eligibility for the zone's incentives in seeking developers—but Pataki did call on Butts as he weighed whether to maintain Cuomo's $100 million commitment to the effort. Pataki's reluctance in part accounted for the long delay before UMEZ began distributing funds in late 1996. Butts shaped the governor's eventual decision to honor his predecessor's pledge. "When the Empowerment Zone was being set up, the governor called me and asked me if I thought the state should really participate," Butts recalled. "I never will forget that. . . . I said that I appreciated him asking for my advice, and to move forward."[59]

The construction of Harlem Center recorded ADC's prominence in Harlem's built environment, at one of the neighborhood's major intersections. No longer occupied only with housing development, the CDC had begun to reshape the landscape in vast strokes. Likewise, the growing power of Butts in Harlem's physical space served as an index of his influence in the political space of Harlem and beyond. Butts, long rumored to be eyeing a run for public office, kept such rumors alive into the late 1990s. "It looks more and more like I would do it," he told a reporter in 1998. That year, Butts appeared on the cover of *New York* magazine, with Sharpton in the background. The headline posed a provocative question: "Which would you choose, Dr. King?" Butts mused about being mayor of his hometown. The reporter considered whether challenging the long-serving Rangel was a more likely possibility. No African American political leader had stepped up since the generation of Dinkins and Rangel, the reporter noted, and Butts's pragmatism, a departure from the approach of his predecessors, could serve as both a liability and an asset on a broader stage.[60]

Though Butts fed such speculation, he played a more prominent political role behind the scenes. He stepped into the rivalry between Giuliani and Pataki in 1998, for instance, labeling the mayor a racist for his administration's approach to policing and cuts to services that benefited the poor. A few months later he officially endorsed Pataki's bid for a second term, angering both African American leaders frustrated with Pataki's own budget cuts and Giuliani, who called for the governor to reject the endorsement. "I can have someone I disagree with, but who helps me a great deal with projects that are important for our community," Butts announced in endorsing the governor. Pataki, rather than rejecting Butts's support, embraced it. "We are unequivocally thrilled to have Reverend Butts's endorsement," Pataki's spokesman said. Butts eventually declined to run for either Rangel's seat or Giuliani's, but his steadfast support for the governor did help gain one new leadership role at the state level. In August 1999, the sixteen-member governing board of the State University of New York at Old Westbury, fifteen of whom were Pataki appointees, nominated Butts as the university's new president. Daniels, the state official who supported Harlem Center and served as a State University of New York trustee, had pushed Butts's candidacy. Despite charges that the decision was politically motivated, a claim that Pataki denied, Butts received approval. He took his new post alongside his position as leader of Harlem's most prominent church and his growing reputation as one of Harlem's most successful builders.[61]

"Real Players" at What Cost?

Early in the new century, the *Amsterdam News* stepped back to survey the church-based CDCs that had been transforming the city's predominantly African American neighborhoods for nearly two decades. "More than 20 years later," the author wrote, "these religious institutions are real players in helping to reshape some of the city's working class neighborhoods, propelling development in places that were once ignored." Exhibit A was Harlem Center, and the reporter turned to Butts. "We think things are going well," Butts explained. "We are involved in total community development, from residential to commercial to educational and cultural." ADC had achieved influence that backers never dreamed of when they launched as a modest, informal venture intended to build stable housing for the church's elderly parishioners. Now, as leaders like Butts gained greater power, Harlem became increasingly diverse economically, and insiders and outsiders both demonstrated a new openness to the private market, organizations like ADC were, indeed, "real players."[62]

Yet if ADC's prominence derived in large measure from its pragmatism in an era of change, serious questions remained about the costs of this new order of development and whether all Harlemites benefited equally. On this front, ADC's experience with Harlem Center again proved instructive. When Abyssinian gained designation for the project to which it had deep political ties, other long-standing CDCs cried foul. Harlem Congregations for Community Improvement, the CDC that had arisen alongside ADC in the late 1980s, had submitted a proposal for the project as well. The organization's director, Preston Washington, objected that ADC had gained favorable treatment through its relationship with Pataki. "I think this was done to position Calvin [Butts] to run for Congress," he explained. "Sixty congregations are going to be overlooked so the project can go to one church, with one preacher." HCC, which was involved with the development of Harlem USA and unsuccessfully sought involvement with this project as well, drew parallels between ADC's success and the just-released state audit of HUDC. "This is more of the same, only now it's colored Republican," an HCC executive claimed. Such complaints surely arose in part from envy, but also from the reality that the changing nature of development rewarded some organizations while leaving others behind. In an increasingly competitive climate, as leaders sought to spur investment in Harlem, the public and private sectors looked to organizations like ADC that built their reputations on ideological flexibility and the ability to get things done.[63]

Moreover, while ADC had achieved the centrality that community-based organizations long sought, the question also remained whether such influence included the high ideals that had inspired demands for community development in the first place. Political pragmatism came at a cost. When neighborhood activists protested against Butts's embrace of Pataki, they did so not merely because of parochial turf battles or personal rivalries, but because they believed such an endorsement had real and damaging consequences in Harlem. Many pointed to the cuts Pataki had instituted in tuition assistance for students attending the state and city university systems. Others wondered how Butts could endorse a leader who had reintroduced the death penalty, expanded the state's investment in prisons, and slashed social service spending. Those on the front lines of such protests included many of Harlem's graying activists, survivors from an earlier era who brought their dissent to the transforming landscape of 125th Street. Several gathered in front of the state office building in late 1998, on the plaza whose pavement covered the earth that had once supported the tents of Reclamation Site #1. "Butts's political opportunism must be challenged by the members of his church and the Harlem community who have provided the base for his emergence as a prominent spokesperson for Harlem," said Jim Haughton, who for decades had fought discrimination in the construction industry. Wilcox, as ever, was among them, and, as ever, spared no mercy in challenging an opponent. "He has put himself in the position of a slave catcher to help Pataki take over Harlem," Wilcox exclaimed.[64]

Yet if Wilcox saw new development on 125th Street as a portent of Harlem's demise, Butts viewed that commercial redevelopment as the most concrete sign that long-standing goals had finally been accomplished. Questioned on his endorsement of Pataki, Butts pointed to one of the projects that his organization had been able to build. "We can . . . say that the developers of the Pathmark supermarket are Black people. In other words, we won the building and the land."[65] Both sides were certain that their view of Harlem was the right one, but in fact their inability to agree suggested the complexity at play in the neighborhood by the late 1990s. Making markets in Harlem, both abstract and literal, brought mixed meanings for the neighborhood's residents. Many welcomed Harlem's entrance into a promised economic mainstream, while others feared that open doors would bring new threats. At the center stood Harlem's community developers, who also had much to gain and much to lose in the neighborhood's transformation.

Conclusion

Between the Two Harlems

IN NOVEMBER 2001, architect J. Max Bond Jr. joined former Upper Manhattan Empowerment Zone (UMEZ) president Deborah Wright, Abyssinian Development Corporation (ADC) executive Darren Walker, and others at an Urban Land Institute event on development in Harlem. The program outlined a boosterish agenda consistent with the orientation of its sponsor. "The purpose of the program is to present a current view of development opportunities in this increasingly vibrant Manhattan community," the announcement explained. "Speakers will address the salient issues driving the current revitalization efforts in Harlem and discuss why these efforts are timely, profitable, and beneficial for New York, Harlem, and the development community." If the program promised discussions consistent with the view of Harlem as a market yet to be fully tapped, however, Bond took the opportunity to raise a series of critical questions about who gained and who lost in Harlem's accelerating transformation. "Who will benefit?" he asked. "Who will profit from growth and change?" Will all Harlemites have access to newly created jobs, Bond wondered, and would the neighborhood's "existing social and cultural institutions" gain too? "There are many other such questions that need to be addressed," Bond told the audience members, "but for me as an architect and urbanist the overarching question is: in what image will Harlem be recreated?"[1]

Indeed, the story of Harlem in the late twentieth century was fundamentally a story about images—about social, political, and architectural visions of the future city and the struggle over which would prevail. Frustration with large-scale, state-led urban redevelopment in the 1960s had prompted often-radical demands for community control over the built environment. Bond had helped to articulate the vision that grew from these demands, a utopian yet seemingly attainable hope that Harlem could be a place built by and for its predominantly low-income residents. These goals gave rise to community-based organizations promising to achieve this radical image. In time, however, they shed such aspirations for a variety of reasons, including their continued dependence on the financial support of the state, the intransigence of community control radicals, the preferences and political orientations of strong leaders, changing sociological understandings of poverty, and the simple fact that profound transformation often required herculean efforts by local activists facing long odds. These causes were subsumed under another, larger factor, one intrinsic to community-based organizations themselves: goals such as community control and community development were inspiring but ambiguous, making them highly subject to the competing interests that filled these decades in Harlem. Indeed, these organizations became the crucibles in which such debates played out, in rhetoric and in Harlem's built environment.

As a result, then, community developers did achieve one of their highest aspirations by the end of the century: to gain a central role in reshaping Harlem. But they came to adopt and realize a vision—of economic integration and commercial redevelopment—that differed dramatically from the ideals that had seeded signal events like the occupation of Reclamation Site #1 and the activism of urban homesteaders. This was a central paradox of these decades: over time, Harlem community organizations with radical origins and their direct successors came to espouse a narrowed, often pragmatic approach to social, political, and spatial transformation. In the process, they produced the Harlem of the new millennium, with new and refurbished housing for middle-class families and shopping centers towering over 125th Street. This outcome suggested the complex history underlying Harlem's much-regarded gentrification in these decades, which was not simply the result of decisions made by outsiders to the neighborhood or the product of external forces, but which grew up from very local roots.

Community development, which had once stood for a radical, communitarian, and collectivist ideal of the future city, instead came to represent an image of Harlem as a place whose revitalization would proceed from its entrance into a so-called economic mainstream. This view predominated by the end of the twentieth century, as public-private development partnerships and income diversification became the watchwords of community developers not only in Harlem but nationwide. Indeed, in articulating his own response to the question he had posed, even Bond blended the radical aspirations that he had voiced in the late 1960s with the vision that had since become pervasive in Harlem. "I believe that we should develop images of what I call the Working City, a city that serves the needs and reflects the imaginations and visions of all its people," Bond explained. "If only Harlem could become an area that retained its rich heritage while providing jobs, good housing, good schools, even better libraries, reliable and efficient municipal services, better parks, and playgrounds." Bond feared Harlem's transformation into a "bourgeois vision of urban paradise, sanitized, full of shops, beautiful people, clean entertainment, museums; but devoid of risk." Yet so too did he acknowledge—and welcome—the present reality, in which middle-class settlement had become typical as both an event and an objective. "Such a community should accommodate people of various incomes. Its population should be diverse," said Bond.[2]

At the helm of UMEZ, too, leadership changes symbolized the broader transformation that had unfolded in Harlem in these forty years and the central role that community-based organizations had played in building it. In early 2003, Kenneth Knuckles became UMEZ's third president, taking his place in the organization's Lenox Avenue office across the street from Harlem Center and just a few doors from where the Architects' Renewal Committee in Harlem (ARCH) had once set up shop. Indeed, Knuckles himself had come to Harlem thirty-five years earlier through the efforts of ARCH. Then a high school dropout, he enrolled in the first class of Architecture in the Neighborhoods, the program that ARCH had launched to increase African American representation in the design professions. Architecture in the Neighborhoods served as the first step in Knuckles's emergence as one of Harlem's leading development officials. The program's greatest success story, Knuckles went on to train as an architect and lawyer, then served as an assistant city housing commissioner, deputy Bronx borough president, commissioner of the New York City Department of General Services, and a vice president of Columbia University. In 2000, he joined the City Planning Commission.

The following year he became a member of the board of UMEZ. In 2002, Mayor Michael Bloomberg elevated him to vice chair of the City Planning Commission.

As UMEZ's new leader, Knuckles pursued an agenda consistent with that of his predecessors, focused on stimulating private development as a means of social and economic transformation. Chain stores, Knuckles argued, both served resident needs and provided employment for a population that he hoped, as did many of his peers, would exhibit increasing income diversity. "Harlem needed economic integration," Knuckles explained. "I think it is a good thing that whites, middle-class Blacks, are moving back to Harlem." In tempering this call with hopes that UMEZ could better engage Harlem's small businesses and residents, however, he revealed his own roots in earlier movements for democratic participation. Knuckles's ascent to the top of UMEZ and the City Planning Commission, the body that ARCH had once targeted with protests at city hall for its lack of diversity, exemplified all the promise and paradoxes intrinsic to the project of community development. At once, he embodied both the considerable legacy and success of radical demands for community control and the remarkably different image of the city that community developers came to construct.[3]

In the first years of the new century, the pursuit of this image would only accelerate in pace and expand in scale. Commercial developments continued to rise on Harlem's major streets, and new middle-class residents found their way to Harlem. Community-based organizations often, though not always, stood at the center of such projects. Private developers and private citizens increasingly joined their efforts. In Bradhurst, the Harlem Congregations for Community Improvement broke ground on a building containing Harlem's second Pathmark supermarket and more than a hundred middle-income cooperative apartments in 2002. UMEZ helped fund an auto mall in 2003, bringing car dealers to the East Harlem Triangle. Touring Harlem, a *New York Amsterdam News* reporter found "on practically every block . . . a plethora of construction activity." A speculative office building and new commercial center joined the other developments that had emerged on 125th Street. A *New York Times* reporter described "A New Harlem Gentry in Search of Its Latte," as he chronicled the life of middle-class, African American residents in the streets around Lenox Avenue, for whom it was ever easier to find a salon, a gift shop, a bistro, or gourmet coffee.[4]

Likewise, long-standing concerns about the direction of Harlem's development would persist at an increased pace and scale. In the new century, organizations like ADC continued to straddle the line between the responsibility
they claimed to existing low-income Harlemites and the middle-income residents they sought to attract. On one hand, ADC proved its commitment to
Harlemites with its continued provision of housing and services for the homeless, a Head Start program, and development of the first public school to open
in Harlem in decades. On the other hand, ADC continued to attract scrutiny
from those same residents in response to its approach to the neighborhood's
built fabric and its increased focus on middle-class homeownership. The organization's planned redevelopment of the Renaissance Ballroom, a neighborhood icon around the corner from Abyssinian Baptist Church, offered one
example. Abyssinian leaders opposed official landmark designation of the
structure, arguing that the status would restrict their plans. ADC intended
to demolish much of the site in order to build a nineteen-story building
with nearly 120 condominiums, four-fifths to be sold at market rate. Leaders
pointed to their normative ideal of a mixed-income community with greater
homeownership to justify the increasing scale of their ambition. But with the
prospect of a new, predominantly middle-income structure towering over a
rapidly gentrifying Frederick Douglass Boulevard and other plans for mod-
erate- and middle-income housing on nearby streets, ADC unsurprisingly
faced criticism about its role and responsibility in the neighborhood. "If you
want to branch out into business and moderate-income housing, that's cool,"
said one Harlem tenant advocate. "But don't forget about the people."[5]

Such concerns proved prescient—and ever more pressing—in the years
that followed. The Renaissance Ballroom project languished in the aftermath
of the 2008 fiscal crisis, while ADC's finances collapsed. The community development corporation (CDC) faced diminishing revenue from its properties
and reduced government support, both consequences of the Great Recession, but also met the backdraft of its own growth strategy, which had increasingly involved heavy borrowing to fund rapid property accumulation.
Questions about the goals, methods, accountability, and spending practices
of ADC's leadership, including Rev. Calvin O. Butts III, only grew in volume
in the 2010s as the organization became overextended and unable to keep up
with its own costs. As Butts sought to save the CDC, he did so with a strategy
that directly tapped into the real estate boom ADC had helped to create in

Harlem, while validating the very criticisms that activists had long voiced: he began to sell the properties that the organization had accumulated in the name of community development. In April 2014, ADC sold the Renaissance Ballroom to a private developer with plans to build an eight-story building with 134 apartments, just one-fifth of which were dedicated to low-income tenants. An even more symbolic move came in early 2015, when the CDC sold the Pathmark supermarket property to one of New York City's largest real estate developers. Compounding questions about whose interests Abyssinian was serving, the Community Association of the East Harlem Triangle, ADC's partner in the project, claimed that it never received its share of the proceeds. By the end of the year, the supermarket, once a symbol of the prominence that community-based organizations had achieved in Harlem, had closed its doors. The "people" were left without the grocery store whose benefits had helped balance the costs of income diversification that CDCs had increasingly pursued. Elsewhere on 125th Street a Whole Foods took form, to serve a very different group of consumers.[6]

Undeniably, if middle-class residents had once been scarce in Harlem—notable in the 1980s for the Beethoven they blasted from their windows as they restored woodwork or their interest in period furniture in a neighborhood confronting the rise of crack cocaine—their presence was not so strange anymore in the new millennium. One newly arrived 125th Street tenant suggested the degree to which Harlem had regained continuity with the rest of Manhattan in the minds of many New Yorkers. In 2001, after leaving office as president of the United States, Bill Clinton rented the penthouse in one of Harlem's tallest buildings for his postpresidential office and the headquarters of his foundation. Community leaders and real estate brokers hoped Clinton's arrival would accelerate the transformation of 125th Street already under way.[7]

The street's ongoing changes brought mixed emotions, however. While some continued to look with optimism on the arrival of retail they had lacked, other longtime Harlemites watched and worried as new amenities displaced the businesses they had depended on. "The majority of the stores, the 99-cent stores, they're gone," one resident explained. "The Laundromat on the corner is gone. The bodegas are gone. There's large delis now. What had been two for $1 is now one for $3. . . . The foods being sold—feta cheese instead of sharp Cheddar cheese. That's a whole other world." These transitions not only affected where one shopped, however; for some, they turned worst fears about neighborhood change into very personal realities. Such was the case for Preston Wilcox, who joined other 125th Street institutions forced to decamp. In early 2005, he received an eviction notice for the office he had occupied for twelve years, as his landlord sought "fair market value" for the space Wilcox had rented at a rate that now seemed unusually low on the changing boulevard. Wilcox moved on from Harlem's main street.[8]

Wilcox passed away the following year, in August, at age eighty-two. "Preston Wilcox was born on Harlem Street in Youngstown, Ohio," read an obituary by the journalist Herb Boyd, "and died last week at his apartment in the village of Harlem." Wilcox had made a life "between the two Harlems," Boyd continued.[9] Though he was referring to the symmetry of Wilcox's place of birth and place of death, and the seeming inevitability of his finding his way to the most famous neighborhood in America, the metaphor could be read differently, too. Wilcox's death marked the end of an era in Harlem, the end of the period chronicled here, a period in which Harlem changed dramatically. In the 1960s, Harlem served as a national emblem of the "urban crisis" wracking predominantly African American communities. By the late 1990s, the neighborhood represented the leading edge of the "Second Renaissance" that touched many such neighborhoods. This renaissance took place amid transformative forces at the local, national, and global levels, including the transnational spread of ideas and economies, the political shift away from a dominant welfare state, and the fall and rise of New York's financial and real estate sectors, but came about in large part through the work of Harlemites like Wilcox who struggled to reimagine and rebuild the neighborhood they called home.

Wilcox offered a creative, often critical voice as such struggles unfolded, a constant who never missed an opportunity to remind Harlemites of the highest ideals that had inspired demands for community control. "He was a challenger, a multifaceted person whom I liked very much," said Harlem politician and businessman Percy Sutton at Wilcox's memorial service. "I didn't know him in his athletic days, but I knew him in his angry days. I will always remember his bringing me clippings, clippings, and more clippings."[10] The movements that Wilcox had inspired built a neighborhood very different from the one he had helped to imagine on blocks like Reclamation Site #1. In his refusal to give up that radical vision as things changed around him, Wilcox could seem quite idealistic, even eccentric, in a neighborhood whose fate community leaders increasingly tied to the goal of economic integration. Yet in an era when such a view of urban revitalization became so common as to go largely unquestioned—ubiquitous not only in the work of CDCs but also enshrined in national policy through programs like HOPE-VI, which replaced public housing with mixed-income developments—Wilcox's dependable advocacy on behalf of Harlem's low-income residents offered a vital counterpoint. Radical activists had offered the possibility that low-income residents in communities like Harlem could be the very roots of a city whose branches would bring benefits to all of its citizens. This view held that longtime Harlemites could provide the foundation for revitalization—that they represented not the problem of cities, but a potential solution.

The most ardent evangelist for this idea no longer could voice it on Harlem's streets, but Wilcox's call remained equally urgent, if not more so, in the era to which these decades served as a prelude. The pace of gentrification became ever quicker in the early twenty-first century in Harlem. Community-based organizations had once wondered about the feasibility of attracting middle-income residents to the neighborhood, but now that they had done so, they wondered if they would be able to manage the rapid change under way and, indeed, maintain the influence they had gained. Harlems nationwide found themselves facing similar questions. On U Street in Washington, DC, for instance, whose past and future mirrored those of 125th Street, expensive apartments, condominiums, and restaurants rose, often bearing names like "The Ellington" and "Marvin" that borrowed from the city's African American history but were too costly for many of its longtime residents. Similarly, Cincinnati's Over-the-Rhine, whose Italianate architecture housed a largely low-income African American enclave in the late twentieth century, found its abandoned structures filling with affluent occupants in the new millennium. On Vine Street, antidisplacement signs and murals stood shoulder to shoulder with new and renovated buildings for young professionals. In these and other neighborhoods, like Bronzeville in Chicago and Bedford-Stuyvesant in Brooklyn, African American residents had built a stronghold during decades of disinvestment, but now found themselves surrounded by accelerating residential and commercial development. As transformation snowballed, the fear of rapid racial and economic change followed closely behind.[11]

In Harlem, where the neighborhood's fame always gave it the added responsibility of a standard bearer and where its Manhattan location meant development pressures came at full volume, residents felt this stress particularly acutely. Columbia University planned a seventeen-acre expansion in 2007, for example, to transform the Manhattanville neighborhood of West Harlem from Broadway to the Hudson River. The following year, the City Planning Commission proposed to rezone 125th Street to enable a greatly expanded scale of development, including skyscrapers up to twenty-nine stories tall. Each revived ghosts from battles long past, eliciting resident protests and turbulent public hearings. Knuckles voted for both plans. Karen Phillips, the former president of ADC who also served on the City Planning Commission, voted against them. Nevertheless, each passed.[12]

Fears about what these decisions would mean for Harlem rose to the surface with new urgency in their aftermath. But just as Harlem's gentrification had deep roots, so too did concerns about its future. Indeed, no sooner had Harlem secured its place as the social, cultural, and political heart of black America in the early twentieth century than observers began to wonder when it would lose that role. "In the make-up of New York, Harlem is not merely a Negro colony or community," wrote James Weldon Johnson during the Harlem Renaissance, "it is a city within a city, the greatest Negro city in the world." Looking out from 1925, Johnson wondered about the future of this place he had come to call home. "The question naturally arises, 'Are the Negroes going to be able to hold Harlem?'" Johnson continued, "When colored people do leave Harlem, their homes, their churches, their investments and their businesses, it will be because the land has become so valuable they can no longer afford to live on it."[13]

This moment would not come soon, Johnson predicted. "The date of another move northward is very far in the future," he wrote. By and large, he was correct. As Harlemites debated the future of their community and their role in rebuilding it in the decades chronicled here, their assumptions proceeded from the power and identity they claimed as a predominantly African American place. Despite disagreeing about Harlem's ideal class makeup, community members had largely agreed that the neighborhood should remain a majority black neighborhood—indeed, America's greatest majority black neighborhood—as they continuously reinvented the space they called home. As the pace of change has quickened in recent years as a consequence of that reinvention, however, this characteristic has come into doubt. Observers have been quick to declare that the end of African American Harlem is near. "No Longer Majority Black, Harlem Is in Transition," read one much-circulated piece in 2010, a claim that depended in large measure on where one drew the boundaries. That year's U.S. Census showed that 36.61 percent of Greater Harlem's residents were African American, while Central Harlem retained a black majority of 58.64 percent. But if Central Harlem remains predominantly African American today, many questions hang in the air about whether this fundamental, defining trait will hold much longer.[14]

In Harlem, answering these difficult questions requires an understanding that Harlemites themselves had helped to seed these changes. In some cases they did so unintentionally, hoping to gain greater control over their community and, in the process, creating the infrastructure that would later support an increasingly gentrified landscape. In other cases, they pursued such changes wholeheartedly, sometimes with the knowledge that they could bring dramatic upheaval to Harlem, but in many cases with the goal of achieving a stable but economically diverse community. Their history demonstrates that the story of gentrification cannot be told only from the point of view of the migrants to neighborhoods like Harlem, nor can it be told through simplistic binaries of good and evil or innocence and guilt. Harlemites helped to produce this urban renaissance from the grass roots. This reality reminds us of the complexity of a process that continues to irrevocably transform Harlem and similar neighborhoods nationwide in the early twenty-first century.

Abbreviations

Archives

ABC   Abyssinian Baptist Church Records, Series XII, Subseries C, Abyssinian Baptist Church, New York, New York

BERC   Black Economic Research Center Records, Manuscripts, Archives and Rare Books Division, Schomburg Center for Research in Black Culture, The New York Public Library, New York, New York

CCC   Christiane C. Collins Collection, Manuscripts, Archives and Rare Books Division, Schomburg Center for Research in Black Culture, The New York Public Library, New York, New York

CHG   Commissioner Harmon Goldstone Papers, City Planning Commission Records, Municipal Archives, New York, New York

CRDN   Civil Rights during the Nixon Administration, 1969–1974 (microform), Black Studies Research Sources, University Publications of America, Bethesda, Maryland

CRH   C. Richard Hatch Private Collection, Potomac, Maryland

CSA/FG   Records of the Community Services Administration, Final Grant and Contract Product Files, 1970–78, National Archives and Records Administration, College Park, Maryland

CSA/RRG   Records of the Community Services Administration, Records relating to Grants, 1981, National Archives and Records Administration, College Park, Maryland

CSA/SF   Records of the Community Services Administration, State Files, 1965–1969, National Archives and Records Administration, College Park, Maryland

DND   Mayor David N. Dinkins Papers, Municipal Archives, New York, New York

DPM   Daniel P. Moynihan Papers, Manuscript Division, Library of Congress, Washington, DC

EIK   Edward I. Koch Mayoral Papers, Municipal Archives, New York, New York

EJL   Edward Joseph Logue Papers, Manuscripts and Archives, Yale University Library, New Haven, Connecticut

FFA   Ford Foundation Archives, Rockefeller Archive Center, Sleepy Hollow, New York

HDA   Harlem Development Archive, Archives and Special Collections Division, City College of New York, New York, New York

JB   Joseph Black Papers, Manuscripts, Archives and Rare Books Division, Schomburg Center for Research in Black Culture, The New York Public Library, New York, New York

JKJ   Senator Jacob K. Javits Collection, Special Collections and University Archives, Stony Brook University, Stony Brook, New York

JLW   John L. Wilson Jr. Papers, Manuscripts, Archives and Rare Books Division, Schomburg Center for Research in Black Culture, The New York Public Library, New York, New York

JMB   J. Max Bond Jr. Papers, Department of Drawings and Archives, Avery Architectural and Fine Arts Library, Columbia University, New York, New York

MCH   Metropolitan Council on Housing Records, Tamiment Library and Robert F. Wagner Labor Archives, New York University, New York, New York

MMW   M. Moran Weston Papers, Rare Book and Manuscript Library, Columbia University, New York, New York

NAR   Nelson A. Rockefeller Papers, Record Group 15: Nelson A. Rockefeller, Gubernatorial, Rockefeller Archive Center, Sleepy Hollow, New York

NLH   Nelam L. Hill Papers, Manuscripts, Archives and Rare Books Division, Schomburg Center for Research in Black Culture, The New York Public Library, New York, New York

NYCS   New York City Seminar, 1971–73, Record Group 16: Institute for Religious and Social Studies, Special Collections, Jewish Theological Seminary, New York, New York

NYF   New York Foundation Records, Manuscripts and Archives Division, The New York Public Library, New York, New York

OCS   Records of the Office of the Cabinet Secretary, Jimmy Carter Presidential Library, Atlanta, Georgia

PW   Preston Wilcox Papers, Manuscripts, Archives and Rare Books Division, Schomburg Center for Research in Black Culture, The New York Public Library, New York, New York

RBF   Rockefeller Brothers Fund Archives, Rockefeller Archive Center, Sleepy Hollow, New York

RF   Rockefeller Foundation Archives, Series 200, Record Group 1.2: Projects, Rockefeller Archive Center, Sleepy Hollow, New York

RL   Ronald Lawson Research Files for the *Tenant Movement in New York City,* Tamiment Library and Robert F. Wagner Labor Archives, New York University, New York, New York

RWG   Mayor Rudolph W. Giuliani Papers, Municipal Archives, New York, New York

SCF   Clipping File, 1925–1974 (microform), Schomburg Center for Research in Black Culture (Alexandria, VA: Chadwyck-Healey, 1986)

UHAB   Urban Homesteading Assistance Board Files, Urban Homesteading Assistance Board, New York, New York

VAF   Vincent Astor Foundation Records, Manuscripts and Archives Division, The New York Public Library, New York, New York

WT   Walter Thabit Private Collection (in possession of Marci Reaven), New York, New York

Periodicals

BE   *Black Enterprise*

CFC   *Consumer-Farmer Cooperator*

CL   *City Limits*

HC   *Harvard Crimson*

HN   *Harlem News*

MT   *Manhattan Tribune*

NYAN   *New York Amsterdam News*

NYDN   *New York Daily News*

NYN   *New York Newsday*

NYP   *New York Post*
NYT   *New York Times*
VV   *Village Voice*
WP   *Washington Post*

Notes

Introduction

1. "Harlem Demonstrators Protest State Building," *NYT*, 1 July 1969, 82; Aubrey Zephyr, "State Office Building: Protestors Vow to Stay," *MT*, 12 July 1969, 13; Simon Anekwe, "Reclamation Site Still 'Occupied,'" *NYAN*, 12 July 1969, 1; Charlayne Hunter, "Harlem Squatters Hold State Site," *NYT*, 4 August 1969; "The Meaning of Reclamation Site1," *HN*, October 1969.

2. See, for example, Amy Waldman, "Where Green Trumps Black and White," *NYT*, 11 December 1999; Bram Alden, "Harlem Building Raises Gentrification Concerns," *Columbia Spectator*, 5 February 2001; Rivka Gewirtz Little, "The New Harlem," *VV*, 17 September 2002; Timothy Williams, "God and Neighborhood: Powerful Harlem Church Is Also a Powerful Harlem Developer," *NYT*, 18 August 2008, B1.

3. "Excerpts from Summary of Urban Panel's Report," *NYT*, 15 December 1968, 70; "Ford to City: Drop Dead," *NYDN*, 30 October 1975, 1.

4. Les Christie, "Cities Are Hot Again," *CNNMoney*, 15 June 2006, http://money.cnn.com/2006/06/15/real_estate/return_to_cities.

5. Kenneth B. Clark, *Dark Ghetto: Dilemmas of Social Power*, 2nd ed. (Hanover, NH: Wesleyan University Press, 1989), xxxvi; Gordon Parks, "A Harlem Family," *Life*, 8 March 1968.

6. Population figures include Central, West, and East Harlem; both median household income figures are in 2010 dollars. Andrew A. Beveridge, David Halle, Edward Telles, and Beth Leavenworth Dufault, "Residential Diversity and Division," in *New York and Los Angeles: The Uncertain Future*, ed. David Halle and Andrew A. Beveridge (New York: Oxford University Press, 2013), 319–323. For "second renaissance" and similar uses, see, for example, Victoria Pope, "Harlem's Next Renaissance," *U.S. News and World Report*, 10 February 1997, 56; Nina Siegel, "Harlem on the Brink," *NYT*, 26 September 1999, 732; Nina Siegel, "For Harlem,

More to a Boom than Shopping Centers," *NYT,* 28 November 1999, ST1; Terry Pristin, "New Cinema and New Hope in Harlem," *NYT,* 1 July 2000, B1; Ruth Evans and Sue Armstrong, "Harlem's Second Coming," *BBC News,* 23 December 2000, http://news.bbc.co.uk/2/hi/americas/1083578.stm; Peter Hellman, "House Proud: Making Family History in Historic Harlem," *NYT,* 17 January 2002, F1; Monique M. Taylor, "A Second Renaissance in Harlem," *Los Angeles Times,* 5 May 2002; Peter Hellman, "Coming Up Harlem," *Smithsonian,* November 2002; C. J. Hughes, "A Neighborhood Worth the Big-Ticket Investment," *NYT,* 5 August 2007, I9.

7. On New York City as a global city, see Saskia Sassen, *The Global City: New York, London, Tokyo* (Princeton, NJ: Princeton University Press, 1991); Janet L. Abu-Lughod, *New York, Chicago, Los Angeles: America's Global Cities* (Minneapolis: University of Minnesota Press, 1999). For accounts of development in New York that consider globalization in relation to national and local contexts, see William Sites, *Remaking New York: Primitive Globalization and the Politics of Urban Community* (Minneapolis: University of Minnesota Press, 2003); Susan Fainstein, *The City Builders: Property Development in New York and London, 1980–2000,* 2nd ed. (Lawrence: University Press of Kansas, 2001). On New York's fiscal crisis, recovery, and changing economy, see Martin Shefter, *Political Crisis/Fiscal Crisis: The Collapse and Revival of New York City* (New York: Basic Books, 1985); John Hull Mollenkopf and Manuel Castells, eds., *Dual City: Restructuring New York* (New York: Russell Sage Foundation, 1991); John Hull Mollenkopf, *A Phoenix in the Ashes: The Rise and Fall of the Koch Coalition in New York City Politics* (Princeton, NJ: Princeton University Press, 1994); Joshua B. Freeman, *Working-Class New York: Life and Labor since World War II* (New York: New Press, 2000); Jonathan Soffer, *Ed Koch and the Rebuilding of New York City* (New York: Columbia University Press, 2010).

8. The large and ever-growing literature on gentrification has tended to emphasize supply-side explanations on one hand, especially focusing on the availability of housing as a profitable means of investment and new flows of global finance capital, and demand-side explanations on the other, especially emphasizing new tastes for urban residence, though these factors are certainly intertwined. The seminal example of the former is Neil Smith, *The New Urban Frontier: Gentrification and the Revanchist City* (New York: Routledge, 1996); a key example of the latter is David Ley, *The New Middle Class and the Remaking of the Central City* (New York: Oxford University Press, 2006). Theoretical and historical accounts of gentrification that acknowledge the importance of both explanations include, among others, Neil Smith and Peter Williams, eds., *Gentrification of the City* (Boston: Allen and Unwin, 1986); Suleiman Osman, *The Invention of Brownstone Brooklyn: Gentrification and the Search for Authenticity in Postwar New York* (New York: Oxford University Press, 2011). What these works share is an emphasis on the role and actions of those who moved *into* neighborhoods. In contrast, the present analysis considers how *existing* residents helped lay the groundwork for demographic and physical change—

though not always intentionally—through neighborhood-level activism with radical roots. Ley also relates gentrification to 1960s-era social movements, but in the context of the gentrifiers rather than the community-based movements I emphasize here. Derek Hyra, *The New Urban Renewal: The Economic Transformation of Harlem and Bronzeville* (Chicago: University of Chicago Press, 2008), offers a multilevel explanation of neighborhood change including the role of community organizations, but focuses on the late twentieth century, thus overlooking the long history I explore here. For a recent history of gentrification that traces the role of existing residents in neighborhood change, but in a very different social context, see Aaron Shkuda, *The Lofts of SoHo: Gentrification, Art, and Industry in New York, 1950–1980* (Chicago: University of Chicago Press, 2016).

9. "Neoliberalism," David Harvey writes, "is in the first instance a theory of political economic practices that proposes that human well-being can best be advanced by liberating individual entrepreneurial freedoms and skills within an institutional framework characterized by strong private property rights, free markets, and free trade. The role of the state is to create and preserve an institutional framework appropriate to such practices." David Harvey, *A Brief History of Neoliberalism* (New York: Oxford University Press, 2005), 2. Neil Brenner and Nik Theodore emphasize the importance of understanding neoliberalism in its specific political, social, and spatial contexts, what they call "actually existing neoliberalism," a goal that is consistent with my own interest in uncovering the social and political processes through which actors on the ground produced the contemporary city. See Neil Brenner and Nik Theodore, "Cities and the Geography of 'Actually Existing Neoliberalism,'" *Antipode* 34, no. 3 (July 2002): 349–379.

10. "Urban renewal" originated as a term in the Housing Act of 1954 as a more comprehensive, sensitive approach to reconstruction than the clearance-oriented "urban redevelopment" established in the Housing Act of 1949. Soon, however, both terms gained essentially the same meaning, as large-scale clearance remained the dominant tactic of publicly funded city rebuilding. The literature on urban renewal is extensive and growing. For contemporary accounts that explain the policy and tenets underlying large-scale redevelopment and its implementation, see Scott Greer, *Urban Renewal and American Cities: The Dilemma of Democratic Intervention* (Indianapolis: Bobbs-Merrill, 1965); James Q. Wilson, ed., *Urban Renewal: The Record and the Controversy* (Cambridge, MA: MIT Press, 1966); Jewel Bellush and Murray Hausknecht, eds., *Urban Renewal: People, Politics, and Planning* (Garden City, NY: Anchor Books, 1967). For some of the many historical accounts that consider the practice of urban renewal in New York City and other American cities, see Robert A. Caro, *The Power Broker: Robert Moses and the Fall of New York* (New York: Alfred A. Knopf, 1974); Jon C. Teaford, *The Rough Road to Renaissance: Urban Revitalization in America, 1940–1985* (Baltimore: Johns Hopkins University Press, 1990); Joel Schwartz, *The New York Approach: Robert Moses, Urban Liberals, and the Redevelopment of the Inner City* (Columbus: Ohio State

University Press, 1993); Alison Isenberg, *Downtown America: A History of the Place and the People Who Made It* (Chicago: University of Chicago Press, 2004); Lizabeth Cohen, "Buying into Downtown Revival: The Centrality of Retail to Postwar Urban Renewal in American Cities," *Annals of the American Academy of Political and Social Science* 611, no. 1 (May 2007): 82–95; Hilary Ballon and Kenneth T. Jackson, eds., *Robert Moses and the Modern City: The Transformation of New York* (New York: W. W. Norton, 2007); Samuel Zipp, *Manhattan Projects: The Rise and Fall of Urban Renewal in Cold War New York* (New York: Oxford University Press, 2010); Michael H. Carriere, "Between Being and Becoming: On Architecture, Student Protest, and the Aesthetics of Liberalism in Postwar America" (PhD diss., University of Chicago, 2010); Christopher Klemek, *The Transatlantic Collapse of Urban Renewal: Postwar Urbanism from New York to Berlin* (Chicago: University of Chicago Press, 2011); Francesca Russello Ammon, *Bulldozer: Demolition and Clearance of the Postwar Landscape* (New Haven, CT: Yale University Press, 2016).

11. For treatments that link urban renewal and public housing to America's urban crisis, see Arnold R. Hirsch, *Making the Second Ghetto: Race and Housing in Chicago, 1940–1960* (New York: Cambridge University Press, 1983); John F. Bauman, *Public Housing, Race, and Renewal: Urban Planning in Philadelphia, 1920–1974* (Philadelphia: Temple University Press, 1987); Howard Gillette Jr., *Between Justice and Beauty: Race, Planning, and the Failure of Urban Policy in Washington, D.C.* (Baltimore: Johns Hopkins University Press, 1995); Thomas J. Sugrue, *The Origins of the Urban Crisis: Race and Inequality in Postwar Detroit* (Princeton, NJ: Princeton University Press, 1996).

12. The best-known critiques of urban renewal, from across the political spectrum, are Jane Jacobs, *The Death and Life of Great American Cities* (New York: Vintage Books, 1961); Herbert J. Gans, *The Urban Villagers: Group and Class in the Life of Italian-Americans* (New York: Free Press of Glencoe, 1962); Martin Anderson, *The Federal Bulldozer: A Critical Analysis of Urban Renewal, 1949–1962* (Cambridge, MA: MIT Press, 1964). Historical accounts of grassroots movements against urban renewal include John Hull Mollenkopf, *The Contested City* (Princeton, NJ: Princeton University Press, 1983); John Emmeus Davis, *Contested Ground: Collective Action and the Urban Neighborhood* (Ithaca, NY: Cornell University Press, 1991); Mandi Isaacs Jackson, *Model City Blues: Urban Space and Organized Resistance in New Haven* (Philadelphia: Temple University Press, 2008); Carriere, "Between Being and Becoming"; Klemek, *Transatlantic Collapse of Urban Renewal;* Jennifer Hock, "Political Designs: Architecture and Urban Renewal in the Civil Rights Era, 1954–1973" (PhD diss., Harvard University, 2012).

13. Daniel T. Rodgers, *Age of Fracture* (Cambridge, MA: Harvard University Press, 2011).

14. On social movements as the end of modern planning, see especially Klemek, *Transatlantic Collapse of Urban Renewal;* Zipp, *Manhattan Projects*. Other works

examine the activism that erupted in urban planning in the 1960s, but either maintain a focus on the profession itself or do not carry the story forward into succeeding decades. See Martin L. Needleman and Carolyn Emerson Needleman,
*Guerrillas in the Bureaucracy: The Community Planning Experiment in the United
States* (New York: John Wiley and Sons, 1974); Lily M. Hoffman, *The Politics of
Knowledge: Activist Movements in Medicine and Planning* (Albany: State University
of New York Press, 1989). In her study of activism in the Cooper Square neighborhood of New York City, historian Marci Reaven explains how citizen participation
became part of the institutional process of planning by the mid-1970s, through
such means as the city's community planning boards. See Marci Reaven, "Citizen
Participation in City Planning: New York City, 1945–1975" (PhD diss., New York
University, 2009). Tom Angotti also focuses on community-generated plans within
the institutional framework of New York City's planning apparatus. See Tom Angotti, *New York for Sale: Community Planning Confronts Global Real Estate* (Cambridge, MA: MIT Press, 2008).

 15. In their seminal statement on Black Power, Stokely Carmichael and Charles
Hamilton wrote, "The concept of Black Power . . . is a call for black people in this
country to unite, to recognize their heritage, to build a sense of community. It is a
call for black people to begin to define their own goals, to lead their own organizations and to support those organizations. It is a call to reject the racist institutions
and values of this society." Stokely Carmichael and Charles V. Hamilton, *Black
Power: The Politics of Liberation in America* (New York: Vintage Books, 1967), 44.
On the history of Black Power and its diverse forms, see Komozi Woodard, *A Na-
tion within a Nation: Amiri Baraka (LeRoi Jones) and Black Power Politics* (Chapel
Hill: University of North Carolina Press, 1999); Robert Self, *American Babylon:
Race and the Struggle for Postwar Oakland* (Princeton, NJ: Princeton University
Press, 2003); Peniel E. Joseph, *Waiting 'Til the Midnight Hour: A Narrative His-
tory of Black Power in America* (New York: Henry Holt, 2006); Hasan Kwame
Jeffries, *Bloody Lowndes: Civil Rights and Black Power in Alabama's Black Belt*
(New York: New York University Press, 2009); Donna Murch, *Living for the City:
Migration, Education, and the Rise of the Black Panther Party in Oakland, Cali-
fornia* (Chapel Hill: University of North Carolina Press, 2010); Peniel E. Joseph,
ed., *Neighborhood Rebels: Black Power at the Local Level* (New York: Palgrave
Macmillan, 2010). On the long history of the civil rights movement, see Jacquelyn
Dowd Hall, "The Long Civil Rights Movement and the Political Uses of the Past,"
Journal of American History 91, no. 4 (March 2005): 1233–1263; Thomas J. Sugrue,
Sweet Land of Liberty: The Forgotten Struggle for Civil Rights in the North (New
York: Random House, 2008). For historical work that casts the militancy of the
late 1960s as the end of a declension narrative, see Hirsch, *Making the Second
Ghetto;* Sugrue, *Origins of the Urban Crisis;* Charles M. Payne, *I've Got the Light of
Freedom: The Organizing Tradition and the Mississippi Freedom Struggle* (Berkeley:
University of California Press, 1995). For accounts that consider the legacy of Black

Power and its demands for community control, see James Edward Smethurst, *The Black Arts Movement: Literary Nationalism in the 1960s and 1970s* (Chapel Hill: University of North Carolina Press, 2005); Noliwe M. Rooks, *White Money/Black Power: The Surprising History of African American Studies and the Crisis of Race in Higher Education* (Boston: Beacon, 2006); Heather Lewis, *New York City Public Schools from Brownsville to Bloomberg: Community Control and Its Legacy* (New York: Teachers College Press, 2013); J. Phillip Thompson III, *Double Trouble: Black Mayors, Black Communities, and the Call for a Deep Democracy* (New York: Oxford University Press, 2006); Fabio Rojas, *From Black Power to Black Studies: How a Radical Social Movement Became an Academic Discipline* (Baltimore: Johns Hopkins University Press, 2007); Devin Fergus, *Liberalism, Black Power, and the Making of American Politics, 1965–1980* (Athens: University of Georgia Press, 2009); Fredrick C. Harris, *The Price of the Ticket: Barack Obama and the Rise and Decline of Black Politics* (New York: Oxford University Press, 2012); Martha Biondi, *The Black Revolution on Campus* (Berkeley: University of California Press, 2012). I take the idea of a "heroic period" of the civil rights movement, framed as a precursor to and in opposition to Black Power, from Peniel E. Joseph, "Waiting Till the Midnight Hour: Reconceptualizing the Heroic Period of the Civil Rights Movement, 1954–1965," *Souls* 2, no. 2 (Spring 2000): 6–17.

16. On the question of what difference the social movements of the 1960s made in America, see—in addition to the many recent works on Black Power listed above—the essays in Van Gosse and Richard Moser, eds., *The World the Sixties Made: Politics and Culture in Recent America* (Philadelphia: Temple University Press, 2003); Michael Kazin, *American Dreamers: How the Left Changed a Nation* (New York: Alfred A. Knopf, 2011); Maurice Isserman and Michael Kazin, "The Failure and Success of the New Radicalism," in *The Rise and Fall of the New Deal Order, 1930–1980,* ed. Steve Fraser and Gary Gerstle (Princeton, NJ: Princeton University Press, 1989); Sara Evans, *Personal Politics: The Roots of Women's Liberation in the Civil Rights Movement and the New Left* (New York: Random House, 1979).

17. For an account of neighborhood change in this period that emphasizes the role of middle-class actors, see Osman, *Invention of Brownstone Brooklyn.* For a history of community-level efforts to rebuild urban centers that takes a largely optimistic view, see Alexander Von Hoffman, *House by House, Block by Block: The Rebirth of America's Urban Neighborhoods* (New York: Oxford University Press, 2003). For accounts that explore the changing nature of community development, focusing especially on economic development, see the essays in Laura Warren Hill and Julia Rabig, eds., *The Business of Black Power: Community Development, Capitalism, and Corporate Responsibility in Postwar America* (Rochester, NY: University of Rochester Press, 2012). For a history of community development in Newark in this period, see Julia Rabig, "Broken Deal: Devolution, Development, and Civil Society in Newark, New Jersey, 1960–1990" (PhD diss., University of Pennsylvania, 2007).

18. Harlem has long fascinated historians, whose works include Gilbert Os-
ofsky, *Harlem: The Making of a Ghetto* (New York: Harper and Row, 1966); David
Levering Lewis, *When Harlem Was in Vogue* (New York: Knopf, 1981); Cheryl
Lynn Greenberg, *"Or Does It Explode?" Black Harlem in the Great Depression* (New
York: Oxford University Press, 1991); Martha Biondi, *To Stand and Fight: The
Struggle for Civil Rights in Postwar New York City* (Cambridge, MA: Harvard Uni-
versity Press, 2003); Shane White, Stephen Garton, Stephen Robertson, and
Graham White, *Playing the Numbers: Gambling in Harlem between the Wars*
(Cambridge, MA: Harvard University Press, 2010); Jonathan Gill, *Harlem: The
Four Hundred Year History from Dutch Village to Capital of Black America* (New
York: Grove, 2011); Kevin McGruder, *Race and Real Estate: Conflict and Coopera-
tion in Harlem, 1890–1920* (New York: Columbia University Press, 2015).

19. Many social scientists flocked to Harlem to study neighborhood change in the
late twentieth and early twenty-first century. Their efforts include John L. Jackson
Jr., *Harlemworld: Doing Race and Class in Contemporary Black America* (Chicago:
University of Chicago Press, 2001); Monique M. Taylor, *Harlem between Heaven
and Hell* (Minneapolis: University of Minnesota Press, 2002); Arlene M. Dávila,
Barrio Dreams: Puerto Ricans, Latinos, and the Neoliberal City (Berkeley: Univer-
sity of California Press, 2004); David Maurrasse, *Listening to Harlem: Gentrification,
Community, and Business* (New York: Routledge, 2006); Lance Freeman, *There
Goes the 'Hood: Views of Gentrification from the Ground Up* (Philadelphia: Temple
University Press, 2006); Hyra, *The New Urban Renewal*; Sharon Zukin, *Naked
City: The Death and Life of Authentic Urban Places* (New York: Oxford University
Press, 2010). On dynamics of immigration in Harlem in this era, see Zain Abdullah,
Black Mecca: The African Muslims of Harlem (New York: Oxford University Press,
2010).

20. Robin D. G. Kelley, *Freedom Dreams: The Black Radical Imagination* (Boston:
Beacon, 2002).

21. The history of the recent past offers both unique opportunities, such as the
chance to interview living figures and access their personal papers, and distinct
drawbacks, such as an archival record that is not yet fully represented at institutions. The growth of media in the late twentieth century, however, and the increasing documentation of events in digital formats provide unique resources
through which to examine these decades. See Claire Bond Potter and Renee C.
Romano, eds., *Doing Recent History: On Privacy, Copyright, Video Games, Institutional Review Boards, Activist Scholarship, and History That Talks Back* (Athens:
University of Georgia Press, 2012).

1. Reforming Renewal

1. Gertrude Wilson, "A Tent in the Rain," *NYAN,* 14 November 1964, 11. Wilson's own story makes her account more complex, for she was a white Upper East

Side resident who wrote with a pen name. Under the banner "White-on-White," her column chronicled the events of the 1960s, especially the civil rights movement, from a novel but sympathetic perspective. See her memoir, Justine Priestley, *By Gertrude Wilson: Dispatches of the 1960s from a White Writer in a Black World* (Edgartown, MA: Vineyard Stories, 2005).

2. C. Richard Hatch, "Pulse of New York's Public: Architect's Views," *NYAN*, 5 December 1964, 10; "Architect's Renewal Committee in Harlem," ca. early 1965, Box 8, Folder 34, NLH. On Gray, see Samuel Kaplan, "Slum Rent Strike Gains Momentum," *NYT*, 1 January 1964, 28; Thomas Sugrue, *Sweet Land of Liberty: The Forgotten Struggle for Civil Rights in the North* (New York: Random House, 2008), 400–410. On Leber, see "Religion: Integration in Chicago," *Time,* 30 September 1957. On Farmer, see Sugrue, *Sweet Land of Liberty,* 144–147, 339–340. On Mayer's work in East Harlem, see Samuel Zipp, *Manhattan Projects: The Rise and Fall of Urban Renewal in Cold War New York* (New York: Oxford University Press, 2010), 332–340.

3. Hatch, "Pulse of New York's Public," 10.

4. For a list of more than one hundred community design centers that followed in ARCH's wake, see "Community Design. Involvement and Architecture in the US since 1963: Projects," *An Architektur,* no. 19 (September 2008), 27–56.

5. Planner Paul Davidoff provided the seminal theoretical work defining "advocacy planning." See Paul Davidoff, "Advocacy and Pluralism in Planning," *Journal of the American Planning Association* 31, no. 4 (November 1965): 331–338. On activism in the profession of planning at this time, also see Robert Goodman, *After the Planners* (New York: Simon and Schuster, 1971); Martin L. Needleman and Carolyn Emerson Needleman, *Guerillas in the Bureaucracy: The Community Planning Experiment in the United States* (New York: John Wiley and Sons, 1974); Lily M. Hoffman, *The Politics of Knowledge: Activist Movements in Medicine and Planning* (Albany: State University of New York Press, 1989).

6. See Hilary Ballon, "Robert Moses and Urban Renewal," in *Robert Moses and the Modern City: The Transformation of New York,* ed. Hilary Ballon and Kenneth T. Jackson (New York: W. W. Norton, 2007), 94. On Moses and urban renewal in New York, also see Joel Schwartz, *The New York Approach: Robert Moses, Urban Liberals, and Redevelopment of the Inner City* (Columbus: Ohio State University Press, 1993); Robert A. Caro, *The Power Broker: Robert Moses and the Fall of New York* (New York: Alfred A. Knopf, 1974); Zipp, *Manhattan Projects;* Christopher Klemek, *The Transatlantic Collapse of Urban Renewal: Postwar Urbanism from New York to Berlin* (Chicago: University of Chicago Press, 2011).

7. Schwartz, *New York Approach,* 175; "Catalog of Built Work and Projects in New York City, 1934–68," in Ballon and Jackson, *Robert Moses and the Modern City,* 244–304; Zipp, *Manhattan Projects,* 157–249, 287.

8. Scott Greer, *Urban Renewal and American Cities: The Dilemma of Democratic Intervention* (Indianapolis: Bobbs-Merrill, 1965), 18, 152; Nicholas Dagen Bloom, *Public Housing That Worked: New York in the Twentieth Century* (Phila-

delphia: University of Pennsylvania Press, 2008), 170–175; Martha Biondi, "Robert Moses, Race, and the Limits of an Activist State," in Ballon and Jackson, *Robert Moses and the Modern City*, 117–120; Schwartz, *New York Approach*, 175; Zipp, *Manhattan Projects*, 114–129, 205–207. On these issues in Detroit and Chicago, respectively, see Thomas Sugrue, *The Origins of the Urban Crisis: Race and Inequality in Postwar Detroit* (Princeton, NJ: Princeton University Press, 1996); Arnold R. Hirsch, *Making the Second Ghetto: Race and Housing in Chicago, 1940–1960* (New York: Cambridge University Press, 1983). On the uses and abuses of "blight," see Wendell E. Pritchett, "The 'Public Menace' of Blight: Urban Renewal and the Private Uses of Eminent Domain," *Yale Law and Policy Review* 21, no. 1 (Winter 2003): 1–52.

9. Zipp offers the most detailed chronicle of public housing construction in East Harlem. See Zipp, *Manhattan Projects*, 258–260; also see Schwartz, *New York Approach*, 116.

10. Schwartz, *New York Approach*, 116; Hilary Ballon, "Harlem Title I" and "North Harlem Title I," in Ballon and Jackson, *Robert Moses and the Modern City*, 255–258. For a discussion of the early history of these blocks, see Sharifa Rhodes-Pitts, *Harlem Is Nowhere: A Journey to the Mecca of Black America* (New York: Little, Brown, 2011), 7–17.

11. Hilary Ballon, "Morningside-Manhattanville Title I," in Ballon and Jackson, *Robert Moses and the Modern City*, 260–261; Schwartz, *New York Approach*, 151–159, 185–189; Michael H. Carriere, "Between Being and Becoming: On Architecture, Student Protest, and the Aesthetics of Liberalism in Postwar America," (PhD diss., University of Chicago, 2010), 182–211.

12. Schwartz highlights the exclusionary aspects of the reconstruction of Morningside Heights, while Ballon and Jackson emphasize their liberal ideals. See Schwartz, *New York Approach*, 151–159; Ballon, "Morningside-Manhattanville Title I," in Ballon and Jackson, *Robert Moses and the Modern City*, 260–261. On the role of renewal in maintaining New York's importance on a global stage, see Zipp, *Manhattan Projects*.

13. Ballon, "Harlem Title I" and "North Harlem Title I," in Ballon and Jackson, *Robert Moses and the Modern City*, 255–258.

14. Zipp, *Manhattan Projects*, 261, 300. The legacy of public housing is extraordinarily complicated and still actively debated among historians, social scientists, and policy makers. See Sudhir Alladi Venkatesh, *American Project: The Rise and Fall of a Modern Ghetto* (Cambridge, MA: Harvard University Press, 2002); Bloom, *Public Housing That Worked*; John F. Bauman, *Public Housing, Race, and Renewal: Urban Planning in Philadelphia, 1920–1974* (Philadelphia: Temple University Press, 1987); Hirsch, *Making the Second Ghetto*.

15. Moses has become the centerpiece of debates over large-scale redevelopment that have continued to the present day, on one hand serving as the symbolic embodiment of government overreach and the negative consequences of liberalism,

and on the other representing the great promise of the postwar state and the appeal of big ideas. The classic negative portrayal of Moses is in Caro, *Power Broker*. Ballon and Jackson provide a corrective to Caro in *Robert Moses and the Modern City*. Also see Zipp, *Manhattan Projects*; Klemek, *Transatlantic Collapse*. Lizabeth Cohen offers a nuanced portrayal of the work of New Haven and Boston redeveloper and Moses contemporary Edward J. Logue in Lizabeth Cohen, "Buying into Downtown Revival: The Centrality of Retail to Postwar Urban Renewal in American Cities," *Annals of the American Academy of Political and Social Science* 611, no. 1 (May 2007): 82–95.

16. Greer, *Urban Renewal and American Cities*, 3; Schwartz writes that Title I projects and their adjoining public housing displaced more than 200,000 New Yorkers and as many as 60,000 jobs. Schwartz's figure does not include displacement from public housing built independently of Title I projects, however, the project type that was most common in Harlem. See Schwartz, *New York Approach*, 295–296.

17. Jane Jacobs, *The Death and Life of Great American Cities* (New York: Vintage Books, 1961): 4; Herbert J. Gans, *The Urban Villagers: Group and Class in the Life of Italian-Americans* (New York: Free Press of Glencoe, 1962); Martin Anderson, *The Federal Bulldozer: A Critical Analysis of Urban Renewal, 1949–1962* (Cambridge, MA: MIT Press, 1964).

18. Zipp offers a detailed account of the work of the East Harlem Project. See Zipp, *Manhattan Projects*, 299–350.

19. See Marci Reaven, "Citizen Participation in City Planning: New York City, 1945–1975" (PhD diss., New York University, 2009), for an excellent discussion of the extended battle over redevelopment in Cooper Square, especially 84–126. Also see Tom Angotti, *New York for Sale: Community Planning Confronts Global Real Estate* (Cambridge, MA: MIT Press, 2008).

20. "Felt Sees Change in Renewal View," *NYT*, 9 May 1961, 36; Zipp, *Manhattan Projects*, 357–360; Christopher Klemek, "Urbanism as Reform: Modernist Planning and the Crisis of Urban Liberalism in Europe and North America, 1945–1975," (PhD diss., University of Pennsylvania, 2004), 147–154.

21. "East Harlem Renewal Backed to Create 'Industrial Triangle,'" *NYT*, 5 October 1961, 30; Charles G. Bennett, "Renewal Backed for 4 City Areas," *NYT*, 22 June 1961, 33.

22. Lawrence O'Kane, "Worst City Slums Due for Renewal in New Program," *NYT*, 14 April 1964, 1; Lawrence O'Kane, "Renewal in Area around Columbia Backed by City," *NYT*, 30 September 1964, 1; Housing and Redevelopment Board, City of New York, *Morningside General Neighborhood Renewal Plan* (New York: Housing and Redevelopment Board, City of New York, 1964), iii–iv, 6.

23. Housing and Redevelopment Board, *Morningside General Neighborhood Renewal Plan*, 25, GN-202 (C), 1–3; Ex. C, 1–3; Ex. D. The portion of West Harlem included in the plan encompassed the area bounded by Morningside Avenue, Eighth Avenue, 111th Street, and 123rd Street.

24. Ibid., GN-202 (C), 3–6; Letter to Friend and Community Leader from Amalia Betanzos, Callender, et al., 17 August 1964, Box 11, Folder 1, MCH.

25. Letter to Friend and Community Leader from Betanzos, Callender, et al., 17 August 1964, Box 11, Folder 1, MCH.

26. "Information: Urban Renewal," ca. October 1964, Box 11, Folder 1, MCH.

27. C. Richard Hatch, interview with author, 2 August 2010; Andrea Lopen, "Harlem's Streetcorner Architects," *Architectural Forum* 123 (December 1965): 50–51.

28. Economic Opportunity Act of 1964, Public Law 88-452, 88th Cong., 2nd sess. (20 August 1964); ARCH, "Organizational Meeting," 12 December 1964, Box 8, Folder 34, NLH. Harlem's major community action agency, Harlem Youth Opportunities Unlimited-Associated Community Teams (HARYOU-ACT), received its first funding under the Economic Opportunity Act in June 1965. See Nicholas Lemann, *The Promised Land: The Great Black Migration and How It Changed America* (New York: Alfred A. Knopf, 1991), 169. On the War on Poverty in local contexts and grassroots efforts to seek community control through it, see Robert Bauman, *Race and the War on Poverty: From Watts to East L.A.* (Norman: University of Oklahoma Press, 2008); William S. Clayson, *Freedom Is Not Enough: The War on Poverty and the Civil Rights Movement in Texas* (Austin: University of Texas Press, 2010); Annalise Orleck and Lisa Gayle Hazirjian, eds., *The War on Poverty: A New Grassroots History, 1964–1980* (Athens: University of Georgia Press, 2011); Wesley G. Phelps, *A People's War on Poverty: Urban Politics and Grassroots Activists in Houston* (Athens: University of Georgia Press, 2014).

29. On the relationship between the liberalism of the New Deal and that of the Great Society, and the characteristics of the War on Poverty in practice, see Robert Self, *American Babylon: Race and the Struggle for Postwar Oakland* (Princeton, NJ: Princeton University Press, 2003), 198–205.

30. "Architect's Renewal Committee in Harlem," ca. early 1965, Box 8, Folder 34, NLH.

31. ARCH, "Organizational Meeting," 12 December 1964, Box 8, Folder 34, NLH; C. Richard Hatch, "Better Cities for Whom? Panel Discussion," *1965 Harvard Urban Design Conference* (Cambridge, MA: Harvard University Graduate School of Design, 1965), 26, 28.

32. Davidoff, "Advocacy and Pluralism in Planning," 331–333.

33. ARCH, "Prospectus: 1965–1966," ca. early 1965, 2, Reel L-227, Log 66-162, FFA; "List of Members—ARCH Millbank [*sic*] Committee," n.d., Box 8, Folder 34, NLH; "ARCH Notes for Harlem Neighborhood Projects," 25 February 1965, Box 8, Folder 34, NLH.

34. "Minister Assails City," *NYT,* 10 August 1959, 20; "Hotel's Tenants Fight Evictions," *NYT,* 4 January 1965, 33.

35. ARCH, "A Review of the Morningside General Neighborhood Renewal Plan," 1 March 1965, Box 6, Folder 7, CCC; ARCH, "A Review of Morningside General Neighborhood Renewal Plan (draft)," 17 January 1965, WT.

36. ARCH staff suggested the blocks immediately north of Morningside Heights along the Hudson River as one area that could support relocation housing. A more novel suggestion involved what to do with Morningside Park. Even as ARCH criticized plans to build a Columbia University gym in the park, they suggested that its northern expanse might be another site for new housing, with lost parkland redistributed throughout adjacent neighborhoods. ARCH, "A Review of the Morningside General Neighborhood Renewal Plan," 1 March 1965, Box 6, Folder 7, CCC; ARCH, "A Review of Morningside General Neighborhood Renewal Plan (draft)," 17 January 1965, WT.

37. Ballon, "Robert Moses and Urban Renewal," 106; Zipp, *Manhattan Projects,* esp. 114–196. The middle class remained the primary target of urban redevelopers not only in New York but in most major cities that practiced urban renewal, in many cases through commercial development (though New York City did not employ urban shopping as a redevelopment strategy). See Alison Isenberg, *Downtown America: A History of the Place and the People Who Made It* (Chicago: University of Chicago Press, 2004), 166–202.

38. ARCH, "A Review of the Morningside General Neighborhood Renewal Plan," 1 March 1965, Box 6, Folder 7, CCC.

39. Ibid.

40. "Morningside Residents Protest Renewal Plan," *NYAN,* 20 March 1965, 26; Lawrence O'Kane, "Morningside Tenants Protest Renewal at City Hall Hearing," *NYT,* 12 March 1965, 17.

41. O'Kane, "Morningside Tenants Protest Renewal," 17. Justifications for institutional expansion voiced in terms of national and international significance were extremely common in the Cold War era, as argued at length in Zipp, *Manhattan Projects.*

42. WHCO members garnered not only an apology from Barzun but also a meeting between community members and representatives from Morningside Heights institutions, where residents pushed leaders to sponsor relocation housing for those displaced by redevelopment. Samuel Kaplan, "Angry Group of 9 Calls on Barzun," *NYT,* 4 May 1965, 45; Samuel Kaplan, "Harlem Residents Ask Columbia's Aid in Their Relocation," *NYT,* 13 May 1965, 41; "ARCH Notes for May, 1965," Box 8, Folder 34, NLH; Edith Pennamon, interview by Sister Ann Richard Brotherton, transcript, 23 July 1971, Box 87, Folder 19, NYCS; ARCH, "ARCH Review 1964/5–1966," ca. September 1966, Reel L-227, Log 66-162, FFA.

43. Amendments at the April Board of Estimate hearing brought the fourteen blocks surrounding Columbia under the plan, with the exception of twenty designated "expansion sites" that accommodated institutional growth but did not help affected tenants; required 25 percent of new and rehabilitated housing each for low- and moderate-income tenants; canceled plans to widen Eighth Avenue; accommodated the possibility of relocation housing north of Morningside Heights; and announced project phasing intended to reduce the burden of displacement.

ARCH and its allies considered these only small concessions, however. See ARCH, "ARCH Notes for May, 1965," Box 8, Folder 34, NLH; "CU's Urban Renewal Plan (GNRP) Amended," *Morningsiders United,* 24 May 1965, Box 11, Folder 1, MCH.

44. C. Richard Hatch, "Architects," *NYAN,* 10 July 1965, 14; Letter to Louis Winnick from Hatch, 17 August 1965, Reel L-227, Log 66-162, FFA; ARCH, "Voluntary Architectural and Planning Services in Neighborhoods," October 1965, Box 1, Folder 2, MCH; ARCH, "ARCH Notes for May, 1965," Box 8, Folder 34, NLH. In 1977, Bailey would write, "I worked both as an architect and as a city planner, much of the time in public agencies, including the New York City Planning Commission and the Boston Redevelopment Authority. It took me a shamefully long time to discover that I was doing more harm there than good. In 1965 I switched sides and spent the five subsequent years fighting City Hall, first with [ARCH]." See Harvard College Class of 1952, *Twenty-Fifth Anniversary Report* (Cambridge, MA: Harvard University Printing Office, 1977), 39.

45. WHCO and ARCH, "West Harlem Urban Renewal Area: Survey and Planning Application," January 1966, CRH; "Memorandum: Creation of a Community Planning Agency in West Harlem," 4 May 1966, Reel L-227, Log 66-162, FFA. On the official requirements of the urban renewal process, see William L. Slayton, "The Operations and Achievements of the Urban Renewal Program," in *Urban Renewal: The Record and the Controversy,* ed. James Q. Wilson (Cambridge, MA: MIT Press, 1966), 189–229, esp. 197.

46. WHCO and ARCH, "West Harlem Urban Renewal Area: Survey and Planning Application," January 1966, 2–5, CRH.

47. On the Housing Act of 1954, see Ashley A. Foard and Hilbert Fefferman, "Federal Urban Renewal Legislation," in Wilson, *Urban Renewal,* 96–103. On the rehabilitation of 114th Street, a project that deserves its own account, see Lawrence O'Kane, "33 Harlem Families Move into a New Life," *NYT,* 5 December 1965, R1; Lawrence O'Kane, "Experimental Block Moving Forward—Slowly," *NYT,* 11 April 1965, R1. For HUD's official chronicle of the project, see U.S. Department of Housing and Urban Development, *The House on 114th Street* (Washington, DC: Government Printing Office, 1968).

48. WHCO and ARCH, "West Harlem Urban Renewal Area: Survey and Planning Application," January 1966, 7, CRH. *Government Programs for Community Development* included information on available policies and case studies describing their use. The case study of the Municipal Loan Program, for instance, described the rehabilitation of a Harlem brownstone on West 132nd Street. The recipient of the loan was "Attorney Charles Rangel," then five years away from election to the House of Representatives from Harlem's congressional district. See ARCH, *Government Programs for Community Development* (New York: ARCH, 1966), 32; ARCH, "Now Available: Government Programs for Community Development," March 1966, Box 1, Folder 2, MCH.

49. House of Representatives Committee on Banking and Currency, *Highlights of the Housing and Urban Development Act of 1965,* 89th Cong., 1st sess., 1965; ARCH, "Summary of the Main Provisions of 'The Housing and Urban Development Act of 1965' Applicable to Harlem," October 1965, Box 1, Folder 2, MCH; C. Richard Hatch, "Notice on Rent Supplements," 23 March 1966, Box 1, Folder 2, MCH; ARCH, "Neighborhood Housing Corporations," 5 May 1966, Reel L-227, Log 66-162, FFA.

50. ARCH, *Tenant Action,* rev. ed. (New York: ARCH, 1966), 21–25; Joel Schwartz, "Tenant Power in the Liberal City, 1943–1971," in *The Tenant Movement in New York City, 1904–1984,* ed. Ronald Lawson with Mark Naison (New Brunswick, NJ: Rutgers University Press, 1986), 183. On the tenants' movement in New York City, see Lawson and Naison, *Tenant Movement in New York City;* Roberta S. Gold, "City of Tenants: New York's Housing Struggles and the Challenge to Postwar America, 1945–1974" (PhD diss., University of Washington, 2004).

51. Thabit reported back to ARCH "that the [*Tenant Action*] handbook has been described to him in terms ranging from 'excellent' to 'great.'" "Tenant Action" [distribution list], March to June 1966, Box 1, Folder 2, MCH; Letter to Gentlemen from Jane Benedict, 11 August 1966, Box 1, Folder 2, MCH; "Tenants Guidebook on Protests Ready," *NYT,* 27 March 1966, 343; "Tenant Action Handbook in 2nd Printing," *NYAN,* 19 March 1966, 35; ARCH, "Confidential: Report to Officers and Executive Committee," 4 November 1966, 7, WT; ARCH, "Notes: ARCH Executive Committee Meeting," 20 January 1966, WT.

52. ARCH, *Tenant Action;* ARCH, "Proposed Program, 1965–66," ca. late 1965, 3, CRH; C. Richard Hatch, "June Newsletter," 8 June 1966, WT; ARCH, "Confidential: Report to Officers and Executive Committee," 4 November 1966, 6–7, WT; ARCH, "ARCH Review 1964/5–1966," November 1966, 5–6, Reel L-227, Log 66-162, FFA; ARCH, "Notes: ARCH Executive Committee Meeting," 20 January 1966, WT; Schwartz, "Tenant Power in the Liberal City," 184–185.

53. ARCH, "Confidential: Report to Officers and Executive Committee," 4 November 1966, 6–7, WT.

54. Ibid., 7; Lopen, "Harlem's Streetcorner Architects," 51; ARCH, "Preliminary Proposal for a Long Range Plan for Harlem," 5 May 1965, Box 8, Folder 34, NLH.

55. ARCH, "Voluntary Architectural and Planning Services in Neighborhoods," October 1965, Box 1, Folder 2, MCH; "Memorandum: Creation of a Community Planning Agency in West Harlem," 4 May 1966, Reel L-227, Log 66-162, FFA. Self finds a similar negotiation in the local implementation of the War on Poverty in Oakland. See Self, *American Babylon,* 199–200.

56. ARCH, "ARCH Review 1964/5–1966," November 1966, Reel L-227, Log 66-162, FFA; ARCH, "ARCH Notes for May, 1965," Box 8, Folder 34, NLH; ARCH, "ARCH Notes for Harlem Neighborhood Projects," 25 February 1965, Box 8, Folder 34, NLH; Hatch, interview with author, 2 August 2010.

57. ARCH, "ARCH Review 1964/5–1966," November 1966, Reel L-227, Log 66-162, FFA.

58. John Kifner, "Poor in Harlem in Their Own H.Q.," *NYT*, 22 February 1966, 22; "Grass Roots Group in Own Headquarters," *NYAN*, 26 February 1966, 7.

59. Kifner, "Poor in Harlem in Their Own H.Q."; Melvin E. Schoonover, *Making All Things Human: A Church in East Harlem* (New York: Holt, Rinehart and Winston, 1969), 44–47; Alice Kornegay, "Sitting-Down Victory," *Annals of the New York Academy of Sciences* 196, no. 2 (April 1972): 66–67.

60. Schoonover, *Making All Things Human*, 47, 133. Schoonover's account of his work in the East Harlem Triangle provides the most thorough history of the community's resistance to urban renewal. See esp. 132–171.

61. Ibid., 134–135, 139–140; Charles G. Bennett, "City Plans Study to Help Harlem," *NYT*, 6 December 1964, 60. Stanley, who later reemerged as Barzun's nemesis in West Harlem, was also involved with this effort. Surveys indicated that 10 percent of residents had drug addictions, another 10 percent suffered from alcoholism, and 15 percent had adult criminal records.

62. Kornegay quoted in Schoonover, *Making All Things Human*, 51, 136–137, 139–143; New York City Planning Commission, CP-16483, 4 October 1961, 16, Box 14, Folder 7, CHG.

63. Schoonover, *Making All Things Human*, 140–150. Schoonover never mentions the sociologist by name, but the *Times* discusses a pending contract with Herbert J. Ganz [*sic*]. See Bennett, "City Plans Study to Help Harlem," 60; Melvin E. Schoonover, "Urban Decay," *NYT*, 17 April 1966, 217.

64. Schoonover, *Making All Things Human*, 152–155; C. Richard Hatch, "June Newsletter," 8 June 1966, WT; ARCH, "Urban Renewal in the East Harlem Triangle," October 1966, 1–2, CRH. Members of the planning committee included Keron Moon, Lucille Washington, Lena Daley, Rosa Brown, Beulah Palmer, Maxine Small, Philip Small, Elaine Auston, Mary Whinen, and Tyrone Georgiou, the last of whom likely worked on ARCH's staff at this time.

65. ARCH, "Urban Renewal in the East Harlem Triangle," October 1966, 9, 11, 13, 20, CRH.

66. Ibid., 5, 9.

67. Ibid., 4, 6.

68. Whitney Young, "World Trade Center for Harlem," *NYAN*, 11 June 1966, 14. Leaders who voted in favor of Young's proposal included Callender, then executive director-designate of the Urban League; State Senator Basil Paterson; and State Assembly members including Shirley Chisholm and Percy Sutton. See "Would Place World Trade Center in Harlem," *NYAN*, 11 June 1966, 4. Young emphasized the connection between his proposal and urban renewal in a letter to the *Times*: "We are in trouble as long as the Negro sees the United Nations put on the East Side to redeem a blighted area and Lincoln Center put on the West Side for the same reason, and yet sees that any suggestion that a major state-supported

facility be placed in Harlem to serve the same purpose is treated as though everybody involved were insane." See Whitney Young, "For World Trade Center in Harlem," *NYT,* 21 July 1966, 25. Also see Maurice Carroll, "Port Authority Is Urged to Build World Trade Center in Harlem," *NYT,* 27 May 1966, 32.

69. "A Good Plan," *NYAN,* 28 May 1966, 16. Callender pushed insistently throughout the summer, finding support especially from state comptroller Arthur Levitt. See "Call Parley on Trade Center as Others Urge Site for Harlem," *NYAN,* 20 August 1966, 1. Also see "Guv Studies Harlem, B-S Possibilities," *NYAN,* 2 July 1966, 3; Will Lissner, "Harlem Studied for State Office," *NYT,* 25 July 1966, 1. Former borough president Constance Baker Motley also supported the plan and had advocated for more public offices in Harlem since 1965, when she was still in office. See "Build the Building," *NYAN,* 6 August 1966, 12; Jonathan Randal, "State Will Erect 23-Story Center on Harlem Site," *NYT,* 18 September 1966, 1; Martin Gansberg, "A New Era Seen for Harlem," *NYT,* 18 September 1966, 44; ARCH, "ARCH Mid-Year Report," ca. June–July 1966, CRH.

70. William Robbins, "Harlem Building to Take 3 Years," *NYT,* 16 October 1966, 80. Sutton initially supported the project but came to see its size as too modest to be consequential. See Randal, "State Will Erect 23-Story Center," 1; "Sutton Calls Rockefeller's Plan for Harlem Offices 'Mere Token Gesture,'" *NYT,* 13 October 1966, 25.

71. ARCH, "Urban Renewal in the East Harlem Triangle," October 1966, 6, 16, CRH.

72. Leonard Buder, "Showcase School Sets Off Dispute," *NYT,* 2 September 1966, 28. Prominent New Orleans–based modernists Nathaniel C. Curtis Jr. and Arthur Q. Davis designed the school.

73. Ibid.; "Integration: The Sorry Struggle of I.S. 201," *Time,* 30 September 1966; Jerald E. Podair, *The Strike That Changed New York: Blacks, Whites, and the Ocean Hill-Brownsville Crisis* (New Haven, CT: Yale University Press, 2002), 33–36. Podair argues that IS 201 marked the start of the community control movement in education and "the last gasp of the integration impulse in the New York City public school system." See Podair, *Strike That Changed,* 34.

74. Bruder, "Showcase School Sets Off Dispute," 28; Podair, *Strike That Changed,* 35; Peter Kihss, "Harlem Teachers Consider Boycott," *NYT,* 19 September 1966, 1; Thomas A. Johnson, "11 Harlem Pickets Seized as 'Disorderly,'" *NYT,* 24 September 1966, 29. CAEHT's offices often provided meeting space for negotiations and a headquarters for demonstrators. See "Meeting Fails to Resolve Dispute over I.S. 201," *NYT,* 18 September 1966, 46. See film of the school and protesters at "Video Clip of I.S. 201 Protests," Harlem CORE, Item #146, accessed November 13, 2014, http://harlemcore.com/omeka/items/show/146. On the transition from civil rights liberalism to Black Power, also see Matthew Countryman, *Up South: Civil Rights and Black Power in Philadelphia* (Philadelphia: University of Pennsylvania Press, 2006); Devin Fergus, *Liberalism, Black Power, and the Making of American Politics, 1965–1980* (Athens: University of Georgia Press, 2009).

75. "'Black Power' Moves into Harlem School Battle," *NYAN*, 24 September 1966, 1. On Carmichael and Black Power in Harlem in general, see Peniel E. Joseph, *Waiting 'Til the Midnight Hour: A Narrative History of Black Power in America* (New York: Henry Holt, 2006). Carmichael's own definitions of Black Power and community control are useful here: "It is a call for black people in this country to unite, to recognize their heritage, to build a sense of community. It is a call for black people to begin to define their own goals, to lead their own organizations and to support those organizations. It is a call to reject the racist institutions and values of this society. . . . *Before a group can enter the open society, it must first close ranks.* By this we mean that group solidarity is necessary before a group can operate effectively from a bargaining position of strength in a pluralistic society" (emphasis in the original). Stokely Carmichael and Charles V. Hamilton, *Black Power: The Politics of Liberation in America* (New York: Vintage Books, 1967), 44. On community control, also see Alan A. Altshuler, *Community Control: The Black Demand for Participation in Large American Cities* (New York: Western, 1970). Negotiations over IS 201 took years to resolve, but ultimately culminated in only a partial victory for those demanding community control: In 1967, the Ford Foundation helped fund governing boards for three districts—IS 201, Two Bridges, and Ocean Hill–Brownsville—that were to give parents, teachers, and community members a voice in the governance of local schools. But this plan took several years to implement, became mired in further controversy, and then was somewhat lost amid the Ocean Hill–Brownsville school strike in 1968, though Triangle activists continued to agitate into 1969. Schoonover provides a thorough account of the IS 201 controversy. See Schoonover, *Making All Things Human*, 111–131. On Ocean Hill–Brownsville, see Podair, *Strike That Changed;* Wendell E. Pritchett, *Brownsville, Brooklyn: Blacks, Jews, and the Changing Face of the Ghetto* (Chicago: University of Chicago Press, 2002), 221–237.

76. Preston Wilcox, "Proposal: Rename the Harlem River Playground to the Alice Kornegay Playground," ca. late 1996, Box 38, Folder 5, PW; Preston Wilcox, "Alice Kornegay: An Unusual Friend," 20 November 1973, Box 10, Folder 3, PW; Podair, *Strike That Changed*, 41; Preston Wilcox, "The Controversy over I.S. 201: One View and a Proposal," July 1966, Box 15, Folder 3, PW (also in *Urban Review* 1 [July 1966]: 12–16); Preston Wilcox, "Architecture: A Palliative for Anger (draft)," ca. mid-1966, Box 10, Folder 6, PW.

77. Preston Wilcox, "Architecture: A Palliative for Anger (draft)," ca. mid-1966, Box 10, Folder 6, PW.

78. On the connections between liberalism and modernism—and the interconnected failures of both—see Carriere, "Between Being and Becoming"; Klemek, "Urbanism as Reform"; Klemek, *Transatlantic Collapse.*

79. ARCH, "Confidential: Report to Officers and Executive Committee," 4 November 1966, 3, WT.

80. CAEHT also hired a firm called Social Dynamics to carry out a socioeconomic study of the neighborhood. See Schoonover, *Making All Things Human*,

155–160; "East Harlem Unit to Plan Renewal," *NYT*, 30 June 1967, 18. For that study, see Social Dynamics Corporation, *The East Harlem Triangle: A Sociological and Economic Study* (New York: Housing and Development Administration, May 1968).

81. ARCH, "ARCH News," April 1967, Box 1, Folder 2, MCH; Letter to Hatch, Edwin Folk, Chester Hartman, and Kenneth Simmons from J. E. H, 30 January 1967, Reel L-227, Log 66-162, FFA; "Urban Planners Get Harlem Aid," *NYT*, 16 April 1967, 70; Jonathan D. Greenberg, *Staking a Claim: Jake Simmons and the Making of an African-American Oil Dynasty* (New York: Atheneum, 1990), 4; C. Richard Hatch, e-mail message to author, 28 February 2011; Kenneth Simmons, "Thoughts on a Strategy for Urban Black Communities" (paper presented at "Conference '67: Survival of the Black Community," San Francisco, 27–29 February 1967), 5–6.

82. Malcolm X, "The Ballot or the Bullet" (lecture, Cleveland, 3 April 1964); also see Sugrue, *Sweet Land of Liberty*, 428.

83. Because of the variable definition of what constitutes a CDC, it is difficult to identify a "first" one, though the Bedford-Stuyvesant Restoration Corporation, founded in Brooklyn in 1966, at least represented the first in New York City, with Harlem's effort close behind. On early CDCs, see Geoffrey Faux, *CDCs: New Hope for the Inner City* (New York: Twentieth Century Fund, 1971), 65–82; Laura Warren Hill and Julia Rabig, eds., *The Business of Black Power: Community Development, Capitalism, and Corporate Responsibility in Postwar America* (Rochester, NY: University of Rochester Press, 2012). On the Bedford-Stuyvesant Restoration Corporation, see Kimberley Johnson, "Community Development Corporations, Participation, and Accountability: The Harlem Urban Development Corporation and the Bedford-Stuyvesant Restoration Corporation," *Annals of the American Academy of Political and Social Science* 594 (July 2004): 109–124; Brian Purnell, "'What We Need Is Brick and Mortar': Race, Gender, and Early Leadership of the Bedford-Stuyvesant Restoration Corporation," in Hill and Rabig, *The Business of Black Power*, 217–244.

84. Columbia University Development Planning Workshop and Harlem Development Committee (CUDPW/HDC), "A Demonstration Economic Development Program for Harlem: Draft Proposal for a 12-Month Demonstration Grant under Section 207 of the Economic Opportunity Act of 1964," 4 April 1967, CRH; Preston Wilcox, "Appendix: Resident Participation in the Harlem Corporation," 14 April 1967, Box 14, Folder 18, PW.

85. CUDPW/HDC, "A Demonstration Economic Development Program for Harlem," 4 April 1967, CRH.

86. "Statement of CAP Grant," 14 June 1967, Box 59, Folder "Harlem Commonwealth Council—News Clippings 1968—1 of 2," CSA/SF; Memo to R. Sargent Shriver from Maurice A. Dawkins, 29 June 1967, Box 59, Folder "Harlem Commonwealth Council—News Clippings 1968—2 of 2," CSA/SF; CUDPW/HDC, "A Demonstration Economic Development Program for Harlem," 4 April 1967, CRH;

Preston Wilcox, "Appendix: Resident Participation in the Harlem Corporation," 14 April 1967, Box 14, Folder 18, PW.

87. "2 Named by ARCH," *NYAN*, 10 June 1967, 6; Hatch, interview with author, 2 August 2010; C. Richard Hatch, "Some Thoughts on Advocacy Planning," *Architectural Forum* 128 (June 1968): 73. Hatch's article was based on a lecture he had given at Cornell in April 1968. Letter to Ellen Berkeley from Hatch, 24 April 1968, CRH.

88. Hatch, interview with author, 2 August 2010; ARCH, *HN,* October 1967.

2. Black Utopia

1. Albert Murray, "Image and Likeness in Harlem," *Urban Review* 2, no. 2 (June 1967): 15. Also see Murray's 1970 revision, "Image and Unlikeness in Harlem," in *The Omni-Americans: New Perspectives on Black Experience and American Culture* (New York: Outerbridge and Dienstfrey, 1970), 71–77.

2. On Murray's rejection of black nationalism, see Daniel Matlin, *On the Corner: African American Intellectuals and the Urban Crisis* (Cambridge, MA: Harvard University Press, 2013), 215–217.

3. Stokely Carmichael and Charles V. Hamilton, *Black Power: The Politics of Liberation in America* (New York: Vintage Books, 1967), 55.

4. J. Max Bond Jr., "A Critical Look at Tema," in *Housing and Urbanization: Report on the Postgraduate Urban Planning Course (1967–68, Term 1–2)* (Kumasi, Ghana: Faculty of Architecture, University of Science and Technology, [1968?]), n.p. Bond's essay appears to have been based on a tutorial he taught on the same subject, likely in the first semester of that school year.

5. "Max Bond: 1935–2009, A Celebration," 12 May 2009, program from memorial service held at Cooper Union, New York (in author's possession). On J. Max Bond Sr., see Eric Pace, "J. Max Bond, Sr., 89, an American Who Headed Liberian University," *NYT,* 18 December 1991. On Ruth Clement Bond, see Margalit Fox, "Ruth C. Bond Dies at 101; Her Quilts Had a Message," *NYT,* 13 November 2005. On Horace Mann Bond, see Special Collections and University Archives, "Horace Mann Bond Papers, 1830–1979: Biographical Note," W. E. B. DuBois Library, University of Massachusetts Amherst, accessed 28 April 2011, http://asteria.fivecolleges .edu/findaids/umass/mums411_bioghist.html. On Rufus Clement, see Isabel Wilkerson, *The Warmth of Other Suns: The Epic Story of America's Great Migration* (New York: Random House, 2010).

6. "Max Bond: 1935–2009, A Celebration"; Lynne Duke, "Blueprint of a Life," *WP,* 1 July 2004, C01; James Bows Jr. and J. Max Bond Jr., "Fiery Cross," *HC,* 21 February 1952; Philip M. Cronin, "Leighton Calls Yardling 'Fiery Cross' Deplorable," *HC,* 23 February 1952; "Cambridge Chiefs Weigh Decision in 'Birth' Exhibition," *HC,* 8 November 1952; "Local Committee Backs Permit for 'Birth' Showings," *HC,* 10 November 1952.

7. Kevin K. Gaines, *American Africans in Ghana: Black Expatriates and the Civil Rights Era* (Chapel Hill: University of North Carolina Press, 2006), 4–5, 136–178.

8. Ibid., 10, 141; Carmichael and Hamilton, *Black Power,* 16–17, 161; Bond, "A Critical Look at Tema"; Kenneth Simmons, "Thoughts on a Strategy for Urban Black Communities" (paper presented at "Conference '67: Survival of the Black Community," San Francisco, 27–29 February 1967), 5–6. See also Robert Self, *American Babylon: Race and the Struggle for Postwar Oakland* (Princeton, NJ: Princeton University Press, 2003), 228; Thomas Sugrue, *Sweet Land of Liberty: The Forgotten Struggle for Civil Rights in the North* (New York: Random House, 2008), 341–343.

9. Duke, "Blueprint of a Life"; David Spencer, "School Strike: A Parent's View," *HN,* October 1967, 1; Roy Innis, "Black $$$ Power," *HN,* November 1967, 1; J. Max Bond Jr., "From the Publisher," *HN,* October 1967, 2.

10. "Mrs. Atkins Cited for Community Work," *HN,* December 1967; George H. Favre, "Urban Issues Bring Splits in Ranks of City Planners," *Christian Science Monitor,* 11 May 1968. On the centrality of participatory democracy in the New Left and its varying forms and contradictions, see James Miller, *"Democracy Is in the Streets": From Port Huron to the Siege of Chicago* (New York: Simon and Schuster, 1987), 141–154.

11. ARCH, "ARCH Review 1964/5–1966," ca. November 1966, Reel L-227, Log 66-162, FFA; Letter to Sir from Bond, 13 February 1968, Box 3, Folder 9, JB.

12. ARCH, "ARCH Review 1964/5–1966," ca. November 1966, Reel L-227, Log 66-162, FFA; ARCH, "Waiver of Notice: Meeting of the Board of Directors," 25 January 1968, WT; United Block Association, "How to Form a Block Association," n.d., Box 20, Folder 35, RL; Manuscripts, Archives, and Rare Books Division, "Kenneth Marshall Papers, 1951–1977," Schomburg Center for Research in Black Culture, accessed 29 April 2011, http://www.nypl.org/archives/3808; David E. DesJardines, "John Oliver Killens," in *The New Georgia Encyclopedia,* August 22, 2013, http://www.georgiaencyclopedia.org/nge/Article.jsp?id=h-1234; Robert Thomas Jr., "John Henrik Clarke, Black Studies Advocate, Dies at 83," *NYT,* 20 July 1998; Preston Wilcox, "Appendix: Resident Participation in the Harlem Corporation," 14 April 1967, Box 14, Folder 18, PW; Memo to Bob Emond, Pat Patrick, and Dick Fullmer from Harry Carpenter, 19 March 1968, Box 59, Folder "Harlem Commonwealth Council—News Clippings 1968—1 of 2," CSA/SF.

13. Charles E. Jones, "From Protest to Black Conservatism: The Demise of the Congress of Racial Equality," in *Black Political Organizations in the Post-Civil Rights Era,* ed. Ollie A. Johnson III and Karin L. Stanford (New Brunswick, NJ: Rutgers University Press, 2002), 80–98; George Barner, "CORE Changes to Implement Policies," *NYAN,* 30 December 1967, 1; Earl Caldwell, "CORE Picks Harlem Militant for Its No. 2 National Position," *NYT,* 28 December 1967, 21; "CORE's Acting Leader," *NYT,* 26 June 1968, 33; Memo to Emond from Carpenter, 6 March 1968, Box 59, Folder "Harlem Commonwealth Council—News Clippings 1968—1 of 2," CSA/SF. Innis remains director of CORE to this day.

14. J. Max Bond Jr., "From the Publisher," *HN,* October 1967, 2; J. Max Bond Jr., "Speech to: Architects and Planners against the War in Viet Nam," 3 May 1968, Box 15, Folder 15, JMB.

15. David Bird, "Sewage Plant Approval Delayed for Harlem; New Sites Studied," *NYT,* 5 April 1968, 29; "Motorcade to Show Sewer Opposition," *NYAN,* 20 April 1968, 2; ARCH, "Lindsay's New Sewage Plant to Smell Up Harlem," *HN,* June 1968, 8.

16. Ralph Blumenthal, "Columbia Scores Gym-Plan Critics," *NYT,* 15 February 1966, 31; C. Richard Hatch, "No Park Gymnasium," *NYT,* 1 February 1966, 34. The Columbia gym saga was both long and complex. For historical accounts, see Michael H. Carriere, "Between Being and Becoming: On Architecture, Student Protest, and the Aesthetics of Liberalism in Postwar America" (PhD diss., University of Chicago, 2010); Stefan M. Bradley, *Harlem vs. Columbia University: Black Student Power in the Late 1960s* (Urbana: University of Illinois Press, 2009). For an official account, see Fact-Finding Commission on Columbia Disturbances, *Crisis at Columbia: Report of the Fact-Finding Commission Appointed to Investigate the Disturbances at Columbia University in April and May, 1968* (New York: Vintage Books, 1968).

17. "Anti-Gym Pickets at Columbia Burn Trustee Hogan in Effigy," *NYT,* 12 November 1967, 66; ARCH, "The Battle of Morningside Park," *HN,* June 1968; ARCH and WHCO, *West Harlem Morningside: A Community Proposal* (New York: ARCH and WHCO, 1968), 5; Horace Foster, "Why? An Epic of Today," *HN,* June 1968.

18. Starr quoted in Favre, "Urban Issues Bring Splits"; "Advocacy Planning: What It Is, How It Works," *Progressive Architecture,* September 1968, 110.

19. Letter to Sir from Bond, 13 February 1968, Box 3, Folder 9, JB.

20. Arthur L. Symes and Rae Banks, *Architecture in the Neighborhoods* (New York: ARCH, Cooper Union School of Art and Architecture, and New York Chapter of the American Institute of Architects, November 1968), 4, 6–7, 15, 19–20; Arthur Symes, "Architecture in the Neighborhoods," *HN,* May 1969, 7; "An Art and Architecture Training Program," Box 2, Folder 14, JLW; Arthur Symes, interview with author, 30 July 2010; Lynn Haney, "Training of Blacks as Architects Increasing," *NYT,* 15 March 1970, 354.

21. ARCH, "Curriculum Advisory Committee for a Technical Training School," 10 June 1965, WT; Symes and Banks, *Architecture in the Neighborhoods,* 15; "ARCH-Cooper Union Training Program," 1968, Box 106, Folder 714, Record Group 3.1, RBF; Kenneth Knuckles, interview with author, 4 February 2011; Knuckles and Symes quoted in "Negro Architects Helping Harlem Plan Its Future," *NYT,* 16 March 1969, 57.

22. "Demand Voice on Planning Commission," *HN,* December 1968.

23. "Planning Commission Still Ignores Blacks, Puerto Ricans," *NYAN,* 5 April 1969, 4; Melvin Dixon, "Blast Lindsay on Plan Commission," *NYAN,* 2 August 1969, 1; "Press Release: Citywide Coalition Demands Appointments of Black and Puerto Rican Representatives to City Planning Commission," 25 July 1969,

Box 31, Folder 8, MCH; Symes, interview with author, 30 July 2010. Lindsay appointed Chester Rapkin and Gerald Coleman to these positions. See "Lindsay Snubs Community," *HN,* March 1969; "Appoint First Black to Commission," *MT,* 6 September 1969.

24. David K. Shipler, "Coalition 'Appoints' 3 Nonwhites to City Plan Group as a Protest," *NYT,* 13 August 1969, 44; Melvin Dixon, "Unplanning City Planning," *NYAN,* 23 August 1969, 1; Melvin Dixon, "Planning Power Ceremony Held," *NYAN,* 16 August 1969, 1; Edward C. Burks, "Two Named to Plan Commission, One Will Be First Negro on Board," *NYT,* 29 August 1969; Symes, interview with author, 30 July 2010. On the Real Great Society/Urban Planning Studio, see Luis Aponte-Parés, "Lessons from El Barrio—the East Harlem Real Great Society/Urban Planning Studio: A Puerto Rican Chapter in the Fight for Urban Self-Determination," *New Political Science* 20, no. 4 (1998): 399–420.

25. "Lindsay Snubs Community," 4; Pat Patterson, "Michael Opposes Urban Renewal," *MT,* 13 September 1969.

26. Patterson, "Michael Opposes Urban Renewal"; Symes, "Architecture in the Neighborhoods."

27. Bond quoted in Priscilla Tucker, "Poor Peoples' Plan," *Metropolitan Museum of Art Bulletin* 27, no. 5 (January 1969): 268.

28. Carmichael and Hamilton, *Black Power,* 164–165.

29. J. Max Bond Jr., "Speech to: Architects and Planners against the War in Viet Nam," 3 May 1968, Box 15, Folder 15, JMB.

30. Larry Neal, "The Black Arts Movement," in *The Black Aesthetic,* ed. Addison Gayle Jr. (New York: Doubleday, 1971), 272–273; Addison Gayle Jr., "Introduction," in Gayle, *The Black Aesthetic,* xxiv. Neal originally published his manifesto in *Drama Review* 12 (Summer 1968): 29–39. On the many forms, variations, and geographic sites of the Black Arts Movement, see James Edward Smethurst, *The Black Arts Movement: Literary Nationalism in the 1960s and 1970s* (Chapel Hill: University of North Carolina Press, 2005). Max Bond's wife, Jean Carey Bond, was on staff at the journal *Freedomways,* which Smethurst describes as an important link between an older generation of African American cultural figures and the new tendencies present in the Black Arts Movement. See Smethurst, *The Black Arts Movement,* 125–127.

31. Neal, "The Black Arts Movement," 272; Amy Abugo Ongiri, *Spectacular Blackness: The Cultural Politics of the Black Power Movement and the Search for a Black Aesthetic* (Charlottesville: University of Virginia Press, 2010), esp. 7, 22, 105; Smethurst, *Black Arts Movement,* 68.

32. Bond quoted in Tucker, "Poor Peoples' Plan," 265–266; Bond, "A Critical Look at Tema." Bond remained interested in communitarian approaches to the city, as he explained in a January 1974 interview with Reed:

REED: I see a theme running through your remarks, Mr. Bond, that if you change the economic system, there will be a flowering of architecture.

BOND: Yes.

REED: A more socialistic—?

BOND: Yes. An economic system adapted to the means of the people.

See "Max Bond and Carl Anthony on Afro-American Architecture: An Interview by Ishmael Reed," *Yardbird Reader* 4 (1975): 20. On the role of communitarian socialism in utopian schemes, see Dolores Hayden, *Seven American Utopias: The Architecture of Communitarian Socialism, 1790–1975* (Cambridge, MA: MIT Press, 1976).

33. Bond quoted in Tucker, "Poor Peoples' Plan," 266–267. For Jacobs's "ballet of the good city sidewalk," see Jane Jacobs, *Death and Life of Great American Cities* (New York: Vintage Books, 1961), 50–54.

34. Samuel Zipp characterizes the clearance-oriented development approach of modernism as "the ethic of city rebuilding." Christopher Klemek describes it as a central aspect of the "urban renewal order." Samuel Zipp, *Manhattan Projects: The Rise and Fall of Urban Renewal in Cold War New York* (New York: Oxford University Press, 2010); Christopher Klemek, *The Transatlantic Collapse of Urban Renewal: Postwar Urbanism from New York to Berlin* (Chicago: University of Chicago Press, 2011).

35. Bond quoted in Tucker, "Poor Peoples' Plan," 268; "Max Bond and Carl Anthony," 17.

36. ARCH and WHCO, *West Harlem Morningside,* 19; ARCH, *East Harlem Triangle Plan* (New York: ARCH, 1968).

37. ARCH and WHCO, *West Harlem Morningside,* 19; ARCH, *East Harlem Triangle Plan,* 37, 43. Implementation of the plan for the East Harlem Triangle over the following decades relied for the most part on Section 8 low-income-housing funding. CAEHT rehabilitated nine buildings with 189 apartments at E. 130th Street and Lexington Avenue in 1968, and built new housing with 169 apartments on Lexington Avenue between 128th and 129th Streets in 1972 (Jackie Robinson Houses); 246 apartments between 126th and 127th Streets, Lexington to Park Avenues in 1975 (1775 Houses); 147 apartments between 127th and 128th Streets, Lexington to Park Avenues in 1979 (AK Houses); 131 apartments between 129th and 130th Streets, Lexington to Park Avenues in 1984 (MS Houses); and 39 apartments at 126th Street and Lexington Avenue in 1990 (Tweemill House). See "The Community Association of the East Harlem Triangle: Improvements Developed by, Sponsored by and Assisted by the Association," 18 July 1989, Box 18, Folder 7, PW; "39 Units in Harlem: Housing for the Handicapped," *NYT,* 4 November 1990.

38. Jacobs, *Death and Life of Great American Cities,* 270–290.

39. ARCH, *East Harlem Triangle Plan,* 46–48.

40. ARCH, *East Harlem Triangle Plan;* ARCH and WHCO, *West Harlem Morningside,* 34–35; ARCH, "The Battle of Morningside Park," 6.

41. ARCH and WHCO, *West Harlem Morningside,* 30; ARCH, *East Harlem Triangle Plan.*

42. ARCH and WHCO, *West Harlem Morningside*, 29–30; ARCH, *East Harlem Triangle Plan*, 46; "Advocacy Planning: What It Is, How It Works," 110; Bond quoted in Tucker, "Poor Peoples' Plan," 267.

43. "126th Street" (map), Box 52, Folder 1946, Series 33, NAR; "Background: Demolition Ceremonies for Construction of State Office Building and Cultural Center in Harlem, New York City," 7 June 1967, Box 52, Folder 1945, Series 33, NAR; "Excerpts of Remarks by Governor Nelson A. Rockefeller Prepared for Delivery at Demolition Ceremony for the Harlem State Office Building," 7 June 1967, Box 52, Folder 1945, Series 33, NAR; Martin Gansberg, "Governor Flunks Test as Wrecker," *NYT*, 8 June 1967, 50.

44. William Robbins, "Harlem Building to Take 3 Years," *NYT*, 16 October 1966, 80; "Advocacy Planning: What It Is, How It Works," 110; Bond, "Speech to: Architects and Planners against the War in Viet Nam," 3 May 1968, Box 15, Folder 15, JMB.

45. Smethurst, *The Black Arts Movement*, 163–164; Sharifa Rhodes-Pitts, *Harlem Is Nowhere: A Journey to the Mecca of Black America* (New York: Little, Brown, 2011), 172–173; Jonathan Gill, *Harlem: The Four Hundred Year History from Dutch Village to Capital of Black America* (New York: Grove, 2011), 372–373; Charlayne Hunter, "The Professor," *New Yorker*, 3 September 1966, 28–29; Charlayne Hunter, "Lull," *New Yorker*, 11 November 1967, 51–53. Governor Rockefeller promised Michaux that the state would relocate the National Memorial African Bookstore after demolition, but relocation never took place. Richard E. Mooney, "State Project Begins in Harlem," *NYT*, 12 October 1967, 47. Richard B. Moore ran the Frederick Douglass Book Center on the same block. It also served as an important intellectual resource for radicals, with a focus on the African diaspora. See Mel Tapley, "Richard Moore: Pioneer Activist," *NYAN*, 23 September 1978, B3; J. M. Floyd-Thomas, "Moore, Richard B.," in *Encyclopedia of the Harlem Renaissance*, vol. 2, ed. Cary D. Wintz and Paul Finkelman (New York: Routledge, 2004), 808–809.

46. Imamu Amiri Baraka, *The Autobiography of LeRoi Jones/Amiri Baraka* (New York: Freundlich Books, 1984), 208; Neal quoted in Smethurst, *The Black Arts Movement*, 164.

47. ARCH, "The Provision of Urban Design and Planning Services to Low Income Communities," ca. August 1968, Box 8, Folder 34, NLH; "We Don't Need That Damn State Building in Harlem," ca. May 1968, Folder "Harlem—State Office Building," SCF.

48. Joseph P. Fried, "Investors Plan Business Center on Harlem Block," *NYT*, 20 August 1968, 1; George Barner, "Skyscraper for Harlem Draws Cheers, Jeers," *NYAN*, 24 August 1968, 1; Joseph P. Fried, "Skyscraper for Harlem Is Protested," *NYT*, 22 August 1968, 39; Simon Anekwe, "Agin' It," *NYAN*, 24 August 1968, 1; "Harlem Labeled City's 'Junkyard,'" *NYT*, 24 August 1968, 30.

49. Symes quoted in Aubrey Zephyr, "Core Scores State Building," *MT*, 12 April 1969, 7; "Who Needs a State Building? Harlem Needs a High School!!" ca.

spring 1968, Folder "Harlem—State Office Building," SCF; Committee for a Harlem High School, "The Case for a Harlem High School," February 1969, Box 7, Folder 7, JMB; "We Don't Need That Damn State Building in Harlem," ca. May 1968, Folder "Harlem—State Office Building," SCF; "Want Autonomous School System," *NYAN*, 25 January 1969, 1; "Harlem Demands Own Schools," *NYAN*, 8 March 1969, 1; Mooney, "State Project Begins in Harlem," 47. Initially, high school proponents went by the clunky name "State Building-NO! High School-YES! Committee," but a more organized effort proceeded as the Committee for a Harlem High School, a group in which ARCH was an active member. Proponents gained a $150,000 budget allocation from the city in 1969 for preliminary planning for a Harlem high school, a victory that observers credited to ARCH's work on behalf of the campaign. See "A Public High School in the Works for Harlem," *NYAN*, 29 March 1969, 1.

50. Harlem Assertion of Rights, Inc., "Report on Proposed State Office Building," ca. March 1969, Box 25, Folder 170, MMW; C. Gerald Fraser, "Malcolm X Memorial Services and Protest Mark Date of Death," *NYT*, 22 February 1969, 22; "Office Ruined; No Arrest," *NYAN*, 1 March 1969, 1.

51. Sylvan Fox, "Warnings Halted Harlem Project," *NYT*, 4 July 1969, 1; Basil Paterson, "The Story about the State Bldg.," *NYAN*, 12 July 1969, 1; "Harlem Demonstrators Protest State Building," *NYT*, 1 July 1969, 82.

52. Community Coalition, "Press Release," 7 July 1969, Box 25, Folder 170, MMW; "Official Position of the Community Coalition," July 1969, Box 25, Folder 170, MMW. The Community Coalition aligned various groups that had been protesting against the state office building. See Juana Clark, "The Coalition Tells Its Side," *NYAN*, 2 August 1969, 1.

53. William Borders, "State Postpones Harlem Building," *NYT*, 3 July 1969; "State Building Now Postponed," *NYAN*, 5 July 1969, 1; Community Coalition, "Press Release," 7 July 1969, Box 25, Folder 170, MMW; Aubrey Zephyr, "State Office Building: Protestors Vow to Stay," *MT*, 12 July 1969, 13; Joseph Lelyveld, "Only Beaches Have Look of the Fourth," *NYT*, 5 July 1969; Michael McCardell and Stephen Brown, "Harlem State Site Stirs Up Controversy," *NYDN*, 13 July 1969. City officials finally lowered the flag on August 29. See Charlayne Hunter, "Heckscher Lowers Controversial Flag in Harlem," *NYT*, 30 August 1969.

54. C. Gerald Fraser, "Harlem Youth Lead Building Protest," *NYT*, 5 July 1969, 23; Emile Milne, "Building 'Will Go Up' despite Harlem Live-In," *NYP*, 1 August 1969, 54; Community Coalition, "Look What's Happenin' on *Our* Land," July 1969, Box 57, Folder "Harlem, New York State Office Building 1969," Subseries 1, Series 10, JKJ.

55. Ernest Johnson, "Resurrection City, Harlem, Is Digging In," *NYP*, 22 July 1969; Charlayne Hunter, "Harlem Squatters Hold State Site," *NYT*, 4 August 1969. On Resurrection City, see John Wiebenson, "Planning and Using Resurrection City," *Journal of the American Institute of Planners* 35, no. 6 (1969): 405–411; Charles

Fager, *Uncertain Resurrection: The Poor People's Washington Campaign* (Grand Rapids, MI: William B. Eerdmans, 1969); Jill Freedman, *Old News: Resurrection City* (New York: Grossman, 1970).

56. Community Coalition, "Press Release From: Community Coalition," 7 July 1969, Box 25, Folder 170, MMW; "It's about Working Together: Community News from Reclamation Site #1," ca. July 1969, Folder "Harlem—State Office Building," SCF; "The 'Sight' and the Site," *NYAN,* 9 August 1969, 1; Simon Anekwe, "Reclamation Site Still 'Occupied,'" *NYAN,* 12 July 1969, 1; Betty Reid, "Dr. Weston's Plan Gives People Part of Economic Action," *New York Courier,* 26 July 1969, 1; Hunter, "Harlem Squatters Hold State Site"; "The Meaning of Reclamation Site1," *HN,* October 1969; Symes, interview with author, 30 July 2010. Historian Frederick Douglass Opie has described the political and cultural importance accorded to "soul food" as a specifically African American cuisine in the Black Power era. See Frederick Douglass Opie, *Hog and Hominy: Soul Food from Africa to America* (New York: Columbia University Press, 2008), 121–138.

57. McCardell and Brown, "Harlem State Site Stirs Up Controversy"; "The 'Sight' and the Site," 1; Peter Siskind, "Growth and Its Discontents: Localism, Protest, and the Politics of Development on the Postwar Northeast Corridor" (PhD diss., University of Pennsylvania, 2002), 259.

58. McCardell and Brown, "Harlem State Site Stirs Up Controversy"; James E. Booker, "For Release after 12 Noon," 13 July 1969, Box 25, Folder 170, MMW; Paul L. Montgomery, "150 Black Groups March on Afro-American Day," *NYT,* 22 September 1969; "Does Harlem Need a State Office Building?," *MT,* 26 July 1969, 3. The *Amsterdam News* found similar results in a September 1969 man-on-the-street survey, with almost all of twelve respondents stating full or partial support for the occupants of Reclamation Site #1. See "Community Reaction on the Site Seizure," *NYAN,* 27 September 1969, 1.

59. "Does Harlem Need a State Office Building?" *MT;* Hunter, "Harlem Squatters Hold State Site"; Community Coalition, "Look What's Happenin' On *Our* Land," July 1969, Box 57, Folder "Harlem, New York State Office Building 1969," Subseries 1, Series 10, JKJ.

60. "Hearings Held on Site," *NYAN,* 16 August 1969, 1; ARCH, "Position Paper on Reclamation Site #1," 8 August 1969, Box 7, Folder 7, JMB; "Alternatives to the SOB," *HN,* October 1969; Clark, "The Coalition Tells Its Side"; Symes, interview with author, 30 July 2010.

61. ARCH, "Position Paper on Reclamation Site #1," 8 August 1969, Box 7, Folder 7, JMB; "Alternatives to the SOB"; Clark, "The Coalition Tells Its Side."

62. "The Meaning of Reclamation Site1"; Herbert Mills, "Against Building," *NYAN,* 13 September 1969, 1; "If You Had a Choice of Colors . . . ," ca. August 1969, Folder "Harlem—State Office Building," SCF. The *Amsterdam News* announced ARCH's "Illustration A" as the "People's Choice." See "'The People's Choice,'" *NYAN,* 20 September 1969, 45.

63. ARCH, "Position Paper on Reclamation Site #1," 8 August 1969, Box 7, Folder 7, JMB; "The Meaning of Reclamation Site1."

3. Own a Piece of the Block

1. Thomas A. Johnson, "Harlem Squatters Ousted; 9 Arrested," *NYT,* 24 September 1969, 1.

2. Johnson, "Harlem Squatters Ousted"; Herbert Mills, "Site Squatters Have Their Say," *NYAN,* 4 October 1969, 1.

3. Thomas A. Johnson, "Harlem Activists Explain Stand on State's Building," *NYT,* 28 September 1969, 67; ARCH, "Summary of ARCH's Position," December 1969, Box 303, Folder 691, EJL.

4. ARCH, "Summary of ARCH's Position," December 1969, Box 303, Folder 691, EJL.

5. On the many forms that community development took in this era, see Laura Warren Hill and Julia Rabig, eds., *The Business of Black Power: Community Development, Capitalism, and Corporate Responsibility in Postwar America* (Rochester, NY: University of Rochester Press, 2012). In his examination of Harlem and Philadelphia in this period, historian Peter Siskind contends that Harlem's moderates opportunistically "deepened their participation" in the neighborhood's political life through the formation of the state-sponsored Harlem Urban Development Corporation. While Siskind argues that "the fundamental orientation of public development policies remained largely unchanged," I contend that the new prominence of community-based organizations in development marked a profound qualitative transformation, though one that often had paradoxical consequences. See Peter Siskind, "Growth and Its Discontents: Localism, Protest, and the Politics of Development on the Postwar Northeast Corridor" (PhD diss., University of Pennsylvania, 2002), 258–313, esp. 260–261, 278.

6. Eleanor L. Brilliant, *The Urban Development Corporation: Private Interests and Public Authority* (Lexington, MA: Lexington Books, 1975), 13–14. On Logue, see Lizabeth Cohen, "Buying into Downtown Revival: The Centrality of Retail to Postwar Urban Renewal in American Cities," *Annals of the American Academy of Political and Social Science* 611, no. 1 (May 2007): 82–95. On redevelopment in New Haven, see Samuel Kaplan, "New Haven Pursuing the Dream of a Slumless City," *NYT,* 7 September 1965, 41. On redevelopment in Boston, see Thomas H. O'Connor, *Building a New Boston* (Boston: Northeastern University Press, 1993).

7. Letter to Friend from Gans, February 1966, Box 65, Folder 38, MCH. ARCH participated in the creation of the Council for New York Housing and Planning Policy, the organization that spearheaded opposition to Lindsay's appointment of Logue. For the report they prepared, see Michael D. Appleby, *Logue's Record in Boston: An Analysis of His Renewal and Planning Activities* (New York: Council for New York Housing and Planning Policy, 1966).

8. Cohen, "Buying into Downtown Revival," discusses Logue's versatility in experimenting with commercial redevelopment. Lizabeth Cohen, *Saving America's Cities: Ed Logue and the Struggle to Renew Urban America in the Suburban Age* (New York: Farrar, Straus & Giroux, forthcoming) will examine Logue's entire career.

9. Brilliant, *Urban Development Corporation*, 67–71.

10. Memo to Marshall from Logue, 10 July 1969, Box 303, Folder 689, EJL; Bill Kovach, "State Unit Offers Aid on Facilities for Harlem Site," *NYT*, 19 September 1969, 1; Letter to Marshall from Logue, 16 September 1969, Box 303, Folder 689, EJL.

11. Siskind, "Growth and Its Discontents," 269; Louella Jacqueline Long and Vernon Ben Robinson, *How Much Power to the People? A Study of the New York State Urban Development Corporation's Involvement in Black Harlem* (New York: Urban Center at Columbia University, 1977), 32–33, 36–37; Brilliant, *Urban Development Corporation*, 86; Murray Illson, "Building Backed by Harlem Group," *NYT*, 12 September 1969.

12. Long and Robinson, *How Much Power to the People?*, 37; Thomas A. Johnson, "Harlem Squatters Stay at Office Site," *NYT*, 23 September 1969, 35; Memo to "The Entire Membership of the MIA" from Gunther, 1 August 1969, Box 302, Folder 657, EJL; Letter to Marshall from Logue, 16 September 1969, Box 303, Folder 689, EJL. Logue wrote to Sutton, "I am enthusiastic about the possibility of UDC's developing and carrying out a program for this remaining portion of the block . . . only if whatever program is developed is what the Harlem community wants and only if there is a representative group of community leaders who will serve as an advisory committee." See Letter to Sutton from Logue, 2 October 1969, Box 302, Folder 656, EJL.

13. Carl McCall, "Chronology of Events," December 1969, Box 303, Folder 691, EJL; Memo to William Chaffee and William Hayden from Logue, 15 October 1969, Box 303, Folder 689, EJL.

14. Memo to "Attached List" from Logue, 6 November 1969, Box 303, Folder 689, EJL; "The Approach to Our Committee of 15 . . . ," November 1969, Box 302, Folder 656, EJL. On the structure of UDC's subsidiaries, see Brilliant, *Urban Development Corporation*, 57–64.

15. Memo to Paterson et al. from Logue, 8 December 1969, Box 303, Folder 689, EJL; Report to Rockefeller et al. (draft), 4 December 1969, Box 303, Folder 689, EJL; Letter to Rockefeller from Logue, 24 December 1969, Box 303, Folder 691, EJL.

16. Memo to Paterson et al. from Logue, 8 December 1969, Box 303, Folder 689, EJL; Report to Rockefeller et al. (draft), 4 December 1969, Box 303, Folder 689, EJL; Memo to Robert McCabe et al. from Logue, 17 November 1969, Box 303, Folder 689, EJL.

17. Carl McCall, "Chronology of Events," December 1969, Box 303, Folder 691, EJL.

18. Ibid.; ARCH, "Summary of ARCH's Position," December 1969, Box 303, Folder 691, EJL; Letter to Logue from Cenie J. Williams, 2 December 1969, Box 303, Folder 689, EJL; Memo to Logue from McCall, 16 December 1969, Box 303, Folder 689, EJL.

19. "Harlem's Convention," *NYAN*, 20 December 1969, 18; ARCH, "Summary of ARCH's Position," December 1969, Box 303, Folder 691, EJL.

20. Letter to Rockefeller from Sinclair, 21 January 1970, Box 302, Folder 657, EJL; Carl McCall, "Chronology of Events," December 1969, Box 303, Folder 691, EJL; Letter to Marshall from Logue, 3 April 1970, Box 302, Folder 658, EJL; Memo to Logue from Dan Miller, 3 February 1970, Box 302, Folder 657, EJL; "Meeting between the Ministerial Interfaith Association . . . ," 16 March 1970, Box 7, Folder 4, NLH; Siskind, "Growth and Its Discontents," 277-278; Memo to William Hayden from Miller, 30 March 1970, Box 302, Folder 658, EJL; Memo to "General Meeting of the Harlem UDC Negotiating Committee" from Central Steering Committee, 30 April 1970, Box 303, Folder 668, EJL; "Harlem-UDC Negotiating Committee Election Ballot," 22 May 1970, Box 303, Folder 668, EJL. Miller, Logue's aide at UDC, encouraged Gunther to contact Bond, Carl Anthony, and Symes of ARCH; Callender; and Vernon Ben Robinson, all representing a more radical viewpoint than Gunther's allies, but Gunther does not seem to have followed his advice. See Letter to Gunther from Miller, 18 June 1970, Box 7, Folder 4, NLH.

21. Memo to Logue from Miller, 19 May 1970, Box 303, Folder 668, EJL.

22. Emile Milne, "A Plot Aimed at Haryou?," *NYP*, 16 July 1970, 12; Memo to Logue from Miller, 16 June 1970, Box 302, Folder 658, EJL.

23. ARCH, "Summary of ARCH's Position," December 1969, Box 303, Folder 691, EJL.

24. Geoffrey Faux, *CDCs: New Hope for the Inner City* (New York: Twentieth Century Fund, 1971), 5-6, 27.

25. "A Demonstration Economic Development Program for Harlem," 4 April 1967, 3-4, CRH. On cooperative economic approaches as a motivation for CDCs, see Laura Warren Hill and Julia Rabig, "Toward a History of the Business of Black Power," in Hill and Rabig, *The Business of Black Power*, 30.

26. On Garvey and his plan to sell shares in the Black Star Line, see Jonathan Gill, *Harlem: The Four Hundred Year History from Dutch Village to Capital of Black America* (New York: Grove, 2011), 211-212, 245-252; Sharifa Rhodes-Pitts, *Harlem Is Nowhere: A Journey to the Mecca of Black America* (New York: Little, Brown, 2011), 162-212; Robert A. Hill, ed., *The Marcus Garvey and Universal Negro Improvement Association Papers*, vol. 1, 1826-August 1919 (Berkeley: University of California Press, 1983), 507-508.

27. Lizabeth Cohen, *Making a New Deal: Industrial Workers in Chicago, 1919-1939* (New York: Cambridge University Press, 1990), 147-154; Juliet E. K. Walker, *The History of Black Business in America: Capitalism, Race, Entrepreneurship*

(New York: Macmillan Library Reference, 1998); Hill and Rabig, "History of the Business of Black Power," esp. 15–21.

28. Columbia University Development Planning Workshop and Harlem Development Committee (CUDPW/HDC), "A Demonstration Economic Development Program for Harlem: Draft Proposal for a 12-Month Demonstration Grant under Section 207 of the Economic Opportunity Act of 1964," 4 April 1967, 4, CRH; "HCC/LDC Progress Report," 1970, Box 58, Folder "Harlem Commonwealth Council 1969–77," Subseries 1, Series 10, JKJ; Roy Innis, "Separatist Economics: A New Social Contract," in *Black Economic Development,* ed. William F. Haddad and G. Douglas Pugh (Englewood Cliffs, NJ: Prentice-Hall, 1969), 52–53.

29. "HCC/LDC Progress Report," 1970, Box 58, Folder "Harlem Commonwealth Council 1969–77," Subseries 1, Series 10, JKJ; Center for Community Economic Development, "Census of Special Impact Program CDCs," 1975, Box 8, Folder "CCED—Census of SIP CDCs," CSA/FG; Barry Stein, *Harlem Commonwealth Council: Business as a Strategy for Community Development* (Cambridge, MA: Center for Community Economic Development, 1974).

30. Ronald P. Smolin, "A Ghetto's Quest for Economic Growth," *Communities in Action* 5, no. 1 (February 1969): 5; "HCC/LDC Progress Report," 1970, Box 58, Folder "Harlem Commonwealth Council 1969–77," Subseries 1, Series 10, JKJ.

31. HCC, in partnership with Columbia University, received almost $400,000 in 1967, and HCC alone received an additional $400,000 in 1969. "Statement of CAP Grant," 14 June 1967, Box 59, Folder "Harlem Commonwealth Council—News Clippings 1968—1 of 2," CSA/SF; Letter to Donald Simmons from Theodore Berry, 6 January 1969, Box 79, Folder "New York—Harlem Commonwealth Council—1969," CSA/SF; "Interviews: WCO," 22 July 1968, Box 43, Folder 356, RF.

32. Innis, "Separatist Economics," 52; Hill and Rabig, "History of the Business of Black Power," 25–33.

33. On Nixon's urban policy and interest in Black Power and black capitalism, see Thomas Sugrue, *Sweet Land of Liberty: The Forgotten Struggle for Civil Rights in the North* (New York: Random House, 2008), 442–443; Robert E. Weems, with Lewis A. Randolph, *Business in Black and White: American Presidents and Black Entrepreneurs in the Twentieth Century* (New York: New York University Press, 2009), 110–156; Dean Kotlowski, "Black Power—Nixon Style: The Nixon Administration and Minority Business Enterprise," *Business History Review* 72, no. 3 (Autumn 1998): 409–445; Roger Biles, *The Fate of Cities: Urban America and the Federal Government, 1945-2000* (Lawrence: University Press of Kansas, 2011), 160–199.

34. Sugrue, *Sweet Land of Liberty,* 430–431; Benjamin Looker, "Visions of Autonomy: The New Left and the Neighborhood Government Movement of the 1970s," *Journal of Urban History* 38, no. 3 (May 2012): 577–598.

35. On Nixon's May 1968 meeting with Innis, see Weems and Randolph, *Business in Black and White,* 117. On the Community Self-Determination Act, see

Innis, "Separatist Economics," 57–59; Weems and Randolph, *Business in Black and White,* 134. While Nixon was eager to meet with Innis during his candidacy, Innis had less luck once Nixon was in office. Nixon's staff recognized Innis's tacit support for Nixon during the campaign and his value as a link to black leadership, but did not feel that a postelection meeting would be necessary or wise, in part because of Innis's seeming political opportunism. See Telegram to Nixon from Innis, 24 February 1969, Reel 1, Frame 816, CRDN; Memo to Hugh Sloan from Daniel P. Moynihan, 7 March 1969, Reel 1, Frame 814, CRDN; Memo to Sloan from Robert J. Brown, 3 April 1969, Reel 1, Frame 809, CRDN.

36. On the Special Impact Program, see Faux, *CDCs,* 85; Alice O'Connor, "Swimming against the Tide: A Brief History of Federal Policy in Poor Communities," in *Urban Problems and Community Development,* ed. Ronald F. Ferguson and William T. Dickens (Washington, DC: Brookings Institution Press, 1999), 105–108. On Kennedy's work in Bedford-Stuyvesant, see Kimberley Johnson, "Community Development Corporations, Participation, and Accountability: The Harlem Urban Development Corporation and the Bedford-Stuyvesant Restoration Corporation," *Annals of the American Academy of Political and Social Science* 594 (July 2004): 109–124.

37. "Social Development," 1 May 1975, 1, Reel 1912, PA730-0054, FFA; "Interview with James H. Dowdy: President of HCC," *Alternatives,* July–August 1976; "Dropout Tells Students How to Succeed," *NYAN,* 14 October 1972, A10; Robin Schatz and Christine Dugas, "The Hollow Dream: Harlem Commonwealth Council Was Supposed to Serve the Community; Some Say It Served Mostly Its Leader," *NYN,* 23 December 1991, 27; James H. Dowdy, "Dollars and Sense," *NYAN,* 6 March 1971, 4; "HCC/LDC Progress Report," 1970, Box 58, Folder "Harlem Commonwealth Council 1969–77," Subseries 1, Series 10, JKJ.

38. Letter to John Adams from Dowdy, 17 July 1972, Box 7, Folder "Harlem Commonwealth Council—1972," Subseries 5, Series 4, JKJ; "Distribution of SIP Funds," *Center for Community Economic Development Newsletter,* January 1975, Box 9, Folder "CCED—Newsletters," CSA/FG; "Special Impact Program Funding Data," *Center for Community Economic Development Newsletter,* December 1977–January 1978, Box 11, Folder "CCED—Newsletters," CSA/FG.

39. Telegram to Bertrand Harding from Charles E. Goodell, 18 December 1968, Box 79, Folder "New York—Harlem Commonwealth Council—1969," CSA/SF; Letter to Bennett Cerf from Dennis Allee, 15 September 1969, Box 58, Folder "Harlem Commonwealth Council 1969–77," Subseries 1, Series 10, JKJ; Letter to Jacob Javits from Dowdy, 26 September 1973, Box 57, Folder "Harlem 1971–1978," Subseries 1, Series 10, JKJ; Memo to Javits from Paul L. Gioia, 4 October 1973, Box 57, Folder "Harlem 1971–1978," Subseries 1, Series 10, JKJ; Memo to Javits from Gioia, 15 November 1973, Box 57, Folder "Harlem 1971–1978," Subseries 1, Series 10, JKJ; Letter to Javits from Dowdy, 22 November 1973, Box 57, Folder "Harlem 1971–1978," Subseries 1, Series 10, JKJ.

40. Willie L. Hamilton, "The Story of Two Harlem Buildings," *NYAN*, 5 December 1970, 1; Willie L. Hamilton, "Council Wants to Buy 125th St. Office Building," *NYAN*, 3 October 1970, 1. Two-thirds of the $751,000 that HCC put up to buy a 50 percent share came from a SIP grant. See Charlayne Hunter, "New Office Building in Harlem, First in Years, Opening Friday," *NYT*, 16 May 1971, 1.

41. HCC exercised their option to purchase the remaining 50 percent share in the Commonwealth Office Building in 1972. "Diversified Corp. to Buy Commonwealth Council Stk," *NYAN*, 30 December 1972, B7; "Building Bought by Harlem Group," *NYT*, 19 December 1972, 47; Dowdy quoted in Hunter, "New Office Building in Harlem"; HCC, "The Land Bank Program," January 1972, Reel 1912, PA730-0054, FFA.

42. Center for Community Economic Development, "Census of Special Impact Program CDCs," 1975, Box 8, Folder "CCED—Census of SIP CDCs," CSA/FG; Hunter, "New Office Building in Harlem"; Stein, *Harlem Commonwealth Council*, 7–8; "Largest Manufacturing Firm Bought for $1m," *NYAN*, 12 August 1972, A3; Commonwealth Holding Company, "An Analysis of the Acquisition of the Shultz Company, Inc.," June 1972, Box 7, Folder "Harlem Commonwealth Council—1972," Subseries 5, Series 4, JKJ; HCC, "Fourth Quarter Narrative Submitted to the Office of Economic Opportunity," June 1972, Box 7, Folder "Harlem Commonwealth Council—1972," Subseries 5, Series 4, JKJ.

43. "Harlem Commonwealth Council Local Development Corp." (advertisement), *NYAN*, 3 June 1972, A3; Simon Anekwe, "To Open Stock to Public," *NYAN*, 29 May 1971, 1.

44. Long and Robinson, *How Much Power to the People?*

45. Bond Ryder Associates, "Preliminary Program Analysis: Harlem Centre," ca. March 1970, 1–20, Box 242, Folder 148, EJL.

46. ARCH, "Summary of ARCH's Position," December 1969, Box 303, Folder 691, EJL; "125th Street Corridor," *HN*, December 1971.

47. Letter to Wood from A. C. O'Hara, 2 December 1971, Box 303, Folder 691, EJL; Letter to O'Hara from Wood, 13 December 1971, Box 303, Folder 691, EJL. Logue and the HUDC Negotiating Committee agreed on Wood as president after a yearlong search that also considered HUD assistant secretary Sam Jackson and Harlem attorney Paterson. Wood had been codirector of the National Committee against Discrimination in Housing and earlier focused on housing discrimination as the national housing director of the NAACP. See "Jack E. Wood, Jr., NCHD Executive Co-Director," May 1971, Box 302, Folder 660, EJL; Memo to Kimball from Miller, 22 June 1971, Box 7, Folder 7, NLH.

48. Memo to Logue from Miller, 5 January 1972, Box 303, Folder 691, EJL; Memo to HUDC Board of Directors from Wood, 14 February 1972, Box 7, Folder 9, NLH.

49. "Memorandum of Understanding between the New York State Urban Development Corporation and the Harlem-UDC Negotiating Committee" (draft),

29 April 1971, Box 7, Folder 2, NLH. Also see "Memorandum of Understanding between the New York State Urban Development Corporation and the Harlem-UDC Negotiating Committee," 15 May 1970, Box 7, Folder 3, NLH.

50. Memo to HUDC Board from Wood, 7 January 1972, Box 8, Folder 1, NLH; Letter to Rockefeller from Logue, 23 February 1972, Box 303, Folder 691, EJL. Subsequent correspondence by the governor's staff referred to the proposal only as a "hotel/convention center." Letter to Rockefeller from Robert R. Douglass, 6 May 1972, Box 303, Folder 691, EJL.

51. Letter to Miller from Wood, 31 March 1972, Box 303, Folder 691, EJL; W. Joseph Black, "Cultural Development Program" (draft), 8 October 1973, 3, 19, Box 7, Folder 3, and Box 8, Folder 2, JB. Black served on HUDC's Cultural Task Force. See "HUDC Harlem Cultural Center," 6 December 1972, Box 7, Folder 3, JB.

52. Bond Ryder Associates, "Preliminary Program Analysis: Harlem Centre," ca. March 1970, 9, Box 242, Folder 148, EJL.

53. Memo to Wood from Logue, 4 August 1972, Box 303, Folder 691, EJL; Memo to HUDC Staff from Charles J. Hayes, 5 May 1972, Box 7, Folder 13, EJL; Memo to HUDC Staff from Hayes, 30 May 1972, Box 7, Folder 13, NLH; Memo to HUDC Staff from Hayes, 5 June 1972, Box 7, Folder 13, NLH; Memo to Files from Nadine Thompkins, 9 November 1972, Box 8, Folder 18, NLH; Memo to W. Joseph Black from Thompkins, 15 January 1973, Box 7, Folder 3, JB. As late as November 1974, HUDC leaders continued to mention the cultural component of the program in their correspondence with Logue, and Logue remained steadfast in his refusal to consider it. "There is no, repeat no, educational/cultural component as a state project in any program for the State Office Building. I am somewhat surprised this is still showing up," he wrote Cogsville, HUDC's general manager. See Memo to Cogsville from Logue, 12 November 1974, Box 303, Folder 693, EJL.

54. HUDC, "Meeting of the Board of Directors, Minutes," 7 September 1972, Box 7, Folder 11, NLH; Memo to Miller from Kimball, 23 June 1971, Box 7, Folder 7, NLH.

55. HUDC, "Meeting of the Board of Directors, Minutes," 9 May 1973, Box 7, Folder 12, NLH; Siskind, "Growth and Its Discontents," 282; HUDC, "Meeting of the Board of Directors, Minutes," 7 June 1973, Box 7, Folder 7, NLH.

56. Letter to Jack Wood from George B. Godwin Jr., 1 June 1973, Box 303, Folder 692, EJL; HUDC, "Meeting of the Board of Directors, Minutes," 7 June 1973, Box 7, Folder 7, NLH. Board members at this time were Victor G. Alicea, Roberto Anazagasti, John Bess, Amalia Betanzos, Judge Herbert B. Evans, State Senator Robert Garcia, Nathaniel Gibbon, Msgr. John J. Gillen, Assemblyman Jesse Gray, Richard Greene, Rev. James Gunther, William R. Hudgins, Mary Iemma, Rev. William James, Arnold P. Johnson, Alice Kornegay, Dr. Arthur Logan, Dorothea Merchant, Assemblyman George Miller, Congressman Charles Rangel, Thomas V. Sinclair, Assemblyman Mark Southall, Hope R. Stevens, Hilda E. Stokely, Councilman Charles Taylor, State Senator Sidney Von Luther, and Livingston L. Wingate.

See Letter to Delegates and Friends from Wood, 29 September 1973, Box 7, Folder 4, JB.

57. Memo to Logue from Wood, 14 June 1973, Box 302, Folder 663, EJL; HUDC, "Meeting of the Board of Directors," 12 July 1973, Box 7, Folder 10, NLH.

58. Memo to Logue from Wood, 14 June 1973, Box 302, Folder 663, EJL.

59. There is no indication that Wood seriously entertained these entreaties. See Letter to Wood from Gunther et al., 23 August 1973, Box 7, Folder 29, NLH; Transfiguration Lutheran Church, "Central 125th Street Redevelopment," Box 7, Folder 27, NLH.

60. Letter to Ronald Gault from Dowdy, 16 January 1975, Reel 1912, PA730-0054, FFA; "Harlem Commonwealth Council, Auditor's Report," 31 October 1973, Reel 1912, PA730-0054, FFA.

61. Memo to All Staff from Thompkins, 12 July 1972, Box 7, Folder 12, NLH; Letter to Dowdy from Wood, 21 August 1972, Reel 1912, PA730-0054, FFA; Letter to Gault from Dowdy, 16 January 1975, Reel 1912, PA730-0054, FFA; Letter to Gault from Dowdy, 18 December 1973, Reel 1912, PA730-0054, FFA.

62. Letter to Gault from Dowdy, 16 January 1975, Reel 1912, PA730-0054, FFA.

63. "Harlem Commonwealth Council, Auditor's Report," 31 October 1973, Reel 1912, PA730-0054, FFA; "Ben's Lumber Yard," *Alternatives,* December 1973; "Ben's Lumber Yard, Inc.," *Alternatives,* October 1977, 5; Stein, *Harlem Commonwealth Council,* 13.

64. In recounting HCC's history, Dowdy alluded to the independence that federal funding enabled: "I think that we have to take in consideration that HCC came along at a unique time, at a time when the government decided that it would put some monies out there as part of the self determination act for what they call socio-economic development, which gave us a chance to invest the money that was granted to us into profit making types of operations." "Interview with James H. Dowdy," *Alternatives,* July–August 1976, 3.

65. Nishani Frazier, "A McDonald's That Reflects the Soul of the People: Hough Area Development Corporation and Community Development in Cleveland," in Hill and Rabig, *The Business of Black Power,* 81–84; Harry E. Berndt, *New Rulers in the Ghetto: The Community Development Corporation and Urban Poverty* (Westport, CT: Greenwood, 1977), 125.

66. Letter to Gault from Dowdy, 16 January 1975, Reel 1912, PA730-0054, FFA; "Harlem YWCA Is Sold," *NYAN,* 19 October 1974, A13; "Commonwealth Buys YWCA Building," *NYAN,* 21 September 1974, A2. HCC never completed plans for senior housing, in part due to a long-running dispute with the members of the Allah Nation of Five Percenters who had long maintained a school on the site. See Charles Kaiser, "Muslim Sect Protests a Plan for Housing on Site of Its Harlem School," *NYT,* 13 October 1977, 28.

67. HCC, "Progress Report," 1975, Box 58, Folder "Harlem Commonwealth Council 1977," Subseries 1, Series 10, JKJ; "Commonwealth Council Aids Logan Hos-

pital," *NYAN*, 8 February 1975, A5; Memo to Project Committee from Dowdy, 11 November 1974, Box 27, Folder 9, BERC; Letter to William O. Allen from Dowdy, 12 December 1974, Box 27, Folder 9, BERC. The hospital and associated housing were never built.

68. Letter to Gault from Dowdy, 18 December 1973, Reel 1912, PA730-0054, FFA; "Interview with James H. Dowdy," 3.

69. "What's the Harlem Commonwealth Council Doing for Me?," *NYAN*, 14 September 1974, D7. A 1973 analysis of SIP recipients found that HCC's emphasis on profits eclipsed its interest in job creation: "Hiring of residents in non-manager positions has risen over the year and a half evaluation indicating that some attention is being paid to who is benefiting from SIP. Economic objectives still hold high priority, however, since HCC is now hiring fewer of the unemployed population than indicated in the original site visit. . . . HCC's intent is venture profitability first, individual benefits later." See ABT Associates Inc., *An Evaluation of the Special Impact Program: Final Report*, vol. 3, *Analysis of 33 Grantees* (Cambridge, MA: ABT Associates, 1973), 145.

70. Memo to Files from Gault, 10 August 1976, Reel 1912, PA730-0054, FFA; HCC, "Progress Report," 1975, Box 58, Folder "Harlem Commonwealth Council 1977," Subseries 1, Series 10, JKJ; "Harlem Commonwealth Council Buys Hotel in St. Thomas," *Alternatives*, June 1974; "Interview with James H. Dowdy," 3; J. Zamgba Browne, "Harlem Commonwealth Selling Virgin Island Hotel," *NYAN*, 10 July 1976, A1.

71. "Profits Come to Harlem," *NYAN*, 26 September 1970, 52; Anekwe, "To Open Stock to Public," 1; Stein, *Harlem Commonwealth Council*, 16–17; HCC, "Progress Report," 1975, Box 58, Folder "Harlem Commonwealth Council 1977," Subseries 1, Series 10, JKJ.

72. Letter to Gault from Dowdy, 16 January 1975, Reel 1912, PA730-0054, FFA.

73. "The Top 100," *BE*, June 1978, 75; Stein, *Harlem Commonwealth Council*, 22; "Interview with James H. Dowdy," 7; "Harlem Commonwealth Council, Inc. . . . An Historical View," *Alternatives*, October 1977, 6.

74. HCC's board was to consist of thirty members: twelve from among the original founders or board-chosen successors; eight from the United Block Association, a clearinghouse for neighborhood block associations; and ten from various Harlem community organizations such as the NAACP, the Urban League, and churches. In actuality, HCC's board included eighteen members in 1975: founders Isaiah Robinson, England, Rolle, Jonnie Marshall (in place of her deceased husband Kenneth Marshall), Arthur Hill, and Wilcox; economist Robert S. Browne, Rev. Frederick E. Dennard; engineer Ewell W. Finley; Kornegay; former building inspector John H. Guilford III; area community organizers Pedro Velez, Freddie Brown, and Allen Hodge; and four representatives from the United Block Association: Sandy Sanford, Audrey Dunner, Alice Adams, and Wallace Andrews. See Center for Community Economic Development, "Community Development

Corporations," 1975, Box 9, Folder "CCED—CDCs," CSA/FG; HCC, "Progress Report," 1975, Box 58, Folder "Harlem Commonwealth Council 1977," Subseries 1, Series 10, JKJ. On the issue of representation on CDC boards of directors, see Rita Mae Kelly, *Community Control of Economic Development: The Boards of Directors of Community Development Corporations* (New York: Praeger, 1977).

75. Berndt, *New Rulers in the Ghetto*, 125. Also see Robert L. Allen, *Black Awakening in Capitalist America* (New York: Doubleday, 1969), from which Berndt drew his conclusion.

76. Stein, *Harlem Commonwealth Council*, 17.

77. Clinton Cox, "Harlem Commonwealth Council Fails to Sell Shares to Residents," *NYAN*, 29 January 1977, A1. On HCC's acquisition of the Washburn Wire Factory, see Charlayne Hunter-Gault, "Purchase in Harlem of a Big Plant Is Set as an Economic Spur," *NYT*, 24 December 1976, 31; "HCC Acquires $6 Million Washburn Wire Company," *NYAN*, 17 September 1977, A3.

78. James H. Dowdy, "Dollars and Sense," *Alternatives*, May 1977, 2.

79. Isaiah E. Robinson Jr., "On Harlem Commonwealth Stock," *NYAN*, 5 February 1977, A2.

80. Brilliant, *Urban Development Corporation*, 132–156, 173–180; Siskind, "Growth and Its Discontents," 281.

81. Joshua B. Freeman, *Working-Class New York: Life and Labor since World War II* (New York: New Press, 2000), 256–287; Memo to Logue from Cogsville, 27 March 1974, Box 303, Folder 693, EJL; Memo to Logue from Cogsville, 11 October 1974, Box 303, Folder 693, EJL; Memo to Cogsville from Logue, 12 November 1974, Box 303, Folder 693, EJL; HUDC, "Proposal: For Financial Assistance for the 125th Street Commercial Center Development," February 1976, Document #11, HDA; Siskind, "Growth and Its Discontents," 281–283. In 1976, HUDC proposed building a temporary cultural pavilion on the vacant site, but this too never materialized. See Project for Public Spaces Inc., *125th Street Study*, ca. 1976, Box 5, Folder 122, HDA.

82. Susan Horn-Moo, "CDCs and the Community Services Act," *Center for Community Economic Development Newsletter*, January 1975, 1–5, Box 9, Folder "CCED—Newsletters," CSA/FG; "Social Development," 1 May 1975, 2, Reel 1912, PA730-0054, FFA; Letter to Robert S. Browne from Dowdy, 29 August 1975, Box 27, Folder 10, BERC; James H. Dowdy, "Dollars and Sense," *Alternatives*, January 1976.

83. Under SIP, HCC received $1,223,000 in FY1977, at least $3 million and up to $5.6 million in FY1978 as a twenty-four-month grant, and an additional $150,000 in FY1979. "Special Impact Program Funding Data," *Center for Community Economic Development Newsletter*, December 1977–January 1978, Box 11, Folder "CCED Newsletter," CSA/FG; Community Services Administration (CSA), "Grant Announcement," 15 September 1978, Box 58, Folder "Harlem Commonwealth Council 1978–79," Subseries 1, Series 10, JKJ; CSA, "Grant Announcement," 28 September 1978, Box 57, Folder "Harlem 1971–1978," Subseries 1, Series 10, JKJ;

CSA, "Grant Announcement," 30 September 1979, Box 58, Folder "Harlem Grants 1979," Subseries 1, Series 10, JKJ; CSA, "Grant Announcement" (2), 30 September 1979, Box 58, Folder "Harlem Grants 1979," Subseries 1, Series 10, JKJ; "Let Community Development Develop," *NYT,* 6 February 1978, A18.

84. J. Zamgba Browne, "Harlem Council Unveils Plans for Shopping Mall," *NYAN,* 22 January 1977, A1; HCC, "125th Street Multi-use Commercial Center: A Proposal," October 1976, Box 58, Folder "Harlem Commonwealth Council 1969–77," Subseries 1, Series 10, JKJ; Memo to Bruce Kirschenbaum from John Comerford, 25 May 1978, Box 353, Folder "Harlem, NY Urban Development Corporation, 1978 [2]," OCS; Donald J. Cogsville, "An International Trade Center for Harlem," *Alternatives,* August 1979, 9.

85. Letter to Robert T. Hall et al. from Kirschenbaum, 4 October 1979, Box 353, Folder "Harlem, NY Urban Development Corporation, 1979 [1]," OCS; Letter to Carter from Rangel, 26 June 1978, Box 353, Folder "Harlem, NY Urban Development Corporation, 1978 [2]," OCS; Letter to Carter from Rangel, 12 April 1978, Document #19, HDA. On Carter's urban policy, see Thomas J. Sugrue, "Carter's Urban Policy Crisis," in *The Carter Presidency: Policy Choices in the Post-New Deal Era,* ed. Gary M. Fink and Hugh Davis Graham (Lawrence: University Press of Kansas, 1998), 137–157. In 1980, HUDC's then-chairman Hope Stevens denounced the aloofness of the international trade center project in resigning from the organization. "His letter raised other issues including some about the International Third World Trade Center, particularly the issue of exclusion of 'the people of the community from participation in programming for the success of the projects,'" the *Amsterdam News* reported of his resignation letter. Stevens had only become chairman of HUDC the previous year, replacing Herbert Evans, who had been chairman since HUDC's foundation. Stevens's tenure proved short and rocky, in large part because he openly criticized the organization's dominant and secretive leadership. See Simon Anekwe, "Hope Stevens Resigns as Chairman of HUDC," *NYAN,* 3 May 1980, 3; Simon Anekwe, "Crisis Rocks HUDC Board," *NYAN,* 15 March 1980, 1.

86. Simon Anekwe, "Funds for 125th Street Mall up to Carter," *NYAN,* 17 November 1979, 2; Jack Watson, "Introductory Remarks," 8 November 1979, Box 245, Folder "Harlem Trade Center (2)," OCS.

87. "Harlem Third World International Trade Center Complex," no. 1, 1979, Box 8, Folder 30, NLH; HCC, "125th Street Multi-use Commercial Center: A Proposal," October 1976, Box 58, Folder "Harlem Commonwealth Council 1969–77," Subseries 1, Series 10, JKJ.

88. "Morningside Park 'Take Part' Workshop," April 1973, Box 7, Folder 2, CCC; Untitled document (begins "The Architects' Renewal Committee in Harlem, Inc."), ca. early 1973, Box 8, Folder 34, NLH; Letter to Jim Coleman from McRae, 14 March 1973, Box 6, Folder 3, CCC; Letter to Alvin R. Arnett from Mary A. Dowery, 7 February 1974, Box 24, Folder "Architect's Renewal Committee in

Harlem (ARCH)—1974," Subseries 3, Series 4, JKJ; Letter to Javitz [*sic*] from Dowery, 11 February 1974, Box 24, Folder "Welfare Reform—Architects' Renewal Committee in Harlem (ARCH)—1974," Subseries 3, Series 4, JKJ; Arthur Symes, interview with author, 30 July 2010; Memo to Coalition for Morningside Park and ARCH from ARCH, 8 November 1973, Box 6, Folder 3, CCC; "HUD Money," 19 November 1973, Box 6, Folder 3, CCC; Letter to Javitz [*sic*] from Dowery, 1 March 1974, Box 24, Folder "Architect's Renewal Committee in Harlem (ARCH)—1974," Subseries 3, Series 4, JKJ; Memo to RBF Files from Marilyn W. Levy, 15 November 1974, Box 106, Folder 716, Record Group 3.1, RBF; Memo to RBF Files from Levy, 25 November 1974, Box 106, Folder 716, Record Group 3.1, RBF.

89. Letter to Neighbor from Dowdy, 29 October 1980, Box 27, Folder 12, BERC; James H. Dowdy, "Dollars and Sense," *Alternatives,* April 1981, 2; "Proposed Item for Directors Status Report to White House/OMB," ca. September 1981, Box 4, Folder "Major CAA Grants," CSA/RRG; "The Community Services Administration: A Job Well Done," *Alternatives,* October 1981, 4; Anthony DePalma, "East Harlem TV Deal Unraveling: Proposal to Convert Washburn Factory Snarled in Litigation," *NYT,* 15 June 1986, R6. Even with Reagan's elimination of the Community Services Administration, Dowdy remained optimistic that HCC would be able to survive with income from its enterprises and with the assistance of foundations and private financial institutions, which had lent to HCC in the past. See Simon Anekwe, "Despite Ron Reagan HCC Is Alive and Well," *NYAN,* 24 October 1981, 6.

90. *Newsday* reported that Dowdy drove a Mercedes-Benz paid for by the Shultz Company, an HCC subsidiary; used subsidiary employees for improvement of his own home; and formed his own construction company that did work for Ben's Lumber Yard. Additionally, reporters wrote that Dowdy squeezed funds out of subsidiaries for general HCC operating costs, unreasonably raised prices charged to customers, and borrowed against HCC's investments excessively and unwisely. For instance, Dowdy borrowed a million dollars against the land on which HCC planned to build the shopping center, money he intended to use to move Shultz out of Harlem, to Corning, New York. By the early 1990s, Acme Foundry and Ben's Lumber Yard had both closed and Shultz was on its last legs. See Schatz and Dugas, "The Hollow Dream," 27; HCC, "For Immediate Release," 20 December 1991, Box 8, Folder 4, PW. By 1976, Wood had become fed up with the strong-willed HUDC board's dominance and exclusion of its CEO. "That operating procedure . . . could profoundly affect the standard of professional integrity and accountability I have sought to maintain throughout my career," Wood wrote in resigning. While Wood had tried to resist the excesses of his board, Cogsville came under heavy scrutiny from community members for his dominant style, secretiveness, consolidation of power, and manipulation of the board. See Letter to Evans from Wood, 14 June 1976, Box 8, Folder 25, NLH; Peter Ixoel, "Donald Cogsville and the HUDC," *NYAN,* 18 July 1981, 4; Peter Noel, "HUDC: Scandal Revisited," *NYT,* 19 September 1981, 2.

91. Letter to Rudolph Giuliani from HCC, 7 December 1993, Box 35, Folder 7, PW. HCC's directors had begun preparations in the late 1970s to form a foundation to provide grants and seed money to Harlem residents and community organizations, a venture intended to address the fact that the organization had never sold ownership shares or shared its profits, but it, too, failed to get off the ground in the 1980s. See Black Economic Research Center (BERC), "Considerations Relative to the Creation of a Foundation by Harlem Commonwealth Council," February 1978, Box 27, Folder 11, BERC; "Meeting of the Foundation Committee of Harlem Commonwealth Council," 13 July 1979, Box 27, Folder 12, BERC.

92. Schatz and Dugas, "The Hollow Dream," 27; Letter to Isaiah Robinson from Wilcox, 11 January 1996, Box 8, Folder 4, PW.

4. The Urban Homestead in the Age of Fiscal Crisis

1. "The Gang Lords!," *Supergirl*, August 1973, 1–14.

2. "Renigades Housing Movement," January 1974, Box 20, Folder 21, RL.

3. Ibid.; "Youth Gang Turns to Housing Reconstruction," *CFC*, January 1974, 4.

4. On middle-class residential rehabilitation, see Suleiman Osman, *The Invention of Brownstone Brooklyn: Gentrification and the Search for Authenticity in Postwar New York* (New York: Oxford University Press, 2011).

5. The notion that the 1970s played a fundamental transitional role is pervasive in recent American political and social history. See, for example, Judith Stein, *Pivotal Decade: How the United States Traded Factories for Finance in the Seventies* (New Haven, CT: Yale University Press, 2010); Bruce J. Schulman, *The Seventies: The Great Shift in American Culture, Society, and Politics* (New York: Free Press, 2001); Andreas Killen, *1973 Nervous Breakdown: Watergate, Warhol, and the Birth of Post-sixties America* (New York: Bloomsbury, 2006); Bruce J. Schulman and Julian E. Zelizer, eds., *Rightward Bound: Making America Conservative in the 1970s* (Cambridge, MA: Harvard University Press, 2008). In conceptualizing the transition from the 1960s to the 1980s, I find especially useful Philip Jenkins's notion of a "follow through as much as a reaction," a gradual transition from the liberalism of the 1960s to the conservatism of the 1980s instead of an abrupt break or backlash. See Philip Jenkins, *Decade of Nightmares: The End of the Sixties and the Making of Eighties America* (New York: Oxford University Press, 2006), 20–21.

6. ANHD, "A Survival Program for New York City's Low- and Moderate-Income Housing and a Proposal for Funding the Administrative Costs of Neighborhood-Based Community Housing Groups," ca. 1975, 4, Reels 2964 and 3055, PA750-0367, FFA; Frank P. Braconi, "In re *In Rem*: Innovation and Experience in New York's Housing Policy," in *Housing and Community Development in New York City: Facing the Future,* ed. Michael H. Schill (Albany: State University of New York Press, 1999), 94; Ruth W. Messinger, "For Immediate Release," 12 April 1978, Box 5, Folder "In Rem Organizational '78," MCH; "Harlem Strategy," ca. 1983, Box 61,

Folder 18, City Hall Staff—David Jones, EIK; Richard Schaffer and Neil Smith, "The Gentrification of Harlem?," *Annals of the Association of American Geographers* 76, no. 3 (September 1986): 360.

7. ANHD, "A Survival Program," ca. 1975, Reels 2964 and 3055, PA750-0367, FFA; Braconi, "In re *In Rem*," 94–95; "ANHD" (brochure), ca. 1978, Box 68, Folder 6, MCH; William Julius Wilson, *The Truly Disadvantaged: The Inner City, the Underclass, and Public Policy* (Chicago: University of Chicago Press, 1987), 46–55; Ronald Lawson with Reuben B. Johnson III, "Tenant Responses to the Urban Housing Crisis, 1970–1984," in *The Tenant Movement in New York City, 1904–1984*, ed. Ronald Lawson with Mark Naison (New Brunswick, NJ: Rutgers University Press, 1986), 210–211; Ronald Lawson, "Owners of Last Resort: The Track Record of New York's Early Low-Income Housing Cooperatives Created between 1967 and 1975," *Review of Radical Political Economics* 30, no. 4 (1998): 64. Lawson has argued that rent control was largely a red herring, since abandonment was concentrated in neighborhoods where rent tended to remain below the limits allowed under rent control. See Lawson, "Owners of Last Resort," 81.

8. "Renigades Housing Movement," January 1974, Box 20, Folder 21, RL; "Cleanup Project Gets a 'Good Job' from Mayor," *NYT*, 22 April 1968, 40; Murray Schumach, "E. 103rd St. Leads Way for a Big Cleanup Job," *NYT*, 18 April 1968, 49; Rita Reif, "Self-Help Housing: Within Limits, It Works," *NYT*, 11 July 1976, 188; Lawson and Johnson, "Urban Housing Crisis," 221–222; Philip St. Georges, "They Shall Rebuild the Ruined Cities: Urban Homesteading and Sweat Equity in New York City" (unpublished manuscript, 1973), 27–101.

9. Joel Schwartz, "Tenant Power in the Liberal City, 1943–1971," in Lawson and Naison, *Tenant Movement in New York City*, 190–191.

10. "West Side Squatters Facing Eviction," *MT*, 16 January 1971, 8; Harold Holzer, "What Next for West Side Urban Renewal?," *MT*, 19 June 1971, 3; Operation Move-In, "Don't Let Them Throw Us Out," June 1971, Box 28, Folder 18, MCH; Verna Thomasson, "Operation Move-In, 1971: Moving On," *MT*, 12 June 1971, 7; "Squatters' Site Is Now Community," *NYP*, 2 July 1971, 13.

11. Bryna Taubman, "An Apt. Rescues a Family," *NYP*, 2 May 1970; "Operation 'Move-In:' Squatters' Rights for Urban Poor," *MT*, 23 May 1970, 5; "Come to the Paint-In," May 1971, Box 28, Folder 18, MCH; "Victory for Columbia Squatter," *MT*, 12 June 1971, 13.

12. The saga of Site 30 continued for years, and officials never built the promised low-income housing. The site remained empty into the 1980s, and though courts ruled in favor of low-income housing, the Koch administration revised plans for the increasingly affluent neighborhood in 1983, proposing a predominantly market-rate project with affordable units reserved for the elderly. Joseph P. Fried, "Police Arrest 32 at Squatter Site," *NYT*, 18 November 1970, 51; Maurice Carroll, "Neighbors of West Side Squatters Argue at Hearing," *NYT*, 15 October 1971, 16; "Welfare Study Approved Here," *NYT*, 12 November 1971, 35; Richard J. Meislin,

"Praise-and-Protest Rally Held in a West Side Lot," *NYT,* 26 July 1976, 46; Linda Greenhouse, "Top Court Backs Housing Project on the West Side," *NYT,* 8 January 1980, B1; Lee A. Daniels, "City Proposes Housing for Disputed West Side Site," *NYT,* 6 September 1983, B7; "Urban Renewal Site's Last Argument," *NYT,* 20 November 1983, R9; St. Georges, "They Shall Rebuild the Ruined Cities," 151–152; "Morningside Homesteaders Take to Rocking Chairs," 2 October 1971, Box 11, Folder 4, MCH; Schwartz, "Tenant Power in the Liberal City," 190.

13. Act of May 20, 1862 (Homestead Act), Public Law 37-64, *U.S. Statutes at Large* 12 (1862): 392; Wayne King, "Homesteaders Combating Urban Blight," *NYT,* 16 September 1973, 1; Emily Lieb, "'A Street's Last Chance': The Dollar Houses and the Great New Baltimore" (unpublished paper presented at the Massachusetts Historical Society, Boston, MA, 26 February 2010).

14. Osman, *The Invention of Brownstone Brooklyn,* 192–195; Neil Smith, "Gentrification, the Frontier, and the Restructuring of Urban Space," in *Gentrification of the City,* ed. Neil Smith and Peter Williams (Boston: Allen and Unwin, 1986), 15–20.

15. Runyon noted, however, that their protest would be nonviolent. "Morningside Homesteaders Take to Rocking Chairs," 2 October 1971, Box 11, Folder 4, MCH. If Runyon's invocation of "homesteaders" in an urban context was not the first such use, it preceded the mainstream adoption of the term. The chairman of the National Urban Coalition also raised the idea of urban homesteading in late 1971. See "The National Urban Coalition: Steering Team Meeting," 19 September 1972, Box 12, Folder 17, JMB.

16. "Youth Gang Turns to Housing Reconstruction," 4; Owen Mortz, "Gangway! 320G Loan to Refit a Tenement," *NYDN,* 25 January 1974, 4; UHAB, *Sweat Equity Homesteading of Multifamily Housing in New York City* (New York: UHAB, 1977), 3; St. Georges, "They Shall Rebuild the Ruined Cities," 137–166.

17. The tenements had sat empty for ten years when the mosque commenced their homesteading project. UHAB, "Self-Help Housing and Neighborhood Development (New Draft)," ca. 1980, UHAB; Charles Laven, "Self-Help in Neighborhood Development," in *The Scope of Social Architecture,* ed. C. Richard Hatch (New York: Van Nostrand Reinhold, 1984), 104–117. Laven's article, the most extensive description of the homesteading project of the Mosque of the Islamic Brotherhood, appeared in a book edited by C. Richard Hatch, the founder of the Architects' Renewal Committee in Harlem.

18. Letter to Greg Farrell from United Harlem Growth, 12 August 1976, Box 196, Folder 3, NYF; David Robinson, "Building for Self and Community in Harlem," *CFC,* January 1977, 3.

19. Carl Callender, a legal aid attorney in Harlem, estimated that he had helped incorporate twenty such cooperatives by late 1972. See Robert E. Tomasson, "Tenants Look to Ownership as Housing Decays," *NYT,* 17 September 1972, R1. See Robert Kolodny, *Self-Help in the Inner City: A Study of Lower Income Cooperative*

Housing Conversion in New York City (New York: United Neighborhood Houses of New York, 1973), 61–67, for an account of one such low-income cooperative conversion in Harlem.

20. Memorandum to Persons Involved in Dweller-Control Housing from the Organizing Committee, 15 March 1973, UHAB; Joseph P. Fried, "Episcopalians Plan Slum Rehabilitation," *NYT*, 1 November 1973, 10; Cathedral Church of St. John the Divine, *A Proposal for the Urban Homesteading Assistance Board, U-HAB* (New York: Cathedral Church of St. John the Divine, 1974). Criticism centered on the church's affiliation with Morningside House, a home for senior citizens that held nearby buildings vacant and planned to evict squatters. See Marie Runyon, "Squatters and Community Backers Stage March on St. John's Cathedral," *Heights and Valley News,* May 1974, Box 28, Folder 17, MCH; "Bishop Moore's War on the Poor," April–May 1974, Box 25, Folder 4, MCH; "Morningside Squatters Say Cathedral Uses Scare Tactics," 9 May 1974, Box 25, Folder 4, MCH. Eloise Ferguson, an early employee of UHAB, had previously worked as the building manager of the Triangle Apartments, the first housing built by the Community Association of the East Harlem Triangle, and served on CAEHT's board of directors. See UHAB, "1974 Annual Report," January 1975, 16, Box 8, Folder "Urban Homesteading Assistance Board, Donald Turner [sic], 117," RL.

21. ANHD, *A Decade of Making a Difference: 10th Anniversary Program* (New York: ANHD, 1985), 13; "The Association of Neighborhood Housing Developers, Inc.," 8 November 1974, Box 137, Folder 922, Record Group 3.1, RBF.

22. St. Georges, "They Shall Rebuild the Ruined Cities," 102, 203–204.

23. UHAB, "Demolition Handbook," April 1978, UHAB; UHAB, *Sweat Equity Homesteading,* 21, 26.

24. On the neighborhood movement and the restoration of brownstones by middle-class residents, see Osman, *The Invention of Brownstone Brooklyn,* 122–124, 233–269; Suleiman Osman, "The Decade of the Neighborhood," in Schulman and Zelizer, *Rightward Bound,* 106–127.

25. "Renigades Housing Movement," January 1974, Box 20, Folder 21, RL; Philip St. Georges, "Renigades Update," *CFC,* January 1977, 7; Jose J. Colon and Eulogio Cedeno, "The Renigades Housing Movement, Inc.," *CFC,* January 1978, 2; K. Ahmad Tawfiq, "Community Groups Reclaim Housing through Sweat Equity," *CFC,* January 1977, 5; Letter to Farrell from United Harlem Growth, 12 August 1976, Box 196, Folder 3, NYF.

26. Renigades Housing Movement et al., "Proposal for an Urban Homesteading-Construction and Building Management Job Training Program," 24 September 1974, 1, 10, Reels 2964 and 3055, PA750-0367, FFA; ANHD, "A Survival Program," ca. 1975, 6–7, Reels 2964 and 3055, PA750-0367, FFA; Letter to Farrell from United Harlem Growth, 12 August 1978, Box 196, Folder 3, NYF; Mortz, "Gangway!," 4; "Renigades Project—Progress Report," *CFC,* January 1975, 3; Tawfiq, "Community Groups Reclaim Housing," 5.

27. Philip St. Georges, "Urban Homesteading-Sweat Equity," *CFC*, January 1975, 3.

28. "Harlem Restoration Project," May 1977, Box 57, Folder "Harlem 1971–1978," Subseries 1, Series 10, JKJ; "Harlem Restoration Project, Inc.," ca. September 1977, Box 57, Folder "Harlem 1971–1978," Subseries 1, Series 10, JKJ; "The Harlem Restoration Project, Inc.: Progress Report," December 1977, Box 57, Folder "Harlem 1971–1978," Subseries 1, Series 10, JKJ. The Harlem Restoration Project persisted at least into the late 1990s. One reporter estimated that by the late 1980s, the Harlem Restoration Project had provided temporary employment for 500 former inmates. See Kathleen McGowan, "A Hard Fall in Harlem," *CL*, 1 October 1997.

29. John Sheils, "Flats for the Homeless," *NYDN*, 21 January 1987; "Building in East Harlem Renovated by Youths," *NYN*, 2 March 1989; "Introduction to Youth-Build," ca. 1990, Reel 6190, PA900-1207, FFA. The Youth Action Program completed their second project in 1987 at 248 East 119th Street, across the street from the Renigades' original project.

30. On the use value of housing in the context of self-building, see Becky M. Nicolaides, *My Blue Heaven: Life and Politics in the Working-Class Suburbs of Los Angeles, 1920–1965* (Chicago: University of Chicago Press, 2002), 29; Dennis Conway, "Self-Help Housing, the Commodity Nature of Housing and Amelioration of the Housing Deficit: Continuing the Turner-Burgess Debate," *Antipode* 14, no. 2 (September 1982): 40–46; Richard Harris, "Self-Building in the Urban Housing Market," *Economic Geography* 67, no. 2 (January 1991): 1–21. On the lack of profit in low-income cooperative conversion, see Robert Kolodny, *Multi-family Housing: Treating the Existing Stock* (Washington, DC: National Association of Housing and Redevelopment Officials, 1981), 58. On "housing as a verb" and the link between self-building and the ideal of control, see John F. C. Turner, "Housing as a Verb," in *Freedom to Build: Dweller Control of the Housing Process,* ed. John F. C. Turner and Robert Fichter (New York: Macmillan, 1972), 151, 153; William C. Grindley, "Owner-Builders: Survivors with a Future," in Turner and Fichter, *Freedom to Build,* 19.

31. Memorandum to Persons Involved in Dweller-Control Housing from the Organizing Committee, 15 March 1973, UHAB; Ian Donald Terner and Robert Herz, "Squatter-Inspired," *Architectural Design,* August 1968, 367. For more on Terner, who tragically died in the same April 1996 plane crash that killed Secretary of Commerce Ron Brown, see Orville Schell, "A Miracle a Day," *San Francisco Examiner Magazine,* 4 August 1996, 14–17, 20–23.

32. Laven, "Self-Help in Neighborhood Development," 110, 112; Luise Haladay, a homesteader at 948 Columbus Avenue, quoted in UHAB, *The Urban Homesteading Assistance Board, 1974–1984: A Retrospective Report and Review* (New York: UHAB, 1986), 14.

33. Ted Wolner, "Pioneers on the Urban Frontier: Can Homesteading Save Your Neighborhood?" *Wisdom's Child,* 17 February 1975; St. Georges, "They Shall

Rebuild the Ruined Cities," 195; Irving Spiegel, "Gang Shows Off Housing Project," *NYT*, 11 May 1975, 94.

34. St. Georges, "They Shall Rebuild the Ruined Cities," 42–101.

35. Lawson and Johnson, "Urban Housing Crisis," 220–223; Lawson, "Owners of Last Resort," 65–68; St. Georges, "They Shall Rebuild the Ruined Cities," 42–101; UHAB, *Sweat Equity Homesteading,* 6–7. On early low-income cooperative conversions in New York, see Kolodny, *Self-Help in the Inner City.*

36. St. Georges, "They Shall Rebuild the Ruined Cities," 102–169, quote on 137; UHAB, *Sweat Equity Homesteading,* 6; Lawson and Johnson, "Urban Housing Crisis," 222–223; Kolodny, *Multi-family Housing,* 56.

37. St. Georges quoted in Wolner, "Pioneers on the Urban Frontier," 9.

38. Ramon Rueda and Joan Allen, "Rebuilding the Bronx through Sweat and Cooperation," *CFC*, January 1977, 3; New York Foundation, "Cathedral of St. John Devine [*sic*] (Sponsor for United Harlem Growth) 8–1," 19 October 1976, Box 196, Folder 3, NYF; Letter to Nancy Castleman from Marvin Goldberg, 11 February 1977, Box 196, Folder 3, NYF; St. Georges, "Renigades Update," 7; Tawfiq, "Community Groups Reclaim Housing," 5; Kolodny, *Multi-family Housing,* 63; Letter to Ann Monahan from Laven, 24 January 1977, Box 72, Folder "Housing Rehabilitation and Conservation 1977," Subseries 1, Series 10, JKJ; "Davis-Bacon Summary," 21 December 1976, Box 72, Folder "Housing Rehabilitation and Conservation 1977," Subseries 1, Series 10, JKJ; Task Force on City-Owned Property, "A Housing and Neighborhood Development Strategy for City-Owned Properties," 29 March 1978, 24–26, Box 63, Folder 16, MCH; Laven, "Self-Help in Neighborhood Development," 109–110. The Consumer-Farmer Foundation grew out of the Consumer-Farmer Milk Cooperative Inc., an organization that began in the 1930s to provide reasonably priced milk. When the cooperative ceased operations in the early 1970s, Meyer Parodneck, its founder, turned its assets toward support for low-income housing. The Consumer-Farmer Foundation eventually became the Parodneck Foundation for Self-Help Housing and Community Development. On the history of the organization, see "Over Spilt Milk," NY Food Museum website, accessed 19 April 2013, http://www.nyfoodmuseum.org/milk/index.php.

39. Lawson and Johnson, "Urban Housing Crisis," 223. St. Georges joined UHAB as a field coordinator and later led the organization; he had been involved with UHAB from the time the Cathedral Church of St. John the Divine proposed its creation. UHAB, "1974 Annual Report," January 1975, 15, Box 8, Folder "Urban Homesteading Assistance Board, Donald Turner [*sic*], 117," RL; Cathedral Church of St. John the Divine, *A Proposal for the Urban Homesteading Assistance Board, U-HAB.*

40. "The Housing Wheel," *NYT,* 29 November 1974, 38; ANHD, "A Program for Tenants and Community Organizations to Assume Control and Management of City-Owned Residential Buildings," 17 December 1974, Box 137, Folder 922, Record Group 3.1, RBF; ANHD, "A Survival Program," ca. 1975, 8, Reels

2964 and 3055, PA750-0367, FFA; Lawson and Johnson, "Urban Housing Crisis," 223; Donald Terner, "Tenant Leader Questionnaire: Section 1B (History)," 3, Box 8, Folder "Urban Homesteading Assistance Board, Donald Turner [sic], 117," RL; Joseph Kahn, "'Sweat' Tour for Sutton," *NYP*, 8 January 1975; UHAB, *Urban Homesteading Assistance Board*, 15; Tawfiq, "Community Groups Reclaim Housing," 5.

41. On Beame's austerity budget and the fiscal crisis in general, see Joshua B. Freeman, *Working-Class New York: Life and Labor since World War II* (New York: New Press, 2000), 256–287. On cuts to low-income rehabilitation funding, see Lawson and Johnson, "Urban Housing Crisis," 234.

42. "City Homesteaders," *NYT*, 3 August 1975, 27; ANHD, "Eighteen-Month Report Covering the Period July 1, 1975 to December 31, 1976," 31 March 1977, Reels 2964 and 3055, PA750-0367, FFA.

43. On President Carter's interest in self-help and neighborhood-based urban policy, see Thomas J. Sugrue, "Carter's Urban Policy Crisis," in *The Carter Presidency: Policy Choices in the Post-New Deal Era*, ed. Gary M. Fink and Hugh Davis Graham (Lawrence: University Press of Kansas, 1998), 142–146.

44. Rose quoted in "City's Rehab Program Could Ease National Problems," *NYAN*, 27 November 1976, A7; UHAB, *Sweat Equity Homesteading*, i; Letter to Monahan from Laven, 24 January 1977, Box 72, Folder "Housing Rehabilitation and Conservation 1977," Subseries 1, Series 10, JKJ; "Davis-Bacon Summary," 21 December 1976, Box 72, Folder "Housing Rehabilitation and Conservation 1977," Subseries 1, Series 10, JKJ; New York Foundation, "Cathedral of St. John Devine [sic] (Sponsor for United Harlem Growth) 8–1," 19 October 1976, Box 196, Folder 3, NYF. The HUD Multifamily Urban Homesteading Demonstration eventually added Williamsburg and Ocean Hill–Brownsville, both in Brooklyn. See UHAB, *Urban Homesteading Assistance Board*, 14.

45. Sugrue, "Carter's Urban Policy Crisis," 145; Michael Sterne, "A Loan and Some 'Sweat Equity' Create an Oasis amid Desolation," *NYT*, 7 October 1977, 54. Lawson writes that a 1976 ANHD survey found average external funding of $282,000 among its affiliates; a 1980 survey of the remaining organizations found average external funding had grown significantly, to $718,000 per organization. See Lawson and Johnson, "Urban Housing Crisis," 235–236. On the People's Development Corporation, see Rueda and Allen, "Rebuilding the Bronx," 1, 3, 7.

46. Freeman, *Working-Class New York*, 274–275; Michael Goodwin, "City-Owned Houses Come Complete with Pandora's Box," *NYT*, 7 January 1979, E6; Lawson and Johnson, "Urban Housing Crisis," 239–240; Ruth W. Messinger, "For Immediate Release," 12 April 1978, Box 5, Folder "In Rem Organizational '78," MCH; Alan S. Oser, "City Urged to Move Faster in Selling Foreclosed Housing," *NYT*, 21 November 1980, B9. Though city-owned units included those taken under urban renewal and other eminent-domain claims, the vast majority constituted in rem foreclosures. See Kolodny, *Multi-family Housing*, 46.

47. Metropolitan Council on Housing, "A Program for Housing in the Public Domain," Box 5, Folder "In Rem Organizational '78," MCH; Task Force on City-Owned Property, "A Housing and Neighborhood Development Strategy for City-Owned Properties," 29 March 1978, Box 63, Folder 16, MCH; Ruth W. Messinger, "For Immediate Release," 12 April 1978, Box 5, Folder "In Rem Organizational '78," MCH. By late 1977, Margaret McNeil of WHCO had become president of ANHD. See Mitchell Sviridoff, "Recommendation for Grant/DAP Action," 11 October 1977, Reels 2964 and 3055, PA750-0367, FFA.

48. Josh Martin, "Can HPD Handle In Rem Crisis?," *Westsider*, 2 November 1978, 3; Steven Katz and Margit Mayer, "Gimme Shelter: Self-Help Housing Struggles within and against the State in New York City and West Berlin," *International Journal of Urban and Regional Research* 9, no. 1 (March 1985): 24–28; Lawson and Johnson, "Urban Housing Crisis," 240–241; "Review by Congressman S. William Green of New York City's Community Block Grant Funded Program for City-Owned Abandoned Buildings," 28 February 1979, Box 63, Folder 15, MCH; Susan Baldwin, "Auction Moratorium Voted," *CL*, November 1978, 3. On Koch's first year as mayor, see Jonathan Soffer, *Ed Koch and the Rebuilding of New York City* (New York: Columbia University Press, 2010), 145–160.

49. Lee A. Daniels, "City Sells Four Buildings That Will Go to Tenants," *NYT*, 29 November 1980, 25; "Harlem and the Mayor," *NYAN*, 6 December 1980, 16; Alan S. Oser, "Approach to Rehabilitation of West Harlem's Housing," *NYT*, 10 October 1980, A23; Susan Baldwin, "Managing West Harlem," *CL*, May 1983, 28–31; Roger Wilkins, "Experiment to Curb Blight: Let Tenants Run Buildings," *NYT*, 20 April 1979, A19; Jonathan Steinberg, "How City Tenant Groups Take Steps toward Ownership," *NYT*, 9 September 1979, R1. The city paid for necessary rehabilitation in buildings in the Tenant Interim Lease program. See Lawson and Johnson, "Urban Housing Crisis," 240–241.

50. Task Force on City-Owned Property, "Statement on the Proposed Public Auction Policy," 10 August 1979, Box 5, Folder "In Rem Organizational '79," MCH; City of New York Department of Housing Preservation and Development, *In Rem Housing Program: Second Annual Report* (New York: City of New York Department of Housing Preservation and Development, October 1980); Kolodny, *Multifamily Housing*, 50.

51. Task Force on City-Owned Property, "Statement on the Proposed Public Auction Policy," 10 August 1979, Box 5, Folder "In Rem Organizational '79," MCH; Memo to Koch from Gliedman, 12 December 1980, Box 175, Folder 5, Departmental Correspondence—HPD, EIK; City of New York, *In Rem Housing Program*, 32–33; "New City Auction Policy Takes Aim at Slumlords," *CL*, March 1980, 12, 23; Task Force on City-Owned Property, "Revised Auction Procedures," 21 April 1980, Box 5, Folder "In Rem Organizational 1981–80," MCH.

52. Task Force on City-Owned Property, "Statement on the Proposed Public Auction Policy," 10 August 1979, Box 5, Folder "In Rem Organizational '79," MCH;

City of New York, *In Rem Housing Program,* 26; Lawson and Johnson, "Urban Housing Crisis," 241.

53. Task Force on City-Owned Property, "Statement on the Proposed Public Auction Policy," 10 August 1979, Box 5, Folder "In Rem Organizational '79," MCH; Memo to Koch from Gliedman, 17 March 1980, Box 175, Folder 3, Departmental Correspondence—HPD, EIK; Memo to Koch from James Capalino, 29 May 1980, Box 154, Folder 2, Departmental Correspondence—DGS, EIK; Memo to Capalino from Koch, 2 June 1980, Box 154, Folder 2, Departmental Correspondence—DGS, EIK; Ronald Smothers, "City Is Proposing Lottery on Sales for Brownstones," *NYT,* 24 December 1980, B3; Simon Anekwe, "Is It: Discrimination?," *NYAN,* 1 August 1981, 1.

54. Lena Williams, "Middle-Class Blacks Return to Harlem," *NYT,* 21 August 1976, 47; Cathy Chance, "People Returning to Harlem," *NYAN,* 17 March 1979, 29; Earl Caldwell, "Harlem Is Jumpin' to a New Buy-Buy Blues Beat," *NYDN,* 28 April 1979, 18; Soffer, *Ed Koch,* 65, 256. On the architectural history of brownstones in Harlem, see Michael Henry Adams, *Harlem Lost and Found: An Architectural and Social History, 1765–1915* (New York: Monacelli, 2002), 74–121.

55. Smothers, "City Is Proposing Lottery," B3; Caldwell, "Harlem Is Jumpin'," 18.

56. Three members of Community Board 10 abstained from the vote. "Harlem Housing," *NYAN,* 25 April 1981, 16; Susan Baldwin, "A Game of Numbers in Harlem," *CL,* June–July 1981, 5.

57. Anti-lottery Committee of Harlemites, "Will We Lose Harlem?," July 1981, Box 35, Folder 7, PW; Anti-lottery Committee of Harlemites, "Are We Going to Give Up Harlem without a Fight???," June 1981, Box 35, Folder 7, PW.

58. Lee A. Daniels, "City to Sell Harlem Brownstones by Lottery," *NYT,* 24 July 1981, A1; Susan Baldwin, "Furor over Harlem's Lottery," *CL,* August–September 1981, 9.

59. Edward Koch, "Koch and Stein React to Brownstone Issue," *NYAN,* 1 August 1981, 3; Letter to Clark Whelton from Koch, 15 December 1982, Box 90, Folder 11, Departmental Correspondence, City Hall Staff—Clark Whelton, EIK. On Koch's neoliberal orientation, see Soffer, *Ed Koch.*

60. Calvin O. Butts III, "Harlem Housing Hassle," *Big Red,* 20 June 1981; Lloyd Williams, "The Harlem Brownstone Dilemma," *NYAN,* 9 May 1981, 15; Preston Wilcox, "We'll Get the Rest of the Story," *Big Red,* 20 June 1981, 14.

61. Wilcox, "We'll Get the Rest of the Story"; Anti-lottery Committee of Harlemites, "How New York City Proposes to Sell Harlem Brownstones," *New York Voice,* 23 May 1981; Baldwin, "Game of Numbers," 4. $18,000 in 1981 is equivalent to approximately $47,400 in 2016. $50,000 in 1981 is equivalent to approximately $131,600 in 2016. See Consumer Price Index Inflation Calculator, accessed 24 May 2016, http://www.bls.gov/data/inflation_calculator.htm.

62. Anti-lottery Committee of Harlemites, "How New York City Proposes"; Preston Wilcox, "Toward Turf Control: A Step toward Positive Communal Action,"

12 March 1980, Box 35, Folder 7, PW. Wilcox, who ran a news service called AFRAM, reissued this document with copies of the Anti-lottery Committee's "How New York City Proposes to Sell Harlem Brownstones."

63. "Koch Says Lotteries to Sell City Housing Are Not Ruled Out," *NYT,* 28 July 1981, B3; Earl Caldwell, "A New Breed of Deal Strikes Harlem," *NYDN,* 25 July 1981, 16.

64. Simon Anekwe, "Odds Favor Residents 3–1 in Brownstone Sale," *NYAN,* 3 October 1981, 3; Memo to Nathan Leventhal from Gliedman, 18 November 1981, Box 175, Folder 9, Departmental Correspondence—HPD, EIK; Susan Baldwin, "Thousands Seek Harlem Brownstones," *CL,* November 1981, 13; Susan Baldwin, "The Next Step for Harlem Brownstones," *CL,* March 1982, 6.

65. Lee A. Daniels, "12 Win City Brownstones in Harlem," *NYT,* 10 February 1982, B3; "Boarded Up for Now, These Brownstones Will Be Future Homes for Three Housing Lottery Winners," *Alternatives,* June 1982, 1; Baldwin, "The Next Step for Harlem Brownstones," 6; Jonathan Gill, *Harlem: The Four Hundred Year History from Dutch Village to Capital of Black America* (New York: Grove, 2011), 179.

66. Daniels, "12 Win City Brownstones," B3.

67. The *Times* estimated that the average financing for purchase and renovation, a combination of city funds and federal Community Development Block Grants, added up to around $130,000 per lottery winner. "Dispute Snags Renovation of Harlem Brownstones," *NYT,* 22 May 1983, 42; "What to Preserve in Harlem," *NYT,* 25 May 1983, A26. The State Historic Preservation Office clarified that their intention was not to undermine the provision of affordable housing but to follow federal guidelines that required consideration of alternatives before historic resources were demolished. They eventually agreed with the city that the brownstones were so dilapidated inside that there "was nothing left to preserve," as the *Times* stated. See "City to Proceed in Refurbishing of Harlem Units," *NYT,* 29 June 1983, B1; Orin Lehman, "Harlem Brownstone Renovation: No State-Erected Hurdles," *NYT,* 1 June 1983, A22.

68. All ownership information is taken from New York City Department of Finance, Digital Tax Map Online (http://gis.nyc.gov/dof/dtm/mapviewer.jsf), cross-checked with public listings in the White Pages (http://www.whitepages .com). See deed records for the following twelve homes sold in the brownstone lottery: 28 West 119th Street; 30 West 119th Street; 32 West 119th Street; 65 West 119th Street; 78 West 119th Street; 26 West 120th Street; 80 West 120th Street; 82 West 120th Street; 1 West 121st Street; 217 West 139th Street; 473 West 141st Street; 317 Convent Avenue. Owners signed identical deeds in 1984 taking ownership under the terms of the lottery for all homes except 1 West 121st Street, which remained in the city's possession until 1998. Addresses are from Anekwe, "Odds Favor Residents."

69. Bernard Cohen, "Rehabilitating Sweat Equity—Part I," *CL*, February 1980, 2; Lawson and Johnson, "Urban Housing Crisis," 244–245.

70. Katz and Mayer, "Gimme Shelter," 31–32; Baldwin, "Managing West Harlem," 29; Lawson and Johnson, "Urban Housing Crisis," 239, 242; Rick Cohen, "Neighborhood Initiatives: What Hath Reagan Wrought?," *CL*, August–September 1983, 22–23; Brian Sullivan, "Off-Target Federal Funds," *CL*, November 1982, 17.

71. Alan S. Oser, "The Slow Transfer from City to Private Ownership," *NYT*, 11 September 1981, B6. As of January 1982, officials estimated that the city owned 8,500 buildings, 4,700 vacant and 3,800 occupied. See City of New York, "For Release," 25 January 1982, Box 63, Folder 16, MCH; "Summary of the Central Harlem Redevelopment Strategy," August 1982, Box 176, Folder 3, Departmental Correspondence—HPD, EIK. By February 1986, the city claimed it had sold sixty-two Harlem buildings with a total of 1,400 apartments through DAMP and that another twenty-nine Harlem buildings with 549 units remained in DAMP. "Central Harlem Redevelopment Strategy Housing (Draft)," 27 February 1986, Box 95, Folder 2, Departmental Correspondence—City Planning Commission, EIK.

72. Lawson, "Owners of Last Resort," 68–75; Jacqueline Leavitt and Susan Saegert, *From Abandonment to Hope: Community Households in Harlem* (New York: Columbia University Press, 1990); Terence Samuel, "African Blend," *Crisis*, September/October 2005, 35; Laven, "Self-Help in Neighborhood Development," 112; Cohen, "Rehabilitating Sweat Equity," 2; Deed (Lot 21, Block 1784), 31 July 1985, New York City Department of Finance, Digital Tax Map Online, accessed 18 December 2011, http://gis.nyc.gov/dof/dtm/mapviewer.jsf; Deed (Lot 21, Block 1784), 30 July 2002, New York City Department of Finance, Digital Tax Map Online, accessed 18 December 2011, http://gis.nyc.gov/dof/dtm/mapviewer.jsf; UHAB, *Self Help: In Our Own Words, 1974–1988* (New York: UHAB, 1988).

73. Lee A. Daniels, "Town Houses in Harlem Attracting Buyers," *NYT*, 21 August 1983; Carlyle C. Douglas, "City Taking Bids for 149 Vacant Harlem Buildings," *NYT*, 11 May 1985, 29; Carlyle C. Douglas, "149 Win in Auction of Harlem Houses," *NYT*, 17 August 1985, 46; Carlyle C. Douglas, "The Brownstone Project in Harlem Raises Hopes and Fears," *NYT*, 15 September 1985, E22; Simon Anekwe, "Samuel Hailed for Brownstone Sales," *NYAN*, 7 September 1985, 19.

5. Managing Change

1. Letter to Lehman from Wilcox, 3 November 1988, Box 36, Folder 1, PW.

2. Ibid.

3. Letter to Wilcox from Lehman, 30 December 1988, Box 36, Folder 1, PW.

4. For a history of this era as a period of fragmentation, see Daniel T. Rodgers, *Age of Fracture* (Cambridge, MA: Harvard University Press, 2011).

5. Preston Wilcox, "Toward a '1,000' Club," 4 April 1989, Box 36, Folder 1, PW.

6. Elliott D. Lee, "Will We Lose Harlem?," *BE*, June 1981, 191–200; Peter Bailey, "Can Harlem Be Saved?," *Ebony*, January 1983, 80–84.

7. Craig Unger, "Can Harlem Be Born Again?," *New York*, 19 November 1984, 28–36. On *New York* magazine's role as booster of middle-class resettlement in New York's neighborhoods, see Suleiman Osman, *The Invention of Brownstone Brooklyn: Gentrification and the Search for Authenticity in Postwar New York* (New York: Oxford University Press, 2011), 207.

8. Unger, "Can Harlem Be Born Again?," 34; Margot Hornblower, "Painful 'Renaissance' in Harlem," *WP*, 31 July 1984, A1.

9. Unger, "Can Harlem Be Born Again?," 34; Hornblower, "Painful 'Renaissance' in Harlem"; Edmund Newton, "How We Found and Bought Our Dream House," *BE*, October 1984, 46–48.

10. Hornblower, "Painful 'Renaissance' in Harlem"; Newton, "Our Dream House." Strife between new homeowners and existing tenants was common in gentrifying neighborhoods. See Osman, *Invention of Brownstone Brooklyn*, 265–267. On the conflicts between new middle-class African American gentrifiers and longtime low-income residents in Chicago, see Mary Pattillo, *Black on the Block: The Politics of Race and Class in the City* (Chicago: University of Chicago Press, 2007). For a similar account that considers Harlem, see Monique M. Taylor, *Harlem between Heaven and Hell* (Minneapolis: University of Minnesota Press, 2002).

11. Martin Evans, "Harlem 'Renaissance' May Push Out Long-Time Black Residents," *Baltimore Afro-American*, 10 March 1984, 15; Bailey, "Can Harlem Be Saved?"; Frank White III, "The Yuppies Are Coming: Young, Affluent Whites Are Taking Over Urban Ghettos," *Ebony*, April 1985, 155. Also see Hornblower, "Painful 'Renaissance' in Harlem."

12. Unger, "Can Harlem Be Born Again?," 32–33.

13. HUDC, "Harlem Area Redevelopment Study Part 1: Gentrification in Harlem—Issues and Observations," November 1982, Document #54, HDA; HUDC, "Harlem Area Redevelopment Study Part 2: Gentrification in Harlem—Research Findings," November 1982, Document #55, HDA; Richard Schaffer and Neil Smith, "The Gentrification of Harlem?," *Annals of the Association of American Geographers* 76, no. 3 (September 1986): 357–358. The white, non-Hispanic population in Central Harlem increased from 0.62 percent to 1.5 percent between 1980 and 1990; in the same period, the white, non-Hispanic population in Greater Harlem increased from 10.29 percent to 10.85 percent. See Andrew A. Beveridge, David Halle, Edward Telles, and Beth Leavenworth Dufault, "Residential Diversity and Division," in *New York and Los Angeles: The Uncertain Future*, ed. David Halle and Andrew A. Beveridge (New York: Oxford University Press, 2013), 320.

14. Peter Marcuse notes the linkages between gentrification and abandonment; while they tended to occur simultaneously in different parts of a single city, gentrification could also follow abandonment, as occurred at times in Harlem. See Peter Marcuse, "Abandonment, Gentrification, and Displacement: The Linkages

in New York City," in *Gentrification of the City,* ed. Neil Smith and Peter Williams (Boston: Allen and Unwin, 1986), 153–177.

15. The city calculated the population of Community Board 10 as 159,300 in 1970 and 105,800 in 1980. See Memo to Herbert Sturz from Con Howe et al., 23 October 1984, Box 94, Folder 10, Departmental Correspondence—CPC, EIK. The *Times* estimated Central Harlem's 1980 population as 161,498, down from 275,100 in 1970. See Sheila Rule, "Crossroads for Harlem," *NYT,* 21 November 1980, B3.

16. Lucius P. Gregg, "Establishing a Fund for Housing and Economic Development in Central Harlem," October 1986, Box 43, Folder 423, Reel MN54125, Deputy Mayor Lynch Subject Files, DND. The poverty threshold for a four-person family in 1980 was $8,414; for a two-person family the threshold was $5,363. See U.S. Census Bureau, Poverty Thresholds 1980, accessed 11 March 2012, http://www.census.gov/hhes/www/poverty/data/threshld/thresh80.html.

17. City of New York Department of Housing Preservation and Development, *In Rem Housing Program: Sixth Annual Report* (New York: City of New York Department of Housing Preservation and Development, 1984), 35; Gregg, "Establishing a Fund"; Michael Goodwin, "Census Finds Fewer Blacks in Harlem," *NYT,* 30 May 1981, 27; David Levering Lewis, "'Harlem Today Resembles Nothing So Much as France after the Great War,'" *NYT,* 10 May 1981, E19. See also David Levering Lewis, *When Harlem Was in Vogue* (New York: Knopf, 1981).

18. Douglas Montero, "Crack, Super Drug Hits New York City Streets," *NYAN,* 8 February 1986, 1; Jane Gross, "A New, Purified Form of Cocaine Causes Alarm as Abuse Increases," *NYT,* 29 November 1985, A1; Gina Kolata, "On Streets Ruled by Crack, Families Die," *NYT,* 11 August 1989, A1.

19. Gross, "Cocaine Causes Alarm"; Peter A. Cooper, "Community under Siege: The AIDS Epidemic in Harlem, Part One," *NYAN,* 23 July 1988; Peter A. Cooper, "Community under Siege: The AIDS Epidemic in Harlem, Part Two," *NYAN,* 30 July 1988, 4; Harold L. Jamison, "5,000 AIDS Cases Reported in Harlem," *NYAN,* 23 July 1988, 4; Charles Baillou, "Drugs, AIDS Killing Off Harlem Youths," *NYAN,* 30 July 1988, 34.

20. Lewis, "'Harlem Today Resembles.'"

21. Jonathan Gill estimates that Harlem had "more than four hundred Christian institutions" by the late twentieth century. See Jonathan Gill, *Harlem: The Four Hundred Year History from Dutch Village to Capital of Black America* (New York: Grove, 2011), 457.

22. Bond quoted in Lee, "Will We Lose Harlem?," 196.

23. Preston Washington, "What Can We Be Thankful For?," *NYAN,* 27 November 1982, 38; Preston Washington, *God's Transforming Spirit: Black Church Renewal* (Valley Forge, PA: Hudson, 1988), 99–100; White, "The Yuppies Are Coming," 155; "Block 2007," ca. 1988–1989, Box 42, Folder 41, ABC; "Adam Clayton Powell Jr. Bould." (map), ca. 1988–1989, Box 42, Folder 41, ABC.

24. Washington, *God's Transforming Spirit,* 99–108. Rev. Donald Morlan guided Memorial Baptist Church's entry into housing development through his position as a public mission staff member with the American Baptist Churches of Metropolitan New York. Morlan had served as the minister at Chambers Memorial Baptist Church immediately after Rev. Melvin Schoonover, and also worked closely with the Community Association of the East Harlem Triangle (see Chapter 1).

25. While Abyssinian Baptist Church remained one of the city's largest churches in the mid- to late 1980s, with 4,000 members, congregants increasingly came from outside Harlem as middle-class families moved to surrounding suburbs. See Howard W. French, "Restoring Abyssinian Church's Stature," *NYT,* 27 February 1988, 33. As of 1989, the average age of Abyssinian members exceeded sixty years old. See Charles Green and Basil Wilson, *The Struggle for Black Empowerment in New York City: Beyond the Politics of Pigmentation* (New York: Praeger, 1989), 69. Letter to Yvonne Lee from Nelam Hill, 5 June 1984, Box 2, Folder 15, NLH; "Abyssinian Housing for the Elderly: Site Plan," Box 2, Folder 15, NLH; Letter to Joseph Monticciolo from Charles Reiss, 5 June 1984, Box 2, Folder 15, NLH; Simon Anekwe, "Harlem Church to Build $5m Housing for Seniors," *NYAN,* 18 October 1986, 18; Robert A. Clemetson and Roger Coates, eds., *Restoring Broken Places and Rebuilding Communities: A Casebook on African-American Church Involvement in Community Economic Development* (Washington, DC: National Congress for Community Economic Development, 1993), 32–33.

26. Washington, *God's Transforming Spirit,* 12, 112; Douglas Martin, "Preston R. Washington, 54, Minister in Harlem, Is Dead," *NYT,* 4 July 2003, B8; "Vitae: Preston Robert Washington," Reel 6380, PA930-0878, FFA; Preston Washington, "Who Must Develop Harlem?," *NYAN,* 6 June 1987, 17; J. Zamgba Browne, "Transit Depot Plan Draws Anger," *NYAN,* 21 November 1987, 3. The Metropolitan Transit Authority canceled plans for the bus depot a few months later. See Simon Anekwe, "City Drops Garage Plans for Harlem-on-Hudson," *NYAN,* 20 February 1988, 5.

27. Gill, *Harlem,* 180, 198, 300–302, 306–307; French, "Restoring Abyssinian Church's Stature"; Laura Middleton, "Rev. Butts Sees Installation More as Community Celebration," *NYAN,* 11 November 1989, 5.

28. Proctor quoted in French, "Restoring Abyssinian Church's Stature"; Butts quoted in Hornblower, "Painful 'Renaissance' in Harlem"; Clemetson and Coates, *Restoring Broken Places,* 33–34; Letter to Butts from John M. Jeffries, 27 October 1987, Box 42, Folder 28, ABC; ADC, "1996 Harlem Renaissance Day of Commitment," 14 June 1996, Box 42, Folder 33, ABC.

29. Letter to Butts from Jeffries, 27 October 1987, Box 42, Folder 28, ABC; ADC, "ADC Plans for 1994–95," ca. 1994, Box 211, Folder "Grants Files, 1994, Abyssinian Development Corporation," VAF; CCHD and HUDC, "Public Presentation on the Bradhurst Neighborhood Revitalization Plan," 23 June 1989, Box 2, Folder 5, JLW; Sam Roberts, "Poor Gain, Rich Gain a Lot," *NYT,* 20 March 1994, CY6; Sam

Roberts, "Gap between Rich and Poor in New York City Grows Wider," *NYT*, 25 December 1994, 33.

30. The city's reluctance to name CCHD as developer of the Bradhurst project seemed to largely hinge on the involvement of HUDC, which the ministers of HCCI also had mixed feelings about. But HUDC claimed the support of Harlem's major political brokers, including Representative Rangel, and HCCI joined forces. Officials initially proposed giving CCHD a 175-unit "pilot project," an offer that CCHD rejected. After Rangel began to apply public pressure in 1989, the city awarded CCHD control over the entire Bradhurst project. See Keith Moore, "A Harlem Coalition Has Ideas," *NYDN*, 2 November 1988, MJ1; Simon Anekwe, "Harlem Coalition Has Housing Plan," *NYAN*, 12 November 1988, 1; Letter to Abraham Biderman from Dinkins, 15 November 1988, Box 187, Folder 2, Departmental Correspondence—HPD, EIK; Letter to Rangel from Biderman, 2 June 1989, Box 187, Folder 6, Departmental Correspondence, EIK; Keith Moore, "2 Locking Horns over Harlem Turf," *NYDN*, 15 June 1989, MJ1; Simon Anekwe, "Bradhurst Plan Gets Green Light," *NYAN*, 25 November 1989, 1; J. Phillip Thompson III, *Double Trouble: Black Mayors, Black Communities, and the Call for a Deep Democracy* (New York: Oxford University Press, 2006), 213-215.

31. For an overview of urban policy during the Reagan presidency, see Roger Biles, *The Fate of Cities: Urban America and the Federal Government, 1945-2000* (Lawrence: University Press of Kansas, 2011), 250-286; Demetrios Caraley, "Washington Abandons the Cities," *Political Science Quarterly* 107, no. 1 (Spring 1992): 1-30.

32. On CDCs in the 1980s, see Neil R. Peirce and Carol F. Steinbach, *Corrective Capitalism: The Rise of America's Community Development Corporations* (New York: Ford Foundation, 1987), 29-35; Avis C. Vidal, *Rebuilding Communities: A National Study of Community Development Corporations* (New York: Community Development Research Center, New School for Social Research, 1992), 36-37; Alexander Von Hoffman, *House by House, Block by Block: The Rebirth of America's Urban Neighborhoods* (New York: Oxford University Press, 2003). On CDCs and African American churches, see Michael Leo Owens, "Doing Something in Jesus' Name: Black Churches and Community Development Corporations," in *New Day Begun: African American Churches and Civic Culture in Post-Civil Rights America*, ed. R. Drew Smith (Durham, NC: Duke University Press, 2003), 215-247; June Manning Thomas and Reynard N. Blake Jr., "Faith-Based Community Development and African-American Neighborhoods," in *Revitalizing Urban Neighborhoods*, ed. W. Dennis Keating, Norman Krumholz, and Philip Star (Lawrence: University Press of Kansas, 1996), 131-143. On East Brooklyn Churches, South Bronx Churches, and the Nehemiah Homes, see Von Hoffman, *House by House*, 66-73; Green and Wilson, *Struggle for Black Empowerment*, 77-81; Samuel G. Freedman, *Upon This Rock: The Miracles of a Black Church* (New York: HarperCollins, 1993).

33. Julie Hack, "A Plan to Revive a Harlem Neighborhood," *NYN*, ca. February 1989, included in HUDC, "Bradhurst Revitalization Planning Document," 1990, Document #101, HDA; Abyssinian Baptist Church, "Abyssinian House Status Report," ca. 1988, Box 42, Folder 41, ABC.

34. "Abyssinian Studio," ca. late 1987, Box 42, Folder 43, ABC.

35. Anekwe, "Harlem Coalition Has Housing Plan"; Roger N. Scotland, "Raising Lazarus: The Resurrection and Transformation of Harlem," in *Signs of Hope in the City,* ed. Robert D. Carle and Louis A. DeCaro Jr. (Valley Forge, PA: Judson, 1999), 191–192; CCHD and HUDC, "Public Presentation on the Bradhurst Neighborhood Revitalization Plan," 23 June 1989, Box 2, Folder 5, JLW. $25,000 in 1988 equals approximately $50,550 in 2016; $11,000 equals approximately $22,250; and $35,000 equals approximately $70,800. See U.S. Department of Labor, Bureau of Labor Statistics, CPI Inflation Calculator, accessed 24 May 2016, http://www.bls .gov/data/inflation_calculator.htm.

36. Abyssinian Baptist Church, "Abyssinian House Status Report," ca. 1988, Box 42, Folder 41, ABC; Clemetson and Coates, *Restoring Broken Places,* 33–34; "Abyssinian Development Corporation Funding Proposal, Executive Summary," ca. 1990–1991, 5, Box 185, Folder "Grants Files, 1991, The Abyssinian Development Corporation," VAF. $24,000 to $54,000 in 1990 equals approximately $44,000 to $98,850 in 2016. See U.S. Department of Labor, Bureau of Labor Statistics, CPI Inflation Calculator.

37. Abyssinian Baptist Church, "Abyssinian House Status Report," ca. 1988, Box 42, Folder 41, ABC; "Abyssinian Studio," ca. late 1987, Box 42, Folder 43, ABC; CCHD and HUDC, "Public Presentation on the Bradhurst Neighborhood Revitalization Plan," 23 June 1989, Box 2, Folder 5, JLW; HUDC, "Bradhurst Revitalization Planning Document," 1990, Document #101, HDA.

38. Elizabeth Wood, *A New Look at the Balanced Neighborhood* (New York: Citizens' Housing and Planning Council, 1960), 7–12. I am grateful to Mariana Mogilevich for bringing this source to my attention.

39. Eleanor L. Brilliant, *The Urban Development Corporation: Private Interests and Public Authority* (Lexington, MA: Lexington Books, 1975), 19, 31, 68, 79; "UDC and Frawley Plaza," ca. 1970, Box 27, Folder 7, BERC; Donald J. Cogsville, "Housing: 1985 and Beyond," *Harlem Urban Development Corporation News* 1, no. 3 (April 1985).

40. On the early history of African American homeownership in Harlem, see Kevin McGruder, *Race and Real Estate: Conflict and Cooperation in Harlem, 1890–1920* (New York: Columbia University Press, 2015), 176–206. McGruder, incidentally, was a longtime staff member at the Abyssinian Development Corporation.

41. William Julius Wilson, *The Truly Disadvantaged: The Inner City, the Underclass, and Public Policy* (Chicago: University of Chicago Press, 1987), 8. Unless otherwise noted, citations refer to this edition. Historian Michael Katz ascribed the rise of the term "underclass" to articles in the late 1970s in *Time* magazine and

then to the work of Ken Auletta in the early 1980s, but notes that the influence and visibility of *The Truly Disadvantaged* escalated the so-called underclass debate. Wilson provided a liberal response to a discussion that had largely been dominated by conservative analyses that focused on cultural explanations of urban poverty. But despite Wilson's focus on both structure and culture, discussion of the underclass still tended to emphasize behavioral explanations, a fact that led Wilson to effectively renounce the term in 1990. See Michael B. Katz, "The Urban 'Underclass' as a Metaphor of Social Transformation," in *The Underclass Debate: Views from History,* ed. Michael B. Katz (Princeton, NJ: Princeton University Press, 1993), 3–23; William Julius Wilson, "Reflections on a Sociological Career That Integrates Social Science with Social Policy," *Annual Review of Sociology* 37 (2011): 1–11; Jason DeParle, "What to Call the Poorest Poor?" *NYT,* 26 August 1990, E4; Herbert J. Gans, "Deconstructing the Underclass: The Term's Dangers as a Planning Concept," *Journal of the American Planning Association* 56, no. 3 (1990): 271–277.

42. Wilson, *The Truly Disadvantaged,* 39–46.

43. Ibid., 7, 46–62.

44. Ibid., 58, 61.

45. Ibid., 3–19; Rodgers, *Age of Fracture,* 122–125; Wilson, "Reflections on a Sociological Career," 7; Robert Greenstein, "Prisoners of the Economy," *NYT,* 25 October 1987, BR1; Don Wycliff, "Q&A: William Julius Wilson: How the Urban Poor Got Poorer," *NYT,* 29 November 1987, E9; HUDC, "Building Harlem for Harlem through Unity: A Community-Wide Conference on Development," 11–13 March 1988, Document #92, HDA.

46. "Building Harlem for Harlem through Unity," *NYAN,* 26 March 1988, 29. Wilson notes this common interpretation of his work, especially in such later policies as the U.S. Department of Housing and Urban Development's HOPE VI program, which replaced public housing with mixed-income developments. Wilson offered his own policy suggestions in *The Truly Disadvantaged,* which emphasized broad structural transformation through the universal expansion of economic opportunity. Such policies were to enable greater social and geographic mobility among the very poor. Wilson is careful to point out that he never called for the displacement of low-income residents as a means of reducing concentrations of poverty. See William Julius Wilson, "Reflections on Responses to *The Truly Disadvantaged,*" in *The Truly Disadvantaged: The Inner City, the Underclass, and Public Policy,* 2nd ed. (Chicago: University of Chicago Press, 2012); Wilson, *The Truly Disadvantaged,* 140–164.

47. Butts quoted in J. Zamgba Browne, "Abyssinian Housing Project Ready for Tenancy," *NYAN,* 3 July 1993, 40; "Become a Harlem Homeowner at West One Three One Plaza," ca. 1993, Box 42, Folder 30, ABC; "To: Prospective Applicants for Dime Mortgages for the West One Three One Plaza Condominiums," ca. 1993, Box 42, Folder 30, ABC; Clemetson and Coates, *Restoring Broken Places,* 34.

48. "Become a Harlem Homeowner at West One Three One Plaza," ca. 1993, Box 42, Folder 30, ABC; "Stop Paying Rent!," ca. 1993, Box 42, Folder 30, ABC; "Harlem Bound!," ca. 1993, Box 42, Folder 30, ABC; "West One Three One Plaza: Condominiums in the Heart of Harlem," ca. 1993, Box 42, Folder 30, ABC; "Harlem Bound! West 131 Plaza Condominiums," ca. 1993, Box 42, Folder 30, ABC.

49. "West One Three One Plaza: Upper Manhattan's Best Kept Secret," ca. 1993, Box 42, Folder 30, ABC; "Harlem Bound!," ca. 1993, Box 42, Folder 30, ABC; "West One Three One Plaza: Condominiums in the Heart of Harlem," ca. 1993, Box 42, Folder 30, ABC; "Stop Paying Rent!," ca. 1993, Box 42, Folder 30, ABC; "Become a Harlem Homeowner at West One Three One Plaza," ca. 1993, Box 42, Folder 30, ABC; Shankar Vedantam, "Dream Homes in Harlem," *NYN*, n.d., Box 211, Folder "Grants Files, 1994, Abyssinian Development Corporation," VAF.

50. CCHD and HUDC, "Public Presentation on the Bradhurst Neighborhood Revitalization Plan," 23 June 1989, Box 2, Folder 5, JLW; "Abyssinian Development Corporation" (brochure), ca. 1991, Box 185, Folder "Grants Files, 1991, The Abyssinian Development Corporation," VAF.

51. Wilson, *The Truly Disadvantaged,* 60; Shankar Vedantam, "Dream Homes in Harlem," *NYN,* n.d., Box 211, Folder "Grants Files, 1994, Abyssinian Development Corporation," VAF; CCHD and HUDC, "Public Presentation on the Bradhurst Neighborhood Revitalization Plan," 23 June 1989, Box 2, Folder 5, JLW.

52. CCHD and HUDC, "Public Presentation on the Bradhurst Neighborhood Revitalization Plan," 23 June 1989, Box 2, Folder 5, JLW; "Bradhurst Project Fact Sheet," ca. 1989, Reel 6380, PA930-0878, FFA; Wilson, *The Truly Disadvantaged,* 56.

53. ADC, "Seventh Annual Samuel D. Proctor Phoenix Awards," 28 March 1996, Box 42, Folder 34, ABC.

54. Phase I included studios and one-, two-, and three-bedroom units. Five additional units housed building superintendents. "Bradhurst Project Fact Sheet," ca. 1989, Reel 6380, PA930-0878, FFA; "The Bradhurst Project," ca. 1989, Reel 6380, PA930-0878, FFA. In 2016 dollars, two-bedroom unit income ranges for moderate, low-income, and very low-income families equal, respectively, $44,400 to $78,150; $31,600 to $46,900; and up to $29,400. See U.S. Department of Labor, Bureau of Labor Statistics, CPI Inflation Calculator.

55. HCCI, "Ford Foundation: Report #1," 30 November 1993, Reel 6380, PA930-0878, FFA; HCCI, "Celebrating 20 Years of Service," 2006, Box 14 (no folder), HDA; HCCI, "Organizational Goals and Activities, 1992–1995," ca. early 1992, Reel 6380, PA930-0878, FFA; HCCI, "Organizational Profile," 1994, Reel 6380, PA930-0878, FFA.

56. HUDC developed the apartments of Bradhurst Phase I and Phase II, and HCCI took possession upon completion, becoming the buildings' landlord. ADC, "New York Foundation Interim Report," July–October 1992, Box 40, Folder 12, NYF; *Synergy* 1, no. 2, 14 December 1995, Box 211, Folder "Grants Files, 1994, Abyssinian Development Corporation," VAF; "Abyssinian Development Corporation," ca. 1995,

Box 211, Folder "Grants Files, 1994, Abyssinian Development Corporation," VAF; ADC, "Seventh Annual Samuel D. Proctor Phoenix Awards," 28 March 1996, Box 42, Folder 34, ABC; ADC, "1996 Harlem Renaissance Day of Commitment," 14 June 1996, Box 42, Folder 33, ABC; "Abyssinian Development Corporation Funding Proposal, Executive Summary," 1990–1991, Box 185, Folder "Grants Files, 1991, The Abyssinian Development Corporation," VAF; Abyssinian Baptist Church, "1992–1993 Annual Report," 32, Box 194, Folder "Grants Files, 1992, Abyssinian Development Corporation," VAF.

57. Alan S. Oser, "How Sharp Cuts in Federal Help Will Affect Housing," *NYT*, 2 October 1981, A31; Robert Pear, "Housing Aid for Poor," *NYT*, 6 March 1982, 9; Gerald M. Boyd, "Housing Vouchers Supported by U.S.," *NYT*, 12 December 1983, A23; Anthony DePalma, "Are Rent Vouchers a Boon or a Bust?," *NYT*, 1 November 1987, R1; Elizabeth Roistacher and Emanuel Tobier, "Housing Policy," in *Setting Municipal Priorities: American Cities and the New York Experience*, ed. Charles Brecher and Raymond D. Horton (New York: New York University Press, 1984), 464–466; Edward Koch, "Ten Year Plan Speech," ca. 1988, Box 186, Folder 8, Departmental Correspondence, EIK.

58. Jonathan Soffer, *Ed Koch and the Rebuilding of New York City* (New York: Columbia University Press, 2010), 290–304; New York City Department of Housing Preservation and Development (HPD), "The 10 Year Plan," 1989, UHAB. The range of income categories varied depending on who was defining them. Koch suggested that low-income housing target those earning less than $19,000 annually; moderate-income housing target those earning from $19,000 to $32,000; and middle-income housing target those earning over $32,000. The Association of Neighborhood Housing Developers, which often criticized Koch's Ten Year Plan for seeming to benefit wealthier residents than officials had promised, stated that the categories should target those earning up to $14,999 (low income), $15,000 to $24,999 (moderate income), and $25,000 to $48,000 (middle income). See Edward Koch, "Ten Year Plan Speech," ca. 1988, Box 186, Folder 8, Departmental Correspondence, EIK; Association of Neighborhood Housing Developers, "Summary Analysis of City's New Vacant City-Owned Buildings and Construction Management Programs," 1988, Box 68, Folder 6, MCH.

59. HPD, "The 10 Year Plan," 1989, UHAB. On the state Low Income Housing Trust Fund, see "Cuomo Tackles the Housing Crisis," *NYAN*, 20 July 1985, 12; "Notice of Availability of Funds under the New York State Low Income Housing Trust Fund," *NYAN*, 17 August 1985, 10.

60. Rebecca Reich, "Foundation Dollars for Nonprofit Housing," *CL*, March 1988, 25–27; Doug Turetsky, "The Go-Betweens," *CL*, June–July 1991, 8–10; Mitchell Sviridoff, "The Local Initiatives Support Corporation: A Private Initiative for a Public Problem," in *Privatization and the Welfare State*, ed. Sheila B. Kamerman and Alfred J. Kahn (Princeton, NJ: Princeton University Press, 1989). On the Low Income Housing Tax Credit, see Kenneth T. Rosen and Ted Dienstfrey, "The

Economics of Housing Services in Low-Income Neighborhoods," in *Urban Problems and Community Development,* ed. Ronald F. Ferguson and William T. Dickens (Washington, DC: Brookings Institution Press, 1999), 449–453; David J. Erickson, "Community Capitalism: How Housing Advocates, the Private Sector, and Government Forged New Low-Income Housing Policy, 1968–1996," *Journal of Policy History* 18, no. 2 (2006): 167–204; HPD, "The 10 Year Plan," 1989, UHAB.

61. Margaret Mittlebach, "Suburbs in the City," *CL,* May 1991, 12–16; Charles J. Orlebeke, *New Life at Ground Zero: New York, Homeownership, and the Future of America's Cities* (Albany, NY: Rockefeller Institute Press, 1997), 84–86; HPD, "The 10 Year Plan," 1989, UHAB. On Bond's early work on this site, known as Frederick Douglass Circle, see Shadrach Woods and Bond/Ryder Associates, "Frederick Douglass Circle Development: Cathedral Parkway Urban Renewal Area, Density, Massing and Programming Study," March 1970, Box 31, Folder 11, JMB.

62. Lynne B. Sagalyn, "Explaining the Improbable: Local Redevelopment in the Wake of Federal Cutbacks," *Journal of the American Planning Association* 56, no. 4 (1990): 429. On the "patchwork" of funding supporting CDCs, see James DeFilippis, "Community Control and Development: The Long View," in *The Community Development Reader,* ed. James DeFilippis and Susan Saegert (New York: Routledge, 2008), 32; Avis C. Vidal, "CDCs as Agents of Neighborhood Change: The State of the Art," in *Revitalizing Urban Neighborhoods,* ed. W. Dennis Keating, Norman Krumholz, and Philip Star (Lawrence: University Press of Kansas, 1996), 149–163.

63. HPD, "The 10 Year Plan," 1989, UHAB.

64. Emily M. Bernstein, "A New Bradhurst," *NYT,* 6 January 1994, B1; Erika Mallin, "The Bradhurst Battles," *CL,* April 1992, 18–21.

65. Memo to Dinkins from Washington and Jones, 31 March 1992, Reel 6380, PA930-0878, FFA; "Harlem Churches for Community Improvement Present and Future Plans for Community and Housing Development," ca. April 1991, Box 110, Folder 5, NYF; "Fact Sheet: Reverend John J. Sass Houses," n.d., Reel 6380, PA930-0878, FFA; "Interim Report of the Harlem Churches for Community Improvement Inc.," 29 February 1992, Box 110, Folder 5, NYF; HCCI, "Organizational Profile," 1994, Reel 6380, PA930-0878, FFA; HCCI, "Organizational Goals and Activities, 1992–1995," ca. early 1992, Reel 6380, PA930-0878, FFA.

66. "Abyssinian Development Corporation Funding Proposal, Executive Summary," ca. 1990–1991, Box 185, Folder "Grants Files, 1991, The Abyssinian Development Corporation," VAF; Abyssinian Baptist Church, "1992–1993 Annual Report," Box 194, Folder "Grants Files, 1992, Abyssinian Development Corporation," VAF; "Abyssinian Development Corporation," ca. 1995, Box 211, Folder "Grants Files, 1994, Abyssinian Development Corporation," VAF; HPD, "The 10 Year Plan," 1989, UHAB; "Become a Harlem Homeowner at West One Three One Plaza," ca. 1993, Box 42, Folder 30, ABC; "To: Prospective Applicants for Dime Mortgages for the West One Three One Plaza Condominiums," ca. 1993, Box 42, Folder 30, ABC.

67. Owens, "Doing Something in Jesus' Name," 233.

68. HCCI, "Organizational Profile," 1994, Reel 6380, PA930-0878, FFA; "Harlem Religious Groups Unite in Prayer for AIDS," *NYAN*, 22 September 1990, 16.

69. DeFilippis, "Community Control and Development," 31-33; New York City Housing Partnership, "Harlem and Affordable Housing: A 'Partnership' Perspective," n.d., Box 42, Folder 42, ABC.

70. "Harlem Churches for Community Improvement," 7 June 1990, Box 110, Folder 5, NYF; Memo to Files from M. G. B., 5 August 1991, Box 110, Folder 5, NYF.

71. "Harlem Churches for Community Improvement," 6 June 1991, Box 110, Folder 5, NYF; Robert McNatt, "Karen A. Phillips," *Crain's New York Business*, 11 February 1991; Avis C. Vidal, Arnold M. Howitt, and Kathleen P. Foster, *Stimulating Community Development: An Assessment of the Local Initiatives Support Corporation* (Cambridge, MA: State, Local, and Intergovernmental Center, Kennedy School of Government, Harvard University, 1986), appendix B; "75 Most Influential Women," *Crain's New York Business*, 25 March 1996, W3.

72. ADC, "1996 Harlem Renaissance Day of Commitment," 14 June 1996, Box 42, Folder 33, ABC; Memo to Wayne Winborne and Lynn Walker from John Koprowski, 30 March 1993, Reel 6380, PA930-0878, FFA; Ford Foundation, "Recommendation for Grant/FAP Action," 17 June 1993, Reel 6380, PA930-0878, FFA. HCCI eventually hired a former staffer from the New York City Human Resources Administration for the CFO position. See "Harlem Churches for Community Improvement, Inc. Report to the Ford Foundation," ca. mid-1994, Reel 6380, PA930-0878, FFA.

73. "Harlem Churches for Community Improvement," 7 June 1990, Box 110, Folder 5, NYF; HCCI, "Ford Foundation: Report #1," 1 June 1993–30 November 1993, Reel 6380, PA930-0878, FFA; HCCI, "Board of Directors, 1993–1994," Reel 6380, PA930-0878, FFA; Clemetson and Coates, *Restoring Broken Places*, 35.

74. ADC, "New York Foundation Final Report," November 1992–March 1993, Box 40, Folder 12, NYF; Memo to Phillips from Bailey, 30 June 1994, Box 40, Folder 12, NYF.

75. Memo to Phillips from Bailey, 30 June 1994, Box 40, Folder 12, NYF; Task Force on City-Owned Property, "Final Report to the New York Foundation," August–November 1994, Box 167, Folder 1, NYF. On political demobilization in community organizations during this period, see Adolph Reed Jr., *Stirrings in the Jug: Black Politics in the Post-segregation Era* (Minneapolis: University of Minnesota Press, 1999), 126–127.

76. Ghislaine Hermanuz, "Infill Housing: A Remedy to Harlem's Deterioration," in *Reweaving the Urban Fabric: Approaches to Infill Housing*, ed. Deborah Norden (New York: New York State Council on the Arts, 1988), 14–15.

77. "Interim Report of the Harlem Churches for Community Improvement Inc.," 29 February 1992, Box 110, Folder 5, NYF; "Abyssinian Development Corporation Funding Proposal, Executive Summary," ca. 1990–1991, 5, Box 185, Folder

"Grants Files, 1991, The Abyssinian Development Corporation," VAF; "Abyssinian Development Corporation," ca. 1995, Box 211, Folder "Grants Files, 1994, Abyssinian Development Corporation," VAF; "The Bradhurst Project," ca. 1989, Reel 6380, PA930-0878, FFA; HCCI, "Celebrating 20 Years of Service," 2006, Box 14 (no folder), HDA; HUDC, "Bradhurst Revitalization Planning Document," 1990, Document #101, HDA.

78. HCCI, "Organizational Profile," 1994, Reel 6380, PA930-0878, FFA; Letter to Howard Phipps from Susan Henshaw Jones, 21 September 1992, Box 191, Folder "Grants Files, 1991, New York Landmarks Conservancy, Folder 2," VAF; "Creating Homes in Vacant Landmarks," *New York Landmarks Conservancy,* Winter/Spring 1997, 3, Box 208, Folder "Grants Files, 1993, New York Landmarks Conservancy," VAF.

79. Shawn G. Kennedy, "Landmarks: Now It's Harlem's Turn," *NYT,* 12 May 1991; Letter to Phillips from Constance Hildesley, 12 July 1991, Box 194, Folder "Grants Files, 1992, Abyssinian Development Corporation," VAF; Foresight Preservation Fund Inc., Jack Freeman Associates Inc., and Michael Kwaltler and Associates, *Landmarks Preservation Study (Prepared for Abyssinian Development Corporation),* 9 September 1992, 1, Box 194, Folder "Grants Files, 1992, Abyssinian Development Corporation," VAF; Letter to Laurie Beckelman from Butts, 28 October 1991, in Foresight Preservation Fund Inc. et al., *Landmarks Preservation Study,* Box 194, Folder "Grants Files, 1992, Abyssinian Development Corporation," VAF; Letter to Beckelman from Phillips, 28 October 1991, in Foresight Preservation Fund Inc. et al., *Landmarks Preservation Study,* Box 194, Folder "Grants Files, 1992, Abyssinian Development Corporation," VAF.

80. Washington and McNeil quoted in Mark W. Griffith and Errol T. Louis, "Harlem: A New Renaissance?," *CL,* October 1990, 18–19.

81. Ibid.; ADC, "1996 Harlem Renaissance Day of Commitment," 14 June 1996, Box 42, Folder 33, ABC; City College of New York, *Changing Streetscapes: New Architecture and Open Space in Harlem,* 2005, http://digital-archives.ccny.cuny.edu/exhibits/ChangingStreetscapes/exhibit.pdf; ADC, "Seventh Annual Samuel D. Proctor Phoenix Awards," 28 March 1996, Box 42, Folder 34, ABC.

6. Making Markets Uptown

1. "In the Zone: Who's Empowered," *NYT,* 20 October 1996, CY8.

2. Letter to Parsons from Harlem Unity Committee for Social Justice, 23 October 1996, Box 35, Folder 7, PW.

3. Letter to Harlem Unity Committee from Parsons, 1 November 1996, Box 35, Folder 7, PW; Letter to Harlem Unity Committee from Wright, 28 October 1996, Box 35, Folder 7, PW.

4. David W. Dunlap, "Retailers Have Harlem on Their Mind," *NYT,* 10 November 1996, R1.

5. In his study of urban transformation in Bronzeville (Chicago) and Harlem, sociologist Derek Hyra offers a theoretical framework emphasizing the importance of examining the interconnection of forces at the global, national, municipal, and community levels. My argument is consistent with his point that African American–led organizations played a larger role in development than scholars have often acknowledged, and that class plays an important part in determining the nature of their work, but he focuses on their impact on housing, only nodding to their role in commercial development. See Derek Hyra, *The New Urban Renewal: The Economic Transformation of Harlem and Bronzeville* (Chicago: University of Chicago Press, 2008), esp. 17–28, 129–150. For other treatments of Harlem in this decade, see Arlene M. Dávila, *Barrio Dreams: Puerto Ricans, Latinos, and the Neoliberal City* (Berkeley: University of California Press, 2004); John L. Jackson Jr., *Harlemworld: Doing Race and Class in Contemporary Black America* (Chicago: University of Chicago Press, 2001); David Maurrasse, *Listening to Harlem: Gentrification, Community, and Business* (New York: Routledge, 2006).

6. Sharon Zukin also notes the role of the public sector in the project of "making markets" in Harlem in this period, though she does not emphasize the centrality of community based organizations in this transformation. See Sharon Zukin, *Naked City: The Death and Life of Authentic Urban Places* (New York: Oxford University Press, 2010), esp. 77–87.

7. Omnibus Budget Reconciliation Act of 1993, Public Law 103-66, 103rd Cong. (10 August 1993); Michael B. Katz, *The Price of Citizenship: Redefining the American Welfare State,* updated ed. (Philadelphia: University of Pennsylvania Press, 2008), 123–129; Roger Biles, *The Fate of Cities: Urban America and the Federal Government, 1945–2000* (Lawrence: University Press of Kansas, 2011), 324–326; Memo to Peter Powers from Alice Tetelman, Bill Daly, and Helen Mathis, 25 January 1994, Box 02/01/1/099, Folder 291, Deputy Mayor Powers, RWG.

8. Peter Hall, *Cities of Tomorrow,* updated ed. (Oxford, UK: Blackwell, 1996), 355–358; Katz, *Price of Citizenship,* 126; Biles, *Fate of Cities,* 325. For a history of Enterprise Zone legislation at both the state and federal levels, see Karen Mossberger, *The Politics of Ideas and the Spread of Enterprise Zones* (Washington, DC: Georgetown University Press, 2000), 54–94.

9. Omnibus Budget Reconciliation Act of 1993; Letter to Gore from Dinkins, 15 December 1993, Box 02/11/007, Folder 218, Deputy Mayor Dyson, RWG; Memo to Powers from Tetelman, Daly, and Mathis, 25 January 1994, Box 02/01/1/009, Folder 291, Deputy Mayor Powers, RWG; Peter Marcuse, "Playing the Rangel Angle," *NYN,* 18 February 1994, 66; Memo to Jay A. Rosenberg from Len Wasserman, 11 March 1994, Box 02/11/007, Folder 218, Deputy Mayor Dyson, RWG; Thomas J. Lueck, "3 Empowerment Areas Must Create a Wish List," *NYT,* 27 December 1994, B3. Seventy-four cities competed for designation as Empowerment Zones. The law also authorized the creation of ninety-five smaller "Enterprise Communities" that received fewer benefits. See Biles, *Fate of Cities,* 326.

UMEZ administered 83 percent of the total budget of the New York Empowerment Zone; the Bronx Overall Economic Development Corporation managed the remainder for the South Bronx area. See Lily Hoffman, "The Marketing of Diversity in the Inner City: Tourism and Regulation in Harlem," *International Journal of Urban and Regional Research* 27, no. 2 (June 2003): 289.

10. HUDC, "Briefing Information Presented to Ronald H. Brown, Secretary, U.S. Department of Commerce," 22 October 1993, Box 36, Folder 2, PW.

11. Ibid.; "New York City Empowerment Zone: Harlem, the South Bronx," 29 June 1994, section II, 24, Document #116, HDA.

12. "New York City Empowerment Zone: Harlem, the South Bronx," 29 June 1994, section II, 23, Document #116, HDA; HUDC, "Briefing Information Presented to Ronald H. Brown," 22 October 1993, Box 36, Folder 2, PW; Memo to Distribution from Kimberly D. Hardy, 29 July 1997, Box 02/09/009, Folder 241, Deputy Mayor Washington, RWG; "Welcome from the President of Wave Hill," 30 June 1997, Box 02/09/009, Folder 241, Deputy Mayor Washington, RWG; "East Harlem Revitalization Project at 125th Street and Third Avenue," ca. April 1995, Box 02/09/008, Folder 326, Deputy Mayor Reiter, RWG.

13. HUDC, "Briefing Information Presented to Ronald H. Brown," 22 October 1993, Box 36, Folder 2, PW; Letter to Rudy Washington and Randy Levine from Parsons and Wright, 20 November 1997, Box 02/09/009, Folder 240, Deputy Mayor Washington, RWG; Deborah C. Wright, "Upper Manhattan: The Future's Looking Up!," *EZ Works* 2, no. 1 (Winter 1998): 2.

14. Michael E. Porter, "The Competitive Advantage of the Inner City," *Harvard Business Review*, May–June 1995, 55. Also see Zukin, *Naked City*, 78.

15. Porter, "Competitive Advantage," 55–56, 58.

16. Ibid., 65, 67.

17. Elisabeth Bumiller, "Harlem on Her Mind: Preacher's Daughter Takes Wall St. Sensibility Uptown," *NYT*, 28 March 1997, B1; Deborah C. Wright, "Money Isn't Everything," *NYT*, 13 July 2008. After leaving UMEZ in 1999, Wright returned to the private sector as CEO of Carver Bancorp, an African American–owned bank based in Harlem.

18. "UMEZDC Board of Directors," Box 02/09/1/005, Folder 160, Deputy Mayor Reiter, RWG.

19. Letter to Harlem Unity Committee from Wright, 28 October 1996, Box 35, Folder 7, PW.

20. Wright quoted in Kirk Johnson, "Uneasy Renaissance on Harlem's Street of Dreams," *NYT*, 1 March 1998, 1.

21. Letter to Wright from Harlem Unity Committee, 20 November 1996, Box 35, Folder 7, PW.

22. For the early shopping mall plans of HCC, see HCC, "125th Street Multiuse Commercial Center: A Proposal," October 1976, Box 7, Folder 24, NLH; HUDC and HCC, "125th Street Shopping Mall Complex," 1978, Document #22a, HDA.

23. Robin Schatz and Christine Dugas, "The Hollow Dream: Harlem Commonwealth Council Was Supposed to Serve the Community; Some Say It Served Mostly Its Leader," *NYN,* 23 December 1991, 27; Letter to Wilcox from Isaiah E. Robinson (and appended Wilcox response), 3 January 1996, Box 8, Folder 4, PW.

24. HCC, "For Immediate Release," 20 December 1991, Box 8, Folder 4, PW; Memo to Carl Weisbrod, Tony Mannarino, and Patricia Zedalis from Lance Ruiz Carlile and Julio Peterson, 20 December 1991, Box 02/11/011, Folder 415, Deputy Mayor Dyson, RWG; Memo to Levine from Charles Millard, 21 May 1998, Box 02/03/008, Folder 323, Deputy Mayor Levine, RWG; "Close Up," *EZ Works* 2, no. 1 (Winter 1997): 4; J. Zamgba Browne, "$56 Mil. Mall Planned for Harlem's 125th St.," *NYAN,* 23 March 1996; Wright quoted in Dunlap, "Retailers Have Harlem on Their Mind."

25. Norris quoted in Browne, "$56 Mil. Mall Planned"; Norris quoted in "Retail Complex in Harlem Takes a Big Step Forward," *NYT,* 19 March 1996; Greenwald quoted in John Holusha, "Around 125th Street, New Interests and Optimism," *NYT,* 12 April 1998; Norris quoted in Dunlap, "Retailers Have Harlem on Their Mind"; Richard Parsons, "Message from the Chairman," *EZ Works* 2, no. 2 (Summer 1998): 2.

26. "Today, Breaking Ground" (advertisement), *NYT,* 27 July 1998, D12; "Harlem USA: Breaking New Ground," *EZ Flash,* August 1998, 1. Though Harlem USA did eventually attract a roster of prominent tenants, the developers encountered some delays in gaining enough commitments to secure financing. See John Holusha, "Harlem U.S.A. Project Is Progressing, but Tempo Lags," *NYT,* 26 March 1997, B8.

27. Terry Pristin, "First Store Opens at the First Shopping Mall in Harlem," *NYT,* 3 February 2000, B8; T. D. Moore, "Harlem USA Opens Its Doors: HMV Comes to Harlem in Grand Style," *NYAN,* 4 May 2000, 3; Terry Pristin, "New Cinema and New Hope in Harlem," *NYT,* 1 July 2000, B1.

28. Y. Salaam, "HMV Records to Be Part of Harlem USA," *NYAN,* 25 September 1997, 4; Mamadou Chinyelu, *Harlem Ain't Nothin' but a Third World Country: The Global Economy, Empowerment Zones and the Colonial Status of Africans in America* (New York: Mustard Seed, 1999), esp. 45–49; Sharpton quoted in Victoria Pope, "Harlem's Next Renaissance," *U.S. News and World Report,* 10 February 1997, 56.

29. Letter to Thomas Wahman from Melvin Schoonover, 12 March 1968, Box 82, Folder 3, NYF; CAEHT, "Annual Report," 1 July 1972–30 June 1973, City Hall Library, New York. On the federal housing moratorium and CAEHT, see Robert E. Tomasson, "Freeze on Funds Shatters a Dream in East Harlem," *NYT,* 28 January 1973, 369.

30. City of New York Department of Consumer Affairs, "The Poor Pay More . . . for Less: Part 1: Grocery Shopping," April 1991, Box 02/09/008, Folder 326, Deputy Mayor Reiter, RWG; Terry Pristin, "A Supermarket as a Spur for Change," *NYT,*

28 April 1999, B1; Memo to Carl Weisbrod, Mannarino, and Zedalis from Carlile and Peterson, 20 December 1991, Box 02/11/011, Folder 415, Deputy Mayor Dyson, RWG.

31. Memo to Barry Sullivan, Carl Weisbrod, Wasserman, et al., from Ann Weisbrod, 30 November 1993, Box 02/11/011, Folder 415, Deputy Mayor Dyson, RWG; The Retail Initiative, "A Blueprint for Inner City Retail Development," n.d., Box 02/09/007, Folder 252, Deputy Mayor Reiter, RWG; Pristin, "A Supermarket as a Spur for Change"; "EDC Pathmark Deals," 30 May 1995, Box 02/01/1/008, Folder 274, Deputy Mayor Campbell, RWG; "Project Financing Summary," n.d., Box 02/11/011, Folder 415, Deputy Mayor Dyson, RWG.

32. City of New York Department of Consumer Affairs, "The Poor Pay More . . . for Less: Part 1: Grocery Shopping," April 1991, Box 02/09/008, Folder 326, Deputy Mayor Reiter, RWG; Community Food Resource Center Inc., "Competition Lowers Prices," ca. early 1995, Box 02/01/1/13, Folder 479, Deputy Mayor Campbell, RWG.

33. HUDC, "The Harlem Survey," ca. 1994, 18–19, Box 36, Folder 2, PW; Boston Consulting Group and Initiative for a Competitive Inner City, *The Business Case for Pursuing Retail Opportunities in the Inner City* (Boston: Boston Consulting Group, June 1998), 1–2, 5, 8.

34. Wilcox quoted in Herb Boyd, "A Supermarket Behemoth Plans a Landing in Harlem," *NYAN*, 28 August 1997, 3; Williams quoted in Eric L. Smith, "Harlem Renaissance—Take Two," *BE*, 1 February 1997.

35. Sonia Reyes, "Pathmark Problems," *NYDN*, 21 October 1994; Sarah Jay, "Pathmark Plans Cheer Shoppers, but Shake Shopkeepers," *NYT*, 3 October 1994; Joyce Purnick, "Plans for Supermarket Caught Up in Politics," *NYT*, 24 April 1995, B3; Jim Sleeper, "Pols Wrong to Fight Pathmark," *NYDN*, 18 April 1995, 22; E. R. Shipp, "Harlem Needs Pathmark, Not Polemics," *NYDN*, 19 April 1995; Memo to Powers, John Dyson, et al., from Clay Lifflander, 2 August 1995, Box 02/09/008, Folder 326, Deputy Mayor Reiter, RWG; Pristin, "A Supermarket as a Spur for Change."

36. "BRISC Lending Begins," *EZ Works* 2, no. 1 (Winter 1997): 1. For a list of UMEZ aid through late 1998, see "Upper Manhattan Empowerment Zone Summary of Initiatives," ca. late 1998, Box 02/08/019, Folder 562, Deputy Mayor Washington, RWG.

37. Hughes eventually launched her own funding effort, with the goal of community ownership through the sale of modestly priced stock in her business. Abby Ellin, "A Harlem Power Zone Weakens Some," *NYT*, 4 January 2000, B4; Dorothy Pitman Hughes, *Wake Up and Smell the Dollars! Whose Inner-City Is This Anyway!* (Los Angeles: Amber Books, 2000), 109.

38. Schlesinger Associates, "Attached Are the Results . . . ," March 1995, Box 02/01/1/008, Folder 274, Deputy Mayor Campbell, RWG; Letter to Powers from Stan Sorkin, 21 June 1995, Box 02/01/1/008, Folder 274, Deputy Mayor Camp-

bell, RWG; "The Pathmark in East Harlem: Misperceptions and Facts," ca. 1994, Box 02/11/011, Folder 415, Deputy Mayor Dyson, RWG.

39. Baruch College, "Pathmark Urban Store in New York City," 2 February 1988, Box 02/09/008, Folder 326, Deputy Mayor Reiter, RWG; Abeles, Phillips, Preiss & Shapiro, "Retail Impact of a Proposed Pathmark Supermarket on East 125th Street," November 1992, Box 02/09/008, Folder 326, Deputy Mayor Reiter, RWG; Pristin, "A Supermarket as a Spur for Change."

40. On the preference for chain retail in African American communities, see Lizabeth Cohen, *Making a New Deal: Industrial Workers in Chicago, 1919–1939* (New York: Cambridge University Press, 1990), 152–154. On the response of existing residents to increasing retail and service options in gentrifying neighborhoods, see Lance Freeman, *There Goes the 'Hood: Views of Gentrification from the Ground Up* (Philadelphia: Temple University Press, 2006), 61–72. Pristin, "A Supermarket as a Spur for Change"; "Harlem Pathmark Super Center: Grand Opening Celebration," 30 April 1999, Box 42, Folder 43, ABC.

41. Lawrence Van Gelder, "Alice Kornegay, 65, Advocate for East Harlem Housing Group," *NYT,* 2 May 1996, D23.

42. "Path(mark) to Progress," *NYDN,* 30 May 1995, 20.

43. ADC, "The Abyssinian Development Corporation Announces They Have Expanded and Relocated" (press release), Abyssinian Development Corporation website, 13 September 2004, http://www.adcorp.org/news/pdfs/ADC_Move_press _release.pdf; Charles V. Bagli, "Plan Set for Retail Complex on State Land in Harlem," *NYT,* 4 November 1999, B9; "$85M Harlem Center Development to Revitalize Local Economy," *Real Estate Weekly,* 3 May 2000.

44. HUDC, "The International Trade Center," ca. 1978, Box 8, Folder 30, NLH; HUDC, "Harlem Third World International Trade Complex," ca. mid-1979, Box 8, Folder 30, NLH.

45. Letter to Edward Koch from Rangel, 26 June 1978, Box 247, Folder 1, Departmental Correspondence, Public Officials, EIK; HUDC, "Harlem Third World Trade Institute," ca. early 1987, Box II:2514, Folder 4, DPM; "UDC Seeks Developers for Harlem Center," *New York Construction News,* 10 November 1986; New York State Urban Development Corporation and HUDC, "Draft: Harlem International Trade Center Request for Proposals," September 1987, Box II:2514, Folder 4, DPM; Letter to Daniel Patrick Moynihan from Rangel, 14 December 1987, Box II:2514, Folder 4, DPM; Letter to James Baker from Rangel, 20 February 1987, Box II:2514, Folder 4, DPM; Harlem International Trade Center Corporation, "The Harlem International Trade Center," ca. early 1988, Box II:2514, Folder 4, DPM; "Developers Chosen for Harlem International Trade Center," *Real Estate Weekly,* 5 July 1989; Letter to Moynihan from Gene A. Norman, 5 July 1989, Box II:2514, Folder 4, DPM; Letter to Moynihan from Rangel, 12 October 1990, Box II:2514, Folder 4, DPM. Rangel's close ties to the project as well as his efforts to move it through Congress were made apparent in a letter he wrote to House Committee on Ways

and Means chairman Dan Rostenkowski. "Thanks for all of your support for the trade center," he wrote. "We haven't named it yet so please let us know whether you prefer Rostenkowski or just plain old 'Rosty.'" See Letter to Rostenkowski from Rangel, 18 October 1989, Box II:436, Folder 2, DPM.

46. Jennifer Lin, "From Harlem, a Plan to Lure the World's Trade," *Philadelphia Inquirer,* 27 August 1989, 1-H; Letter to Paul O'Dwyer from Norman, 18 October 1990, Box 4, Folder 42, UN and Consular Corp./Com. O'Dwyer General Correspondence, DND; Letter to George Pataki from Rangel, 15 November 1995, Box 02/09/005, Folder 190, Deputy Mayor Reiter, RWG; Kevin Sack, "New York Voters End a Democratic Era," *NYT,* 9 November 1994, A1; Jacques Steinberg, "How the Voters in the Suburbs Boosted Pataki," *NYT,* 13 November 1994, WC1.

47. Kevin Sack, "Neither Pataki nor Giuliani Will Turn Other Cheek," *NYT,* 19 November 1994, 28; James Dao, "The Endgame: For Pataki, Fighting Giuliani Became the Way to Fight Cuomo," *NYT,* 10 November 1994, B15; James Dao, "In a Final Budget Proposal, Pataki Sticks with His Cuts," *NYT,* 3 March 1995, B6.

48. Dao, "Pataki Sticks with His Cuts"; Brett Pulley, "End of Urban Agency Draws Fears of Neglect," *NYT,* 30 March 1995, B3; Brett Pulley, "Governor Closes Harlem Development Agency," *NYT,* 31 August 1995, B3.

49. David W. Dunlap, "Building a Business-Friendly New York," *NYT,* 4 June 1995, RNJ1; Temporary Commission of Investigation of the State of New York, *An Investigation into the Creation of the Harlem Urban Development Corporation and Its Operations from 1981–1995* (New York: State of New York Commission of Investigation, April 1998), 1.

50. Matthew Purdy, "Audits Indicate Misuse of Funds by Aid Agency in Harlem," *NYT,* 1 May 1997, B1; Temporary Commission of Investigation, *Creation of the Harlem Urban Development Corporation,* esp. 1–31.

51. Temporary Commission of Investigation, *Creation of the Harlem Urban Development Corporation,* 18–20, 112–118; Memo to Frank Mahoney from Ihor Ferencevych, 5 February 1996, Box 02/08/003, Folder 74, Deputy Mayor Washington, RWG; Purdy, "Audits Indicate Misuse of Funds."

52. Dunlap, "Building a Business-Friendly New York"; Letter to Pataki from Rangel, 15 November 1995, Box 02/09/005, Folder 190, Deputy Mayor Reiter, RWG. The project's backers claimed that they had in fact secured commitments from private-sector tenants like Motown Records, Equitable Insurance, and *Essence* magazine, but the state nonetheless terminated the project. See Robin Pogrebin, "State Pulls Plug on Trade Center," *NYT,* 17 December 1995, CY6.

53. Pogrebin, "State Pulls Plug on Trade Center."

54. Calvin O. Butts, interview by Julian Bond, ca. 2008, Explorations in Black Leadership, University of Virginia, accessed 1 November 2012, http://www .virginia.edu/publichistory/bl/index.php?fulltranscript&uid=43; Ari L. Goldman, "Calvin Butts: Maverick's Power Rises," *NYT,* 9 August 1987, 28; Calvin Sims, "Butts Comes Under Fire for Endorsement of Perot," *NYT,* 14 July 1992, B3; Larry Olmstead,

"From Powerful Pulpit, a Moral Warrior Takes Aim," *NYT*, 5 June 1993, 23; Robert D. McFadden, "Prominent Harlem Minister Says He Will Back Pataki," *NYT*, 11 October 1998, 39; Cathy Connors, "Rev. Calvin Butts Breaks with Tradition, Endorses Congressman Charles Rangel," *NYAN*, 7 May 1994, 1; Charisse Jones, "Pataki Takes His Campaign Message to Harlem Church," *NYT*, 10 October 1994, B6. Butts later expressed regret for endorsing Perot, especially because doing so undermined his chance to gain political capital with Clinton. See Olmstead, "From Powerful Pulpit."

55. Robin Pogrebin, "The Political Dance of Calvin Butts," *NYT*, 3 December 1995, CY4.

56. McFadden, "Prominent Harlem Minister"; Craig Horowitz, "The Anti-Sharpton," *New York*, 26 January 1998; Greg Thomas, "Pataki's Man in Harlem," *VV*, 28 January 2003.

57. State of New York, ESDC, and Harlem Community Development Corporation, "Harlem Center Mall: Request for Proposals," 16 February 1996, Box 02/08/003, Folder 74, Deputy Mayor Washington, RWG; David W. Dunlap, "The Changing Look of the New Harlem," *NYT*, 10 February 2002, J1.

58. Rangel and Butts quoted in Jane H. Lii, "Act 2 for Prime Site, and Butts Is Supporting Player," *NYT*, 8 June 1997, CY6; Butts quoted in George Rush and Joanna Molloy with Baird Jones, "Butts Takes a Malling over Harlem Project," *NYDN*, 13 May 1997.

59. Peter Noel, "The Battle for Harlem," *VV*, 2 June 1998; Dunlap, "Changing Look of the New Harlem"; Butts quoted in Thomas, "Pataki's Man in Harlem."

60. Noel, "The Battle for Harlem"; Horowitz, "The Anti-Sharpton."

61. Dan Barry, "Butts, Harlem's Prominent Pastor, Calls Giuliani a Racist," *NYT*, 21 May 1998, 35; David M. Halbfinger, "With Attack on Giuliani, Pastor Returns to Fiery Past," *NYT*, 22 May 1998, B4; J. Zamgba Browne, "Butts: Why Pataki? Black Leaders Question Motives," *NYAN*, 15 October 1998, 1; Abby Goodnough, "Mayor Faults Pataki Approval of Harlem Minister's Support," *NYT*, 12 October 1998, B5; Randal C. Archibold, "Pastor of Harlem Church Nominated to Head SUNY at Old Westbury," *NYT*, 7 August 1999, B3. Butts's criticism did not come without costs, as Giuliani withdrew the city's support from the Harlem Center project in the aftermath of the accusation. The state ended up constructing the building around the parking garage on the site, which occupied the city-owned portion of the land. See Herb Boyd, "Harlem Center Mall Sacrificed; Butts-Giuliani 'Racist' Feud at Core," *NYAN*, 4 February 1999, 1; Bagli, "Plan Set for Retail Complex," B9.

62. Jamal E. Watson, "Black Churches Develop Congregations, Corporations," *NYAN*, 24 July 2003, 1.

63. Rush, Molloy, and Jones, "Butts Takes a Malling."

64. Browne, "Butts: Why Pataki?," 1; Haughton and Wilcox quoted in Peter Noel, "The Sins of Reverend Calvin Butts," *VV*, 27 October 1998.

65. Browne, "Butts: Why Pataki?"

Conclusion

1. "ULI New York: Rescheduled Program!!," 19 November 2001, Box 11, Folder 9, JMB; "ULI New York—11-19-01, Harlem: Evolution of Revitalization, Remarks—Max Bond," November 2001, Box 11, Folder 9, JMB.

2. "ULI New York—11-19-01, Harlem: Evolution of Revitalization, Remarks—Max Bond," November 2001, Box 11, Folder 9, JMB.

3. Jamal E. Watson, "Harlem Empowered," *NYAN*, 29 April 2004; Yvonne Delaney, "Knuckles Buckles Down at the Helm of UMEZ," *NYAN*, 13 February 2003, 6; Kenneth Knuckles, interview with author, 4 February 2011.

4. Terry Pristin, "Construction Is to Start in Fall on Central Harlem Supermarket," *NYT*, 3 July 2002, B6; Yvonne Delaney, "Bradhurst Court Breaks Ground, New Pathmark to Open," *NYAN*, 21 November 2002, 5; J. Zamgba Browne, "Auto Dealership Breaks Ground," *NYAN*, 26 June 2003, 3; Yvonne Delaney, "125 Building Boom," *NYAN*, 21 March 2002, 1; John Leland, "A New Harlem Gentry in Search of Its Latte," *NYT*, 7 August 2003, F1. For other coverage of new middle-class, African American residents in Harlem, see Lisa W. Foderado, "For Affluent Blacks, Harlem's Pull Is Strong," *NYT*, 18 September 1998, A1; Peter Hellman, "Making Family History in Historic Harlem," *NYT*, 17 January 2002, F1.

5. Alan Feuer, "Stress of Harlem's Rebirth Shows in School's Move to a New Building," *NYT*, 2 February 2004, B1; Timothy Williams, "God and Neighborhood: Powerful Harlem Church Is Also a Powerful Harlem Developer," *NYT*, 18 August 2008, B1; Robin Finn, "Nurturing a New, yet Old, Vision of Harlem," *NYT*, 22 August 2008, B4; Demetria Irwin, "Landmarking the Black Cultural Capital of the World," *NYAN*, 20 March 2008, 1; Christopher Gray, "Adam Clayton Powell Boulevard: A Harlem Landmark in All but Name," *NYT*, 18 February 2007, I7.

6. Graham Rayman, "The (Very) Earthly Pursuits of Rev. Calvin O. Butts III," *VV*, 17 April 2013; Kia Gregory, "In Harlem, Renaissance Theater Is at the Crossroads of Demolition and Preservation," *NYT*, 19 December 2014; Melanie Grayce West, "Pathmark Closure Jars East Harlem," *Wall Street Journal*, 17 November 2015; Aaron Elstein, "Rev. Calvin Butts Seeks Salvation for the Church-Based Organization That Resurrected Harlem," *Crain's New York Business*, 22 November 2015.

7. Amy Waldman, "In Harlem, a Hero's Welcome for New Neighbor Clinton," *NYT*, 31 July 2001; Susan Saulny, "Government Signs Lease for Harlem Office," *NYT*, 18 April 2001; Terry Pristin, "Harlem Hopes Move Spurs a Revival," *NYT*, 17 February 2001, B6.

8. Timothy Williams, "Mixed Feelings as Change Hits 125th Street," *NYT*, 13 June 2006, B1; Herb Boyd, "Harlem Legend Faces Eviction," *NYAN*, 19 May 2005, 10.

9. Herb Boyd, "Harlem Legend, Preston Wilcox, Passes," *Black World Today*, 18 August 2006.

10. Herb Boyd, "Preston Wilcox Praised at Memorial," *NYAN*, 24 August 2006.

11. Stephen A. Crockett Jr., "The Brixton: It's New, Happening, and Another Example of African-American Historical 'Swagger-Jacking,'" *TheRootDC*, 3 August 2012; Sarah Wesseler, "Over-the-Rhine," *Satellite*, September 2013.

12. Trymaine Lee, "Bracing for the Lion," *NYT*, 22 July 2007, O1; Charles Bagli, "At Raucous Hearing, City Panel Approves Columbia's Plan for Expansion in Harlem," *NYT*, 27 November 2007, B3; Timothy Williams, "City's Sweeping Rezoning Plan for 125th Street Has Many Concerned," *NYT*, 21 February 2008, B3; Demetria Irwin, "City Planning Commission Approves 125th Street Rezoning," *NYAN*, 13 March 2008, 28.

13. James Weldon Johnson, "Harlem: The Cultural Capital," in *The New Negro: An Interpretation*, ed. Alain Locke (New York: A. and C. Boni, 1925), 301, 308.

14. Johnson, "Harlem: The Cultural Capital," 308; Sam Roberts, "No Longer Majority Black, Harlem Is in Transition," *NYT*, 6 January 2010; Les Payne, "Is Harlem No Longer Black?," *Root*, 8 January 2010; Andrew A. Beveridge, David Halle, Edward Telles, and Beth Leavenworth Dufault, "Residential Diversity and Division," in *New York and Los Angeles: The Uncertain Future*, ed. David Halle and Andrew A. Beveridge (New York: Oxford University Press, 2013), 320.

Illustration Credits

Figure I.1. Cartography by Garrett Nelson and Rebecca Summer.

Figure 1.1. West Harlem Community Organization and Architects' Renewal Committee in Harlem, "West Harlem Urban Renewal Area: Survey and Planning Application," January 1966, C. Richard Hatch Private Collection, Potomac, Maryland. Courtesy of C. Richard Hatch. Redrawn by Garrett Nelson and Rebecca Summer.

Figure 1.2. Architects' Renewal Committee in Harlem, "Urban Renewal in the East Harlem Triangle," October 1966, C. Richard Hatch Private Collection. Courtesy of C. Richard Hatch.

Figure 1.3. "Harlem's Besieged Showplace," *Architectural Forum* 125, no. 4 (November 1966): 48. Photograph by George Cserna. Courtesy of the Avery Architectural and Fine Arts Library, Columbia University.

Figure 2.1. *Bond Ryder Associates AIA,* ca. 1969, Box 1, Folder 20, J. Max Bond Jr. Papers, Department of Drawings and Archives, Avery Architectural and Fine Arts Library, Columbia University, New York. Courtesy of Davis Brody Bond.

Figure 2.2. Architects' Renewal Committee in Harlem and West Harlem Community Organization, *West Harlem Morningside: A Community Proposal* (New York: Architects' Renewal Committee in Harlem and West Harlem Community Organization, 1968), 48. Photograph by Tyrone Georgiou. Courtesy of Arthur L. Symes.

Figure 2.3. Arthur L. Symes and Rae Banks, *Architecture in the Neighborhoods* (New York: Architects' Renewal Committee in Harlem, Cooper Union School of Art and Architecture, and New York Chapter of the American Institute of Architects, November 1968), 22. Courtesy of Arthur L. Symes.

Figure 2.4. Architects' Renewal Committee in Harlem and West Harlem Community Organization, *West Harlem Morningside: A Community Proposal* (New York: Architects' Renewal Committee in Harlem and West Harlem Community Organization, 1968), 42. Courtesy of Arthur L. Symes.

Figure 2.5. Architects' Renewal Committee in Harlem, *East Harlem Triangle Plan* (New York: Architects' Renewal Committee in Harlem, 1968). Courtesy of Arthur L. Symes.

Figure 2.6. Architects' Renewal Committee in Harlem, *East Harlem Triangle Plan* (New York: Architects' Renewal Committee in Harlem, 1968). Courtesy of Arthur L. Symes.

Figure 2.7. Architects' Renewal Committee in Harlem, *East Harlem Triangle Plan* (New York: Architects' Renewal Committee in Harlem, 1968). Illustration by E. Donald Van Purnell. Courtesy of Arthur L. Symes.

Figure 2.8. Architects' Renewal Committee in Harlem and West Harlem Community Organization, *West Harlem Morningside: A Community Proposal* (New York: Architects' Renewal Committee in Harlem and West Harlem Community Organization, 1968), 38. Courtesy of Arthur L. Symes.

Figure 2.9. Architects' Renewal Committee in Harlem and West Harlem Community Organization, *West Harlem Morningside: A Community Proposal* (New York: Architects' Renewal Committee in Harlem and West Harlem Community Organization, 1968), 34. Illustration by E. Donald Van Purnell. Courtesy of Arthur L. Symes.

Figure 2.10. Architects' Renewal Committee in Harlem, *East Harlem Triangle Plan* (New York: Architects' Renewal Committee in Harlem, 1968). Illustration by E. Donald Van Purnell. Courtesy of Arthur L. Symes.

Figure 2.11. Collection of the author.

Figure 2.12. *Harlem News,* October 1969. Photograph by Doug Harris. Courtesy of Arthur L. Symes.

Figure 2.13. *Harlem News,* October 1969. Photograph by Doug Harris. Courtesy of Arthur L. Symes.

Figure 2.14. *Harlem News,* October 1969. Photograph by Doug Harris. Courtesy of Arthur L. Symes.

Figure 2.15. Architects' Renewal Committee in Harlem, "Position Paper on Reclamation Site #1," 8 August 1969, Box 7, Folder 7, J. Max Bond Jr. Papers, Avery Architectural and Fine Arts Library, Columbia University, New York, New York. Courtesy of Arthur L. Symes.

Figure 2.16.   Folder "Harlem—State Office Building," Clipping File, 1925–1974, Schomburg Center for Research in Black Culture, New York Public Library.

Figure 3.1.   Thomas A. Johnson, "Harlem Squatters Ousted; 9 Arrested," *New York Times*, 24 September 1969, 1. Patrick A. Burns/*The New York Times*/Redux.

Figure 3.2.   Bond Ryder Associates, "Preliminary Program Analysis: Harlem Centre," ca. March 1970, Box 242, Folder 148, Edward Joseph Logue Papers, Manuscripts and Archives, Yale University Library, New Haven, Connecticut. Courtesy of Davis Brody Bond.

Figure 3.3.   HUDC, "The International Trade Center," ca. 1979, Box 8, Folder 30, Nelam L. Hill Papers, Manuscripts, Archives and Rare Books Division, Schomburg Center for Research in Black Culture, New York Public Library, Astor, Lenox and Tilden Foundations. Courtesy of the Harlem Community Development Corporation.

Figure 3.4.   Harlem Commonwealth Council, "125th Street Multi-use Commercial Center: A Proposal," October 1976, Box 58, Folder "Harlem Commonwealth Council 1969–77," Subseries 1, Series 10, Senator Jacob K. Javits Collection, Special Collections and University Archives, Stony Brook University, Stony Brook, New York. Courtesy of Davis Brody Bond.

Figure 4.1.   Charles Laven, "Self-Help in Neighborhood Development," in *The Scope of Social Architecture*, ed. C. Richard Hatch (New York: Van Nostrand Reinhold, 1984), 107. Photograph by Beverly Hall. Courtesy of the New Jersey Institute of Technology.

Figure 4.2.   Urban Homesteading Assistance Board, *Third Annual Progress Report* (New York: Cathedral House, April 1977). Courtesy of the Urban Homesteading Assistance Board.

Figure 4.3.   Urban Homesteading Assistance Board, *The Urban Homesteading Assistance Board, 1974–1984: A Retrospective Report and Review* (New York: UHAB, 1985), 34. Photograph by Frederic Ohringer. Courtesy of the Urban Homesteading Assistance Board.

Figure 4.4.   Charles Laven, "Self-Help in Neighborhood Development," in *The Scope of Social Architecture*, ed. C. Richard Hatch (New York: Van Nostrand Reinhold, 1984), 109. Photograph by Beverly Hall. Courtesy of the New Jersey Institute of Technology.

Figure 4.5.   Urban Homesteading Assistance Board, *The Urban Homesteading Assistance Board, 1974–1984: A Retrospective Report and Review*

(New York: UHAB, 1985), 50. Courtesy of the Urban Homesteading Assistance Board.

Figure 4.6.   Charles Laven, "Self-Help in Neighborhood Development," in *The Scope of Social Architecture,* ed. C. Richard Hatch (New York: Van Nostrand Reinhold, 1984), 112. Photograph by Beverly Hall. Courtesy of the New Jersey Institute of Technology.

Figure 4.7.   Lee A. Daniels, "City to Sell Harlem Brownstones by Lottery," *New York Times,* 24 July 1981, A1. Chester Higgins, Jr./*The New York Times*/Redux.

Figure 4.8.   Charles Laven, "Self-Help in Neighborhood Development," in *The Scope of Social Architecture,* ed. C. Richard Hatch (New York: Van Nostrand Reinhold, 1984), 107. Photograph by Beverly Hall. Courtesy of the New Jersey Institute of Technology.

Figure 5.1.   Photograph by author.

Figure 5.2.   Photograph by author.

Figure 5.3.   Photograph by author.

Figure 6.1.   Harlem Urban Development Corporation, "New York City Empowerment Zone: Harlem, the South Bronx," 29 June 1994, following Sec. I, p. 6, Avery Architectural and Fine Arts Library, Columbia University, New York, New York. Courtesy of the Harlem Community Development Corporation.

Figure 6.2.   *New York Times,* 27 July 1998, D12. Courtesy of the Upper Manhattan Empowerment Zone Development Corporation.

Figure 6.3.   Photograph by author.

Figure 6.4.   Photograph by author.

Figure 6.5.   Photograph by author.

Acknowledgments

As a historian of the built environment, I am keenly aware that to understand places, we must understand the people who inhabit them. And to understand people, we must understand the places they inhabit. Likewise, researching and writing this book has been an endeavor equally dependent on people and places, one that would not have been possible without the support of both. My gratitude goes first, then, to the place at the center of this study—Harlem. Learning its streets and buildings, meeting its residents in person and in the archives, and engaging deeply with its history has in many ways changed my life, and certainly changed the way I see. Needless to say, without Harlem this project could not have existed. I hope that those who enter its blocks always look and listen closely.

The people who enabled this project as mentors, friends, and supporters comprise a much longer list, and one inclusive of all the places I inhabited as I wrote this book. I am tremendously grateful to the advisers and colleagues who supported its initial conception and subsequent development. I count myself extremely fortunate for having had the opportunity to work with Lizabeth Cohen at Harvard University. Liz has been a dedicated, generous mentor and supportive friend, whose mix of criticality and kindness shaped this project—and its author—in immeasurable ways. I aspire to her model of the balanced, insightful, and productive scholar. I am likewise grateful to K. Michael Hays, Sandy Zipp, and Neil Brenner. Their expertise sharpened the spatial, theoretical, and historical analysis at the heart of this study, while their kindness, energy, humor, and friendship gave me the confidence to see myself as their colleague. At the University of Wisconsin–Madison, where I completed a postdoctoral fellowship, William Jones took me on as his mentee. He eagerly supported the project already under way while pushing me to refine it. For his advice on life and work, and his continued friendship, I am very grateful. Like the story told in the book, this project also has deep roots. While I was still an undergraduate, Yve-Alain Bois, Margaret Crawford,

Neil Levine, and Bill Wilson all helped me to see myself as a scholar and a historian. More than this, they taught me to look closely, question the obvious, and search deeply for answers. I see their fingerprints all over this book.

Generous funding and administrative support enabled me to conduct this research, provided time to write, and allowed my work to reach a wide audience. I am extremely grateful for the support of Harvard University Press and my editor, Andrew Kinney, who has listened carefully to my ambitions for the book while guiding me in revision. Katrina Vassallo, Stephanie Vyce, and numerous other staff members at HUP have made production efficient and satisfying. An A. W. Mellon Postdoctoral Fellowship at the Center for the Humanities and Department of History at Wisconsin provided an intellectual community that I could never have imagined beforehand. On the beautiful shores of Lake Mendota, my project improved with the input of new friends, colleagues, and students. Wisconsin offers a model of the engaged, sophisticated public university that must be preserved in our society. I will be forever thankful for my time there. My project would truly not have been possible without the generous assistance of the Graduate School of Arts and Sciences at Harvard University and the Charles Warren Center for Studies in American History, which both facilitated my research and enabled me to study and learn. In particular, I wish to acknowledge the support of Arthur Patton-Hock, Larissa Kennedy, and the directors of the Warren Center. I likewise appreciate the generous assistance of the Taubman Center for State and Local Government at the Harvard Kennedy School; the Real Estate Academic Initiative, Center for American Political Studies, and Graduate Student Council at Harvard; and the Rockefeller Archive Center, all of which likewise provided vital financial support. My gratitude extends also to the University of New Mexico, especially the School of Architecture and Planning, Geraldine Forbes Isais, and John Quale. I have benefited from their support for my research and willingness to allow me to explore new ideas in my teaching. I appreciate the patience of my colleagues and students as I finished this book. Lastly, I wish to thank the Society of Architectural Historians, which generously funded the book's image program with an SAH/Mellon Author Award. I am grateful for the society's interest in my work and know the book benefits tremendously from the illustrations their support enabled.

A number of individuals and organizations have provided permissions and assistance in support of those illustrations and other aspects of the book. In particular, I would like to thank Arthur Symes and C. Richard Hatch, both formerly of the Architects' Renewal Committee in Harlem (ARCH); Holly Stern and the New Jersey Institute of Technology; Carole Ann Fabian, Janet Parks, Nicole Richard, and Margaret Smithglass of the Avery Architectural and Fine Arts Library; Elizabeth Frenchman and Davis Brody Bond; Rosemary Morrow at Redux Pictures; Andy Reicher and the Urban Homesteading Assistance Board; Curtis Archer and the Harlem Community Development Corporation; Eunice A. Jackson at Empire

State Development; and Blair Duncan and the Upper Manhattan Empowerment Zone Development Corporation. Some portions of Chapters 1 and 2 of this book were previously published in "'The Search for New Forms': Black Power and the Making of the Postmodern City," *Journal of American History* 103, no. 2 (2016): 375–399. I am grateful to the journal for allowing their use here.

This book would have been impossible to write without the archives on which its arguments are based. I extend immense thanks to the archivists and institutions that enabled it. At the Schomburg Center for Research in Black Culture, located in the heart of Harlem and designed by J. Max Bond Jr., I am grateful to the staff of the Research and Reference Division and the Manuscripts, Archives, and Rare Books Division, especially Steven Fullwood. Tal Nadan, Thomas Lannon, and Laura Morris welcomed and guided me at the Manuscripts and Archives Division of the New York Public Library. I am likewise grateful to the staff of the Tamiment Library and Robert F. Wagner Labor Archives at New York University, particularly Peter Filardo. Janet Parks, Shelley Hayreh, and Jason Escalante in the Department of Drawings and Archives at the Avery Architectural and Fine Arts Library allowed me to be among the first to study Bond's papers. At the beautiful Rockefeller Archive Center, I benefited from the assistance of Michele Hiltzik and Camilla Harris. I also wish to thank Idelle Nissila-Stone, who made the Ford Foundation Archives available to me when they were still housed at the foundation's headquarters. My gratitude also includes Kristen Nyitray at the Special Collections and University Archives at Stony Brook University; Sydney Van Nort at the Archives and Special Collections at City College of New York; Keith Schuler at the Jimmy Carter Presidential Library; the late Leonora Gidlund and the staff of the New York City Municipal Archives; and Kevin McGruder, who generously helped me access the records of Abyssinian Baptist Church. My thanks go also to the staffs of the Columbia University Rare Book and Manuscript Library, the National Archives and Records Administration, the Library of Congress, the Special Collections of the Jewish Theological Seminary, and the Manuscripts and Archives at Yale University Library. I want to extend special thanks to the staff of the Urban Homesteading Assistance Board, especially Andy Reicher and Dana Variano, who welcomed me into their office and allowed me free rein in their file room. My book benefited tremendously from their graciousness.

I am equally fortunate to have had the chance to discuss my research with some of those who appear in this story and to record oral histories with them. In particular, I am grateful to Arthur Symes, Kenneth Knuckles, Ghislaine Hermanuz, Forrester Lee, and Natsu Ifill. I must extend special gratitude to Maureen and C. Richard Hatch, who welcomed me into their home, shared their stories, and allowed me access to their files. They offered a firsthand glimpse into the origins of ARCH that shaped my project profoundly. I wish to also thank Marci Reaven, who shared her collection of the papers of Walter Thabit; Steven Caputo, who generously shared his own research on ARCH; and Gail Radford, who dug up old research files on my behalf. Michael Henry Adams and Sharifa Rhodes-Pitts, writers, activists, and Harlemites both, allowed me to see Harlem through their eyes. Friends provided hospitality that made my research trips to New York and other cities both productive and fun. I appreciate the generosity of Liz Cohen and Herrick Chapman, Frank and Lori Giblin, Bobby and Michelle Hulme-Lippert, Ashwin Jacob, the Mogilevich family, Paolo Roy and Danielle Stelly, and Angela Starita.

Many others shaped my work, knowingly and unknowingly, in innumerable ways. For critical feedback, advice, guidance, and support, I am grateful to Francesca Ammon, Martha Biondi, Eve Blau, Howard Brick, Michael Carriere, Nancy Cott, Susan Fainstein, Marta Gutman, Dianne Harris, Laura Warren Hill, Timothy Hyde, Meg Jacobs, Matt Lasner, Edward Linenthal, Lisa McGirr, Suleiman Osman, Antoine Picon, Aaron Shkuda, David Smiley, Tom Sugrue, Komozi Woodard, anonymous reviewers of the *Journal of American History,* and the anonymous readers who reviewed this manuscript for Harvard University Press. For invitations to share my work publicly and receive helpful criticism, I thank Harvey Jacobs, Reinhold Martin, Jonathan Massey, Adam Tanaka, and Meredith Ten-Hoor. At Harvard University, members of Liz Cohen's dissertation workshop were wonderful colleagues, friends, and teachers. I would like to thank Anne Blaschke, Casey Bohlen, Eli Cook, Claire Dunning, Bryant Etheridge, Maggie Gates, Jane Hong, Ariane Liazos, Anna Lvovsky, Noam Maggor, Betsy More, Shaun Nichols, Chris Phillips, Josie Rodberg, Josh Segal, Stephen Vider, Clinton Williams, and Ann Wilson. In the doctoral program in Architecture, Landscape Architecture, and Urban Planning, I benefited from the intellectual comradeship and personal support of Sai Balakrishnan, Jana Cephas, Kenny Cupers, John Davis, Lisa Haber-Thomson, Max Hirsh, Jennifer Mack, Anna Bergren Miller, Maria Moran, Sunny Park, Bill Rankin, Rebecca Ross, Ivan Rupnik, Fallon Samuels, Jesse Shapins, Nick Smith, David Theodore, Olga Touloumi, and Delia Wendel. I extend special thanks to Barbara Elfman, who ensured that our program ran smoothly and has continued to support me both personally and professionally. At the University of Wisconsin–Madison, I was welcomed into several vital and active intellectual communities that helped me develop my work, including the Center for Culture, History, and Environment; Center for the Humanities; Department of History; and Department of Urban and Regional Planning. Anna Andrzejewski, Kathryn Ciancia, Jessica Courtier, Bill Cronon, Sean Dinces, Sarah Florini, Spring Greeney, Sara Guyer, Daegan Miller, Gregg Mitman, Mary Murrell, Garrett Nelson, Amanda Rogers, Becca Summer, and Jerome Tharaud deserve special gratitude as colleagues and friends. At the University of New Mexico, Andrew Sandoval-Strausz has been an incisive and supportive interlocutor whose critical feedback improved this book at its late stages.

Friends and family have supported me during what has been the thrilling and, at times, difficult process of writing this book. They have distracted me when I needed it and provided advice when I needed that. The solitude of research and writing is alleviated by such intellectual and personal care. I am especially grateful to Heather and Jamie Hannon, Blake and Phyllis Johnson, Elisa Minoff and Ramesh Nagarajan, Mariana Mogilevich, Ross Mulcare and Erin Quinn, Sam Rosenfeld and Erica De Bruin, Rachel Silver and Nathan Englander, Brandon Terry, and Johanna Winant and Geoff Hilsabeck. Danny Warshawsky, Paul Weaver, and Sammy Ford have stuck with me for a long time. I am tremendously grateful for not one but two sets of parents and siblings who have been patient with me, kept my best interests in mind, and always provided abundant care. My love and gratitude go to Ann and John McCulla, Bridie McCulla and Francesco Da Vela, and James McCulla, my in-laws. My parents have always asked me what I hope to accomplish and helped me to achieve it; my sister and her family have cheered me along the way. Thank you, with love, to Steven and Shelley Goldstein and Rebecca, David, Lewis, Nathan, and Audrey Silber.

I save my final—and greatest—gratitude for two companions who have experienced this book at every stage and made room for it in our family. I would be remiss to not specifically thank Kitty, our gray cat, who often shows little regard for what I happen to be working on but is nevertheless eager to entertain, distract, and comfort. She has occasionally added words to my chapters and is never shy to demand treats; she has offered frequent comic relief and provided levity in difficult times. My other close confidant in this journey, Theresa McCulla, has been my steadfast supporter, insightful editor, inspiring colleague, patient partner, and devoted friend. She has encouraged me to follow my curiosity and unfailingly believed in me. It is my tremendous fortune to be married to someone so brilliant, kind, and funny. We have together experienced tremendous highs and crushing setbacks during the last few years, none greater than the birth and death of our twin daughters, Ruth and Marian, during the final stages of completing this manuscript. Theresa's love and fortitude have kept us afloat, and I know that brighter days lay ahead. I dedicate this book to Theresa with all of my love.

Index

Page numbers in italics refer to illustrations.